HEALING LITURGIES
FOR THE SEASONS OF LIFE

HEALING LITURGIES
FOR THE SEASONS OF LIFE

ABIGAIL RIAN EVANS

Westminster John Knox Press
LOUISVILLE • LONDON

Book design by Teri Kay Vinson
Cover design by Pam Poll Graphic Design

First edition
Published by Westminster John Knox Press
Louisville, Kentucky

This book is printed on acid-free paper that meets the American National Standards Institute Z39.48 standard. ♾

PRINTED IN THE UNITED STATES OF AMERICA

04 05 06 07 08 09 10 11 12 13 — 10 9 8 7 6 5 4 3 2 1

Library of Congress Cataloging-in-Publication Data

Evans, Abigail Rian.
 Healing liturgies for the seasons of life / Abigail Rian Evans.— 1st ed.
  p. cm.
 Includes bibliographical references.
 ISBN 0-664-22482-2 (alk. paper)
  1. Occasional services. I. Title.

BV199.O3E93 2004
265'.82—dc21

2003053751

To my parents, Marian Schall Rian (1906–1994) and
Edwin Harold Rian (1900–1995), who cared for me and my sisters,
Marian and Roanne, whenever we were sick,
and through their love and example showed
Christ's victory over every circumstance of life.

Contents

Preface

God comes to thee, not as in the dawning of the day, not as in the bud of Spring, but as the sun at noon to illustrate all shadows . . . all occasions invite his mercies and all times are his seasons.
    —Richard London, quoted by John Donne, A Manual for Ministry to the Sick

Healing Liturgies for the Seasons of Life is the third book in a series of three. All three books are based on a theology of healing that is rooted in the Judeo-Christian concept of health and wholeness. With the patient as the focus of the healing, the first book, *Redeeming Marketplace Medicine,* recommends a collaborative approach to health care involving the disciplines of medicine and religion. The second book, *The Healing Church,* begins with a history of the church's healing ministry and describes health ministries that involve educational, support/ advocacy, and direct health care approaches. It concludes with a description of practical programs that illustrate these areas. I have purposely placed *Healing Liturgies for the Seasons of Life* as the last book in this series because liturgical healing ministry is often the least understood. Unfortunately, healing liturgies have, on occasion, been based on a misapplication of a theology of miraculous healing, as well as the inappropriate exclusion of medical means and other health resources. In other words, some faith healers have indicated that personal faith alone is the cause for healing. This idea is inconsistent with the Judeo-Christian concept of health and wholeness and the healing ministry of Jesus.

I want to be clear from the beginning that this is not a book about the history of worship or a general discussion of liturgy but principally a collection of liturgies for the various seasons of life—liturgical passages, if you will. There is no promise of some miraculous properties to these liturgies; the Spirit of God and the faith of the worshiper are what give them the power. These liturgies themselves will not provide healing but may open up a person or the community to God's healing. The liturgies can be one of God's instruments, though we need to acknowledge that God needs no means to release God's healing. We are never in complete control of what happens in worship; the Spirit blows where it will.

THESIS OF THIS BOOK

The thesis of this book is that God's gift of healing is available during all seasons of a person's life and that the power of hope and healing may be affirmed and redirected through liturgical services, sacraments, and rites. It is important, not only psychologically but also spiritually, to mark the passages of life and times of crisis.

The liturgical calendar is a well-regulated and accepted part of worship for many traditions. In addition, our lives have an internal rhythm that is marked, for instance, by waking and sleeping. Chronological seasons are also reflected in the passage of our life from birth to childhood, adolescence, and young, middle, and older adulthood. In this book no ages are assigned to these stages, since when one enters a phase of life varies from one individual to another.

The liturgies in this book reflect on the natural rhythms of life and the crises we experience, providing another way of ordering our worship life. Christian worship may minister to us during times of crisis and unique events or circumstances.[1] "The mountain peaks and valleys of life are occasions for Christian worship just as surely as are the flat plains of day-by-day living. The crisis points of life are marked when the community of faith gathers around individuals to express its love as people pass through various stages."[2] Pastoral care precedes and follows worship. The two are intimately connected. Each section of the book has a brief introduction to highlight the experience of those passing through that stage of life. This material can be used as part of the congregational education prior to conducting the liturgies. It is hoped that this brief material will be expanded by those conducting the educational programs.

The liturgies for seasons of crisis include those for individuals (body, mind, or spirit) and for external crises of a community, nation, or the world. The more difficult the crisis, the more detailed and carefully patterned is the ritual. The seasons are: life-altering illness, life-threatening illness, death and dying, broken world, and deliverance. This fits with my thesis that healing in the passages and crises of life is enhanced by a liturgical response. Liturgies provide a way for people to process their grief and give a framework that connects one's faith to the process of healing.

Worship moves us from self-absorption to focus on God and other people. The interplay between life and liturgy is quite important; it is my hope that these liturgies will help strengthen that connection. Worshiping with other Christians should be as natural and vital as the air we breathe—it is not a luxury but a necessity. As people come together in worship around the major events of life, they will be bound together in unique ways. It is hoped that clergy and others will see the importance of including all God's people, bringing those often marginalized by society, such as people with disabilities, mental illness, and addiction, into the center of the church's life.

This book may also contribute to liturgical renewal, not simply by replacing contemporary worship for traditional services but by breaking down that false dichotomy and rediscovering the importance of seeking God, the transcendent, through all changes of life. In addition, the existence and offering of these liturgies bear witness to God's presence in the tides and seasons of life, the joys and the sorrows, connecting as well with those in pain. Some claim that liturgical renewal will revitalize the church, linking worship, edification, and evangelism.[3] The purpose here is not precisely this but instead to reconnect people to God rather than the church—though the latter may be an indirect result, as most of these liturgies are to be held in the sanctuary with members of the congregation, rather than in the home. These are not to be private services for individual family members but celebrated in the context of a fellowship of believers. The premise is that there is power in *koinonia*—two or three gathered in Christ's name. In a few instances, the liturgies may be held in the home, retirement community, hospital, and so forth. However, this book can also be used devotionally by persons in crisis.

DEFINITION OF TERMS

Since this book deals with liturgies, perhaps brief definitions of *liturgy* and *healing liturgy* might be helpful. *Liturgy* is a public, as opposed to a private, gathering of Christ's faithful for worship of God—"Christ is not an abstraction but a reality when a community gathers to be signs of Christ's presence with one another."[4] Just as God is present to us in our joy and suffering, so we serve the same function to each other as we gather as the body of Christ to publicly witness and, in doing so, participate in our neighbor's suffering by accepting it; thus we transform it (make it whole) through our faith in the cross. Liturgy has consequences for life, and life has consequences for liturgy. The term *church* in Greek, *ekklesia*, means "those called out," for example, the gathered, the assembly. Liturgy is the ordering of this household through prescribed written services. "The liturgy is the most perfect manifestation of the Church."[5]

Liturgy in these last decades has provided as well an opportunity for women to take a leading role in developing liturgies. Teresa Berger argues that "women-identified liturgies" are a place for theological reflection. This illustrates the rediscovery of the relationship between worship and theology. "Since the publication of Geoffrey Wainwright's *Doxology: The Praise of God in Doctrine, Worship and Life* two decades ago,[6] a growing number of Protestant theologians have joined the many Orthodox and Catholic theologians who consciously draw on liturgical materials for their work. . . . Although there are distinct differences between theologians as to how *lex orandi* and *lex credendi* are to be related—from claims to the priority of doxology over theology, to the subordination of the liturgy to dogma, to an interpretation of worship as theology—all these proposals are part of the (re-)turn to the liturgy that so profoundly marked recent theological work."[7]

Worship is our praise to God as Romans 12 expresses it, our living sacrifice, the work of the people. Rituals are the forms we follow, for example, as part of our worship service. They may contain rites that become sacraments (outward sign of inward change), such as baptism and the Lord's Supper for Protestants. Rituals can be "the symbolic use of bodily movement and gesture in a social situation to express and articulate meaning."[8] Some scholars such as Colin Lanceley, Australian artist, have equated ritual with a form of collage. "The elements of ritual are like the layers or surfaces of a collage; you can put them together or break them apart, but the constituents do not equal the whole."[9]

Healing liturgies are worship services that focus on our movement toward wholeness while acknowledging our brokenness and need for God. While it is true that all worship can be a healing experience, special liturgies emphasize as preeminent this aspect of worship. It is parallel to the practice of prayer, which is at all times and places, including worship, but we still recognize the importance of special prayer services.

It is important to note that the general use of the term *healing liturgies* does not necessarily mean that a person is sick; rather, these services may bring people to greater wholeness. Healing liturgies are not confined to people facing imminent death—a shift already made by Vatican II in the change from extreme unction back to the original sacrament of healing. They are for those in different places of physical and spiritual need. We use not only sacraments for healing but various rites and services that allow us to gather as a worshiping community, inviting the presence of Christ and the action of the Holy Spirit.

My hope is that these liturgies will be used widely in the life of the church and in the community at large. They are appropriate for various seasons of the life cycle as well as during times of personal and community crisis. They can be adapted or used in their entirety to meet people's needs and conditions in the life of the church and in the world at large, or used in circumstances different from their original purpose. The most important thing in adapting these liturgies is that they should arise from the context of the worshipers and speak to their condition. I attended many churches that celebrated these liturgies and was greatly blessed. Not only is contemporary liturgy wonderful but the beauty of the language of the great prayers of the church may also speak to us today.

Besides services for different chronological seasons and times of crisis, this book presents general healing services from various denominations and traditions to reflect the diversity of expressions of faith that now exists. These general services reflect the reality that we need healing at all times and places, not just in moments of crisis. The book also includes individual prayers and litanies, not just complete worship services. Of course, this collection of liturgies is not exhaustive. Other sources are available, such as Roman Catholic blessings at athletic events and graduation and numerous prayers for the sick in the Anglican prayer book.

STYLE AND FORMAT OF THE LITURGIES

This book includes healing liturgies currently in use in a wide variety of Christian faith communities. The denomination of origin is indicated by each liturgy, but no liturgy is limited to use in that tradition. In fact, several have been written by Presbyterians or Roman Catholics for an ecumenical setting. Certain nonliturgical denominations, such as Baptist or Pentecostal, are underrepresented not because they do not value healing services but because they seldom use printed services.

The reader will notice in these collected liturgies a tremendous variation in language, theology, and style. Both ancient and contemporary liturgies are included from different Protestant denominations as well as Roman Catholic and Free Church traditions. Several services are interfaith, reflecting global and community-wide situations. Terms used for the clergy also vary: *celebrant, priest, pastor, minister,* and *leader.*

Some liturgies are feminist and use inclusive language for God and people, whereas others use only male pronouns. A few contain theology with which I might disagree—for instance, the translation in James 5, *presbyteros,* as "priests" rather than "elders." A few have a Latino or African American character. These liturgies were purposely not changed; in most cases they are under copyright, and they have been left in their original form to reflect the diversity in various Christian traditions. In a few instances, I have expanded the liturgies where copyright permission allowed and a brief addition seemed warranted. Music was another area of expansion: the hymns selected for several of the liturgies do not appear in the common hymnbook of that denomination. In those cases, other sources of the hymn have been cited to provide a guide. In many cases, only hymn names were listed in the original liturgy and were researched to provide a source. In several instances the service indicates music with no specific hymn listed, so hymns were found to fit the theme. The bibliographic information on the hymnals listed follows the Acknowledgments.

One of the challenges in selecting these liturgies was to find those that mark passages of people's lives while retaining the focus on worshiping God. Worship cannot be too cozy or popular. For example, I am opposed to applauding in church—it is God, not people, whom we are praising and honoring. Worship should be the food that sustains the soul, the inner spirit. The purpose of my book is to provide bread for the journey. It is precisely at the difficult times of life that we need healing. In all may God's name be praised.

Acknowledgments

When I first envisioned this book on healing liturgies five years ago, I never realized what extensive work would be involved in finding liturgies to mark the passages of life and, even more, in obtaining permission to use these liturgies. The latter was complicated by the fact that many of the services had multiple copyright holders for the various parts of the service. A single liturgy could require up to ten different permissions since it was of a composite nature. The notes reflect the hundreds of sources that were used so that permission to print these liturgies would come from the original copyright holder. Without the diligent work of a number of outstanding research assistants over several years, this never could have been accomplished.

First and foremost, I thank Raimundo Barreto, who has done so much of the work on this book. As well, many others assisted in bringing it to publication—Jane Brady; Dorothy LaPenta; Myesha Hamm; Amanda Wanschura; Jane Ferguson, who helped find liturgies and worked on the final editing; Marian Hays, professional musician, who helped with the music selections; and of course my excellent assistant, Janice Miller, who has worked tirelessly on so many aspects of this book, including the final manuscript. A special thanks also to Martin Tel for putting the finishing touch on the music selections, and Michael Atzert, while an M.Div. student, for handling all the necessary office details. My gratitude goes to President Thomas Gillespie and Dean James Armstrong of Princeton Seminary for years of support and encouragement.

I also thank the American Bible Society, who granted permission for use of *Good News Bible* line drawings. I am grateful to the church members and pastors who wrote and conducted these services and to the churches who comforted those for whom these liturgies were written. They are a great cloud of witnesses to the healing presence of our Savior, Jesus Christ, the power of the Holy Spirit, and the love of God our parent.

Hymnals Used in Liturgies

AAHH   Rev. Dr. Delores Carpenter, ed., *African American Heritage Hymnal* (Chicago: GIA Publications, 2001).

AMR   *Hymns Ancient and Modern Revised* (London: Hymns Ancient and Modern Ltd./The Canterbury Press, 1950).

ASB   *Alternative Service Book of 1980* © Central Board of Finance of the Church of England.

BH   *Baptist Hymnal 1991* (Nashville: Broadman & Holman Publishers, 1991).

CCH   *Catholic Community Hymnal* (Chicago: GIA Publications, 1999).

CH   Gayle Schoepf, chair, Hymnal Development Committee, *Chalice Hymnal* (Christian Church, Disciples of Christ) (St. Louis: Chalice Press, 1995).

CMP   Peter Horrobin and Greg Leavers, comps., *Complete Mission Praise* (Great Britain: Marshall Pickering, 1999).

H82   James Litton et al., The Joint Commission on Revision of the Hymnal, *The Hymnal 1982* (New York: Church Hymnal Corp., 1985).

HAM   Hymnal Committee, *Hymns Ancient and Modern New Standard* (Words Edition) (Norwich, Norfolk: Hymns Ancient & Modern Ltd., 1989).

HPW   Emerson C. Frey, chair, Editorial Committee, *Hymns for Praise and Worship* (Brethren in Christ) (Nappansee, Ind.: Evangel Press, 1984).

H:WB   Rebecca Slough, ed., *Hymnal: A Worship Book* (Elgin, Ill.: Brethren Press; Newton, Kans.: Faith and Life Press; Scottdale, Pa.: Mennonite Publishing House, 1992).

LEVS   Horace C. Boyer, *Lift Every Voice and Sing II: An African American Hymnal* (New York: Church Hymnal Corp., 1993).

LH   *The Lutheran Hymnal, Lutheran Worship, Hymnal Supplement 98* (St. Louis: Concordia Publishing House, 1998).

LW   Inter-Lutheran Commission on Worship, *Lutheran Book of Worship,* 5th printing May 1982 (Minneapolis: Augsburg Publishing House; Philadelphia: Board of Publication, Lutheran Church in America, 1978).

MAR   *Maranatha! Music Praise Chorus Book* (Nashville: Word Publishing Group, 1989).

NCH   James W. Crawford, chair, Hymnal Committee, *New Century Hymnal* (United Church of Christ) (Cleveland: Pilgrim Press, 1995).

PrH   Melva W. Costen, chair, Hymnal Committee, *The Presbyterian Hymnal* (Louisville, Ky.: Westminster/John Knox Press, 1990).

PsH   Emily R. Brink, ed., The Revision Committee, *Psalter Hymnal* (Christian Reformed Church) (Grand Rapids: CRC Publications, 1987).

SB   Ito Loth, ed., Apec Editorial Committee, *Sound the Bamboo: CCA Hymnal 2000* (Taiwan: Taiwan Presbyterian Church Press, 2000).

SNC   *Sing! A New Creation* (Grand Rapids: Calvin Institute of Christian Worship, CRC Publications; New York: Reformed Church Press, 2001).

S&P   *Songs and Prayers from Taizé,* GIA Publications, Inc., 1992, ISBN 0941050343.

TFF   *This Far by Faith: An African American Resource for Worship* (Minneapolis: Augsburg Fortress, 1999).

TFWS   *The Faith We Sing* (*United Methodist Hymnal* supplement) (Nashville: Abingdon Press, 2000).

UMH   Reuben P. Job, chair, Hymnal Revision Committee, *The United Methodist Hymnal* (Nashville: United Methodist Publishing House, 1989).

W&R   George H. Shorney et al., *Worship and Rejoice* (nondenominational) (Carol Stream, Ill.: Hope Publishing Co., 2001).

WIII   Robert J. Batastini, ed., *Worship III* (Chicago: GIA Publications, 1986).

WL&P   John L. Hooker, Episcopal Church, *Wonder, Love and Praise: A Supplement to the Hymnal 1982* (New York: Church Publishing, 1997).

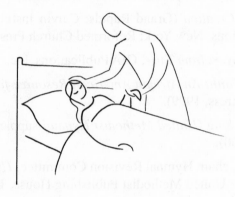

"Even if I go through the deepest darkness . . ."
(Ps. 23:4)

Healing Liturgies: An Analysis

*T*he healing liturgies in this book are rooted in a theology of the incarnational and historical God, who is intimately involved in our daily lives. Although the liturgies speak for themselves, it may be helpful to discuss how they fit into the general ministry and worship life of the church. In addition, their various components are important to understand. The preparation and education before holding these services is also crucial. This educational prelude may be almost as important as the services themselves. Follow-up and pastoral care should also form part of the overall context of these liturgies.

DEFINING HEALING

Understanding what healing means is central to planning a healing service. Healing is any activity that moves an individual or community toward "wholeness," a concept rooted in a Christian perspective of the integration of body, mind, and spirit with God at the center and the source of all healing. It is the affirmation of one's potential within the limits of the human condition. All are in permanent need of God's grace and therefore are in need of healing.

At the heart of the Christian theology of healing is the problem of pain, suffering, and death. There are indeed times when suffering actually becomes part of the healing process, but even at these times, Christian hope should pervade the person or community in need of healing. Healing may be what resolves a crisis. In times of crisis, many disciplines (social worker, pastor, physician, therapist) may be called on to collaborate in order to support healing. There are certain times in each person's life, or in the life of loved ones or communities, when woundedness seems especially acute and attention to God's healing power and grace is needed. Woundedness and suffering can take many forms—cancer, cystic fibrosis, Alzheimer's, depression, memories of abuse, alcoholism, divorce, unemployment. But no matter what our pain, we need to pass through it before we can be restored to wholeness, though complete wholeness is possible only in eternity.

Healing is more than curing and includes caring, sustaining, comforting, counseling, and transforming. Healing in one sense is becoming all we were meant to be, becoming fully alive, becoming fully ourselves within the limits of our particular condition. From a Judeo-Christian perspective, healing is seen not only as an individual concern. People should also be cognizant of the well-being and health of neighbor, community, world, and the environment in which we all live. In a community context, healing may also entail freedom from oppression that renders some members of society powerless and marginalized.

ROLE OF HEALING LITURGIES

It is unfortunate that too often Christians have misunderstood the power and purpose of healing liturgies. While healing liturgies are frequently special services that take place outside the context of weekly worship, the traditional Sunday-morning service can be an occasion for promoting spiritual and emotional well-being. This is not to discount special worship experiences using such rites as laying-on of hands and anointing with oil. Indeed, such practices have ancient roots in the Christian tradition. But healing liturgies should not be relegated solely to services conducted outside the routine worship life of the community; doing so carries with it certain dangers of separation and sensationalism. Rather, concern for the well-being of the community and its members should be incorporated into the ongoing worship life of the congregation. Some people treat worship like a sacred parenthesis that has nothing to do with the rest of their lives.[1] That is why I have taken the everyday events of life and tried to find ways of marking them liturgically, so that celebration, sorrow, recognition, and healing can take place. These new liturgies in a way take words and liturgical acts as reflecting a new reality and expressing power in and of themselves.[2]

Through the observance of the church year, the worship life of the local congregation can touch the full range of emotional and spiritual situations in which church members find themselves. It offers a wide range of possible sustenance and healing through liturgical means. Bible study, discussion, prayer, reflection, readings about healing ministry, and different liturgies are all part of the necessary education when healing services are first being introduced in a church.

PLACE OF SYMBOLS AND RITUALS

Symbols are very important in healing liturgies, as they add a dimension of meaning. They testify to the transforming power of what is taking place. Symbols are complex; icons, banners, altars or ceremonial spaces, special gestures, and objects all form part of the symbols of liturgy. The complex nature of symbols invokes an attitude of faith.[3] Symbols are multi-dimensioned. They resonate with deep imaginative need and intentions that are not easily translated into words. Water, for example, says something to the eternal dimensions of our origins, so its use in baptisms invokes strong remembrances that we cannot adequately articulate. Carl Jung, in his theory of "archetypes," spoke of such symbols as water, fire, a breeze, or a sip of wine, which have meanings that cannot be verbalized.[4]

It is important to grasp that symbols are archaic, complex, and many-dimensioned: archaic in the sense that we invoke a promise made long ago, for example, in the Communion, remembering the death and resurrection of Jesus Christ that brings us new life. We need to recognize the past deed and the difference it makes in our life to fully appreciate what has happened to us.[5] The notion of readiness connotes that we are able to appreciate the signs, actions, and sharing of worship. Ritual action brings together imagery and social meaning.[6] Liturgy involves not only words but also ritual action. In this sense, ritual is a symbolic action. "A symbol is one thing 'thrown with' another. *Syn* is the Greek word for 'with,' *bolein* means to 'throw.' A symbol is something which, having been 'thrown with' something else, stands for that other thing."[7]

"Symbols not only stand for objects but can evoke feelings, call forth memories long buried, and combine references in a way that makes the world new."[8] The identity between a thing and a symbol is so deep that some theologians do not refer to sacraments as symbols at all, lest they be confused with arbitrary symbols.[9] Chris Harris discusses the two poles of a symbol, namely, the sensory and ideological poles. The sensory pertains to the emotional dimension and the ideological with the more abstract.[10]

Symbols also pull together the reality of the community bringing us into God's presence.[11] Erik Erikson talks of the "ontogeny of ritualization," a term deriving from two Greek words, *onto* and *genesis,* meaning the coming into being of the individual we were meant to be. For Erikson, aspects of ritualization are repetition, relation, and reasons. Practices, in other words, become second nature. It is not possible to really participate in healing liturgies without some knowledge of the Christian faith; otherwise the symbols will be empty and healing cannot truly take place. Another way of expressing this is that these liturgies cannot be placed in a vacuum unconnected to a faith structure. Rituals, for Erikson, take place between persons, so they are relational.[12]

There are also ceremonies and rituals that embody spiritualities, such as the sign of peace expressing fellowship in Christ. "In recent years, the passing of the peace has again become a prominent sign of reconciliation and love as Christians embrace one another or shake hands during worship."[13] Other rituals, such as genuflection before the sacrament, forming of a circle, coming forward for Communion, and lighting of candles, symbolize deeper realities. These various ceremonies can reinforce the central focus or message of the service. Objects, for example, may form an important part of a funeral.[14]

LANGUAGE AND SILENCE AS SYMBOL

Part of what we are discussing in terms of symbols is the power and use of language, which can enrich liturgy. Language involves gesture and words, which are intertwined with each other. Liturgical language uses active, performative words that do not simply describe or communicate existing situations but actually create new situations. In some ways, a liturgical text is similar to the script of a drama. Reading a script is one-dimensional—to come alive, action, gesture, and movement must accompany it.

In liturgy, gestures and words go together. The gesture itself may be powerful enough to make its own statement. For example, the sign of the cross made over a person or an object, without any words, effectively conveys a blessing. Bowing before the altar needs no words for its power. In the Roman Catholic ordination rites, the bishop lays his hands on the head of the ordinand in silence. This in itself contains a prayer for consecration by the Holy Spirit; then a spoken prayer follows. The silent gesture and the spoken words together constitute the act of ordination.

Respect for the power of language also involves an equal respect for silence, without which sounds are a meaningless jumble. By silence, we acknowledge the limitations of words. Silence may lead us directly into God's presence. Rests in music, spaces in architecture, pauses in poetic lines are as important as the notes, the masses, and the articulated syllables. Silences as much as sound convey strong meaning beyond words. At times profound revelation is wordless. We recall the words of the Elijah story: after the wind and the fire comes the still, small voice of God.

PREPARATION FOR HEALING SERVICES

Preparation for healing services involves several parts: education of the congregation, training of leaders and participants, and publicity.

EDUCATION OF THE CONGREGATION

The first step in education for healing services is for the leadership to know the community and people who come for healing. Selecting the services that match the needs of individuals and congregations is important. Some Christians resist scripted services, which they think keep tight rein on the Spirit. They believe that each time Christians unite, the Holy Spirit reinvents worship; but even those Christians may develop a pattern.[15] For example, in the Black Baptist Church one observes a certain formula of music, dynamic preaching, and extensive congregational participation. If there were no "Amens," the pastor would think he or she was in the wrong church. Conversely, other Christians, such as Episcopalians or Roman Catholics, may feel ill at ease in the absence of a more formal approach to liturgy. It is hoped that the variety of these liturgies reflects the reality of the infinite ways the Holy Spirit moves through our worship.

Despite the attraction of liturgies for the various passages of life, some parishioners will resist them. Often people resist changes in worship because of deep issues. Worship renewal must be for the right reasons, not simply to draw a crowd. Taking time for preparation and education of the congregation can enrich the experience considerably.

Robin Green, author of *Only Connect: Worship and Liturgy from the Perspective of Pastoral Care,* for example, recounts vignettes of members resisting the introduction of passing the peace in the church because of intimacy issues. The members were squeamish about becoming involved with those around them even in this seemingly slight way. Education may not address all the issues of resistance because the causes are often emotional rather than rational. Active listening, patience, and understanding are crucial.[16] William Willimon, dean of the chapel and professor of Christian Ministry at Duke University, Durham, North Carolina, describes one congregation that, through education, eventually instituted the passing of the peace when they recognized this rite as a way of breaking down barriers of isolation and individualism, and of creating community.[17]

The congregation should be educated about the nature of the services to be conducted. Unfortunately, false expectations and misunderstandings often surround healing services—hopes of miraculous physical healings or sudden healing of past pain and abuses should be offered not as the norm but as the exception. The tension exists between the firm belief that with God all things are possible and awe in the face of both the mystery of suffering and God's power to speak through our brokenness. A Christian theology of health, healing, sickness, and suffering should be taught through sermons and Christian education classes as a way of preparing people for these healing services.

In any service, God's healing power is present and some healing will happen, even if it is only acceptance of our pain or a sense of God's sustaining presence in the midst of it. As important as education is, one must always remember that God's Spirit is surprising and unexpected in its power and possibilities. The Holy Spirit cannot be contained within our plans. An attitude of openness is essential.

TRAINING OF LEADERS AND PARTICIPANTS

Preparation is essential both for the leaders and the participants in a worship service. In *A Manual for Ministry to the Sick,* edited by Martin Dudley, there are prayers to prepare the leader that are a necessary part of visitation of the sick, as well as leading healing liturgies.[18] The leader, in turn, needs to prepare the participants by praying with them and addressing expectations.

Church members may have unexpected gifts for healing ministry that God may raise up for times of need. "One is struck by the variety of ministries that appears in the New Testament. All seem structured on a pragmatic basis: a need is apparent and a ministry to meet it develops. There is a need to distribute food so that the twelve can be free to devote themselves 'to prayer and to serving the word' (Acts 6:4) and so the seven are chosen." There is some fluidity in the ministries as they are developed. For example, Stephen certainly does not limit himself to the job description of waiting on tables as a ministry. A common characteristic is that though there are varieties of services "to each is given the manifestation of the Spirit for the common good" (1 Cor. 12:7).[19] So in leadership of healing services, people may have gifts of music, anointing, praying, and so forth.

Leadership is an important consideration in planning a healing service. Although it is not an ironclad rule, involving laity in the leadership can enrich the service tremendously. However, they should receive some education and preparation for this role. While Protestants make much of the theology of the laity, it is not often practiced in worship leadership. Especially in healing liturgies, the sharp distinction between clergy and laity does not hold true. There is now a movement even in the Church of England for nonordained members to lead healing services, as members discover their gifts for healing.[20] Whether the leaders are lay or clergy, preparation and planning, for even seemingly free-form or "spontaneous services," are important. This frees one to focus on the Holy Spirit's presence as an instrument of God's healing power. There is now a movement that emphasizes more flexibility to healing services and the gifts of healing being reemphasized by charismatic groups within congregations.

The ministry to the sick is an illustration of the empowerment of the laity in leadership because the community renders service to the sick person. Likewise, the ill render service in their vulnerability and weakness, by giving witness to the power of the risen Lord in testimony to the church. This is tied to our recommendation that lay people take a very active role in the leadership of these services, as well as the sick individuals themselves. These services expand to a ministry of empowerment as both rely on God's grace in the midst of suffering.[21] Justice issues and worship are concerned not only with the content of the service but with who is involved in the leadership. Too often certain people, for example, persons with disabilities, have been excluded from leadership because the pulpit is inaccessible. It is important to involve those with the particular condition or crisis that is highlighted in the service. This is not only to avoid paternalism or a we/they dividing of so-called well and sick folks but also because we are bound together in our mutual brokenness and need for God's grace. "He/she is only whole who shares in the brokenness of others."[22] This approach is especially important for services involving those with disabilities, mental illness, or addiction, who may be generally shunned by society.

The distinction between leader and participant is not always sharply drawn in healing liturgies. For example, "At the Time of Divorce" has parts spoken by the parents, and the only role of the clergy is a blessing at the close of this short service. This blending of roles is actually a common feature in many of the liturgies, as healing services are much more participatory by their very nature. The congregation should not be an audience but participants.

What the leaders wear can also send a message. What leaders choose to wear is not inconsequential for a healing service.[23] Whether street or business dress, jeans or vestments, clothing conveys something about the style of worship. Dressing with care shows that as a leader you care. The vestments of the priest/pastor can convey high church with elaborate vestments that might separate the people from the celebrant or might contribute to a sense of the holy mystery.

In addition to training the leaders, preparation for the participants is important. Many people who attend a healing service do just that—attend rather than participate. However, the story of Peter's mother-in-law gives an insight into the proper mode of response. "The fever left her, and she began to serve them" (Mark 1:29–31). Her response to healing was to serve others. The story of the ten lepers is also instructive. The one who received healing and returned to give thanks is a model response. Gratitude and service are the best attitudes or responses to healing. The healing liturgy itself can help encourage this sense of service by responses of music and the spoken word, where participants pray to help others and testify to a sense of God's presence and power. How unfortunate that many people who come to a service with a variety of needs, upon being filled take these gifts for granted and do not think to help others.

PUBLICITY ABOUT SERVICES

Once a congregation has decided to hold one of these services, how it is publicized is part of the education about its meaning. One must be careful that people attending these services do not view themselves as more spiritual or religious, with special gifts and graces. I cannot emphasize strongly enough the importance of these services being seen as an integral part of the life of the church and not some extra or add-on activity. In the same way that the healing ministry of the church must be central, so must be these services. In announcing them, care should be taken in how the invitation is offered and the service publicized. Use phrases like "As part of the continual ministry of this church, we are offering times of worship for those with a variety of needs, especially those recovering from addiction, for example, or suffering with AIDS." Here, however, caution is needed not to structure the service so that those without these conditions will not feel free to come; rather, they should come in solidarity with others, bound together in mutual brokenness.

COMPONENTS OF HEALING LITURGIES

There are various parts of healing liturgies, which vary according to the subject, type, and setting of the service. However, I will comment on some general components: the gathering rite, proclamation of the Word, prayer, sacraments, and music.

THE GATHERING RITE

As people gather for worship, one of the important parts of the service is calling people to praise and glorify God, the ruler of all. Times of meditation in silence or printed prayers for reflection may assist the centering. Soft music may help people open themselves to God's presence. Although many services start with a call to worship, it is important to note that God is always present; it is we who need to be attentive to God's word to us. In some traditions, on entering the church the sign of the cross is made as the first step of preparation. A greeting may be given or announcements made, and an opening song or instrumental prelude may draw people into the worship. A sense of mystery or expectation may be created.

PROCLAMATION OF THE WORD

An important part of any healing service is the proclamation and living out of a wholistic theology of health. This theology should highlight an integrated *Weltanschauung* (worldview) that clarifies values and priorities and enhances self-esteem. It envisions a community where healing, wholeness, and harmony all constitute health. It is presented through the reading of the Scriptures and/or preaching and exposition of Scripture. Genuine spirituality is built on the Scriptures; they can be read out loud or meditated on, as in the ancient practice of *lectio divina*.[24] Christ, the Word, should be at the center of the service.

PRAYER

Prayer is not only part of any healing service but should surround those preparing for a healing ministry. Prayer forms a central part of any healing service. Having a clear theology of prayer is crucial. Corporate prayer may speed recovery as well as promote healthy attitudes in those praying; we place ourselves in God's service when we pray for someone else. We may begin with petitionary prayer, which leads us into a deeper relationship with God where God's will is our deepest desire (Matt. 26:39). God always hears our petitions but does not automatically grant them in the way we might desire. However, when God's spirit infuses us, our whole outlook can be changed. "Confidence in prayer is therefore a Christian hallmark."[25]

The Bible has no lack of clarity as to when we should pray—always, pray without ceasing. The key passage is in 1 Thessalonians 5:17. We should pray daily, when we are in need, on occasions of joy and thanksgiving. Prayer is a deep, interior attitude, not just saying prayers but a habitual forefront and background of great living. We are constantly sending up prayers to God, but that does not mean that if all of life is a prayer, we do not need times of prayer, because private prayer can become merely a tuning in to our own inner voice, not the voice of God. The biblical account refers to specific times when Christ prayed: Mark 1:35 recounts, "In the morning, while it was still very dark, he got up and went out to a deserted place, and there he prayed." His disciples saw him praying so often that they finally asked him to teach them how to pray, from which comes the Lord's Prayer. Jesus told many parables about prayer; one is recorded in Luke 18:1: "Jesus told them a parable about their need to pray always and not to lose heart." We read of the great saints of the church who set aside specific times each day to pray, and Dietrich Bonhoeffer, for example, believed it was essential to begin each day early in the morning with prayer.

Also, there are specific occasions of need when we should pray. The problem with "need prayers" is that if we have not prayed daily, we are not in the habit of knowing where to turn for help. We need to cultivate the habit of prayer. Instead, we use prayer as a hotline to God and call collect. Then we wonder why nothing happens. We are so accustomed to working things out on our own that we find it hard to confess our need. However, there is nothing wrong with asking God to respond to a particular need. In fact, we are urged to do this by James 5:13: "Are any among you suffering? They should pray." First Kings 17 and 18 recounts the story of Elijah and his prayers in a specific time of need, that is, when he petitioned for Israel to stop worshiping Baal and return to the true God. He requested God work a miracle through the rain and fire so that Israel would believe in the true God, YHWH.

Every time Christ had an agonizing decision to make, he prayed—facing his temptation in the desert, in Gethsemane, during his transfiguration, on the cross. Even in times of physical exhaustion, after he had been healing, preaching, feeding the multitudes, Matthew 14:23 tells us, "After saying farewell to them, he went up on the mountain to pray" (Mark 6:46). And again later, "he would withdraw to deserted places and pray" (Luke 5:16).

Knowing how to pray is essential. First, we must pray in faith. If we do not believe in God, there is no point in praying. Prayer is involvement with God—an act of faith that there is a personal God who cares and is listening. This does not mean that we cannot pray for God to increase our faith but that we talk to God, not the sun or a mountain or a statue. This underscores the need for daily prayer in order to develop an increasingly intimate *relationship* with God.

Second, we pray for God's will to be done. Too often our prayer life is weak because we stay in the aggressive workaday world. We are still trying to force our selfish will on the world. Prayer is looked on only as an additional way of getting what we want. A fallback position to be used when other methods have failed, the whole tone is: God, get me what I want. We hold our wish, the object of our desire, in the center of our prayer—it obsesses and controls us. This kind of prayer can ruin us. We should not come to God saying God's will be done and secretly desiring our own will. Jesus said the pure in heart will see God. Søren Kierkegaard said that purity of heart is to will one thing, the will of God.[26]

Third, when we pray, we should ask anything of God. When we pray in faith and for God's will, there is nothing we cannot request. "Ask, and it will be given you; search, and you will find" (Luke 11:9). Again, Jesus says in the Gospel of John, "If you ask anything of the Father in my name, he will give it to you. Until now you have not asked for anything in my name. Ask and you will receive, so that your joy may be complete" (John 16:23). What a glorious promise we have in 1 John: "And this is the boldness we have in him, that if we ask anything according to his will, he hears us" (1 John 5:14).

Last, in remembering how to pray, we should pray for others. James tells us to pray for one another. The heart of prayer is intercessory. The Bible is full of admonitions to pray for others—for example, Paul writing to the Thessalonians: "To this end we always pray for you, asking that our God . . . will fulfill by his power every good resolve and work of faith" (2 Thess. 1:11). Jesus saved his worst ridicule for the man who went up and prayed for himself. Have you ever felt yourself upheld by a circle of prayer? What power is released through the prayers of others on our behalf?

A central element of healing prayer is confession, repentance, and forgiveness. In the early church, the elders came not simply to visit but to pray, and to encourage others to pray, for healing. "Therefore confess your sins to one another, and pray for one another, so that you may be healed. The prayer of the righteous is powerful and effective" (James 5:16). An important component of prayer is confession. We need to remove guilt and resentment by receiving God's pardon. This clears the way for the inner healing power of the person *vis medicatrix naturae*—force of natural healing. When we take seriously mutual forgiveness, then we free God's power to pour through us and genuinely pray for one another. The knowledge that a whole group is praying for your recovery can have tremendous power.

When the invitation for healing prayers is offered, one cannot be sure who will come forward. We all have hidden inner wounds that may be revealed at the invitation for healing in a sacred space. It may be strangers who have simply felt an impulse to come to church, or people known to the parish for years who seem healthy and carefree and who pour out anguished prayers for healing, for conditions of which we were totally unaware. (As well, people may come forward to request prayers for friends or family members.) Be prepared for these deep revelations and needs that may occur at invitations to share prayer requests.

SACRAMENTS

The sacraments are the means by which God's grace is offered to a repentant humanity and are signs of God's ongoing activity in the world. They are gifts from God, available to all who accept the new life that God offers in Christ. Through their regular administration, members of the church community are reminded of the life of grace and obedience to which they are called. The sacraments signify and seal God's power and gifts that the church uses in healing: they remind us of Christ's gifts to us and the incarnational reality of the spiritual. They reaffirm the believer's dependence on grace and symbolize hope.

God is everywhere. However, on this earth God also reveals God's self in particular places, that is, in the sacraments. The sacraments become windows into heaven. Sacraments reflect God's love and presence with us. The sacraments of baptism and the Lord's Supper are observed in all Christian traditions. In addition, others include the rite of healing as a sacrament, which is discussed in chapter 5, "Illness: As Life-Threatening."

It is no accident that in the Presbyterian Church we refer to the clergy as ministers of Word and Sacrament. This indicates the centrality of sacraments in the life of the church. We do not celebrate the sacraments alone but in the presence of God's people. By offering God prayers and praises, we acknowledge whose we are.

MUSIC

Music is an essential part of these liturgies; it may be God's word to us. Music provides an aesthetic, intangible link to the spiritual experience. In the following poem, "Praises of God," James Montgomery is echoing Job and the songs heard by St. John the Divine (Rev. 19:6–7):

Songs of praise the angels sang,
Heaven with alleluias rang,
When creation was begun,
When God spake and it was done.

And at the end:

> Heaven and earth must pass away,
> Songs of praise shall crown that day,
> God will make new heavens and earth,
> Songs of praise shall hail their birth.[27]

One of the most important aspects of worship is music. As we survey the Bible, we see the truth of that reality. A number of passages speak of the singing of hymns, even in such uncomfortable places as the Philippian jail (Acts 16:25). Ephesians and Colossians mention singing: "As you sing psalms and hymns and spiritual songs among yourselves, singing and making melody to the Lord in your hearts . . ." (Eph. 5:19; cf. Col. 3:16). We have glimpses of various hymn texts in the Bible, although these are difficult to identify with certainty. Several passages probably began as hymns. The christological hymn in Philippians (Phil. 2:6–11) is a most likely candidate, as are the hymns in Romans (Rom. 11:33–35), Colossians (Col. 1:15–20), Ephesians (Eph. 5:14), and possibly the hymn on love in 1 Corinthians (1 Cor. 13). The first two chapters of Luke contain the hymns of Elizabeth (1:42–45), Mary (1:46–55), Zechariah (1:8–79), and Simeon (2:29–32). All these hymns combine the language of Jewish history and the personal experience of the singer. They easily lend themselves to corporate singing and have been so used for centuries. The book of Revelation is also full of songs: 4:11; 5:9–10; 11:17–18; 15:3–4.[28]

Early Christians, such as Clement of Alexandria (ca. 150–215 C.E.), found in such psalm verses as 33:3, referring to a "new song," a foreshadowing of the songs of Christianity occasioned by the coming of Christ, himself the New Song. Clement's explanation is that the first letter of Jesus' name, *iota*, which signifies ten, is implied in the ten-stringed instrument of Psalm 33:2, which reveals "Jesus, the Word, manifested in the element of the decad." Christ, metaphorically New Song, establishes order, harmony, and concord. He ordered "the universe and tuned the discord of the elements in one harmonious arrangement."[29] Church fathers such as Jerome accepted the Pauline injunction to use "psalms, hymns, and spiritual songs" (Eph. 5:18–20; Col. 3:16–17), making melody in our hearts.

The language of liturgy as it ascends toward God may turn to music to release a power, giving wings to the word.[30] "Because of this powerful, domineering energy that erupts into song, we naturally expect liturgical texts to involve song. As well, the sermons of nonliturgical African-American preachers and many Pentecostals have a cadence. These preachers whose sermons must bear much of the burden of worship move, as the emotion builds, from mere prose into a sing-song punctuated with a kind of humming, a clear rhythm that captivates the congregation in its driving energy and musical cadence."[31]

The hymns and other music of the worship services should focus on the music as well as the text. "We must look at the words, to be sure, but we must also look at the music to which the words are set and examine the interplay between them. Even then we have not yet done enough, for we must also examine the movements that the text and the melodies require, suggest or inspire. What do the ministers and the congregation *do* before, during, after these texts are sung? Only by answering such questions can we have a comprehensive and satisfactory analysis of the liturgy."[32]

Churches need continually to use fresh words and music to praise God, however, so many new compositions confuse praise with "happiness." In their book *Reaching Out without*

Dumbing Down, which offers a "theology of worship for the turn-of-the-century culture," authors Marva Dawn and Martin Marty lament, "Some worship planners and participants think that to praise God is simply to sing upbeat music; consequently, many songs that are called 'praise' actually describe the feelings of the believer rather than the character of God."[33]

" 'Praise' that uses only 'upbeat' songs can be extremely destructive to worshipers because it denies the reality of doubts concerning God, the hiddenness of God, and the feelings of abandonment by God that cloud believers going through difficult times." Many people who only hear happy songs may leave with huge feelings of inadequacy. " 'Why do I feel so discouraged? I know I should praise God, but I just can't,' they say. That is because the worship has not dealt with their feelings of guilt, their doubts and fears, their sense of hypocrisy and sinfulness."[34]

There are certain dangers of narcissism or feeling good in contemporary society and worship where God recedes into the background. Worship should not focus "on me and my feelings," as this makes us think first of self rather than of God. Some modern music does not focus on praising God but on how well we are loving God.[35] The chief function of church music should be to add a deeper dimension of involvement to worship. "By now almost every choir room must have a sign quoting Augustine to the effect that the one who sings prays twice."[36] Church music adds emotion and beauty to the service.

Liturgical music can express a spirituality of sober restraint, as in German chorales; otherworldly peace, as in the Gregorian chant; or contact with contemporary American culture through jazz or "praise" music. The choice of instrument can also reflect different spiritual experiences; for example, organ, guitar, harp, and piano all set a different tone and mood for the service.[37]

It is not only the professional musician but also congregational song that can give everyone the opportunity to offer to God the best music he or she can create. Congregational hymn singing of great music is one of the hallmarks of the Protestant Reformation. Martin Luther encouraged the development of congregational hymnody as a means for worshipers to engage actively in worship. Hence, it became a significant feature of Protestant life.[38]

Many scholars see deeper into the role of music. Hymn singing provides a way of knowing through action.[39] As a form of ritual behavior, it refocuses attention on the "doing" aspects of the singers' actions and sets these events on a par with drama, dance, and sporting events.[40] For some, such as George Steiner, the singing of religious texts opens one up to a type of "real presence" that is almost sacramental.[41]

"Music and the metaphysical, in the root sense of that latter term, music and spiritual feeling, have been virtually inseparable. It is in and through music that we are most immediately in the presence of the verbally inexpressible but wholly palpable energy that communicates to our senses and to our reflection what little we can grasp of the naked wonder of life; this is a sacramental notion."[42] This energy itself has a healing dimension.[43]

CONCLUSION AND DISMISSAL

Worship should end with an act of closure—final hymns and a benediction, periods of silence. Instrumental music or changes in the lighting have been used to signal the end to a service. Sometimes people choose to remain in the sanctuary to reflect on the worship experience, so the sanctuary should remain open at least thirty minutes after the conclusion of the service.

FOLLOW-UP AFTER THE SERVICE

As deep emotions surface during these healing liturgies, recognition of the need for pastoral care should form part of the planning. Sometimes it is helpful to have a notepad available to jot down the need for follow-up with particular individuals. Clergy should be trained so that they can appropriately respond to the needs that surface. Elders or church leaders should be ready to assist. Especially qualified are Stephen Ministers, who are church members who have received certified training in one-on-one caring. Long-term counseling may be needed to help the person to process all that has happened. Names for referral should be researched ahead of time. William Willimon has written persuasively of the link between worship and pastoral care. Worship itself may be a form of pastoral care. Being attuned to the pastoral needs that lead to participation in healing services, as well as those growing out of these services, is an aspect of this ministry.

SETTING OF SERVICES

ARCHITECTURE

Where liturgy takes place can emphasize different realities of worship. For example, the focus of attention can be the altar, either visible or hidden (as in the case with the Orthodox Church reflecting the mystery of God's presence). Or there may be a visual link between the baptismal font, the altar, and the pulpit. The building structure can contribute to creating a certain mood in worship, and appropriate settings affect the extent of the people's participation. A huge sanctuary with a pulpit at a great distance from the congregation can make participation less likely, or a sanctuary for a thousand in which twenty-five are gathered can create a disheartening atmosphere.[44]

At various periods of history, "so divorced had clergy and people become that a sixteenth-century Catholic bishop could write: 'The people in the church [nave] took small heed what the priest and clerks did in the chancel. . . . It was never meant that the people should indeed hear the Matins or hear the Mass, but be present there and pray by themselves in silence.' The division between nave and chancel, so functional in a monastic church, was a disaster in parish churches but nevertheless imitated with zeal."[45]

The relationship between architecture and worship is complex. Church architecture not only reflects how Christians worship, but architecture also shapes worship or, not uncommonly, misshapes it. It is clear that the building dictates the possibilities for various forms and styles of worship. We may want good singing, but bad acoustics may swallow up each sound.[46] Consideration of physical worship space can be a holy act.

ENVIRONMENTAL DETAILS

Being a leader for a healing service requires consideration of the environmental details of the service. This refers not only to the physical objects of the service but to the overall sanctuary, room, or chapel, that is, the place of worship. Appealing to all the senses is part of a wholistic service, where a climate of expectancy and openness is suggested. This can occur in ornate settings of the Roman Catholic, Orthodox, or Anglican sanctuary; the intimate setting of a felowship hall; the simple setting of the Quaker meetinghouse or the Taizé tent. No detail is too small for attention—lighting, ventilation, comfort and placement of chairs, sound system. There should be no rushing in a few minutes before the time for the service, full of distractions and stress, as the worship space as well as the worship leader needs to be ready. It is a great privilege to conduct a healing service, but with that comes responsibility of preparation at every stage.

The church itself stands as a symbol of God's presence. As a pastor in New York City at Broadway Presbyterian Church, I remember a woman across the street from the church who asked if I could do her mother's funeral. I was a bit surprised, as I never knew her mother or any members of her family. I learned that her mother was a lapsed Jew who had heard our church bells in the last years of her life. The daughter said they were a source of comfort to her. Since she and her mother belonged to no religious community, she thought it would be fitting to have her mother's funeral in our church.

Some of the liturgies in this book take place in the home, but they should always have members of a church present, and the space in whatever ways possible should be sanctified. Knowing the setting—for instance, whether small children and friends will be present in the house—is important so that the service can incorporate these realities. A few liturgies are set for outdoors. Those locations should be checked for noise level, privacy, and accessibility. Services on the beach, for example, may require special permissions.

SACRED ART

Sacred art is an expression of faith, so that we see the God whom we love reflected in the mystery behind the picture. Icons are perhaps the most powerful form of sacred art, which deepens our encounter with the divine. The icon "expresses artistically the principle that the truth of being is an event of communion between persons."[47] The icon actually places the viewer "inside" the icon, providing a window into the person depicted. It provides a means by which the object viewed is in a sense "reconstructed in the consciousness of the viewer."[48] Art engages the affective level of the person; it appeals to a different level of our understanding and so is a complement to theology. One thinks of Piero della Francesca's Resurrection mosaic, where Christ trods boldly upon death, proclaiming his victory; or the Boticelli Madonna, which reflects Mary as the mother of God.[49]

A more contemporary use of art is banners, which can be hung almost anywhere in the church. Increasingly we see a move to large-scale banners, fifteen feet or so in length, which can be changed for different liturgical seasons or moods within a liturgy.[50] They provide a marking of the liturgical seasons as well as celebratory feelings.

Different objects are used at various seasons, such as an Advent wreath with four candles, a Lenten veil, palm branches, a paschal candle, a star, a crown of thorns, tongues of flame, and so on. These objects can be sanctified to a sacred use. The lack of things also is a powerful form of communication.[51] For example, the absence of any flowers and candles on Good Friday sends a deep message.

Seasons of Life

"I will praise you, Lord . . ."
(Ps. 9:1)

"Teach them to your children."
(Deut. 11:19)

Chapter 1

Childhood/Adolescence

Father, bless to me the dawn,
Bless to me the coming morn.
Bless all that my eyes will see.
Bless all that will come to me.
Bless my neighbor and my friend.
Bless until our journey's end.
Bless the traveler to our shore.
Bless the stranger at our door.
Bless to me the opening year.
Bless all who to me are dear.
Bless, O Lord, this day of days.
Bless with riches all our ways.
    —David Adam, *"Consecration," in* Tides and Seasons[1]

INTRODUCTION

Pathologists and educators have long told us of the importance of the early years in shaping who we are as adults. The liturgies in this chapter begin with "Blessing of the Children" and then move to different passages of adolescence, including the difficult time of divorce that affects about one in two families in the United States. Many parents ignore conversations about divorce with their children, who either end up blaming themselves or never deal with the pain of their broken family. Hence, for example, it is hoped that the liturgy "At the Time of Divorce" (p. 25) can help ease the transition and recognize the loss that children experience. Giving children the support they need in their own crises and passages is an essential part of their future health.

Erik Erikson, in his classic work *Childhood and Society,* has developed what he calls the eight stages of human life.[2] These stages are summarized as follows: (1) infant—trust versus mistrust; (2) toddler—autonomy versus shame and doubt; (3) preschooler—initiative versus guilt; (4) school-age child—industry versus inferiority; (5) adolescence—ego identity versus role confusion; (6) young adult—intimacy versus isolation; (7) middle adult—generativity versus stagnancy; and (8) older adult—ego integrity versus despair. The reader will note that many liturgies in this book address the experiences of these stages. I discuss the later stages in chapter 2. The first stage is basic trust versus mistrust. "Trust born of care is, in fact, the touchstone of the actuality of a given religion."[3] Here Erikson is discussing the first stage of infancy, that of developing trust, which provides the foundation for all future relationships. The liturgy of the "Blessing of the Children" reflects our responsibility and care for our children to build a foundation for their trust.

In the second stage, autonomy versus shame and doubt, we see the tension between holding on and letting go; autonomy is preserved by a sense of justice.[4] He refers to different levels of experiencing, behaving, and inner states. Addressing the issues of shame are important as doubts enter. Here we find the ratio of love/hate, cooperation/willfulness, freedom of self-expression and its suppression.[5]

The third stage is initiative versus guilt. The young child tests what it means to go forth to conquer, sometimes finding that others have been there first. This is juxtaposed on one side with withdrawing from the conquered territory, on the other side, forging ahead.[6] This stage "also sets the direction toward the possible and the tangible which permits the dreams of early childhood to be attached to the goals of an active adult life."[7]

The truly tragic fact of childhood is that for some it is a time of abuse, so that the normal development of a child is thwarted. The replacement of trust with fear leaves lifetime scars. Donald Capps's incisive work on this subject, *The Child's Song: The Religious Abuse of Children,* lifts up the work of Alice Miller, whose lifetime work and writing concerned the eradication of child abuse.[8] She argues that child abuse as a learned behavior can be unlearned, hence eradicated. However, she is addressing subtler forms of child abuse, not physical assault or even domination over the child; but rather the squelching of a healthy narcissism in a child. The absence of this narcissism inhibits the child in later developing a healthy desire to share (ages five to six). Another dimension is our unwillingness to criticize parental abuse, substituting instead an idealized childhood.[9] If we agree with this, then perhaps liturgies like the one here, "Darkness and Light: On Child Abuse and Neglect," can contribute one small step to the healing process; though we must heed Capps's warning that sometimes religion itself can become a form of abuse.

Erikson's fourth stage is industry versus inferiority. Here the danger lies in one's identity resting solely in one's work. A sense of skills and abilities begin to surface. Hard work may not always render rewards, and one can have a sense of inferiority.[10] This is a crucial time for self-esteem and self-worth, which, especially for North Americans, later in life is falsely tied only to career and job accomplishments.

The fifth stage, identity versus role confusion, is the time of adolescence when the ego identity is being formed and the promise of a career is on the horizon. In this stage one struggles to assert one's own identity. "Adolescent" now generally refers to someone who has reached puberty, but the new phenomena of "tweens" challenges the conflating of teenagers and adolescents.[11] Writers such as Robert Regan challenge the assumptions of Jean Piaget and Erikson about the progression of these stages.[12]

For girls, the passage to womanhood as signaled by the onset of menstruation too often has been surrounded by secrecy. By marking this important event, as in the liturgy "For My Daughters: Celebration of Your Menarche" (p. 33), girls may feel more empowered and comfortable with this natural rhythm of their bodies. Boys as well experience puberty, which can be an awkward and embarrassing time. By recognizing this passage in the Christian church, as the Jewsh community does with bar mitzvah, it can be regarded with gladness. This may be accompanied with leaving home, a time of ambiguity between asserting one's independence and still feeling the pull of home. The liturgies in this section, "Leaving Home" and "Taking Leave," address the importance of preparing for life's transition to adulthood, and reflect the tension between what to take and what to leave behind. This transition is one not simply of biology but of culture. Turning eighteen or twenty-one or even receiving sufficient training or passing through certain rites is no guarantee of becoming an adult in today's society.

Erikson's descriptions of the stages of life may seem a bit clinical and more straightforward than they really are. As we reflect on the passage of childhood/adolescence, we recognize the gaps that may exist between the privileged and affluent, who have education, money, intact families, and opportunities, and those whose lives are lived in abandoned buildings, on the streets and alleys, running drugs to put bread on the table, with little family who care.

The irony, however, is that despite these disparities many common problems of high-risk sex and drug abuse affect both groups. In fact, kids who run away from home and end up on the streets come from both affluent and poverty-stricken families. What do they share in common? Low self-esteem, lack of healthy values, absence of positive adult role models. Young people, especially black males, are at high risk due to the absence of black role models, which the liturgy "Sons of Thunder" recognizes and to which it provides an important corrective.

The church is in a unique position to help these teens. In fact, hundreds of scientific studies have shown that church-attending youth and those with religious beliefs and practices have a lower incidence of almost all unhealthy behaviors.[13] Factors associated with resilience and positive outcomes are a stable, positive relationship with at least one caring adult; religious and spiritual anchors; high, realistic academic expectations and adequate support; positive family environment; and emotional intelligence and ability to cope with stress.[14]

Many theorists emphasize the importance of adolescents gaining difference and distance from their parents to transcend infantile ties to them. "Individuation during adolescence is defined as a sharpened sense of one's distinctness from others, a heightened awareness of one's self-boundaries . . . individuation in adolescence means that individuals now take increasing responsibility for what they do and what they are, rather than depositing this responsibility on the shoulders under whose influence and tutelage they have grown up."[15] Although these theories may be sound for middle-class youth, what is often missing for troubled youth is parents against whom they can rebel, and the parents' lack of values.

As we look at these various stages, we also realize how our image of God may change and develop. Liturgy can help people develop more adequate images of God. As Erikson expressed it, part of the road to maturity is to free ourselves from inadequate images of God. This is an alternative to some who feel that becoming mature means freeing ourselves from God and religion altogether, which were used as crutches. Perhaps by displaying the breadth of God's presence in the midst of the various crises and seasons of life, one can begin to mature in faith and see God as active at all seasons of life; this would indeed be a mature faith. Feelings of acceptance and forgiveness by God are part of what is needed for a mature faith.[16] This is reflected in Cardinal Newman's prayer: "Lord, do not let me deny in the darkness what I have seen in the light."[17]

Infancy gives rise to the image of God as a "reluctant giver" and slowly moves in the development cycle to God as "unimaginable abundance."[18] In early childhood, the main issue is that of autonomy. The negative image may be of God as the "demanding tyrant"; the experience, of moral negative injunctions such as "thou shalt nots." It is important that the child moves toward a loving image of God despite the prohibitions that may pertain.[19] We move toward the Emmanuel God, who opens the possibilities of the positive moments of life where God appears. At school age, the child learns to work in cooperation with others, though God may be viewed as the bestower of unreal expectations.[20]

For the adolescent, the dominant God image may be that of the "alienating God" who asks worthless acts of self-denial and unquestioned conformity.[21] If this phase is adequately negotiated, it may lead to vocation, which engenders a commitment perhaps to God in a larger sense. In young adulthood one moves from the devouring God, who is jealous of any other attachments, to the God who is the source of abundance of human relationships.[22] In designing education and worship programs, keeping in mind how to help children and youth to mature in their understanding of God is central.

In addition to the changing images of God are the stages of faith development that have become fundamental to much of Christian education. James Fowler's seminal work makes distinctions among religion (cumulative traditions), belief (holding of certain ideas), and faith (relation of trust and loyalty to the transcendent) that are important as we consider the educational dimension to the liturgies in this chapter.[23] A discussion of Fowler's stages of faith provides us another lens through which to view Erikson as well as to interpret the faith struggles of children and adolescents. Fowler's developmental theory was positioned theologically with Richard Niebuhr and Paul Tillich[24] and philosophically with Eric Erikson, Daniel Levinson, Jean Piaget, and Lawrence Kohlberg.[25] Understanding Fowler's stages of faith becomes a helpful foundation for structuring meaningful education and worship for children and adolescents. These faith stages are: primal (infancy), intuitive-projective (early childhood), mythic-literal (childhood and beyond), synthetic-covenantal (adolescence and beyond), individuative-reflective (young adulthood and beyond), and conjunctive (midlife and beyond) and universalizing (midlife and beyond).[26] Adolescence is a time of integrating diverse self-images and is the early stage of synthesis of beliefs and values.

An interesting complement to Fowler's work is Kenda Dean's emphasis on the theological nature of youth's concerns. "Children inquire *about* God; youth inquire *after* God, seeking a relationship, a sacred trust, an anchor that remains steady in winds of change."[27]

Youth ministry requires intentional theological reflection. "We tend to view young people as *consumers* of theology rather than as people who help *construct* religious discourse. We are far more likely to consider youth *objects* of ministry rather than *agents* of ministry; people to be ministered *unto* rather than people Jesus has called into ministry in their own right. We think teenagers need theology added to them, like antifreeze, when they really require a language that claims for Christ the unnamed quest for God that is already well underway."[28] "Ninety-five percent of American teenagers say they believe in God, and half say they attend church weekly—68 percent 'because they want to.' "[29]

What we need to do is understand how each adolescent is a unique child of God, not simply broad developmental differences between genders and across age groups. The presence of a loving community is key. "In youth ministry we are seeking to *theologically* as well as *developmentally* understand the unique needs and desires of every adolescent God brings to us. The most foundational understanding we must carry with us as youth workers, then, is that *both* boys and girls are created in the image of God, 'male and female he created them' (Gen. 1:27)."[30] The church can enhance this process by liturgical markers for children and adolescents.

Many of us are terrified of young people and, since the Columbine High School killings, think only of statistics such as the fact that 17 percent of students have carried a weapon to school.[31] We see adolescents as specializing in risk-taking behaviors. The teenagers of past decades seem to have disappeared with children having children. The birth rate for young teenagers ages fifteen to seventeen was 27.4 per thousand for 2000, but fortunately these rates are declining.[32] Some argue these are lost and broken youth, while others see an optimistic profile of this generation known as "milennias."[33] There are some sobering statistics: in the United States in 1999, 72 percent of all deaths among youth and young adults ages ten to twenty-four resulted from only four causes, all linked to behavior—motor vehicle crashes (31 percent), homicide (18 percent), suicide (12 percent), and other unintentional injuries (11 percent).[34] Seventy percent of high school students have tried cigarette smoking, 81 percent of high school students have tried alcohol, and 47 percent of high school students have tried marijuana.[35] Violent dating relationships also concern us. "Research indicates that 35 percent of teenage couples are involved in a violent relationship and dating violence has been experienced by nearly one out of four teenagers. One study that examined 123 adolescent girls, age 15–19, resulted in 24 percent of respondents saying that they had been victims of dating violence on one occasion and 14.6 percent said they had been victims on several occasions. And, this same study showed that the number one reason for the violence was jealousy."[36] These statistics on adolescents give pause for serious reflection. They challenge the church to do more to prevent self-destructive patterns; to celebrate young people and embrace them into the church community by worship, programs, a ministry of presence, and education for positive values and role models.

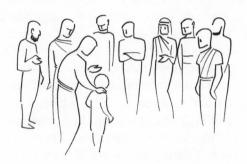

For the Children

"Unless you change and become like children . . ." (Matt. 18:3)

BLESSING OF THE CHILDREN[37]
(Methodist)

THE ACTS OF PRAISE AND PRAYER

GREETINGS

PRELUDE   "Aria on Jewels" by Dale Woods

INVOCATION OF THE HOLY SPIRIT *(please remain standing)*

> **Leader:** "Come," my heart says, "seek God's face!" Your face, Lord, do I seek (Ps. 27:9).
>
> **People:** **We come to this place on this Children's Sabbath to seek God; to glimpse God in the faces of children, to know God in the Spirit who moves among us when we work for children.**
>
> **Leader:** Come to me, all you who are weary and are carrying heavy burdens, and I will give you rest (Matt. 11:28).
>
> **People:** **We come to this place, many of us weary. Weary from the demands of juggling work and family and other responsibilities, weary from long years of working for justice, weary from hopes long delayed for a world in which every child will be healthy and cherished.**

PRAYER AND RESPONSE

> **Leader:** Tender God, we come before you with prayers on our hearts. We seek the balm that only you can provide.
>
> **People:** *(sing)* **There is a balm in Gilead, to make the wounded whole. There is a balm in Gilead, to heal the sin-sick soul.**

22

Leader: We pray for all children, that they may know wholeness in their lives and flourish as God intends. We pray especially for children who are sick or injured, that while they wait for healing, they may know the love and presence of God.

People: *(sing)* **There is a balm in Gilead, to make the wounded whole. There is a balm in Gilead, to heal the sin-sick soul.**

Leader: We pray for families, especially families that know pain—whether of abuse, divorce, violence, drugs, rebellion, lack of resources, lack of time together, or illness—that they may find healing.

People: *(sing)* **There is a balm in Gilead, to make the wounded whole. There is a balm in Gilead, to heal the sin-sick soul.**

Leader: We pray for communities that are divided by racism, violence, selfishness, or ideology, that they may find ways to work together to improve the lives of children, families, and all who live in them.

People: *(sing)* **There is a balm in Gilead, to make the wounded whole. There is a balm in Gilead, to heal the sin-sick soul.**

Leader: We pray for leaders—leaders of our nation, states, and communities, of businesses and congregations, of schools and child care centers, of scout troops and soccer teams, of hospitals and homeless shelters—that they may lead in a way that embraces diversity while promoting unity for the well-being of children and families and communities.

People: *(sing)* **There is a balm in Gilead, to make the wounded whole. There is a balm in Gilead, to heal the sin-sick soul.**

Leader: We pray for ourselves. For the dashed dream, the bruised spirit, the wounded heart, the battered hope. Come touch our hearts with the tenderness and healing that only you can provide, that we may be healed and renewed for the work we are called to do.

People: *(sing)* **There is a balm in Gilead, to make the wounded whole. There is a balm in Gilead, to heal the sin-sick soul.**

BLESSING OF THE CHILDREN
(Please bring your children forward for a blessing.)

HYMN   #191   UMH   "Jesus Loves the Little Children"

Leader: Let the little children come to me; do not stop them; for it is to such as these that the kingdom of God belongs (Mark 10:14b).

People: **We come today carrying children in our hearts—the children we brought into this world, our grandchildren, children we care for in our work, children we speak out for in our witness. Let the children come!**

Leader: O come, let us sing to the Lord; let us make a joyful noise to the rock of our salvation! (Ps. 95:1)

People: We come today with hearts that sing with thanksgiving—thanksgiving for the wonder of childhood, the lives we have touched and that have touched us, the gains for justice, the steps toward peace. Come, let us sing to God!

PROCESSIONAL HYMN *(standing)*   #156   UMH   "I Love to Tell the Story"

BLESSING OF THE CREATURES
(Please bring your animal, plant or symbol thereof forward for a blessing. After the blessings, let the congregation say softly, responsively:)

Leader: Ask of the Beasts and they shall teach you

People: Ask of the Trees and they shall teach you

Leader: Ask of the Beasts and they shall teach you

People: Ask of the Flowers and they shall teach you

All: The beauty of the earth!

PRAYER FOR CHILDREN'S HEALTH
(Offer this or another prayer each day for one week.)

God of healing, I pray for children who are sick or injured, that they may receive the love and care they need. I pray especially for [insert name].

I pray for parents who struggle to get their children the health care they need, that together we find ways to provide the support they need to secure care for their children.

I pray for doctors, nurses, and all health care providers that they will be guided to heal with loving care and skill.

I pray for our society, that we will heal the poverty, injustice, violence, and other wounds that prevent all children from receiving the care, nurture, and resources they need for a healthy start to live out the lives for which they were created.

I pray for myself, that I may be an instrument of your healing love, bringing comfort and care to children.

All this I pray in confidence of your steadfast presence, tender care, and healing love. **Amen.**

LORD'S PRAYER

FIRST LESSON   Isa. 53:7–12

CHORAL ANTHEM   "Jesus Loves Me"   arr. Michael Hassel

SECOND LESSON   Heb. 4:14–16

GOSPEL HYMN   #194   UMH   "Morning Glory, Starlit Sky"
(Please remain standing.)

GOSPEL LESSON   Mark 10:35–45

MEDITATION

MAKING OUR OFFERING
(Naming the ministries of our everyday lives. We take a moment to respond to God's call in our lives. Please offer introductions and brief announcements.)

OFFERTORY   "The King of Love My Shepherd Is"   arr. David Cherwein

DOXOLOGY   "Johnny Appleseed" grace *(sing twice)*

> OOOOOOOOOO, THE Lord's been good to me,
> And so I thank the Lord, for giving me, the things I need,
> The sun, and the moon, and the appleseed!
> The Lord's been good to me. Amen.

UNISON PRAYER

Gracious God, guard the laughter of children. Bring them safely through injury and illness and neglect, so they may live the promises you give.

Do not let us be so preoccupied with *our* purposes that we fail to hear *their* voices or pay attention to their special vision of the truth; but keep us with them, ready to listen and to love even as you have loved us, your grown-up and sometimes wayward children.

HYMN GOING FORTH   #206   UMH   "I Want to Walk as a Child of the Light"

WORDS GOING FORTH *(begin loudly, grow softly—3 times)*

>   **Leader:** May we go forth to celebrate the gifts of each child?

>   **People: May we go forth to heal the hurts of each child?**

>   **Leader:** May we go forth to seek justice for each child?

>   **People: This we ask as ones who are claimed as God's children. Amen.**

POSTLUDE   "Praise God"   arr. Ralph Hastings

AT THE TIME OF DIVORCE[38]
(Ecumenical)

This ritual needs to occur in a place that is 'holy' for the family; that may be in a church, the family's dining room table, or at a favorite outdoor location. It is possible to do this in conjunction with the Ritual of Divorce. The parents make a pledge to the children and give them a gift as a symbol of their vow. The parents may speak in their own words or use the ones below.

MAKING VOWS TO THE CHILDREN
(The mother takes the child [children] by the hand or in her arms and says:)

I promise that I will love you always whether we are together or apart. I will care about everything that happens to you. I will try to help you feel secure when you are afraid, to give you comfort when you are hurt, and to protect you from all harm.

(The mother gives the child a gift, saying:)

This gift is a symbol of what I have promised to you. Whenever you see it, remember my love.

(The father takes the child by the hand or in his arms and says:)

I promise that I will love you always whether we are together or apart. I will care about everything that happens to you. I will try to help you feel secure when you are afraid, to give you comfort when you are hurt, and to protect you from all harm.

(The father gives the child a gift, saying:)

This gift is a symbol of what I have promised to you. Whenever you see it, remember my love.

PRAYING TOGETHER
(The family may kneel together or hold hands as the parents pray:)

Bless us, O God, as we who once lived together now are separated and live apart. Bless our children. Keep them safe from all harm, give them courage to face the pain of this division, and the knowledge that our brokenness is not their fault. Help us to keep the promises we made to them; let us not fail them again; in the name of Jesus Christ we pray. Amen.

BLESSING THE FAMILY
(If this ritual is done in a church in the presence of a priest, the priest then offers them a blessing.)

> **Priest:** The blessing of God,
> whose love gives you life,
> forgives mistakes,
> and heals brokenness,
> be with you now and always.

> **All: Amen.**

HYMN   #518   CH   "This Is a Day of New Beginnings"

CLOSING PRAYER

> Lord, keep us safe this night,
> Secure from all our fears;

May angels guard us while we sleep,
Till morning light appears. **Amen.**[39]

DARKNESS AND LIGHT: ON CHILD ABUSE AND NEGLECT[40]
(Roman Catholic)

THE SERVICE OF DARKNESS
THE COMING OF NIGHT

(People enter a fully lit church where four lighted candles are prominently displayed. Behind the candles is an etching of Jesus. They silently meditate on the following prayer.)

MEDITATIVE PRAYER

> **Leader:** Lighten our darkness, we beseech thee, O Lord; and by thy great mercy defend us from all perils and dangers of this night; for the love of thy only Son, our Savior, Jesus Christ. **Amen.**[41]

OPENING OF SERVICE
(The clergy enter and take their seats quietly. After a few moments of silence the leader rises and addresses the congregation. Note that the three leaders alternate throughout the rest of the service.)

> **Leader One:** For so many children their suffering, their abuse or neglect, was endured in the dark and quiet of the night. Tonight, let us be willing to enter the night with them so that perhaps we can lead them forth into the light. Let us pray, Lord, we would be present with the children of the night. We would hear their voices. We would weave slender threads joining their hearts to our own.

THE EXTINGUISHING OF THE FIRST LIGHT

> **Leader Two:** A father enters his little boy's bedroom. He rapes his son. Tonight that little boy will sleep on his back. If he should roll over his fears will overwhelm him.
>
> The night has come!

(The first candle is extinguished; some of the lights in the church are turned off. A moment of silence is provided for the congregation to reflect and also to experience all the gathering darkness portends.)

> **Leader Two:** A child's spirit cries out:

> **Leader Three:** *(From back of sanctuary a child's voice is heard. Read selected verses from Psalm 18.)*

Leader Two: And somewhere someone is singing:

Congreg.: *(All join in the singing of a lullaby.)*

THE EXTINGUISHING OF THE SECOND LIGHT

Leader One: It's late. A mother enters her home. The smell of alcohol on her is strong. She yells for her children. They pretend they're not there.

The night has come!

(The second candle is extinguished, more lights are turned out and a moment of silence is provided.)

Leader Two: Another child's spirit cries out. *(Read selected verses from Psalm 18)*

THE EXTINGUISHING OF THE THIRD LIGHT

Leader Two: She hears them arguing again. Things get broken. People get hurt. She hears the angry voice and the steps approaching her room. She hides in the closet.

The night has come!

(The third candle is extinguished, more lights turned out and another moment of silence is observed.)

Leader Three: And another child's spirit cries out. *(Read selected verses from Psalm 18.)*

Leader One: And somewhere someone is singing:

Congreg.: *(All sing a lullaby.)*

THE EXTINGUISHING OF THE FOURTH LIGHT

Leader One: And they crucified him, and divided his clothes among them, casting lots to decide what each should take. When it was noon, darkness came over the whole land until three in the afternoon.

The night has come!

(The fourth candle is extinguished, the rest of the lights are turned off. The church is in darkness except for the illumination of the "Jesus" etching. A moment of silence is observed.)

Leader Two: The child of God cries out.

Leader Three: For a last time a child's voice calls out. *(Read Matt. 27:46.)*

(All sit in the dark and the quiet to the point of being uncomfortable, 2–3 minutes.)

THE SERVICE OF LIGHT
THE COMING OF DAY

THE KINDLING OF THE FIRST LIGHT
(A Paschal/Christ Candle is carried in while a few of the church lights are turned on. As the Candle comes forward the presider proclaims the Gospel.)

Leader One: Day has dawned! *(Read Mark 16:9–11.)*

HOMILY
(The presider gives a homily standing at the Paschal/Christ Candle. The focus may revolve around use of Scripture to define how God sees the child, the family and the broader community. May conclude with a reference to how these children—orphans in a profound sense— deserve the sacred portion. Note Deut. 26:4–13.)

PETITIONS
(Each of the religious leaders in attendance comes forward and making use of documents or teachings of their tradition presents a prayer of petition for the congregation's affirmation, which is either sung or spoken.)

PRAYER OF INTERCESSION FOR CHILDREN

> **Presider:** Loving God, you have created us for life together and placed in your midst the young who are symbols of both hope and vulnerability.

> **Congreg.:** **Hear our prayers for all your children: to sustain their hope and joy and youth; to comfort and console their vulnerability. Hear us as we pray for that precious gift of life.**

> **Left:** We pray for children who put chocolate everywhere, who like to be tickled, who stomp in puddles and ruin their new pants, who sneak Popsicles before supper, who erase holes in math workbooks, who can never find their shoes.

> **Right:** And we pray for those who stare at photographs from behind barbed wires, who can't bound down the street in a new pair of sneakers, who have never "counted potatoes," who are born in places where we wouldn't be caught dead, who will never go to a circus, who live in an X-rated world.

> **Left:** We pray for the children who bring us sticky kisses and fistfuls of dandelions, who sleep with the dog and bury goldfish, who hug us in a hurry and forget their lunch money, who cover themselves with Band-Aids and sing off-key, who squeeze toothpaste all over the sink, who slurp their soup.

> **Right:** And we pray for those who never get dessert, who have no safe blanket to drag behind them, who watch their parents die, who can't find any bread to steal, who don't have any rooms to clean, whose pictures aren't on anybody's dresser, whose monsters are real.

> **Left:** And we pray for those who spend all their allowance before Tuesday, who throw tantrums in the grocery store and pick at their food, who like ghost

stories, who shove dirty clothes under the bed and never rinse out the tub, who get visits from the tooth fairy, who don't like to be kissed in front of the carpool, who squirm in church and dream on the phone, whose tears we sometimes laugh at and whose smiles can make us cry.

Right: And we pray for those whose nightmares come in the daytime, who will eat anything, who have never seen a dentist, who aren't spoiled by anybody, who go to bed hungry and cry themselves to sleep, who live and move but have no being.

Left: We pray for the children who want to be carried and for those who must, for those we never give up on and for those who don't get a second chance.

Right: For those we smother and for those who will grab the hand of anybody kind enough to offer it.

Left: We pray for our children, for your children, for all children, for childhood's dreams and nightmares.

Congreg.: **In each child let us behold anew your promise of creation. Sustain these little and not so little ones. By your grace may they live the lives for which they were created.**

TRANSITION

Congreg.: *(A song proclaiming the coming of the light is sung.)*

THE KINDLING OF THE SECOND LIGHT
(A leader of the religious community comes forward and says:)

Leader Two: Small children awaken to a day where there will be no screaming and no hurtful words.

Day has dawned!

(He/she rekindles the second candle and more church lights are turned on.)

Leader Two: And the spirit of a little boy calls out:

Leader Three: *(The voice of a child once again is heard. Read selected verses from Psalm 18.)*

Leader Two: And her spirit sings:

Congreg.: *(The congregation breaks out in the refrain of the song!)*

THE KINDLING OF THE THIRD LIGHT
(A civic leader comes forward and states:)

Leader Two: A little boy rises to a day where love and sex no longer bring him pain and despair.

The day has dawned!

(He/she lights the third candle and more church lights are turned on.)

Leader One: And the spirit of a little girl calls out:

Leader Three: *(Read selected verses from Psalm 18.)*

Leader One: And her spirit sings:

Congreg: *(The congregation breaks out in the refrain of the song!)*

THE KINDLING OF THE FOURTH LIGHT
(A mother and father come forward and state:)

Leader Two: A little girl rises to a day where she does not have to witness rage and violence.

The day has dawned!

(The family lights the fourth candle and the church lights are brought up to full.)

Leader One: A child's spirit calls out:

Leader Three: *(A child's voice is heard for a last time. Read selected verses from Psalm 18.)*

Leader One: And a child's spirit sings:

Congreg: *(The congregation breaks out in the refrain of the song!)*

COMMISSIONING
(The presider explains the commissioning with rainbows using the story of the little girl and her picture of the Rainbow Connection. The members of the congregation are asked to accept this challenge: to be the Rainbow Connection for the children of our abuse and neglect.)

(Each religious leader reads a line of the following commission:)

Leader One: The rainbow spans the sky as a sign of God's everlasting covenant against destruction and chaos. May this bow, fashioned by a child and reflecting his or her fears of the darkness as well as his or her dreams for light, stand as a covenant between you and children. May it be a sacred pledge that you will be that bridge upon which children can walk, sure footed, leading from darkness to light! Amen! Amen!

(The religious leaders move out among the congregation presenting each person with a ribbon bound scroll containing a child's rainbow.)

CLOSING
(The service concludes with the Rainbow Connection Picture being placed next to a picture of Jesus and the entire congregation sings the Rainbow Connection song.[42])

Passage through Adolescence

"Listen to what is wise and try to understand it." (Prov. 2:2)

PASSING FROM GIRLHOOD TO YOUNG WOMANHOOD[43]
(Ecumenical)

A low table is put in the center of a room or worship space, or a cloth laid on the floor. On it is a candle, water, decanter of red wine and small glasses, red ribbon cut into strips of about 25cm., a basket to receive the gifts of the women as they arrive, and the cake or cakes.

INTRODUCTION
(The candle is lit and then the young woman is addressed.)

Mother or Grandmother: N, tonight we have come together to mark an important stage on your life journey.

2nd Woman: We have come as women who love you, family and friends, to acknowledge that you have begun the transition from being a young girl to being a young woman.

3rd Woman: Each of us has experienced the changes that you are now experiencing.

4th Woman: The flow of blood is a symbol of life.

5th Woman: It is also a symbol of all the creativity that is inside us.

6th Woman: It is also uncomfortable at times, and so it reminds us that life is uncomfortable, difficult to deal with at times.

READING   Luke 1:46–55

1st Woman: Mary was a young woman, perhaps not much older than you. God called her as a young woman. He gave her a specific task to do. Each of us is called by God to live our life to the fullest and to be what God wants us to be in God's world. When you hear this Song of Mary being read in the

32

future, may you be reminded that you are also a strong and creative woman, blessed by God, and because of that, able to bring blessing to others.

THE BLESSINGS
(Each woman present gives a blessing by naming something special about the young woman, things that they value in her. After or while giving her the blessing, the ribbon is tied or draped over her, reminders of each blessing and a symbol that we as women are all part of the same life fabric.)

THE WINE
(All drink a glass of wine together.)

THE GIFTS
(Each woman gives a gift-symbol.)

CLOSE
(Celebrate by eating cake and finishing the wine!)

FOR MY DAUGHTERS: CELEBRATION OF YOUR MENARCHE[44]
(Roman Catholic)

INTRODUCTION

C (Celebrant): Today is a day to celebrate, a day of celebration for *N*. We are to show our love for *N* and to thank God for her body, its strength, its growth, its beauty and her ripening and passing into young womanhood.

Let us pray.

All: **Holy Spirit, who lives in each one of us, may *N* through your indwelling come to know herself and live according to her true nature. Let her discover joy, strength, compassion and love.**

Through the love of Christ, Amen.

All: **Hail Mary, full of grace, the Lord is with you,**
Blessed are you among women,
Blessed is the fruit of your womb, Jesus.
Holy Mary, Mother of God,
Pray for us now, and at the hour of our death.
Amen.

THE ANOINTING

C: Today, *N*, blessed are you among women, I anoint you with the oil of gladness. We pray that you may find passion and joy in loving another and in being loved. We pray that, if you choose it, you may know the glory of pregnancy and childbirth, and delight in nourishing your children. We pray that you may discover the unfolding of your own special creativity. We pray that you grow through any pain you may meet, a wiser, braver and stronger woman. Amen.

All: Today, *N*, blessed are you among women.

THE GIFTS

    C: We offer gifts to *N*.

(Mother, grandmother, godparents and friends offer gifts.)

Mother: *N*, I give you this sign of the Moon, a waxing Moon to denote your growth towards fullness.

READING   Eccles. 43:6–9, on the glory of God in nature
(Others may give their gifts and speak their words.)

THE COLLECT

Grandmother: God our mother
        You hold our life within you,
        nourish us at your breast,
        and teach us to walk alone.
        Help us so to receive your tenderness
        and respond to your challenge
        that others may draw life from us,
        in your name. Amen.
               —Janet Morley

OLD TESTAMENT READING
(A godmother reads from the Book of Wisdom 7:24–30 and 8:1.)

    All: Let the Wisdom of God fill our hearts and souls and minds and bodies. Amen.

NEW TESTAMENT READING
(The young woman chooses someone to read Mark 12:30–31.)

    All: Thanks be to God.

HYMN   #279   PrH   "Lord of Our Growing Years"

    C: Women are invited to join in this part of our celebration, which names *N* to womanhood.

(Chalice containing red wine is passed round the circle.)

    C: *N*, I offer you this cup.

All: *(In circle holding hands)* **Blessed be our wombs. May the blood shed bring forth new life. Through the love of Christ. Amen.**

(Turning from center of circle to those outside...)

All: **May our bodies be blessed and glorified. Through the love of Christ. Amen.**

THE PEACE

C: *(All slightly extending arms)* We invite you to join with us in sharing a sign of peace.

(Others come into the circle, exchange a sign of peace, and hold hands.)

All: **We offer our souls and bodies to be a living sacrifice. Send us out into the world in the power of your Spirit to live and work to your praise and glory. Through the love of Christ. Amen.**

BLESSING

C: The blessing of the most Holy Trinity
God unbegotten,
God incarnate,
God among us,
Keep us now and evermore,
Amen.
—Liz Campbell, Women's Agape,
Greenham Community, Sue Newman

TAKING LEAVE[45]
(Presbyterian)

REAFFIRMATION OF BAPTISM
IN THE CONTEXT OF A MOTHER-DAUGHTER RETREAT:
A PRESBYTERIAN GATHERING OF MOTHERS AND DAUGHTERS
CELEBRATING HIGH SCHOOL GRADUATION

GATHERING AROUND THE WORD

PREPARATION FOR WORSHIP   2 Cor. 5:17

CALL TO WORSHIP   Ps. 121

Leader: I lift up my eyes to the hills—from whence will my help come?

All: My help comes from the Lord, who made heaven and earth.

Leader: God will not let your foot be moved, God who keeps you will not sleep.

All: God who keeps Israel will not slumber nor sleep.

Leader: The Lord is your keeper, the Lord is your shade at your right hand.

All: The sun shall not strike you by day, nor the moon by night.

Leader: The Lord will keep you from all evil, God will keep your life.

All: The Lord will keep your going out and your coming in from this time on and forevermore.

HYMN OF PRAISE   #294   PrH   "Wherever I Wander" or "Wherever You Go"   Julie Howard[46]

CALL TO CONFESSION

PRAYER OF CONFESSION *(together)*

God of love, forgive me for unkind words said to (name of mother or daughter), for failing to respect and honor her, for taking her for granted, for the times I was afraid to allow her freedom to grow, for words left unsaid, but felt in the heart.

Gracious God, I ask your forgiveness, for holding on too tightly, for seasons of anger and busyness, for refusing to trust you in the hard and easy times, for insisting that all must be well, for ignoring your voice when you urged me to let go, for taking in all the blessings, but being reluctant to share them, for doubting my inner strength and beauty. Forgive me Lord, for resisting your constant presence on this journey of womanhood to which I have been called. In the name of Jesus Christ, Amen.

WORDS OF FORGIVENESS

Leader: Friends, hear and believe the good news of the Gospel.

All: In Jesus Christ we are forgiven. Thanks be to God. Amen!

THE SERVICE OF THE WORD

THE WORD PROCLAIMED   John 4:4–30
(Meditation on the Woman at the Well)

OUR RESPONSE

REAFFIRMATION OF BAPTISM

Leader: Hear these words from Holy Scripture again: (John 4:13–15)

Let us pray.

O God Most High,
You have made the font of baptism
To be the womb from which we are reborn in the waters of life.
Grant that all who have been born of water and the Spirit
May live in Christ as the first fruits of the new humanity,
Leading others to hope in the rebirth of your whole creation,
And to serve you with joy,
Now and forever.

All: Amen.

Leader: Sisters in Christ
Our baptism is the sign and seal
Of our cleansing from sin
And of our being grafted into Christ.
Through the birth, death and resurrection of Christ,
The power of sin was broken
And God's kingdom entered the world.
Through our baptism we were made citizens of that kingdom,
And freed from the bondage of sin.
Let us celebrate that freedom and redemption
Through the renewal of our baptism.

RENUNCIATION AND AFFIRMATION[47]

Leader: Trusting in the gracious mercy of God,
Do you turn from the ways of sin
And renounce evil and its power in the world?

All: I do.

Leader: Who is your Lord and Savior?

All: Jesus Christ is my Lord and Savior.

Leader: Will you be Christ's faithful disciple,
Obeying his Word and showing his love?

All: I will, with God's help.

AFFIRMATION OF FAITH (*together* using "The Woman's Creed")[48]
(*The Minister places her hand into the water of the font, lifts up the water letting it run through her fingers, letting it fall back into the font, three times. She then makes the sign of the cross over the people, while saying:*)

Remember your baptism and be thankful.
In the name of the Father and of the Son and of the Holy Spirit.
Amen.

(At this time, all the young women come forward to receive a shell, an early church symbol from the rivers and seas where baptism was performed and water was collected. The shell will serve to remind them of their baptism. As they move forward and then back to their places, the mothers, stepmothers or stand-ins join in singing to the daughters the baptismal hymn.)

BAPTISMAL HYMN   #2051   TFWS   *"I Was There to Hear Your Borning Cry"*

CLOSING PRAYER
(Daughters then pray together a closing prayer:)

Loving God, you, who birthed all into being, created women to be life-givers, we thank you for our mothers, our mother's mothers and all those women who play a nurturing role in our lives. In pain and joy they gave us life, encouraged us, and modeled your loving care. Grant us courage to be for those who follow us, what they have been for us— a source of light in the power of your Spirit, that others may see you as our God, our life-giving Source, our holy-available One. We ask this through Jesus, your Son and our brother. **Amen.**

CLOSING HYMN   "Blessing Song"   Marsie Silvestro[49]

BENEDICTION

Leader: Remember Who and Whose you are—Remember your Baptism!!!

CHORAL RESPONSE   #440   LW   *"On Eagles Wings"*

WORSHIP SERVICE DETAILS

This service is held in the greater context of a larger mother-daughter retreat, junior high age and up. Throughout the retreat mothers and daughters will engage in times of study, play, and worship. But this particular worship service of reaffirmation of baptism is only for graduating senior women and their mothers, stepmothers, etc. One aspect of the retreat will be the setting of a suitcase around the main meeting room for each senior girl. During the weekend, various gifts, notes, and mementos from those attending the retreat as well as members of the congregation (ahead of time) will be placed in each senior girl's suitcase as reminders of the blessings they will carry with them as they move on at this time of their lives. The *shell* will be the last thing placed in their suitcase. With a physical shell will be included a paper shell which has been laminated with the church's address, phone number, and e-mail as a sign to the seniors that the church will always be available to them, night or day.

The Leadership of the Worship Service will come from female ordained ministers of Word and Sacrament and elders. Teams of mothers and daughters with gifts appropriate would lead the songs. The songs were chosen specifically for their content and simplicity, as a retreat setting might not be affordable to musical accompaniment. Musical gifts of the women involved would of course be appropriate.

There is always the possibility that there is a graduating senior who does not have a mother. The retreat committee would make plans for that and see to it that a grandmother, aunt, or friend accompanies the woman. The language of the liturgy is also careful to include the possibility of stepmothers, adoptive mothers, etc.

These type retreats and worship services always have the possibility of bringing up strong emotions. The pastors would be aware of the potential need to spend time with individuals or mothers and daughters as they process this transition. The retreat planners and leaders will also be given background information on this important transition time.

SONS OF THUNDER[50]
(Baptist)

IN CELEBRATION OF AFRICAN AMERICAN MALES IN THEIR CHILDHOOD

A RITE OF PASSAGE

PROCESSIONAL   African Drums
(The Elders of the Church [Deacons and Deaconess and church leaders], the Women and Daughters of the Church come forth in African dance.)

INVOCATION   Worship Leader/ Pastor of the Church

THE OCCASION

We are gathered here today in celebration of our young men through their different stages of life. We are here as a testament to our belief that they are our present and future hope for our church, our community, and our nation. We believe that their gifts and talents will make room for them before the great leaders of the globe. We believe that just as we stand in the presence of God, we are standing in the presence of excellence as embodied in these young men.

Yes, today we are here gathered in the name of God, Jesus Christ and the Holy Spirit to celebrate the gift of life in these young men.

PRAYER OF CELEBRATION
(Minister [a brief prayer celebrating the lives of the young men in the program])

AFRICAN DRUM SOLO

CELEBRATION OF BIRTH

(In this portion of the program a couple brings forth a young male baby from one month to two years old.)

**Worship
leader:** Who presents this young male baby to the Lord?

Parents: We present _____ (child's name)

**Worship
    leader:** Do you as the parents make a commitment to love, honor, discipline, protect, and educate this young child?

Parents: We will.

**Worship
    leader:** Will you promise to allow him to enjoy the time as a child?

Parents: We will.

**Worship
    leader:** Will you bring him to church to enjoy the fellowship of a loving community who will be his extended family from now throughout all his life?

Parents: We will.

**Worship
    leader:** Will you provide for this young babe to grow in grace and stature in the Lord by having prayer with him and for him?

Parents: We will.

**Worship
    leader:** Will you not only bring him to Sunday school and church, but also will you commit your own lives to consistent church attendance, Bible Study and family devotions?

Parents: We will.

**Worship
    leader:** And to the community of believers who are gathered in this place today, do you hereby pledge and affirm that you will serve as this child's (name) extended family? Maintaining the traditions of the ancestors that we are all related through Christ and therefore we each bear a responsibility to show love, concern, support—physical and financial—to the development of this child from now until he reaches maturation. And if something happens to his parents, that we as the church will serve as his parents and continue to provide an atmosphere of love?

    All: We will.

PRAYER OF DEDICATION OVER THE MALE BABY CHILD

CELEBRATION OF CHILDHOOD

(The young male children are brought down before the church. The age of the children should be about preschool to the third grade.)

Worship
leader: Today we honor the time of childhood for our young male children. It is a precious time that goes so quickly. Let us as the community of believers understand this moment of curiosity and high energy is a sacred place before God. Do you as the community of believers stand ready, willing and able to provide support, love and care for these young male children of our community?

All: We do.

The children
(together): We are created in the image of God.

Child 1: I am like Moses: One day I will set my people free.

Child 2: I am like Joseph: I dream dreams.

Child 3: I am like Solomon: I seek the wisdom of God.

All: You are created in the image of God. And we love you, each one in your own unique way. We love you as wonderful young men of God. Today we give you the gifts of joy, the gifts of books, and the gift of love, free and unconditional.

(Presentation of the gifts to the young children.)

PRAYER OF DEDICATION OVER THE YOUNG CHILDREN

CELEBRATION OF 4TH GRADE

(All the male children who are in the fourth grade come before the church.)

CELEBRATION IN MUSIC   "Stand"   Donnie McClurkin
"The Man in the Mirror"   Daryl Colley

Worship
leader: We give special honor to our young male children in the fourth grade. We are here today to provide you with a hedge of protection. We know that you face challenges in school and in the community. There are many challenges you may not even understand. But we as the community of faith are here with you and for you.

The statistics show that it is at fourth grade that many young male children decide to drop out of school.

All: We are here with you and for you—to stay in school.

Worship
leader: There are many pressures in the world that would invite you to try drugs even at this tender age. But drugs will destroy you. We want to build you up and encourage you.

All: We are here with you and for you.

Worship
leader: We all are human and all people make mistakes and yes even young folks like you can make mistakes—don't be afraid of trying new things, don't be afraid of failure. If you need some extra help with homework or if you want to play sports and even become artists, let us know. We will help.

All: We are here with you and for you

Youth 1: I am like Malcolm X. I believe I can achieve by any means necessary.

Youth 2: I am like Nelson Mandela. I can withstand the challenges of school. I am patient and can run this race in strength and in grace.

Youth 3: I am like W.E.B. Du Bois. I am part of the talent tenth. I am brilliant. I have a beautiful mind. It is OK to be smart. I can achieve all things through Christ who strengthens me.

All: You are brilliant young men of God and we celebrate and support you. We present to you the gifts of books and the gift of technology (*a calculator or if possible a laptop computer*). Hold on to your God given gift of creativity and laughter to carry you over the waters of trials and tribulations in life.

We are here with you and for you.

CELEBRATION OF YOUTH: RITES OF PASSAGE INTO THE TEEN YEARS

Elder of
the Church: For everything there is a season and a time to every purpose under heaven. This is the season for our young men of the church to take their rightful place in the community and in the church. Let us stand together in honor of our young men.

(The congregation stands while the young men enter into the sanctuary. The group of young men should be divided up so that an equal number comes down each aisle of the church to gather in the front of the altar.)

**Elder of
the Church:** As Jesus said to Peter at the Last Supper, "Listen, Satan has demanded to sift all of you like wheat, but I have prayed for you that your own faith may not fail, and once you have turned back, strengthen your brothers."(Luke 22:31) As it says in Proverbs 4, two is better than one. Therefore stand together as brothers to face the challenges of life.

Over the last few months you have shown Your faith in God, belief in Christ as your Savior and the power of the Holy Spirit in each of your lives. Know this one thing, that God loves you exceedingly and abundantly and beyond your imagination. Jesus is your strong foundation.

Walk in your destiny. Live your destiny. Believe in yourself, as we the elders of this church believe in you.

God has a purpose for your life. Fulfill that purpose in your life.

***Teen
leader 1:** Today we stand on the Promises of God. We give honor to you our elders who have taught us the way of salvation, the challenges of life, and the joy of true worship and service to God and to our community.

***Teen
leader 2:** Today we present ourselves, wholly, as a living sacrifice which is our reasonable service. Today we present our gift of strength for the days of our youth. We present the capacity of our minds to dream and conceive the solutions not only for tomorrow but here today.

All the teens: Today we accept the challenge that is left before us. The challenge to choose Life in Christ and not death in drugs, alcohol, unprotected and careless acts of sex. The challenge of speaking peace to violence. The challenge of seeking peace instead of choosing anger.

Today we choose to learn from the past and not repeat the negative history that has attempted to destroy our community. We embrace the positive streams from our historic past. We stand today building tomorrow as a salute to yesterday.

**Teen
leader 1:** We stand as Moses using what is in our hand to create miracles not only for ourselves, but for our community.

**Teen
leader 2:** We stand as Nehemiah ready to rebuild new walls for our community while fighting the spiritual warfare against those enemies who would destroy both body and soul.

(*Each teen leader makes a presentation from the youth group that represents service to God and to community, as well as the gift of strength and creativity.)

Teen
leader 3: We accept the challenge of Jesus Christ to repent for the kingdom of heaven is at hand. We accept Christ's challenge to do kingdom building right here and right now. We are wise master builders.

The Elder of
the Church: Today we pass on to you, the young men of the the church, the mantle of leadership. Bring all your many gifts unto the storehouse. We look unto you, the young men, to be the Joshua Generation, leading us into the Promised Land. As God was with his servant Moses, so God will be with you.

(The Elders of the Church place a mantle or African print material on each of the young men.)

(Gather all the children from each age group in front of the church. The adults of the church should form a circle around the children for the concluding portion of this Worship service.)

Worship
leader: We are the elders and the family of this church community. We stand here in solidarity with and for these young men. We celebrate their gifts, their talents, and their youth. We encourage them in knowing that even when they fall down, they can stand up. We commit our time, our talents and our resources to the development of these young men of God as they continue in their path from childhood, adolescence and young adulthood.

Young people, know that God has a destiny for you and a plan for your life, a plan of Good and not of Evil. Walk with God as your creator, as your mother and as your father, Christ as your Savior, as your friend. Know this, that as God is with you and for you, so are we, the community of believers.

The male
children: We are the sons of thunder. We walk in the spirit of *HeKima*—wisdom. We know that we are created in the image of God. We feel the love of this our church family and we share our love with you.

Please remember to be patient with us for God is not through with us yet.

As we leave here today, we walk by faith and not by sight. We thank you, our church community for being our cloud of witnesses.

CLOSING PRAYER AND BENEDICTION   Worship Leader

RECESSIONAL   African Drummers
Young Male Children
Elders

GRADUATION AND PROMOTION DAYS[51]
(African Methodist Episcopal)

This particular service is created in an African-American setting but may be adapted for use on any special graduation day. Areas for adaptation will be underlined throughout the text.

OCCASION

Recognition is honorable and helps us to highlight the milestones in our lives. In joy, we celebrate (*graduation or promotion*) of the (*name of the classes or group*) of (*name of church or organization*). Many steps make up the ladder of achievement. That process involves work and much effort by the faculty, staff, and the supportive members of (*church or community*).

The knowledge gained and the lessons learned are tools that help us to be more loving, more Christlike. Today we celebrate all efforts made to nurture and prepare our (*graduates or students being promoted*). This occasion honors the successful. Every time we study God's Word and exercise our understanding in our daily lives we are a success. Education is an act of grace: a gift of God's loving-kindness that can give us insight and joyfulness.

Joyfulness comes as we appreciate people and the gifts of goods and events in our lives. Joyfulness reflects the wonder and awesomeness we encounter as we realize God is for us and with us. The possibilities and enlightenment that occur through the education process show God being with us in concern and love. We take the mantle of education and scholarship in the church and the world and salute those African Americans who have paved the way for us in history and recently: Anna Julia Cooper, scholar; Mary McCleod Bethune, educator and activist; George Washington Carver, scientist and inventor; Richard Allen and Absalom Jones, AME and AMEZ founding bishops; Cornel West, author and philosopher; Henry L. Gates, literary critic; Samuel Proctor, pastor and professor; Calvin Butts, pastor and activist; James H. Cone, theologian; Barbara Harris, Anglican bishop; Jacquelyn Grant, Womanist scholar and theologian; Katie Cannon, Womanist scholar and ethicist; Johnnetta Coles and Marguerite Ross Barnett, university presidents. (*Include current leaders in your own denominational churches and schools and pertinent secular Black schools.*)

We also honor the work and lives of (*name of local and state workers in Christian and secular education*). Their labors and their students' work make this day possible. Education does not mean we are better than others and does not allow us to judge others. Education is a tool for enlightenment and improving the plight of ourselves and others. We take seriously the process of developing the knowledge, the skill, and the mental, spiritual, and emotional characters of all teachers and students to the honor and glory of God. Praise and thanksgiving! Hallelujah!

WELCOME

The psalmist cries out words of gladness in praise of Zion in Psalm 122. The group of pilgrims arrives in Jerusalem and rejoices at the unity the buildings symbolize. We honor and greet all of you whose pilgrimage has allowed you to bless us with your presence. We rejoice that the Lord has brought us together in unity to celebrate (*graduation or promotion*) day. We receive you in gladness and cordiality with open hearts. The pastor, leaders, officers, members, and friends of (*church name or organization*) invite you to participate with us as we honor the (*graduates or students promoted*) this year from (*name of class or church school*).

These students represent the beautiful, the good, and the true in our lives. We are beautiful for we are God's children. We are good in that God made us that way in the beginning and we are called to do good things. One way we know truth is through Christ Jesus. We know truth and beauty as we use all our God-given gifts to help us actively love and make a difference. We welcome you here! We welcome you to explore the good, true, and beautiful within because Christ is here in us and with us. Welcome.

PRAYER

We come as an extended family, to offer praise and thanksgiving for the commitment represented here. We thank you, O God, our Supreme Teacher, for the ministry of church and academic education. We bless your precious name, and ask that you bless those who continuously give and receive knowledge. Help us to appreciate the gifts and marvels of learning and enlightenment. Help us to see that education is a lifelong process that informs all areas of our life.

Lord, we know you hear each idea and concept spoken in your name and each heart that cries out for answers. Help us to think through and ask the questions that help us function lovingly in society toward our sisters and brothers in Christ Jesus.

Help us to study and apply your Word that we may have wisdom and integrity in our beliefs and ethical practices. Help us to take seriously and become actively involved in the education of our children and youth: by showing our children that we love them; by providing an environment that is safe and conducive to study; by teaching our children to read, write, and do math early on; by regularly visiting schools and being active in parent-teacher associations and in our church's Christian education program; by monitoring homework and being interested in the course of studies; by emphasizing scripture and *African American life experiences and heritage daily*; by seeing parenting and education as a ministry. For this insight and all other blessings, we thank you. **Amen.**

LITANY

> **Leader:** O Divine Teacher and Redeemer, we rejoice and are glad for the gifts of knowledge that this day brings and celebrates.
>
> **People: In gracious joy, we lift our voices to proclaim our delight in your many gifts of knowledge and experience. We honor the accomplishments of those recipients who have gone the distance and accomplished much.**
>
> **Leader:** We offer thanks for the gifts of hearing, sight, touch, taste, and smell that strengthen and enhance our education process.
>
> **People: Dear Creator, we thank you for the call you place on our lives to minister to others through teaching and sharing knowledge.**

Leader: Help us to be so grateful for our education that we encourage those who teach and preach; and we inspire others to write our stories, to create, to invent, to start businesses, to learn.

People: We shout hosannas! As we gain knowledge, we experience the truth of Christ, and that truth will set us free.

All: God anoints us and sends us out in truth as disciples and ministers of the Word of Jesus Christ, through the power of the Holy Spirit. We accept the challenge and choose to learn and to celebrate the milestones of learning with the household of faith: the community of believers in Christ Jesus.

Vow of Commitment

Lord God of Deborah and Solomon, teacher of teachers and creator of leaders: we honor the giving and receiving of knowledge and the opportunity to celebrate Christian achievement. In gratitude for your grace that has instituted this program of study, we pledge to excel as we continue to teach and learn wherever our faith journey takes us.

We bless you, O God, for bringing us thus far on our educational journey. We accept your challenge to mold our lives in the ways of Christ: to be disciples and to disciple others. We pledge to use the knowledge and skills received this year in ministry. May we learn and live by the Christian biblical and life principles taught during the (*name of class or group*) at (*church name*). We are grateful to (*names of teachers, sponsors, superintendents, pastors*). In honor of their contributions, nurture, and care, we rededicate our lives to God's service. We vow to continue our studies and association with (*name of class or group*). We confess the experience of grace afforded by the relationships built through group study and the empowerment born of new knowledge. May the Grand Architect of the universe and of all knowledge keep us and protect us.

Suggested Colors
(White and purple are the suggested colors for graduation. White symbolizes purity, peace, light, and illumination. Purple depicts royalty, penitence, power, self-esteem, and depth of feeling.)

Scriptures   Ps. 119:125; Isa. 44:18; Mark 12:14a; 1 Cor. 12:8.

Poem or Reflection

Graduation and Promotion Days

Leader: Announce to the world
The hard work and dedication of
Families and friends
Students and educators:
To better ourselves
And the rest of humanity
For the glory of God.

Ideas, concepts, thoughts,
Visions, drawings, experiments,
Speeches, poems, essays,
Athletic events, a collegiate bowl,
Express part of us
Express part of God
In whose image we are made.

Let's honor education,
Not make it a god.
Let's work passionately,
Let's do well:
Shunning attitudes of
Superiority of judgment.

God's Grace
Bestows our gifts,
Behooves us to excel,
To feel good about ourselves:
With gratitude and purpose,
Share what we have,
Never stop learning,
Never stop caring,
Dream dreams,
Plan well,
Work hard,
Share God.

PRESENTATION OF CERTIFICATES AND DIPLOMAS

LEAVING HOME[52]
(Methodist)

OPENING PRAYER

Gracious and loving God, you have been a good and generous presence in my life. Be here, now, that I may know again the goodness of your care for me, in all things. **Amen.**

SCRIPTURE   Ps. 90:1
Ps. 127
Prov. 31 (if a young girl is leaving home)

THE FOCUS FOR REFLECTION
(Leave-taking. Hurried good-byes to family, friends, and all that is familiar. Whether you're leaving home to go to college for the semester as a resident student or for the day as a commuter, "home" will never be the same again.)

POINTS OF DEPARTURE

> Where we love is home,
> Home that our feet may leave, but not our hearts.
> *—From "Homesick in Heaven" by*
> *Oliver Wendell Holmes*

(Selection from Howard Thurman.)

When the time came to leave for Jacksonville, I packed a borrowed old trunk with no lock and no handles, roped it securely, said my good-byes, and left for the railway station. When I bought my ticket, the agent refused to check my trunk on my ticket because the regulations stipulated that the check must be attached to the trunk handle, not to a rope. The trunk would have to be sent express but I had no money except for a dollar and a few cents left after I bought my ticket.

I sat down on the steps of the railway station and cried my heart out. Presently I opened my eyes and saw before me a large pair of work shoes. My eyes crawled upward until I saw the man's face. He was a black man, dressed in overalls and a denim cap. As he looked down at me he rolled a cigarette and lit it. Then he said, "Boy, what in hell are you crying about?"

And I told him.

"If you're trying to get out of this damn town to get an education, the least I can do is to help you. Come with me," he said.

He took me around to the agent and asked, "How much does it take to send this boy's trunk to Jacksonville?"

Then he took out his rawhide moneybag and counted the money out. When the agent handed him the receipt, he handed it to me. Then, without a word, he turned and disappeared down the railroad track. I never saw him again.[53]

JOURNALING: IDEAS FOR WRITTEN REFLECTION
(Take some time to consider what you want to take with you from home and what you want to leave behind as you head off to school. Make a list of these "intangibles" for yourself. Are some things on your list harder to take with you or to leave behind than you thought they'd be? Reflect on the ways God has been with you on your life's journey this far. Are there people, places, incidents in your life that witness to God's presence with you? How does God's presence in your past affect your feelings about moving on toward an unknown future?)

PRAYERS: FOR THE WORLD, FOR OTHERS, FOR MYSELF[54]

Leader: What should you take and what should you leave behind?

What to take: Memories, love of family and friends, support and encouragement of your church—joy, excitement, hope, expectations—solid beliefs, positive values.

What to leave behind: Worn-out ideas, fear of failure, bad self-image, narrow views, clinging to the past.

Who can help you? Reflect on Ephesians 6, "Put on the whole armor of God." How can you equip yourself for this new passage? Who can be your companions on this exciting journey in your life? Now all of us present pledge to support and encourage N. on this new passage in his/her life and to pray for God's presence on this journey.

Let us pray for (*name of young person*) while forming a circle around him/her.

CLOSING HYMN   #215   SNC   "Take, O Take Me as I Am"

ADDITIONAL RESOURCES

DAILY SCRIPTURE READINGS

Sunday	Gen. 12:1–9
Monday	Exod. 13:18–22
Tuesday	Josh. 24:14–18
Wednesday	Ps. 139:1–12
Thursday	Matt. 7:24–27/Luke 6:46–49
Friday	Luke 8:4–15
Saturday	Phil. 1:3–11

RITUAL PRACTICE

(One tradition that a church might consider in conducting a service for leaving home, for graduating seniors, is used by Covenant Presbyterian Church in Charlotte, North Carolina. Fleece blankets with the name of the church embroidered on the corner are given to each parent of a graduating senior. They literally wrap the blanket around their son or daughter as a symbol of the church's continual presence and concern for them. The young person then takes the blanket with them as a visual reminder of the church's care.)

"Welcome him back."
(Phlm 17)

Chapter 2

Early/Middle Adulthood

INTRODUCTION

In chapter 1 we were discussing Erikson's stages of life from infancy through adolescence. Stages six through eight cover the period from young adulthood to old age. This model helps to provide a perspective for the psychological and spiritual passages that adults experience. The sixth stage is intimacy versus isolation. The "young adult, emerging from the search for and the insistence on identity, is eager and willing to fuse his identity with that of others. He is ready for intimacy, that is, the capacity to commit himself to concrete affiliations and partnerships and to develop the ethical strength to abide by such commitments, even though they may call for significant sacrifices and compromises."[1] It is during this stage that satisfactory experiences of sex are important for strengthening future heterosexual relationships in healthy ways.

The seventh stage is generativity versus stagnation. While we recognize the dependence of children on adults, we often forget the dependence of the older generation on the younger one. During these middle years is the advent of the "sandwich" generation, where the parent may become the child. The liturgy on "Midlife Transition" is designed to ease this passage. The mature person needs to be needed, and maturity needs guidance as well as encouragement from those who are our offspring, whom we have previously nurtured.

"Generativity, then, is primarily the concern in establishing and guiding the next generation, although there are individuals who, through misfortune or because of special and genuine gifts in other directions, do not apply this drive to their own offspring." The concept of generativity also includes productivity and creativity but is not subsumed under them.[2]

The eighth stage is ego integrity versus despair. Only the person who has taken care of things and people and has adapted as well to the triumphs and disappointments of life and has created products and ideas—only in that person may gradually ripen the fruit of Erikson's seven stages, namely, ego integrity. One aspect of this is the ego's need for order and meaning. "It is a post-narcissistic love of the human ego—not of the self—as an experience which conveys some world order and spiritual sense, no matter how dearly paid for. It is the acceptance of one's one and only life cycle as something that had to be and that, by necessity, permitted of no substitutions: it thus means a new, a different love of one's parents. It is a comradeship with the ordering ways of distant times and different pursuits, as expressed in the simple products and sayings of such times and pursuits."[3] In chapter 3 on older adults, I have included a liturgy on celebrating aging as recognition of the positive dimension to this stage.

At this point Erikson believes that "the relation of adult integrity and infantile trust is that healthy children will not fear life if their elders have integrity enough not to fear death."[4] We can honor death and face our fears, sorrows, and hopes by naming them in ways such as those represented by the later liturgies for death and dying, whether it be through a service for the "Withdrawal of Life Support" (p. 300) or "After a Suicide" (p. 319).

Are these generalizations about different passages or stages, whether by Erikson, Gail Sheehy, Levinson, or Fowler, helpful or unhelpful? Do they tend to lump everybody together into a potpourri with which no individual identifies? These stages, passages, and categories might best be described as a way of selecting common experiences around different times in our lives. However, they are not neatly self-contained. For example, teen mothers who ordinarily would have been described under the adolescent stage, due to age, find themselves in the young adulthood group with others who are mothers and birthing.

Middle age is in some sense the "in-between times," where we still remember our youth and are not as oriented to the long-range future but are savoring the moment. Midlife literally indicates that life is half over, but a lot of changes may still be occurring for women who started careers and families later, which today is more common than ever before. The liturgy on midlife transition can, it is hoped, be adapted to the different realities that men and women face. We are both looking back and looking forward. Many of life's major events happen at this season of life—job, marriage, buying a home, having children. It is for this reason the "Renewal of Baptismal Covenant for a Congregation" service is here, as a way of affirming from where we came—children of the covenant promise, reappropriating, rediscovering, reexperiencing whose we are and who we are. (Baptism is a sacrament that engrafts us into the community and is also a healing sacrament, as the water symbolizes new life that washes away our sins. Of course, this service is appropriate for those who were baptized as infants, but similar services of renewal could be constructed for those baptized as teenagers.)

One of the happiest moments in our lives is the birth of our children. This has too often become a medical event rather than a family celebration. Birthing needs to be returned to the family and the church. With women having children later in life, into their forties, the chance of miscarriages and complications increases. Previously, the church has marked the advent of a new child by baptism, a seminal sacrament. However, I have included some additional rites that may be meaningful to parents. I have included both the celebration of birth and also the mourning of a stillborn child, which in the past was rarely even recognized socially or liturgically. As well, the tragedy of abortion has too often been only a politicized event rather than a time of pastoral care, which "After an Abortion" addresses from Protestant perspectives; Appendix A presents the perspective from the Roman Catholic framework, in light of the work of the Sisters of Life covenant community.

Realizing our potential, pursuing our dreams, and becoming who we were meant to be dominate the middle season of life. Daniel Levinson decades ago wrote the classic book *The Seasons of a Man's Life,* where he describes the middle years as the BOOM years (Becoming One's Own Man).[5] Gail Sheehy, in her landmark book *New Passages,* frames this period as traditionally forty to sixty years of age. Her research brought her to a different picture, describing first adulthood (thirty to forty-five) and second adulthood (forty-five to eighty-five and older). Part of what we are discovering is that so-called older adults do not act or feel old. Strict seasons of life, narrowly defined, no longer apply.[6]

"The second half of adult life is not the stagnant, depressing downward slide we have always assumed it to be," Sheehy writes. "Wonderfully zesty women in their forties, fifties, and sixties came up to talk to me after my lectures. I kept asking them how it felt to be here, now, on the cusp of radical changes in the life cycle. Whether they talked about the degrees they were studying for, or the daringness of launching new businesses or digging up fossils in China, or the alcoholism or anger or anxiety they had shed, or the live-out lovers they were enjoying instead of remarriage, they all seemed to be exhilarated about starting over."[7]

It is important that the church learn to listen to women tell of their experiences in midlife, so we can minister effectively to them.[8] Unfortunately, much of developmental theory was rooted in research of males, so women's experiences were not authenticated. Carol Gilligan's landmark book *In a Different Voice* helped change that by describing women's preference for relationships over against the male self-actualization model.[9]

Some women may experience the church as overly patriarchal and oppressive, so pastors need to be especially aware of this reality to make worship as inclusive as possible, not simply of language but of symbols and stories. Language, however, should embrace people in all sorts of circumstances and conditions.

Part of my struggle in the placement of liturgies in various seasons was where to put menopause. Traditionally, it probably fits in late middle age. In one sense this can be a freeing time for women: even though it marks the end of fertility, of menstrual cycles, it is also a deeply meaningful psychological and spiritual passage. "Anthropological accounts have revealed that cultural assumptions about aging and femininity can operate to magnify or ameliorate the physical symptoms. The Chinese, who revere age, for example, do not even have a word for 'hot flashes.' Menopause is not an issue in China, according to Dr. Jane Porcino, who attended the first Chinese-American Women's Conference there in 1990."[10] Of course, with the advent of the surrogate mothers and freezing of eggs, women in menopause can still parent newborns. With the new reproductive technologies, the end of fertility is not really the end.

Although I have not included a liturgy for male menopause, this phenomenon is increasingly recognized. Sheehy has some keen insights about the male in his fifties. She claims that men do not face aging as early as women. "In their First Adulthood most men are on more singular achievement tracks than women are. The tracks are made for them; they know all the stops; they are very aware of whether they're racing ahead or falling behind. Most pour out tremendous energy and often dangerously suppress their emotional needs. At least until their forties men can gain strong personal identities and sense of self-worth simply from engaging their aggressive instincts in a struggle for dominance and position in the social hierarchy."[11]

In middle life, Sheehy says, "a man's suppressed emotional needs usually come to the surface. Yet even as his emotional life is becoming more important to him, his surly teenage children are probably rebelling, his older children are leaving home for good, and his wife is becoming more assertive. If his wife is roughly the same age, she is likely to be either bouncing off the walls with menopausal mood swings or soaring with postponed ambitions, joining nonprofit boards or political campaigns and paying less attention to him than to saving refugees. With all these fears and losses on their minds, what do they worry about first? Losing hair."[12] An understandable fear, considering Sheehy's observation that men wish to retain their prowess in bed and work.[13]

Another reality that affects men, but of course women as well, is corporate downsizing and job loss. The phenomenon of "corporate refugees" is sobering.[14] Liturgies for work are included to acknowledge this painful reality. From my perspective, the spiritual dimension is critical in easing work-related transitions. Paradoxically, a job change can spell greater freedom in our lives. Freedom can be frightening or liberating, and one's spiritual resources can make a difference.

There is, however, an upside to job loss. As the liturgy "Work of Our Lives" helps to redefine what constitutes a job and work, so the homemaker, ditch digger, and corporate executive should be regarded equally. And job security is not the only goal in life. Finding meaning in life is crucial. As one man interviewed by Sheehy reflected on his job loss, " 'I can do anything I want. My God, how can this be?' That freedom is the scariest freakin' thing in the world. It is not easy to transform oneself from an institutionalized team player into a self-promoting entrepreneur."[15]

It makes a huge difference if we understand our work as a vocation, a calling from God, rather than simply a career or a job. For the Christian, there are differences among call, vocation, ministry, profession, and career. Karl Barth (1886–1968), Swiss Reformed theologian, talked about vocation as the place of responsibility within the limits of freedom. So our vocation defines what our call from God is, and by virtue of responding to that call, this is our vocation. This puts certain definitions around our life by being faithful to that call. It is a very interesting juxtaposition of the concepts of freedom and responsibility. Frederick Buechner refers to vocation in several of his books as being where the world's deepest needs meet your heart's desire.[16] Work, then, is cast in a very different light.

Of course, the need to be self-supporting is paramount in our society, and, if one has a family as well, the need to help support and sustain them. Unfortunately, our consumer culture has raised the expectations of what constitutes the basics for a family: two televisions, two cars, every available gadget. Tract mansions for the upper middle class are no longer the exception. All this creates a climate where unemployment or constantly changing jobs is not simply about not being able to pay the bills but represents a whole change in lifestyle, which can threaten one's sense of identity and self-image. Jobs, of course, enable us to have homes, and I have included "Blessing of a New Home" and "Blessing of Domestic Pets" as part of celebrating these important realities in our midlife journey.

Not everyone's experience in these middle years is positive. Some experience illness, job loss, and/or death of parents, as reflected in many of this book's liturgies. Furthermore, some criticize Sheehy's research as overly concentrating on upper-class Anglos and not reflective of everyone's experience. However, there are many occasions and reasons to rejoice—celebrations, if you will. Liturgies that help us mark these seasons also are healing, as they reinforce our movement toward wholeness.

The other dominant theme in this period of life is the creation and, sometimes, the breakdown of the family. One in two marriages end in divorce. Does the church not have some comfort to offer in the face of the pain and failure that result from this? Some people, on remarriage, have written letters to their former spouses telling them of this new step and remembering the good things in their former life together. Most churches in mainline denominations up to thirty or forty years ago scarcely talked about divorce; it carried a terrible stigma. The liturgy for divorcing people has two foci—(1) to ask for forgiveness and realize one's failure and (2) to acknowledge that it is important to move forward in life. I have included liturgies for "The Healing of Relationships" and "Dissolution of Partnerships/Marriage" precisely to facilitate not only comfort but also healing in these areas. Coming to closure about lost relationships and learning to move forward is part of healing.

Middle age is also a time when the spiritual quest deepens, where feeling the pain and avoiding the pain of loss may occur simultaneously.[17] "Walking the Labyrinth," while not strictly a liturgy, is included because it allows one to go on a symbolic journey. Since one walks the labyrinth while meditating and praying, there is both an inward and an outward journey—for many, the marking of a passage, a spiritual discipline. Henri Nouwen, in his book *Reaching Out,* describes a different type of passage.[18] Nouwen was a professor who in his retirement years lived at L'Arche residential community for mentally challenged people, who are paired with companions. L'Arche was founded by Jean Vanier in France in 1964. In *Reaching Out,* Nouwen talks about the three stages—moving from loneliness to solitude, from hostility to hospitality, and from illusion to prayer. This is another way of charting our spiritual life. In the movement from loneliness and isolation to solitude, solitude is not to be avoided. Sometimes we are terrified of being alone, but this is loneliness, not solitude.

The second stage is the movement from hostility to hospitality. We live in a hostile world. All we need to do is turn on the television to hear about new impending disasters; psychologically and spiritually, these are unsettling times. How do we make that movement to hospitality? Before we do so, we have to be at home with ourselves, learning to center on who we are; then we can reach out to the stranger. It is in reaching out to the stranger and inviting people in that some have entertained angels unawares, as the writer of Hebrews tells us (Heb. 13:1–2). Hospitality then replaces hostility.

The third and final stage is moving from illusion to prayer. We have a deep cynicism and suspicion that runs through our psyches in this age. Everything is up for grabs; everything is to be examined. Some people are full of despair and say life is not worth living. How do we hang on to the power and love of God in the midst of the tragedies that surround us?[19] It is only by totally saturating ourselves in prayer. Individual prayer is important, and community prayer in the worship context is powerful.

Birthing

"Mary remembered all these things."
(Luke 2:19)

BLESSING OF A PREGNANT WOMAN[20]
(Episcopal)

The following may be used either privately or at a public service.

GATHERING

We are here today at *N*'s home to celebrate this time of expectancy—waiting for the birth of her child and that of her husband, *N*. Let us praise God for this time.

HYMN   #390   H82   "Praise to the Lord"

SCRIPTURE   Luke 1:39–58

BLESSING OF A PREGNANT WOMAN

O Lord and giver of life, receive our prayer for *N*. and for the child she has conceived, that they may happily come to the time of birth, and serving you in all things may rejoice in your loving providence. We ask this through our Lord Jesus Christ, who lives and reigns with you and the Holy Spirit, one God, now and forever. **Amen.**

(When appropriate, any or all of the following may be added:)

Blessed are you, Lord God. You have blessed the union of *N*. and *N*. **Amen.**

Blessed are you, Lord God. May your blessing be upon *N*. and the child she carries. **Amen.**

Blessed are you, Lord God. May this time of pregnancy be for *N*. and *N*. months of drawing nearer to you and to one another. **Amen.**

Blessed are you, Lord God. May *N*. and *N*.'s experience of birth be full of awe and wonder and the joy of sharing in your creation. **Amen.**

RESPONSE OF EXPECTANT WOMAN

BENEDICTION

Go in peace, rejoicing in the power of the Holy Spirit, confident in the protection of God, thankful for this coming gift of life. **Amen.**

THANKSGIVING FOR WOMEN AFTER CHILDBIRTH[21]
(Anglican)

COMMONLY CALLED
THE CHURCHING OF WOMEN

(The Woman, at the usual time after her Delivery, shall come into the Church decently appareled, and there shall kneel down in some convenient place, as hath been accustomed, or as the Ordinary shall direct: And then the Priest shall say unto her one of the following:)

Gen. 3:16, Lev. 12:6–7, Ps. 50:15 & 116:3–7, Luke 2:21–24, 1 Tim. 2:14–15, Gen. 35:16, Ps. 111:1

Forasmuch as it hath pleased Almighty God of his goodness to give you safe deliverance, and hath preserved you in the great danger of Childbirth; you shall therefore give hearty thanks unto God, and say,

(Then shall the Priest say the 116th Psalm.)

Dilexi quoniam.[22]

Or, Psalm cxxvii. *Nisi Dominus.*[23]

(Then the Priest shall say,)

Let us pray.

>   **Minister:** Lord, have mercy upon us.
>
>   **All: Christ, have mercy upon us.**
>
>   **Minister:** Lord, have mercy upon us.

THE LORD'S PRAYER

(1, 2.) Ps. 86:2   **Minister:** O Lord, save this woman thy servant;

   Answer: Who putteth her trust in thee.

   Minister: Be thou to her a strong tower;

(3,4.) Ps. 61:3   **Answer: From the face of her enemy.**

Minister: Lord, hear our prayer.

(5,6.) Ps. 61:1   **Answer: And let our cry come unto thee.**

Minister: Let us pray.

(1.) Ps. 116:8–19; John 16:21

O almighty God, we give thee humble thanks that thou hast vouchsafed to deliver this woman thy servant from the great pain and peril of Childbirth; Grant, we beseech thee, most merciful Father, that she, through thy help, may both faithfully live, and walk according to thy will, in this life present; and also may be partaker of everlasting glory in the life to come; through Jesus Christ our Lord. **Amen.**

SUGGESTED SCRIPTURE   Deut. 23:23; Chron. 19:9; Ps. 20:2, 119:17, 73:24, 133, 124:8, 143:10; 2 Cor. 5:7; Gal. 2:20; Phil. 4:13; Col. 2:6–7; Heb. 4:16; 2 Pet. 1:10–11
(The woman that cometh to give her thanks, must offer accustomed offerings; and, if there be a communion, it is convenient that she receive the holy communion.)

AN ORDER OF THANKSGIVING FOR THE BIRTH OR ADOPTION OF A CHILD[24]
(Methodist)

Following the birth or adoption of a child, the parent(s), together with other members of the family, may present the child in a service of worship to be welcomed by the congregation and to give thanks to God. Part or all of this order may be included in any service of congregational worship.

Thanksgiving for the birth or adoption of a child may also be offered to God in a hospital or home, using such parts of this order as are appropriate.

It should be made clear to participants that this act is neither an equivalent of nor a substitute for Holy Baptism but has an entirely different history and meaning. This act is appropriate: (1) prior to the presentation of the child for baptism; or (2) if the child has been baptized elsewhere and is being presented for the first time in the congregation where his or her nurture is to take place.

While this order will not normally be the theme of an entire service, one or more of the following Scriptures may, if desired, be read as a lesson or sung as an act of praise and thanksgiving:

Deut. 6:4–9	Diligently teach your children.
Deut. 31:12–13	Do this that children may hear and learn.
1 Sam. 1:9–11, 19b–20, 26–28	Samuel born and lent to the Lord
Psalm 8	O Lord, how majestic is your name.

Gal. 4:4–7	We are God's adopted children.
Matt. 18:1–5	The greatest are humble like children.
Mark 10:13–16	Jesus blesses the children.
Luke 1:47–55	The Canticle of Mary
Luke 2:22–40	The presentation of Jesus in the Temple

(As a Response to the Word or at some other appropriate place within a public worship service, the pastor invites those presenting children to come forward and then continues as follows:)

PRESENTATION AND CALL TO THANKSGIVING
(There may be informal and spontaneous acts of presentation and thanksgiving and/or the following:)

Brothers and sisters in Christ:
The *birth (adoption)* of a child is a joyous and solemn occasion in the life of a family.
It is also an occasion for rejoicing in the church family.
I bid you, therefore, to join with *parent's Name* (and *parent's Name*)
    in giving thanks to God, whose children we all are,
        for the gift of *child's Name* to be their *son/daughter*
(and with *sibling's Name(s)*, for a new *brother/sister*).

PRAYER OF THANKSGIVING AND INTERCESSION
(One or more of the following prayers is offered.)

For the Birth of a Child

O God, as a mother comforts her children,
    you strengthen us in our solitude, sustain and provide for us.
As a father cares for his children,
    so continually look upon us with compassion and goodness.
We come before you with gratitude for the gift of this child,
    for the joy that has come into this family,
    and the grace with which you surround them and all of us.
Pour out your Spirit.
Enable your servants to abound in love,
    and establish our homes in holiness;
through Jesus Christ our Lord. **Amen.**

For a Safe Delivery

Gracious God, we give you humble and hearty thanks
    that you have preserved through the pain and anxiety of childbirth
        your servant *mother's Name*
    and upheld your servant(s) *Names of father and/or other family members.*
They desire (She desires) now to offer you
    their (her) praises and thanksgivings.
Grant in your mercy that by your help

they (she) may live faithfully according to your will in this life,
    and finally partake of everlasting glory in the life to come;
through Jesus Christ our Lord. **Amen.**

For the Adoption of a Child

O God, you have adopted all of us as your children.
We give thanks to you for the child
    who has come to bless *Name(s) of parent(s)*
    (and *Name(s) of siblings*)
    who have welcomed this child as *their* own.
By the power of your Holy Spirit,
    fill their home with love, trust, and understanding;
through Jesus Christ our Lord. **Amen.**

For the Family

Gracious God, from whom every family in heaven and on earth is named:
Out of the treasures of your glory, strengthen us through your Spirit.
Help us joyfully to nurture *child's Name* within your Church.
Bring *him/her* by your grace to *baptism (Christian maturity)*,
    that Christ may dwell in *his/her* heart through faith.
Give power to *child's Name* and to us,
    that with all your people we may grasp
        the breadth and length, the height and depth, of Christ's love
Enable us to know this love,
    and to be filled with your own fullness;
through Jesus Christ our Lord. **Amen.**

(A hymn or response may be sung and a blessing given. All from the United Methodist Hymnal.)

#951	Listings under Doxology
#186	*"Alleluia"*
#53	*"All Praise to You"*
#54	*"All Praise to You"*
#611	*"Child of Blessing, Child of Promise"* (stanzas 2, 4)
#141	*"Children of the Heavenly Father"*
#92	*"For the Beauty of the Earth"* (stanzas 1, 4, 6)
#72	*"Gloria, Gloria"*
#78	*"Heleluyan"*
#84	*"Thank You, Lord"*

AFTER A MISCARRIAGE OR STILLBIRTH[25]
(Anglican Church of Canada)

This service may be offered at the hospital bedside, at home, or in church.

RATIONALE

The church has a responsibility to offer opportunity for grieving, healing, and affirming the life-giving gifts of God to parents who experience the pain and sorrow of a miscarriage or the birth of a stillborn child.

It is important that our words and actions acknowledge this loss. It is appropriate that the memory of this experience is not dismissed or taken lightly. Comments made to the parents should not burden them with guilt or false reassurances.

If there are other children in the family, they also should be enabled to enter into the mystery of this loss and, with their parents, hear the comforting assurance of God's presence and promise in Jesus Christ.

CONCERNING THE SERVICE

Pastoral caregivers, particularly chaplains, should be prepared to offer prayers of comfort and consolation as soon as possible after the miscarriage or stillborn birth. Hospital procedures should include notifying chaplains of miscarriages and stillbirths, so that prayers may be offered in the clinical setting.

In the case of a miscarriage, special prayers and a particular Scripture passage may follow the main service on Sunday or be included in a weekday service. Other family members and close friends may be invited to attend and participate.

SUITABLE READINGS

OLD TESTAMENT READINGS

Isa. 66:7–14	(I will comfort you)
Jer. 31:15–17	(Rachel is weeping for her children)
Ps. 42	(Where now is your God?)
Ps. 91:9–18	(He shall give his angels charge over you)
Ps. 103:8–18	(The Lord is full of compassion)
Ps. 121	(My help comes from the Lord)
Ps. 139:6–18	(Where can I go from your spirit?)
Baruch 4:19–23	(I have put my hope in the Everlasting)

NEW TESTAMENT READINGS

Rom. 8:31–39	(Nothing will separate us from the love of God)
1 John 3:1–2	(We are God's children)

GOSPEL READINGS

Matt. 5:1–10	(Blessed are those who mourn)

Matt. 18:1–5, 10–14   (Not one of these little ones should be lost)
Mark 10:13–16   (Let the little children come to me)
John 10:11–16   (I am the good shepherd)

PRAYERS
(These prayers should be adapted with pastoral discretion and sensitivity to suit the circumstances and place.)

Loving God, we come in shock and sadness.
By grace and power you gave us opportunity
to create new life;
now we feel our human frailty.
Hear our cries of disappointment and anger
because of the loss of this new life.
Be with us as we struggle
to understand the mystery of life and death.
Receive this little one into the arms of your mercy,
to abide in your gracious and eternal love.
May we give ourselves over to your tender care.
In Jesus' name we pray. **Amen.**

Holy God, we bring to you our pain and sorrow:
we grieve the loss of a human life.
Show compassion to this mother *(N)* and father *(N)*,
that they may be comforted by your presence
and strengthened by your Spirit.
Be with this family *(N, other children)* as they mourn,
and draw them close together in your healing love.
May each of us know that in our pain you bring us comfort,
in our sorrow you bring us hope,
and in our dying you promise us new life.
In Jesus' name we pray. **Amen.**

(The mother and/or father may offer a personal prayer or reflection. The following may be found helpful as models.)

Creator God, our wombs bring new life to your world.
My body and soul ache with pain for the loss of this child.
Help me to understand where there is no understanding,
strengthen me now in my vulnerability and weakness,
and bring me peace
that I may know more fully your presence
and your salvation,
in the name of Jesus, the child of Mary. **Amen.**

O God, you have loved *me* into being.
Hear *my* cries for *my* loss.

I wanted to bring new life into the world.
Now *I* want to cry forever
and wash your earth with *my* tears.
Move *me* from this darkness
and bring *me* to the light of your love and peace.
In the name of Mary's son. **Amen.**

God of all creation, *I* wanted this child
with all *my* heart, *my* soul, and *my* body.
I feel guilty even though *I* am not to blame,
I feel unworthy, and alone.
Give *me* strength to trust in your faithfulness,
make *me* open to the comfort of family and friends,
and in time free *me* from the bondage of grief.
Bless *me* with the desire and power
to live again in joyful expectation.
I ask this in the name of your Son,
my friend and *my* Savior. **Amen.**

AFTER A MISCARRIAGE[26]
(Ecumenical)

INTRODUCTION
(When all have gathered, the leader introduces the service in words like:)

- We have come together to mourn the death of our unborn child, a life that had been growing with *N* for . . . weeks.
- We had looked forward to the day when we would have seen *his/her/this* face and form, with joy and wonder in our hearts.
- But now this child has gone from us; we now look forward to that day, in the wisdom of our loving God, when we will meet for the first time. 'Now we see dimly, then we shall see face to face.'
- Jesus wept at the death of his friend Lazarus. Jesus weeps with us now, sharing the loss of our hopes, the loss of our dreams.

READINGS   *Possible options:* Ps. 139:13–16; Isa. 43:1–5; 2 Cor. 5:1; John 14:1–4; Mark 10:13–16; John 7:37–8.

HOMILY
(This may include teaching on grief and God's love. We acknowledge our fears, anger and frustration. We recognize that in the deepest of our sorrows God stands with us. The homily is most effective when it is brief, empathetic, personal and reflects the humanity of the speaker.)

POSSIBLE SYMBOLIC ACTIONS

(Water is a most powerful symbol to enter into here. It speaks of living-giving and death-dealing; of the birth process and the death process. It also can have a soothing, therapeutic effect.

Before the prayers, fill a glass bowl with water, perhaps arranging some greenery around it, and sprinkling a few flower petals on the water. You could also have a candle beside the water. Have a towel handy.

When indicated in the service, the couple come to the bowl and 'enter into' the symbol in some way that seems appropriate to them. They may plunge their hands in and hold them under (a death echo) or swirl them about, or cascade the water from their hands (life). They may gently stroke each other's hands under the water, or simply experience its soothing, supporting quality. They may wish to sign themselves with it.

While there are some words to accompany these actions, they should not be rushed in any way. It is important for the couple to experience the symbol at their own pace.

Others at the service may wish also to share in this symbolic act.)

POSSIBLE WORDS TO USE DURING A SYMBOLIC ACTION
(John 7:38; Rev. 21:1–7 could also be read.)

Though we are saddened that our unborn child was with us for so short a time, we entrust *him/her* into your loving care with all confidence.

Our miscarried child was a gift from you, hear our prayer and look upon *him/her* with love.

Bless this mother. We thank you for her womanliness, her beauty of form and spirit; may her love for her lost child be her strength.

Bless this father. Comfort him in his sadness and grant him peace in your eternal love.

(Those present may wish to voice their own prayers.)

CONCLUSION

> **Leader:** We pray now that:
>
> All who are saddened by the death of this hoped-for child, this couple, their family and friends, may put their hope in Christ and through him and each other, receive comfort, peace and holiness.
>
> **All: Lord, hear us.**
>
> **Leader:** That the power of the Holy Spirit may fill us all with freedom and change our fears into trust.
>
> **All: Lord, hear us.**
>
> **Leader:** We pray too for a blessing on this family if in time other children are entrusted to them.
>
> **All: Lord, hear us.**

Leader: And may God who is all loving, all creative and all healing, bless us forever.

BURIAL
*(Remains, or ashes of remains, if these are available, may be wrapped in leaves or cloth and
buried in the family garden, near a special plant, or a new tree may be planted above them.)*

AFTER AN ABORTION[27]
(Ecumenical)

*The service was prepared for a young woman who had chosen to have an abortion after rape
by her boyfriend. This incident also brought up issues of earlier abuse for her. The service was
held on the day when the baby would have been born.*

OPENING SENTENCE

Leader: The steadfast love of the Lord never ceases, his compassion never fails. We
come together today to mark what might have been the birth of _____'s baby,
we come to share our love and care for _____ and we come trusting in God's
steadfast love and his great compassion for all of us.

We want to think about and offer to God more than just today. We bring
memories of the difficult last months and we want to look forward with
hope to the future.

In the last months, choices have had to be made, choices that have been
hard and choices where there was no perfect solution. At times it's easy to
think we took the wrong path, but then we remember again all the good reasons that took us that way.

Lord we ask you to honor _____'s decision, a decision made out of great
pain, a pain that you know and understand, a pain that you carry with her.
Together we come before you as those who have fallen short of the perfect
love you made us for, yet trusting that each time we turn, you are there to
draw us back to yourself.

And so we pray together,

All: **Eternal God, giver of light and grace,**
we have sinned against you and against our neighbors,
in what we have thought,
in what we have said and done.
We have wounded your love,
and marred your image in us.
We are sorry and ashamed,
and repent of all our sins.
For the sake of your Son Jesus Christ,

> **who died for us,**
> **forgive us all that is past;**
> **and lead us out from darkness**
> **to walk as children of light. Amen.**

Leader: Almighty God have mercy upon us, pardon and deliver us from all our sins, and bring us to eternal life, through Jesus Christ our Lord. **Amen.**

We say together Psalm 23. During this the candle will be lit to remind us of Jesus the shepherd who is also our light.

(During the following prayer the young woman laid a single red rose beside the lighted candle.)

We remember your light and your presence with ____'s baby, a baby given up in love. Lord, as you are the creator of all life so we entrust ____'s baby into your care.

Lord God, by your mighty power you gave us life, and in your love you have given us new life in Christ Jesus. We entrust ____'s baby to your merciful keeping, in the faith of Jesus Christ your Son our Lord, who died and rose again to save us, and is now alive and reigns with you and the Holy Spirit in glory forever. **Amen.**

Gracious God,
in darkness and in light,
in trouble and in joy,
help us to trust your love,
to serve your purpose,
and to praise your name;
through Jesus Christ our Lord. **Amen.**

God in heaven, you gave your Son Jesus Christ to suffering and to death on the cross, and raised him to life in glory. Grant us a patient faith in time of darkness, and strengthen our hearts with the knowledge of your love; through Jesus Christ our Lord. **Amen.**

Lord have mercy upon us.
Christ have mercy upon us.
Lord have mercy upon us.

Leader: Our Father in heaven . . .

O God,
Giver of Life,
Bearer of Pain,
Maker of Love,
you are able to accept in us what we
cannot even acknowledge;

you are able to name in us what we
cannot bear to speak of;
you are able to hold in your memory
what we have tried to forget;
you are able to hold out to us
the glory that we cannot conceive of.
Reconcile us through your cross
to all that we have rejected in our selves,
that we may find no part of your creation
to be alien or strange to us,
and that we ourselves may be made whole.

Through Jesus Christ our lover and our Friend.   **Amen.**

Leader: Lord, as we entrust the past into your loving and compassionate hands we
look with you to the future.

READING   Jairus's daughter: Mark 5:21a–24 and 35b–43

SILENCE

REFLECTION

Leader: Our God is one who draws us on—out of the painful and death-like experiences. To take his hand is to bring all that the past has made us and step out
into his future for us. So he calls each one of us by name, and says *'Talitha
cum,'* that is, 'Get up my child.'

'. . . and he told them to give her something to eat.' Jesus calls us on into the
future and, directly by his love and by the love he gives us through others,
he gives us food to enable us to get up and to step out.

(Communion from the reserved sacrament might follow.)

FINAL PRAYER AND BLESSING

Leader: May God in his infinite love and mercy bring the whole church, living and
departed in the Lord Jesus, to a joyful resurrection and the fulfillment of his
eternal kingdom. And the blessing of God Almighty, the Father, the Son and
the Holy Spirit, be with us and with all whom we love today and always.
Amen.

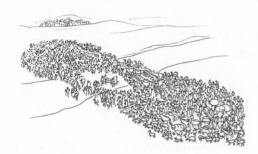

Life Transitions

"The people hurried across the river." (Josh. 4:10)

FOR A NEW DAY

God of Time
God of Space
Fill this moment
With your grace.
God of Motion
God of Peace
From each sin
Give release.
God of Quiet
God of Might
Keep us ever
In your sight.

—David Adam, *"For a New Day"*
in Tides and Seasons[28]

RENEWAL OF BAPTISMAL COVENANT FOR A CONGREGATION[29]
(Presbyterian)

This liturgy is provided for occasions calling for a public reaffirmation of the baptismal covenant, and is included in the order for the Service for the Lord's Day.

(This service is led from the baptismal font or pool, which shall be filled with water.)

SCRIPTURE READING
(After the sermon, the minister, standing at the baptismal font or pool, reads one of the following scripture texts: 1 Cor. 12:12–13; Eph. 4:1–7.)

PROFESSION OF FAITH
(The congregation may stand, as the minister continues:)

Sisters and brothers in Christ,
our baptism is the sign and seal
of our cleansing from sin,
and of our being grafted onto Christ.
Through the birth, life, death, and resurrection of Christ,
the power of sin was broken
and God's kingdom entered our world.
Through our baptism we were made citizens of God's kingdom,
and freed from the bondage of sin.
Let us celebrate the freedom and redemption
through the renewal of the promises made at our baptism.

I ask you, therefore,
once again to reject sin,
to profess your faith in Christ Jesus,
and to confess the faith of the church,
the faith in which we were baptized.

RENUNCIATIONS
(The minister continues, using one of the following:)

1. **Minister:** Trusting in the gracious mercy of God,
    do you turn from the ways of sin
    and renounce evil and its power in the world?

    All: I do.

    Minister: Do you turn to Jesus Christ
    and accept him as your Lord and Savior,
    trusting in his grace and love?

    All: I do.

    Minister: Will you be Christ's faithful disciple,
    obeying his Word and showing his love?

    All: I will, with God's help.

2. **Minister:** Do you renounce all evil,
    and powers in the world
    which defy God's righteousness and love?

    All: I renounce them.

    Minister: Do you renounce the ways of sin
    that separate you from the love of God?

    All: I renounce them.

Minister: Do you turn to Jesus Christ
and accept him as your Lord and Savior?

All: **I do.**

Minister: Will you be Christ's faithful disciple,
obeying his Word and showing his love,
to your life's end?

All: **I will, with God's help.**

3. **Minister:** Trusting in the gracious mercy of God,
do you turn from the ways of sin
and renounce evil and its power in the world?

All: **I do.**

Minister: Who is your Lord and Savior?

All: **Jesus Christ is my Lord and Savior.**

Minister: Will you be Christ's faithful disciple,
obeying his Word and showing his love?

All: **I will, with God's help.**

PROFESSION

Minister: With the whole church,
let us confess our faith.

(The congregation affirms the faith in the words of the Apostles' Creed.)

THANKSGIVING FOR BAPTISM
(Water is poured visibly and audibly into the font. One of the following prayers is then said by the minister:)

1. **Minister:** The Lord be with you.

All: **And also with you.**

Minister: Let us give thanks to the Lord our God.

All: **It is right to give our thanks and praise.**

Minister: We give you thanks, Eternal God,
for you nourish and sustain all living things
by the gift of water.
In the beginning of time,
your Spirit moved over the watery chaos,
calling forth order and life.

In the time of Noah,
you destroyed evil by the waters of the flood,
giving righteousness a new beginning.

You led Israel out of slavery,
through the waters of the sea,
into the freedom of the promised land.

In the waters of Jordan
Jesus was baptized by John
and anointed with your Spirit.

By the baptism of his own death and resurrection,
Christ set us free from sin and death,
and opened the way to eternal life.

We thank you, O God, for the water of baptism.
In it we were buried with Christ in his death.
From it we were raised to share in his resurrection,
through it we were reborn by the power of the Holy Spirit.

Therefore in joyful obedience to your Son,
we celebrate our fellowship in him in faith.
We pray that all who have passed through the water of baptism
may continue forever in the risen life
of Jesus Christ our Savior.
To him, to you, and to the Holy Spirit,
be all honor and glory, now and forever.[30]

All: Amen.

2. **Minister:** The Lord be with you.

    All: And also with you.

Minister: Let us give thanks to the Lord our God.

    All: It is right to give our thanks and praise.

Minister: Eternal and gracious God, we give you thanks.
In countless ways you have revealed yourself in ages past,
and have blessed us with signs of your grace.

We praise you that through the waters of the sea
you led your people Israel out of bondage,
into freedom in the land of your promise.

We praise you for sending Jesus your Son,
who for us was baptized in the waters of the Jordan,
and was anointed as the Christ by your Holy Spirit.
Through the baptism of his death and resurrection

you set us free from the bondage of sin and death,
and give us cleansing and rebirth.

We praise you for your Holy Spirit,
who teaches us and leads us into all truth,
filling us with a variety of gifts,
that we might proclaim the gospel to all nations
and serve you as a royal priesthood.

We rejoice that you claimed us in our baptism,
and that by your grace we are born anew.
By your Holy Spirit renew us,
that we may be empowered to do your will
and continue forever in the risen life of Christ,
to whom, with you and the Holy Spirit,
be all glory and honor,
now and forever.[31]

All: Amen.

LAYING-ON OF HANDS
(The minister may invite persons who wish to receive the laying-on of hands to come and kneel at the font.
The minister lays both hands on the head of each person in turn, while offering one of the following prayers. The sign of the cross may be traced on the forehead of each person. Oil prepared for this purpose may be used.)

1. **Minister:** O Lord, uphold N. by your Holy Spirit.
    Daily increase in *him/her* your gifts of grace:
    the spirit of wisdom and understanding,
    the spirit of counsel and might,
    the spirit of knowledge and the fear of the Lord,
    the spirit of joy in your presence,
    both now and forever.[32]

2. **Minister:** Defend, O Lord, your Servant N.
    with your heavenly grace,
    that *he/she* may continue yours forever,
    and the daily increase in your Holy Spirit more and more,
    until *he/she* comes to your everlasting kingdom.

    Candidate: Amen.

THE PEACE
(The service concludes with the exchange of peace if it was not included earlier in the service.)

Minister: The peace of our Lord Jesus Christ be with you.

All: And also with you.

(It is especially appropriate that the Lord's Supper follow a reaffirmation of the baptismal covenant.)

BIRTHDAY LITURGIES[33]
(Nondenominational)

Families may want to use a birthday liturgy before or after the birthday dinner. All who participate should come prepared with a scriptural verse they have selected to read to the birthday person. A large "Christ candle" is needed, as well as a smaller unlit candle, and for the second service, a stone upon which to strike a match.

BIRTHDAY CELEBRATION

First reader: As we gather together to celebrate your birthday, _____, we want to thank God for giving you to us, and we want to encourage you in fulfilling the purpose for which God created you.

(Light large Christ candle in the center of the table.)

Second reader: We light a candle to symbolize that Jesus is the source of your life, not only because He made you, but because He constantly gives you spiritual life.

Third reader: The Bible tells us that you were created with God's personal attention, Ps. 139:13–16.

Fourth reader: Ps. 22:9–10 tells us that God watched over you when you were young and helpless.

Fifth reader: And now we want to give you some nourishment from the scriptures to strengthen your trust in the Lord and your commitment to fulfill the purpose for which He created you.

(Each person reads the verse they have selected for the celebrated one, going around the table. An unlit candle is passed from reader to reader as the verses are read. After all the verses are read, the unlit candle is placed in the hands of the celebrated one. The following is then read.)

Sixth reader: We ask you, _____, to light your candle from the Christ candle to signify your willingness to begin another year of life, your thankfulness for God's gift of life through Jesus, and your desire to give all that you have and are to the Loving and Sovereign One for another year.

CLOSING SONG   #391   PrH   "Take My Life and Let It Be"

BIRTHDAY LITANY

First reader: "The people walking in darkness have seen a great light; on those living in the land of the shadow of death a light has dawned."

(A match is struck from a stone on the table and the Christ candle is lit.)

Second reader: We light the Christ candle from a spark struck from a stone symbolizing the stone rolled from the tomb.

All: Christ has died, Christ is risen, Christ will come again. Hallelujah!

Third reader: *(Alternative for adults)* As we celebrate your physical birth this evening, _____, we also want to celebrate your spiritual birth. As with Christians of old we present you with a candle to signify your identification with Christ. With the candle we give you some nourishment from the Scriptures.

(Alternative for children) _____, we are glad that God brought you into the world. As we celebrate your birthday we give you a candle and some verses from the Bible.

(As the unlit candle is passed around the table, each person reads a verse they have selected for the celebrated one while holding the candle. As the last one before the birthday person holds the candle, the following is read.)

Fourth reader: Jesus said, "While I am in the world, I am the light of the world."

Fifth reader: Jesus also said, "I have come into the world as a light, so that no one who believes in me should stay in darkness."

(The person beside the celebrated one lights the candle and hands it to him or her as the following is read.)

All: As Jesus said to his followers, we say to you, and hope that it will be true of your life. "You are the light of the world, a city that is set upon a hill cannot be hid. You were once in darkness, but now you are light in the Lord. Walk as a child of the light."

HYMN   #557   W&R   "It Only Takes a Spark"

CLOSING PRAYER

HONORING OUR FIFTIETH YEAR[34]
(Interfaith)

Gaia, Mother Earth, we hear your pain and suffering,
    your struggles for breath and life.
We mourn our careless and heavy footsteps on your body.

All oppressed peoples of the earth, we taste your hunger and
    thirst for justice.
We confess our failures to work for freedom and justice.

Friends and family near and far, we see you reaching for
    understanding and healing.
We regret our actions and inactions, large and small, that
    have brought you sorrow.

RENEWAL OF COMMITMENT
(The woman [or man] celebrating her/his Jubilee describes the ways in which she/he wants her/his next decades to honor her/his bonds with all of creation and its peoples.)

READING   Isa. 65:17–22, 24–25

REFRESHMENTS AND DANCING

BLESSING OF A NEW HOME[35]
(Episcopal)

For there we loved, and where we love is home,
Home that our feet may leave, but not our hearts,
Though o'er us shine the jasper-lighted dome.
        —From "Homesick in Heaven"
        by Oliver Wendell Holmes

GATHERING AND GREETING NEAR THE FRONT HALLWAY AT THE HOME OF ABIGAIL RIAN EVANS, PRINCETON, N.J.
(Hosts will move from area to area in the house while leaders remain near their appointed room. When visitors come to your room, please participate with them in the 'gifting' and the prayers.)

Unison Prayer

Almighty and everlasting God, grant to this home the grace of your presence, that you may be known to N., and the defender of this household. Let the mighty power of your Holy Spirit be present in this place to make it a secure habitation for all who dwell and come or go here; in the Name of Jesus Christ our Lord. **Amen.**

At the Entrance

Leader: Behold, I stand at the door and knock, says the Lord. If you hear my voice and open the door, I will come into the house, and eat with you, and you with me.

People: **The Lord shall watch over your going out and your coming in from this time forth and for evermore.**

Leader: Sovereign God, as you send your servant N. out from this place, be her constant companion in the way, and welcome her upon her return, so that coming and going she may be sustained by your presence, O Christ our Lord. **Amen.**

Nursery Gifting Symbol: Winnie-the-Pooh Bear

Leader: Jesus said, "Let the children come to me, and do not hinder them; for to those like them belongs the kingdom of heaven."

People: Praise the Lord, you children of the Lord. Praise the Name of the Lord.

Leader: O God our Loving Parent, your Son our Savior took young children into his arms and blessed them. Embrace the children and grandchildren who enter this room with your unending love. Protect them from all danger and bring them in safety to each new day. Through Jesus Christ our Lord. **Amen.**

Master Bedroom/Sitting Room Gifting Symbol: Pillow

Leader: Guide us waking, O Lord, and guard us sleeping, that awake we may watch with Christ, and asleep we may rest in peace.

People: I lie down and go to sleep: I wake again, because the Lord sustains me.

Leader: O God of life and love, the true rest of your people: Sanctify to your servant her hours of rest and refreshment, her sleeping and waking. Grant that, strengthened by the indwelling of your Holy Spirit, she may rise to serve you all the days of her life. Through Jesus Christ our Lord. **Amen.**

Guest Room Gifting Symbol: Viking Statue

Leader: Since we are surrounded by so great a cloud of witnesses, let us run with perseverance the race that is set before us.

People: My boundaries enclose a pleasant land: Indeed, I have a goodly heritage.

Leader: Jesus our good Companion, on many occasions you withdrew with your friends for quiet and refreshment: Be with your servants in this place to which they come for fellowship and recreation. Remind N. of her heritage and strengthen her to live faithfully therein. Through Christ our Lord. **Amen.**

Kitchen Gifting Symbol: Bowl of Food

Leader: You shall eat in plenty and be satisfied, and praise the Name of the Lord your God, who has dealt wondrously with you.

People: The eyes of all wait upon you, O Lord: You give them their food in due season.

Leader: O Lord our God, you supply every need of ours according to your great riches: Bless the hands that work in this place, and give us grateful hearts for daily bread; through Jesus Christ our Lord. **Amen.**

Dining Room Gifting Symbol: Dinner Gong

Leader: The living God gave you from heaven rain and fruitful seasons, satisfying your hearts with food and gladness.

People: **God brings forth food from the earth, and wine to gladden our hearts; oil to make a cheerful countenance, and bread to strengthen the heart.**

Leader: Blessed are you, O Lord, Ruler of the universe, for you give us food and drink to sustain our lives. Make us grateful for all your mercies, and mindful of the needs of others; through Christ Jesus our Lord. **Amen.**

Living Room Gifting Symbol: Flower Vase

Leader: Oh, how good and pleasant it is, when God's people live together in unity!

People: **Above everything, love one another earnestly; for love covers a multitude of sins.**

Leader: Give your blessing, Lord, to all who share this room, that they may be knit together in fellowship here on earth, and joined with the communion of your saints in heaven; through Jesus Christ our Lord. **Amen.**

HYMN   "Bless This House"   Tune "Eternal Father Strong to Save"—words by Abigail Rian Evans

Bless this house O Lord we pray
Keep her safe both night and day
Protect her from all dangerous foes
Keep watch o'er all life's ebbs and flows
A place of welcome for our friends
To serve and love all without end.

CONCLUDING BLESSING

Leader: Unless the Lord builds the house, their labor is in vain who build it.

People: **Visit, O blessed Lord, this home with the gladness of your presence, Bless N. with the gift of your love, and grant that all whose lives are touched by this home may grow in the grace and the knowledge and the love of you. Preserve this home in peace, O Jesus Christ, now and forever. Amen.**

Leader: The Peace of the Lord be always with you.

People: **And also with you.**

BLESSING OF DOMESTIC PETS[36]
(Anglican)

CONCERNING THE OCCASION

Animals are a vital part of the creation of which human beings have been given stewardship. They provide us with companionship, and in some cases assist in independent daily living. The rite which follows is intended for use when it is desired to give thanks and to pray for God's blessing on pets and other domestic animals. It is anticipated that a significant number of children will be present, and their participation and leadership should be encouraged. The service may take place on an occasion such as the feast of a saint or a Sunday whose proper readings illustrate the theme. The service may be modified as appropriate to the circumstances.

Portions of this material may be incorporated into the Sunday liturgy of a congregation, but this service should not replace the Sunday liturgy and the readings proper to the day.

THE GATHERING OF THE COMMUNITY
(When the community has gathered the presiding minister says,)

> **Minister:** Let us bless our God,
> creator and giver of all.

> **People: Blessed be God, now and for ever. Amen.**

(A canticle or hymn may follow.)   #105   HAM   "All Creatures of Our God and King"

THE PROCLAMATION OF THE WORD

THE READINGS
(One or more of the following, or another passage, is read.)

Gen. 2:18–20a   (The Lord God formed every animal of the field.)
Gen. 9:8–17   (This is the sign of the covenant . . . between me and every living creature.)
Isa. 11:1–9   (They will not hurt or destroy.)
Matt. 6:25–34   (Look at the birds of the air.)
Matt. 18:10–14   (If a shepherd has a hundred sheep.)
John 10:2–5   (The [shepherd] calls his own sheep by name.)

(Ps. 8 or Ps. 65 may follow the reading.)

(A homily or other reflection on the readings may follow.)

INTERCESSIONS AND THANKSGIVINGS
(A deacon or other member of the community may lead the prayers.)

> **Leader:** We thank you, God, for the gift of life: for the beauty and wonder of creation, and for our own life which comes from you.

People: **Glory to you forever and ever.**

Leader: We thank you for the richness of animal life: for fish and birds, insects, reptiles, and mammals.

People: **Glory to you forever and ever.**

Leader: We thank you for the animals who give us faithful companionship, joy when we are happy and comfort when we are sad.

People: **Glory to you forever and ever.**

Leader: We thank you for calling us to care for these animals. May we learn love and respect for all living things.

People: **Glory to you forever and ever.**

(The minister says the prayer of blessing.)

Blessed are you, living, loving God.
All creation praises you,
yet you have given the earth into our hands.
You made animals as our companions,
that in caring for them
we might learn to love and care
for all your creatures,
and find in them a sign of your grace.
As we fulfill this calling
may we draw close to you,
the giver of all life,
through Jesus Christ our Lord. **Amen.**

(The Lord's Prayer may be said.)
(The minister may dismiss the congregation.)

Minister: Go forth into the world,
rejoicing in the power of the Spirit.

People: **Thanks be to God.**

TURNING SEASON[37]
(United Church of Christ)

PRAYER OF DISCERNMENT FOR THE INDIVIDUAL

CALL TO WORSHIP

SONG   "Turn! Turn! Turn!"[38]

PRAYER

> God, my Source of Strength:
> A season is turning in my life
> Calling me to make ready:
> Walk with me, I pray.
>
> This unmapped course lies divided ahead
> Urging careful determination:
> Walk with me, I pray.
>
> The gate has swung open and everything's loose
> Bidding that something be left behind:
> Walk with me, I pray.
>
> Until the turbulent waters clear
> I reach for your mercy
> And pray for wisdom:
> Walk with me, I pray.
> **Amen.**

READINGS *(while reading selected Scripture, slowly turn)*

> Ps. 143:8, 10
> 1 Cor. 13:12
> Jer. 6:16
> 2 Sam. 22:33–34
> John 14:27

PRAYER FOR THE JOURNEY

> God of Blessing,
> With pilgrim's feet
> I trace this fresh journey
> One step at a time.
>
> With an apprentice's regard
> I seek a clear vision
> One landscape at a time.
>
> With a dancer's heart
> I trust the center to hold
> One leap at a time.

With a mother's tender arms
You cradle my new spirit
One breath at a time.
Amen.

MIDLIFE TRANSITION[39]
(Roman Catholic)

ENVIRONMENT

The theme of this ritual lends itself well to the use of visual symbols. These may be arranged artistically on a table draped with a colorful cloth to create a meditative focal point for the celebration. If the space is flexible enough, a circular seating arrangement is preferable, with the table, the symbol station, forming part of the circle's circumference. With such an arrangement, the symbol station becomes a point of departure and of closure for the circle, itself an appropriate symbol for midlife prayer. If the space is not flexible, however, the symbol station should be placed in the foreground where it will be visible to the entire assembly.

The symbols are often chosen to be suggestive of the passage and the promise of the midlife journey. They might include some of the following: a vase containing bittersweet or some other autumn foliage; a large, attractive clock, preferably in a wooden case; a small pillow on which is placed a pair of leather sandals; a roughly hewn walking staff; a partially opened road map; a cluster of medium-sized stones; a pillar candle; a compass; a wooden cross without a corpus. Other symbols might be chosen instead.

Care should be exercised to ensure a harmonious coordination of size and color among all the elements of the symbol station. The point is to provide a contemplative focal point to feed and nourish reflective prayer.

INTRODUCTORY RITE

GATHERING
(As the assembly gathers, soft instrumental music may be played in the background. When everyone is gathered and seated, the presider and attending ministers enter the assembly and take their assigned places. After a brief time of quiet, one of the ministers lights a candle on the symbol table.)

CALL TO WORSHIP

Presider: My brothers and sisters in Christ, welcome!
Our lives are filled with turning points,
cycles of change and crisis and transformation.
The old passes into ever new beginnings.

We grow, we stand still, we grow again.
As Christians we believe and proclaim
that God's love is always at work within us,
in men and women who believe and trust and hope.
I welcome you now to this time of prayer,
this time to know again the action of God in our lives.
I welcome you to celebrate together
time passing, and time beginning anew.
And I pray that the God of Jesus Christ,
who is ever old and ever new
be with us.

**All: As it was in the beginning,
is now and ever shall be,
world without end. Amen.**

LITURGY OF THE WORD

MEDITATION
(A reader steps to the center of the circle and faces the symbol station. At specified points during the reading of the meditation, the reader turns to the right in a clockwise movement and faces another segment of the assembly. The movement is designed to come full circle when the meditation comes to an end. The reading should be done slowly and with feeling. Eye contact with the assembly is essential.)

Time
turns
taking us
where we would not choose to go.

(Reader turns to the right.)

Suddenly we pass a point
we will never pass again.
Turning points interrupt us—
there must be some mistake.

(Reader turns to the right again.)

Looking back we see them
for what they really are:
bittersweet raw reality,
breakthrough to beatitude,
bedrock that gives us courage

(Reader turns to the right again.)

> to give ourselves away.
> The less we struggle with turning points
> the greater the strength remaining
> to return

(Reader turns again, thus coming full circle.)

> and turn
> again.

SONG   #595   WIII   "There is a Wideness in God's Mercy"
(The assembly is invited to a sung prayer of hope and trust. A text employing the imagery of journey would be ideal.)

PRAYER

Presider: Let us pray.

> God of our past, our present, and our future,
> we know that we do not travel alone,
> for you are with us and within us.
> You are the God of seasons and sojourns,
> of passage and pilgrimage,
> of Exodus and Emmaus.
> Be companion with us all the days of our lives.
> Direct our steps along the path of goodness and growth.
> Be gentle with us through the seasons and the years.
> Give us power to serve others
> in compassion, mercy and love.
> Be for us always a new beginning,
> a fresh springtime,
> and lead us to your eternal day
> with him who is the Rising Dawn,
> Jesus Christ, our Lord.

All: Amen.

READING   Rom. 8:18–27

RESPONSE   based on Eccles. 3:1–11 *(read responsively)*

READING   John 21:18–19

HOMILY
(The homilist may wish to share reflections on the theme of midlife journeying and on the importance of responding to Christ's invitation, "Follow me." It is strongly recommended that the homilist be a person who has personal experience of the midlife transition.)

RITE OF ANOINTING

PRESENTATION OF OIL
(The presentation is made within the context of a meditative reading which may be rendered by a solo voice or by several voices in dialogue.)

>I said to my soul, be still and let the dark come upon you
>Which shall be the darkness of God.

(All lights in the worship space are extinguished except for the single candle on the symbol station.)

>I said to my soul, be still, and not without hope,
>For hope would be hope for the wrong things; wait without love
>For love would be love of the wrong things; there is yet faith
>But the faith and the love and the hope are all in the waiting.
>Wait without thought, for you are not ready for thought:
>So the darkness shall be the light, and the stillness, the dancing.

(Here the reader pauses long enough to create the sensation of "waiting in darkness.")

>What we call the beginning is often the end
>And to make an end is to make a beginning.
>The end is where we start from.

(At this point instrumental music is introduced as background accompaniment to the reading. A solo flute or oboe would serve best.)

>Time present and time past
>Are both perhaps present in time future . . .
>What might have been and what has been
>Point to one end, which is always present.
>At the still point of the turning world . . .
>Neither from nor towards; at the still point, there the dance is . . .
>Where past and future are gathered . . .
>Except for the point, the still point,
>There would be no dance.

(The reading and the music cease simultaneously. There is a brief reflective silence, a still point, before the music resumes. When it does, a minister enters carrying a decanter of oil for the anointing. This ritual action may be a simple processional gesture with the decanter of oil held high, or, if a dancer can be enlisted for this, it may be a more complex dance presentation. The lights are raised as the minister or dancer enters the assembly. The oil is presented to the presider for the blessing.)

BLESSING OF OIL

>**Presider:** Blest be God who has given us healing ointments
>with which to salve the wounds and hurts of life.

Blest be this golden liquid,
pressed from the fruits of the earth
and possessed of powers
to nurture healing and wholeness.
Blest be God whose life-giving Spirit
animates the flowing motion
and the fluid ministrations
of this holy unction.
Blest be God who invites us to receive
the healing touch of divine compassion
in the sacrament of anointing.
Blest too be men and women of faith
who respond to God's invitation.

All: Amen.

(Oil is poured into several earthenware bowls set aside for the purpose and are given to those who will administer the anointing. These proceed to designated stations.)

ANOINTING WITH OIL
(The minister signs the head of each person with oil, saying one of the following prayers:)

Minister: May your journey through midlife
bring you to full maturity in Christ.

[or] Through this holy anointing,
may you realize more fully
your true humanity in God.

Recipient: Amen.

PRAYER AFTER ANOINTING
(When all have been anointed, a prayer of thanksgiving may be offered, or a song sung, or simply some time given to quiet prayer.)

CONCLUDING RITES

CLOSING PRAYER

Presider: Let us now pray.

**All: From God's infinite glory
may our hidden selves grow,
and may Christ live in our hearts through faith
Then, planted in love and built on love,
we will, with all the saints,
have the strength to grasp
the breadth and the length,**

> **the height and the depth,**
> **until knowing the love of Christ**
> **which is beyond all understanding,**
> **we are filled with the utter fullness of God.**
>
> **Glory be to God,**
> **whose power at work within us**
> **can do infinitely more than we can ask or imagine.**
> **Glory be to God from generation to generation**
> **in the church and in Christ Jesus**
> **forever and ever. Amen.**

DISMISSAL

> **Presider:** And so, my friends and fellow voyagers,
> I make but one suggestion:
> Think not today that the past is finished,
> nor even that the future is before us.
> Rather, consider the future and the past with equal mind.
> With God's blessing upon us all,
> I bid you not "Farewell,"
> But "Fare forward."

RECESSIONAL

(The solo instrumental recapitulates the theme introduced during the rite of anointing. The minister/dancer re-enters to beckon the presider and the members of the assembly to follow his/her lead in exiting the worship space. As the community departs, the lights are gradually extinguished until the place of prayer is once again in dark stillness. The music continues for a bit after all have departed. Finally, it ceases. All is stillness.)

PASSAGE TO MENOPAUSE[40]
(Nondenominational)

CALL TO WORSHIP

Our help is in the Name of the Lord who made heaven and earth. Come let us worship our God and King; our Healer and Redeemer.

HYMN   #275   PrH   "God Our Life"

PSALM FOR A WOMAN WHO NO LONGER BLEEDS[41]

> O Divine One,
>   Source of the feminine life-force,
>   I thank you this day

for your life-energy within my body,
for the order of its rhythm and cycles.

Even though I no longer have
My blood time to mark my cycles,
teach me to listen with my inner ear
to the other cycles and patterns
of my body.

As I listen with attentiveness and respect,
May I daily grow in understanding
of how to care for my body
with gentleness and love.

May I always remember
That my femininity
is an integral part of me,
regardless of whether I am fertile or not.

And as I listen with greater reverence
To that rhythm of your life within me,
may I allow the special gifts
of this stage of my life to emerge,
creating space for the wise woman within me
to find fuller expression in my life.

PRAYER OF BLESSING

SCRIPTURE   Prov. 31:10–31

MEDITATION

HYMNS   #276   PrH   "Great Is Thy Faithfulness"
         or
         #261   PrH   "God of Compassion"

BENEDICTION

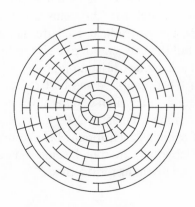

WALKING THE LABYRINTH: A HEALING LITURGICAL PRACTICE[42]
(Nondenominational)

A SACRED PATH TO OUR INNER BEING

Walking the labyrinth is the rediscovery of an ancient spiritual tool that functions as a metaphor for our spiritual journey and inner transformation. As Lauren Artress has put it, walking the labyrinth is the seeking of a sacred path, which can guide us in our search for meaning and purpose in life. To walk a sacred path is to explore our inner sacred space, to understand the invisible world, which opens us to the movement of the Spirit.[43] This medieval practice has been retrieved and is an available spiritual tool today for self-knowledge as well as for spiritual and psychological healing.

BACKGROUND INFORMATION

Labyrinths can be found in most religious traditions in the world and have been known to the human race for at least four thousand years.[44] They are mysterious, because no one knows the origin of their design or why they were created. They have, however, had a religious function for centuries and have been present in Christian churches at least since the construction of the Gothic cathedrals in Europe, where they were strategically placed. Labyrinths were used as a substitute for pilgrimages to the Holy Lands during dangerous times, for example, during crusades, or for those who were too poor to travel.

Labyrinths have to be differentiated from mazes, which are multicursal and offer a choice of paths, multiple entrances, exits, and dead ends. Mazes are often used to challenge our logic. Labyrinths, by contrast, are unicursal, having a well-defined path that leads us into the center and back out again, without any tricks, dead ends, or intersecting paths. Some have referred to this as "sacred geometry."[45] For example, the Chartres-style labyrinth has eleven circuits or concentric circles leading to the twelfth circle in the center.[46] It is aligned with the rose window in the cathedral. This is what sets the labyrinth apart as a spiritual tool. Instead of engaging our logic, our thinking mind, it "invites our intuitive, pattern-seeking, symbolic mind to come forth. It presents us with only one, but profound choice. To enter the labyrinth is to choose to walk a spiritual path."[47] By offering only one way, which leads to its center, the labyrinth becomes a strong symbol of our own journey in search for the center of our lives. Knowing oneself in the mystical traditions entails knowing the Divine. Therefore, the labyrinth invites us, as spiritual seekers, to an inward journey toward God.

Another link between the labyrinth and spiritual disciplines is that of the Christian symbol of the "way," *hodos*. The symbolism of the way is a frequently used metaphor for the Christian path—following Christ. This was foreshadowed in the Hebrew Scriptures—Proverbs 9:6, "way of insight" and Job 24:13, "those who rebel against the light," which is similar to Matthew 21:32 referring to John the Baptist who "came to you in the way *(hodos)* of righteousness. . . ."[48] The way *(hodos)* is referred to in John 14 and Luke 24:35. In Acts 24 the Christians are referred to as members of "the way." In its root sense this word referred to a road or a path one might walk (Matt. 2:12; Mark 11:8). However, it soon took on a metaphorical meaning. There is also the image of the path of wisdom, which for Christians was following Christ. Christ himself declares, "I am the way *(hodos)*, and the truth, and the life" (John 14:6).[49] It seems no accident that these images of journey and the way could give rise to the understanding of the labyrinth as a spiritual practice to symbolize our Christian journey.

The oldest church labyrinth that still exists today was designed between 1194 and 1220 C.E. and is located at Chartres Cathedral, in the central body of the cathedral. "Labyrinth designs have been found on Cretan coins and poetry, on a rock carving in Sardinia dating from 2500–2000 B.C.E., and made of mounded earth in fields in England, Ireland and Scandinavia. Historians believe that labyrinths were walked by pilgrims in medieval times. Some labyrinths are round, some square, some octagonal, and the patterns vary. The paths in some church labyrinths form a cross."[50]

The labyrinth as a spiritual tool was introduced to the American public through the initiative of Lauren Artress, canon pastor of Grace Cathedral, in San Francisco. "A website lists more than one hundred labyrinths in the United States, but there are many more. A woman carries a cloth labyrinth to jails in San Diego for prisoners to walk. Students at several universities in California walk them before exams."[51] Canvas labyrinths are also available through the General Assembly Office of Presbyterian Church (U.S.A.) and at seminaries such as Princeton Theological Seminary, Columbia Seminary, and others.

THE POWER AND MEANING OF THE LABYRINTH

Despite its multiple symbolism, the labyrinth ultimately represents journey: "the journey through life, death and rebirth, the spiritual journey, the initiatory journey."[52] It speaks to us as a powerful symbol of journeying. This journey can either be our whole life or it can represent a particular journey in our present or past life, such as a crisis situation one is facing, the journey through school, one's professional vocation, a relationship, a creative project, and so forth. The labyrinth helps the pilgrim by revealing one's particular journey and how it should be done. It is especially helpful during the season of middle adulthood at times of transition, but it has been effectively used with children, the homeless, and people at all ages and life situations. It can be either a solo journey or a communal one. Hence, it is a community-building experience.

The power of the labyrinth resides in its symbolism and tradition. The labyrinth's form seems to have evolved from "an archetypal symbol known in virtually every culture throughout time: the spiral, the universal symbol of growth and transformation."[53] Furthermore, it is not only a symbol of a sacred journey, but it becomes also a sacred space, where one can feel safe, nurtured, and supported in one's totality.

CREATING A LABYRINTH

Labyrinths can come in several formats, have different dimensions, be portable or permanently designed on the floor of a cathedral, or even be either a walking or a finger labyrinth.[54] Walking labyrinths, however, are more usual. In order to choose the right model for your context it is important to know from the outset what the purpose is for that labyrinth. Once one's intention with the labyrinth is clear, one can choose the appropriate type of labyrinth and the materials to build it, as well as the place where it is going to be set. A labyrinth can be set on a church's floor, at a school, in a meeting room, or in a community center, for instance. However, it is important to provide the amount of space required for comfortable walking (a twenty-five-foot-square minimum). If the labyrinth is permanent, there are a number of ways and materials to mark the walls of the circuit, which include ropes, bricks, mown grass, sand, mounds of earth, paint, stain, tiles, or even wood.[55] The choice of materials will depend on whether the labyrinth will be outdoors or indoors. Creating a total environment for the labyrinth is important, with candles, flowers, meditative music, and chairs or rugs for people to sit on before entering the labyrinth.

Temporary labyrinths can be of two types: "constructed ones that can be dismantled easily and portable ones painted on a variety of fabrics, which can be laid down for walking and stored until the next use." Temporary labyrinths can be placed indoors or out: "in your yard, in parks, at the beach, or on any kind of floor, if the dimensions of the room are at least 25 feet square."[56] Portable labyrinths "can be painted on canvas, sheets, or ripstop nylon, or laminated vinyl-on-vinyl."[57]

Once one has chosen the type, materials, and place for the labyrinth, it is important to consecrate the space where it will be placed. This act of consecrating the labyrinth can include a prayer and a time of meditation on the intention for the labyrinth. Some people also include a ceremony of dedication for the labyrinth when it is used for the first time. The format of this dedication ceremony varies according to the groups. Melissa West, program director of Harmony Hill retreat center, cites a prayer used by Alex Champion every time he first walks a labyrinth: "Thank you for the opportunity to make this labyrinth, and we bless it in the name of All That Is. We surround this labyrinth with a bubble of divine white light filled with love and protection. May all who walk this labyrinth be balanced, centered, and grounded; have peace and happiness; be healed according to their needs; have their hearts filled with unconditional love. May the energy of this labyrinth always be pure and of the highest quality. If anyone walking this labyrinth releases nonbeneficial energy, we humbly ask the local spirits to transform and recycle it. May the experiences of all who walk this labyrinth be for their highest good."[58] This is just a sample of a dedication prayer, which can be adapted or completely changed in accord with each group's spiritual and theological inclinations.

PRAYING THE LABYRINTH

Once a labyrinth is set up, it is important to have a knowledgeable person there to instruct the pilgrims about the mechanics, for example, taking off shoes, a minimum number of people, and so forth. Books and literature on a table about the labyrinth are also helpful.

The labyrinth can be conceived as a prayer of our entire being: body, mind, and spirit; an experience of being strongly connected to God. It can work as a pilgrimage, in which the body prays along with one's entire being, while walking. People have different experiences and perspectives as they walk the labyrinth. Each one experiences different transformations and personal growth. So the walking can be done in various paces, rhythms, and corporal expressions. It is important to let the body tell you how to walk. Thirty minutes is a usual time to allow for the experience.

The Rev. Jill Geoffrion has put together some good suggestions for this journey of prayer into the labyrinth; they reflect her own experience of walking the labyrinth numerous times over several years.[59] She suggests journaling the journey, recording whatever happens, whenever and wherever it happens. The walk to the center of the labyrinth represents a pilgrimage toward a sacred and special encounter with the Divine, whereas the walk out of the labyrinth represents the act of taking what one has received out into the world.

Following Geoffrion's suggestions, the pilgrim can ask some questions as she walks, starting with the reasons why she is making this pilgrimage and for what is she longing. Thus, from the outset, one can state the most important things one is seeking in that pilgrimage. The inner attitude prior to walking the labyrinth must be one of openness and receptivity to God's invitation to the pilgrim, as you ask to what is God inviting you.[60]

"While walking one should try to identify the thoughts, feelings, phrases, images, and questions that are shaping your journey."[61] Then, one can identify the spiritual tools and body movements needed for the personal journey. During the pilgrimage, one must also pay attention to the images that nourish one's soul, by asking what one sees while looking at the labyrinth. One can also ask questions such as: Who am I being called to become in spite of what others think I should be or do? What parts of my life are being brought to the surface? Where do I need to go so that God and I can work together? It is important to listen to God's voice speaking to you, and to rest in the presence of the Divine. The path of the labyrinth inspires trustworthiness, as it takes us to the center, in spite of the changes of direction that take place as we walk. So we need to relax and trust the path.

It is possible to use song, music, poetry, dance, drawing, painting and other artistic expressions while walking the labyrinth, choosing what artistic expression would enhance one's spiritual journey. One also needs to respect others, since this is an intensely personal and inward time. The question is "What is God trying to tell me?" The focus should be on the purpose of the journey; the hopes and assurances that support one's movements of faith.[62]

As Geoffrion points out, there are several other questions that can be asked during the journey: What gifts am I getting from this journey? How am I experiencing God's grace as I walk? At this point, one could recall a deeply meaningful experience with God for which one is grateful. One could sing "Amazing Grace" or another song of gratitude.

One can also walk the labyrinth in search of comfort and psychological healing after hurtful and painful experiences, when one needs the assurance of God's presence with them. As Melissa West has shown, people suffering from severe illness have found comfort and healing in walking the labyrinth. They experience guidance and relaxation. Furthermore, there are some variations of the labyrinth that can be drawn in paper sheets and "walked" with one's fingers. These can be of special help for those who are bedbound. The labyrinth can also be a healing tool for people experiencing grief, anger, and fear, as it connects them to their bigger story.[63]

As the pilgrims walk, they should also pay attention to the way they connect with other pilgrims in the journey. Whose spiritual journeys do I touch as I move with God?[64] How do these journeys interact with my own? How am I connecting to the whole environment around me? What is underneath the labyrinth I am walking? What am I sensing about the connections I am making? At this point one can identify those people who have been God's messengers for them in their journey. Who are those who need my help? Ask for compassion; pray for someone who is in need.

The labyrinth pilgrim can experience the mystery of God's presence in special ways and should express whatever feelings and visions come to mind. Identify those things that have power to move you to tears. Remember recent mental or physical shifts. Identify how God is involved in your mind, body, and experience. Ask for God's help to open your heart and mind to listen to God's voice. Visualize a smooth pathway of creativity flowing through your life. Feel how God has loved you and become open to experience a profound harmony with the Divine. One can ask, what love song is God singing to me? Express your gratitude in a way that feels natural to you.[65]

Throughout the journey one can use texts and prayers from the Bible to express rejoicing, thanksgiving, resting, surrender, petition for an open mind and heart, concerns with those who are in need, fear and anxiety, personal needs and struggles, refreshment, praise and adoration. Remember, the decision to walk the labyrinth represents an intentional encounter with the Divine. So worship the Divine throughout your entire journey.

For more information about the labyrinth, go to the Web site of Grace Cathedral, San Francisco, California, home of Veriditas, the worldwide labyrinth project—www.gracecathedral .org/labyrinth/index.shtml—and the St. Louis Labyrinth Project, source of canvas labyrinths— www.labyrinthproject.com.

Work

*"A working man . . . at least can get a good
night's sleep." (Eccles. 5:12)*

WORK OF OUR LIVES[66]
(Presbyterian)

*(Service of Worship on the theme of work. Labor Day might be an appropriate occasion for
this service.)*

*Invite the children the preceding week to come this Sunday dressed in the "work" clothes
of someone in their family and bring any items such as palm pilots, purses, briefcases, etc.,
which that person might use in their work. Stress that it can be someone employed in a job or
someone who works in the home. (For example, the child might want to dress as a housemother
bringing a duster or kitchen spatula.) In lieu of having all the children dress up, call three or
four children in advance to dress up and they will be the illustration for children's time.*

*The Prayer of St. Francis may be printed in the bulletin for congregants to meditate on
before worship and/or take home as a source prayer for the spiritual works of our lives.*

Any part of this service may be excised to fit your own worship needs.

PRELUDE

CALL TO WORSHIP

> **Leader:** Remember the sabbath day, and keep it holy.
>
> **All: Six days you shall labor and do all your work.**
>
> **Leader:** But the seventh day is a sabbath to the LORD your God; you shall not do
> any work—you, your son or your daughter, your male or female slave, your
> livestock, or the alien resident in your towns.
>
> **All: For in six days the LORD made heaven and earth, the sea, and all that is
> in them, but rested the seventh day; therefore the LORD blessed the
> sabbath day and consecrated it.**

INVOCATION

Creator God, in the work of creation you wrought us with the will to work your will. You have called us to the work of worship that we may be filled with your Spirit's grace. May all the works of your hand be a sign to us of the workings of your Spirit in our hearts and lives and may this time so fill us with your holy joy that we are led to do your work in the world that all creation may serve you in a single voice of eternal praise. In the name of Jesus Christ who was, who is and who is to come. **Amen.**

HYMN

(A hymn might be selected here that praises God for the work of creation such as:
    #483   PrH   "Sing Praise to God Who Reigns Above"
or
    #285   PrH   "God You Spin the Whirling Planets.")

CONFESSION

Lord we confess that often our work is a source of vanity. We toil to make ourselves believe we are worthy. We look with contempt upon those who have no employment and we often revere those with prominent jobs. Remind us that our worth lies not in our work but in the grace of your Son Jesus Christ. Free us to work in whatever fashion you have called us out of joy and thanksgiving for the gift of your love.

ASSURANCE OF FORGIVENESS

> **Leader:** The works of Jesus Christ have freed us from the suffocating weight of sin
>   and freed us to live faithful lives. Hear the good news!

Congregation: God loves us. God forgives us!

PASSING OF THE PEACE

RESPONSE
(Select a sung response that your congregation would be comfortable with, perhaps
    #576   PrH   "Gloria")

SCRIPTURE
(Any number of scriptures could be used for this service, perhaps portions of Gen. 1 & 2, Exod. 20:8–11, Matt. 20:1–16 [parable of the laborers in the vineyard], Rom. 12, or the parable of the talents.)

ANTHEM
(Suggestion: A Prayer of St. Francis. There are many musical arrangements of this prayer, often called "Lord Make Me an Instrument of Thy Peace.")

CHILDREN'S SERMON
(Ask several children to stand before the congregation and explain the clothes and accessories that they are wearing. Then explain to the children that God gives us special clothes and tools

to do work. In the same way God gives each of us the tools of prayer, kind words, kind acts, and a loving heart to do Christ's work of sharing divine love. Explain how every person no matter their status of employed, or unemployed has special work given by God.

Then invite the children and everyone to write on a piece of paper [place this paper either in the bulletin or the pews so that they will already have it] the work that God gives them to do whether it is in the form of employment, of prayer, or volunteer work.

The piece of paper might say on it "God you have called me and blessed me to the work of_____—I pledge to do it in thanks and glory for you." Then everyone during the offering will bring it forward to the communion table during the offering time.)

SERMON
(This message might focus either on themes of the gift of work and the privilege from God giving us a part to play in the symphony of life, or perhaps the overvaluing of work and possessions; develop the theme of viewing all our work as stewardship of our gifts from God as a form of thanks and praise. [Note the root of the Hebrew word for worship is to serve, that is, to work for God.])

HYMN
(This hymn should be chosen to match the theme of the sermon. Suggestions include:
   #238   PrH   "Unless the Lord the House Shall Build"
   #305   PrH   "Jesus Our Divine Companion"
   #369   PrH   "I'm Gonna Live So God Can Use Me.")

LITANY OF THE BLESSINGS OF WORK

Leader: Lord in the work of creation you brought us into existence. You have given a part for each member of creation to play.

All: **For the warmth of brother sun; the light of sister moon; the nourishing blossoming strength of mother earth; for the cooling quenching power of grandmother stream, Christ of all blessings, we praise your name.**

Leader: Lord you have given to some the call to employment. For all their contributions to a productive, bountiful, safe, and joyous community we now bless and praise you.

All: **For the strong true arm of the carpenter, the warm welcoming voice of the receptionist, the keen mind of the scientist, the loving heart of the teacher, the diligent work of the caretaker, the rigorous documents of the lawyer, for all those working to make this world a productive place, Christ of all blessings, we praise your name.**

Leader: Others you called to special tasks with little acknowledgment from the world for their work. Let us now remember them.

All: **For the devoted housewife, the diligent student, the babysitting sister, the committee members and clerks, the community organizers, and the social advocates, Christ of all blessings, we praise your name.**

Leader: For those past their years of employment whose work now resides in their gifts of time devoted to the needs of others we now bless and praise you.

All: **For volunteers dedicated to the needs of others, for the devoted widow who prays for the world, for the grandparents who give time to raise their children's children, for the wisdom of the aged whose work is to share their memories, Christ of all blessings, we praise your name.**

Leader: Lord, there are others who struggle to know your purpose and calling for their lives. For the people in transition, confusion and sometimes pain we importune your special mercies.

All: **For those who have lost their employment, those who have moved from job to job, those who are considering whether to enter or reenter the workforce, we ask for your special blessing of discernment and compassion.**

Leader: We have been told there is a time and a season for all things. You have woven rest into the fabric of creation as a holy calling. May we revel in the joy of relaxation when our work is done and the toil of the day or of our years is over.

All: **May we all rest with the satisfaction of a job well done. May we hear Christ's words, "Well done my good and faithful servant. Enter into the joy of your Lord," as an invitation to us all.**

Leader: Most of all for the work of your Son Jesus Christ our Lord, whose saving acts of love, forgiveness and grace freed us from the burden of works righteousness that we might work in freedom and thanksgiving we praise you.

All: **All glory be to you O God, the creator of all good things and giver of work. Praise to you O Spirit of blessing of strength and giver of wisdom. Thanks be to you O Christ giver of grace and Lord of Peace. Amen.**

PRAYER OF SUPPLICATION

In the beginning Lord you worked your will into the glory that is creation. Upon reflection you declared that it was good. You declared that we should rest to reflect on your wonder. But too often we find no rest in our spirits. We keep working and keep doing, secretly believing that we can do enough to make ourselves worthy. Convict us all of your steadfast love granted freely to all. Some use work as a cover for loneliness and as an excuse to avoid piecing together broken relationships. Give those the courage to confront the difficulties at home that their lives may become whole. For some Lord, work is a wretched burden. They toil endlessly for their families yet are unable to provide for them the necessities of life. We pray that you will show our society how to pay fairly so that a day's wage is a living wage for all. Others bury themselves in meaningless work feeling trapped because of their financial situation. Help all those to either find meaning in the work they do or discover a way out into more fulfilling productive employment. For those who have been released from their employment may they know you love them no less and perhaps even more. For those who work years trying to make the world a better place yet are frustrated by seeming lack of progress, grant them the peace of mind which is deserved from diligent effort. In the work of our lives dear Lord may we sense the privilege of being able to play a part in the grand drama of life you have created. May we be filled with purpose in the true work of our lives which is to celebrate in each thing we do the glory of your gracious name. **Amen.**

OFFERING

(Invitation to offering:) God has blessed the fruits of our labors with the power of money. May we give back to God a portion of this gift to empower the work of the church in the world.

(Choir, congregation, or quartet sings "As Those of Old Their First Fruits Brought" or "Come Sing a Song of Harvest," as the people bring forward their pieces of paper they wrote on during the children's time and place them on the communion table.

After worship assemble all or many of the phrases from the papers creatively on a poster or in the bulletin, frame them and display prominently somewhere in your Narthex or church fellowship hall.)

DOXOLOGY

PRAYER OF THANKSGIVING

HYMN
Suggestions:
    #429   PrH   *"Lord You Give the Great Commission"*
    #480   PrH   *"Praise Our God Above"*
    #415   PrH   *"Come Labor On"*

CHARGE

BENEDICTION

POSTLUDE

HONORING THE OUTWORKERS (SWEATSHOP WORKERS)[67]
(Uniting Church in Australia)

A RITUAL FOR USE IN A SECULAR SETTING

This is focused on the outworkers in the textile industry in Australia but could be adapted for use with other groups who suffer injustice in the workplace.

OPENING
    Outworkers are people worthy of being honored.

Their lives are significant.
Their cause is just.
Let us mark their struggle by pausing and remembering them.

Music   #591   W&R   "Where Cross the Crowded Ways of Life"

WE WOULD LIKE TO DO MORE

> **Leader:** It is hard to see and hear and know the truth about injustice.

> **Voice 1:** We have created societies where money is more important than people.

(Silent reflection)

> **Voice 2:** We look at the images of glamorous models
> rather than the worn-out lives of those who make their clothes.

(Silent reflection)

> **Voice 3:** We choose to forget the cost in the lives of outworkers for the bargains we
> buy.

(Silent reflection)

> **Leader:** But we will do more.
> We can do more.

> **All: Yes, we will and we can!**

STORIES FROM THE WOMEN AND/OR SPEAKER

OUR RESPONSE

> **Leader:** This is the stretched-out life of a woman outworker.

(Two people stretch out a purple cloth across a table and down onto the floor.)

> **Leader:** Let us look at this cloth and imagine what her life might be like.

> **Voice 1:** She is tired, and committed to her family.

> **Voice 2:** She is afraid of her employer because she might lose her work.

> **Voice 3:** She is skilled and faithful.

> **Voice 4:** She is a person of dignity.

> **Leader:** Are there other words we would say about her life?

(People add words.)

> **Leader:** The labels we have brought are the sign that she has finished this piece of work.
> They are our connection with her life.

They may tell us, if we wish to know,
how fairly she has been paid for this work which we now receive.
Let us place our labels on the edge of her life.

(The people place their labels on the end of the cloth.)

Leader: Let us make our commitment: We commit ourselves to search for the truth about injustice and to act in response to that knowledge.

All: **We will not knowingly buy clothes which are the products of exploitation.**
We will stand with outworkers in their struggle
and challenge those who are their oppressors.

SHARING OUR STRENGTH AND HOPE

Leader: At this moment we offer our hope and strength to all outworkers
who are exploited, exhausted, or harassed,
who receive none of the work entitlements which we take for granted:

All: **We celebrate their growing empowerment.**

Leader: We share our hope and strength with those who struggle for justice alongside the outworkers, the Textile, Clothing and Footwear Union, FairWear, Asian Women at Work, and other advocates:

All: **We celebrate their energy, courage and commitment.**

Leader: We support all employers of outworkers, industry bodies,
Governments and policy makers who are moving towards justice:

All: **We celebrate those who are ethical, caring and just.**

Leader: We have hope in the Industrial Relations Commission
as it decides on awards and conditions for working people:

All: **We celebrate its existence and the moments**
when it is the voice for the rights of the people.

Leader: We share hope and energy with each other, that we may be creative agents of change:

All: **We celebrate that this is indeed possible.**

LET US GO OUT

Leader: Let us go out into the world,
Determined to make it a different place for all people.
Let us stand in solidarity with the outworkers
until justice is done.

All: So be it!

MUSIC

WHOLENESS AND HEALING FOR THOSE IN MINISTRY[68]
(Presbyterian)

PRELUDE

THE GATHERING

CALL TO WORSHIP

Those who wait for God shall renew their strength,
they shall mount up with wings like eagles,
they shall run and not be weary,
they shall walk and not faint.

HYMN   #390   PrH   "O Savior, in This Quiet Place"

CONFESSION AND PARDON

CALL TO CONFESSION
(Confession of Brokenness [unison]:)

Eternal Mother of all souls,
in whom we live and move and have our being,
whose face is hidden from us by our pain,
and whose mercy we forget in the blindness of our hearts:
Cleanse us from all our offenses,
and deliver us from proud thoughts and vain desires,
that with reverent and humble hearts
we may draw near to you,
confessing our faults,
confiding in your grace,
and finding in you our refuge and our strength;
through Jesus Christ your Son.

DECLARATION OF FORGIVENESS

Hear the good news!
Who is in a position to condemn?
Only Christ,
and Christ died for us,
Christ rose for us,

Christ reigns in power for us,
Christ prays for us.
Anyone who is in Christ
is a new creation.
The old life has gone;
a new life has begun.
Know that you are forgiven
and be at peace.
Amen.

HYMN   #394   PrH   "There Is a Balm in Gilead"

THE WORD

PRAYER FOR ILLUMINATION

FIRST READING   Gen. 32:24–32

ANTHEM

SECOND READING   Heb. 12:28–13:2

SERMON

HYMN   #408   PrH   "Where Cross the Crowded Ways of Life"

OFFERING OF OUR LIVES TO GOD
(The minister or another leader says:)

I appeal to you therefore,
brothers and sisters,
by the mercies of God,
to present your bodies as a living sacrifice,
holy and acceptable to God, which is your spiritual worship.

ANTHEM
*(Here all present may ponder in silence all that is happening in their lives, and may, with
renewed commitment, offer themselves and their gifts for ministry to the service of Jesus Christ
in the world.)*

INTERCESSION FOR HEALING

(The following prayer of intercession is said:)

God, our creator,

your will for us and for all your people
is health and salvation:
have mercy on us.
Jesus Christ, Son of God,
you came that we might have life
and have it in abundance:
have mercy on us.
Holy Spirit,
dwelling within us,
you make us temples of your presence:
have mercy on us.

RITUAL OF HEALING

THANKSGIVING AND INVOCATION

Gracious God, source of all healing,
in Jesus Christ you heal the sick and mend the broken.
By your Spirit, come upon all who receive the laying-on of hands,
that they may receive your healing touch and be made whole,
to the glory of Jesus Christ our Redeemer.
Amen.

A GUIDED HEALING MEDITATION
(Following the meditation, those desiring the laying-on of hands turn to your neighbor and express your need.)

LAYING-ON OF HANDS

> **Leader:**   Lay a hand on the head of your neighbor and, after a brief silence, say the following prayer:
> *(Name your neighbor)*, May the healing light of Christ bring you whole-ness.
>
> And now with the confidence of the children of God,
> Let us pray:

THE LORD'S PRAYER

DISMISSAL

HYMN   #521   PrH   "You Satisfy the Hungry Heart"

BLESSING

The Healing of Relationships

"Let my people live in peace." (Hos. 2:18)

INTERGENERATIONAL HEALING[69]
(Roman Catholic)

(This ritual is meant to mark the conclusion of a conversation or process in which reconciliation has taken place. For each person there is paper, pen, a package of flower seeds, a small pot and soil for planting. A container that is safe for burning paper to ashes is provided as well.)

OPENING PRAYER

O God, you who desire our healing and peace, be with us as we seek to forgive one another and be reconciled. Soften the hard places in our hearts. Strengthen our resolve to let go of hurt and anger. Open us to the energy of your love and generosity. We count on your grace and power. **Amen.**

READING   Matt. 13:4–9

QUIET MUSIC AND REFLECTION
(During this time each person writes out the things she desires to let go of in the relationship, e.g., past hurts, regrets, disappointments, anger.)

RITE OF FORGIVENESS AND LETTING GO
(Each person tears the paper with the things she is letting go of into pieces, puts them into the container, and watches as they burn to ashes.

In turn each person then asks for and receives forgiveness for some way in which she is aware of hurting the other, e.g., First person: "I have hurt you by my accusations and lack of trust. I ask your forgiveness." Second person: "I forgive you as God has forgiven us both.")

RITE OF STRENGTHENING OF BONDS
(Each person offers the other a package of flower seeds as a symbol of the fresh beginning

104

they hope to find in the relationship. Each mixes part of the ashes with the soil and plants her seeds in it.)

CLOSING PRAYER *(based on Hildegard of Bingen)*

O Holy Spirit, Fiery Comforter Spirit,
Life of the life of all creatures,
Holy are You, You that give existence to all form.
Holy are You, You that are balm for the mortally wounded.
Holy are You, You that cleanse deep hurt.
Fire of love, breath of all holiness, You are so delicious to our hearts!
Bulwark of life, You are the hope of oneness for that which is separate.
Amen.

(Music, Refreshments, and Celebration)

COMMUNAL RECONCILIATION[70]
(Roman Catholic)

Materials Needed

A large pearl for each participant

GREETING

> **Leader:** We gather today in joy knowing that we are a forgiven and forgiving people. We gather to give thanks and praise to God, who has made us fit to share in the inheritance of the holy ones; for God delivered us from the power of darkness through his Son, Jesus, in whom we have redemption and forgiveness of sin.

OPENING SONG   #650   WIII   "O God of Every Nation"

OPENING PRAYER

> **Leader:** May the grace and peace of God our Father be with you.
>
> **All: And also with you.**

> **Leader:** Let us pray:
> Merciful God, you bring us the good news
> that you are a God who forgives.
> Carry this good news
> to all who strive to celebrate your loving mercy.
> Through your bountiful goodness

> pardon our offenses and
> free us from the sins we have committed in our frailty.
> Give us hearts of flesh,
> hearts big enough to welcome you into our lives
> with joy, praise, and thanksgiving,
> through Christ, our Lord.

All: Amen.

SCRIPTURE   Eph. 1:3–7

RESPONSE   Ps. 103:1–5, 8–12

Leader: The Lord is tender and caring.

All: The Lord is tender and caring.

Leader: My soul, bless the Lord,
Bless God's holy name!
My soul, bless the Lord,
hold dear all God's gifts!

All: The Lord is tender and caring.

Leader: Bless God, who forgives your sin
And heals every illness,
Who snatches you from death
And enfolds you with tender care,
Who fills your life with richness
And gives you an eagle's strength.

All: The Lord is tender and caring.

Leader: The Lord is tender and caring,
slow to anger, rich in love.
God will not accuse us long,
nor bring our sins to trial,
nor exact from us in kind
what our sins deserve.

All: The Lord is tender and caring.

Leader: As high as heaven is above the earth,
so great is God's love for believers.
As far as east from west,
so God removes our sins.

All: The Lord is tender and caring.

GOSPEL ACCLAMATION   "Alleluia" *(sung)*

NEW TESTAMENT READING   Matt. 13:44–46

HOMILY

LITANY OF SORROW

Leader: With sorrow for taking God's goodness and kindness for granted,
we pray to the Lord.

All: Lord, have mercy.

Leader: For failing to love as we are commanded,
we pray to the Lord.

All: Lord, have mercy.

Leader: For neglecting to respond to God's grace and inspiration,
we pray to the Lord.

All: Lord, have mercy.

Leader: For not responding to those in need,
we pray to the Lord.

All: Lord, have mercy.

Leader: For giving in to pride and self-pity,
we pray to the Lord.

All: Lord, have mercy.

Leader: For misusing the beauty and resources of the earth,
we pray to the Lord.

All: Lord, have mercy.

Leader: For all our deliberate sins,
we pray to the Lord.

All: Lord, have mercy.

Leader: For not giving thanks every day of our lives,
we pray to the Lord.

All: Lord, have mercy.

Leader: May God have mercy on us, forgive all our sins, and bring us to everlasting
life.

All: Amen.

EXAMINATION OF CONSCIENCE AND CONFESSION OF SINS

Leader: Let us now examine our consciences, and confess our sinfulness to God.

Loving God, you welcome us as wayward children,
you rejoice at our return
like the finder of a long-lost coin or perfect pearl.
For our sake you risked all, sold all,
and purchased us at great price.
Your generosity overwhelms us.
Bless us, merciful God.
Bring us to see you eye to eye, face to face.
And remind us of your amazing promise,
that your forgiveness is always ours,
through Christ Jesus, our Lord and Savior.

All: Amen.

RITUAL ACTION
(Participants are invited to approach the leader and other ministers. If they wish, they may mention a sin for which they are particularly sorry, or they may simply come in silence. As they come forward, the ministers lay hands on them and say,)

God rejoices in your repentance, for you are a Pearl of Great Price.

(They then give each participant a large pearl. During this ritual action, appropriate hymns may be sung or instrumental music may be played.)

ABSOLUTION

Leader: Those who wish to receive the sacramental absolution of the church, please bow your heads.

May God give you pardon and peace
in the knowledge that we walk in the Light of Christ.
Through the ministry of the church,
God has taken from us everything that cannot bear this light.
And through the ministry of that same church,
I absolve you from your sins,
in the name of the Father, and of the Son, and of the Holy Spirit.

All: Amen.

CONCLUDING PRAYER

Leader: Gracious God, by baptism and reconciliation, you have called us to be your light to the world. Let this good work shine forth in us, so that all may glorify you. Go forth, People of Light, God's Pearls of Great Price, in the peace and joy of the Lord.

All: Thanks be to God.

(All exchange a sign of peace.)

CONCLUDING SONG   #654   WIII   "O Day of Peace"

Dissolution of Partnerships/Marriage

"God be with you!" (1 Sam. 20:42)

END OF A CLOSE RELATIONSHIP[71]
(Ecumenical)

The intention of this service is not to celebrate the breakdown of a relationship, but to help people to come to terms with one which has radically changed. For example, it might perhaps be used when a marriage has ended in divorce—when the two people immediately concerned still love and care for one another, but not in the same way. Never in the same way again. It would also be appropriate for a relationship which both parties had intended should lead eventually to marriage, but which somehow had not developed in that way, although both are still friends and wish to remain so. To face facts like this, and to help others to face them too, is not simply to make the best of a bad job. Indeed it can be a lifesaving operation, for nothing can survive destruction which has not been consciously allowed to die, and things cannot be lived which dare not even be thought of. Inevitably, it is rather a sad service; it is certainly a penitential one, and, as such, requires a good deal of courage and resolution on the part of the two people undertaking it. However it is offered in the belief that the acceptance of human failure can itself be a kind of success, in that it provides us with a foundation for new beginnings. This is particularly so in the context of the rite's ability to transform private intention into public reality. In this case public will probably mean a rather restricted congregation, perhaps one that consists of a few relatives and friends; it is not to be expected that a service of this kind will ever really become popular—no one likes to admit failure (the church less than most!). However, there are times when it could prove useful. . . .

Minister: God shows his love for us in that while we were still sinners Christ died for us.

HYMN #370 PrH "Just as I Am, without One Plea" *(spoken or sung)*

> **All: Almighty God, to whom all hearts are open, all desires known, and from whom no secrets are hidden: cleanse the thoughts of our hearts by the inspiration of your Holy Spirit, that we may perfectly love you, and worthily magnify your holy name; through Christ our Lord. Amen.**

Minister: Lord Jesus Christ, you said to your apostles: I leave you peace, my peace I give you. Look not on our sins, but on the faith of your Church, and grant us the peace and unity of your kingdom, where you live for ever and ever.

All: Amen.

READINGS
(Two readings, one chosen by the two people themselves, and one by the minister. The circumstances of the occasion may suggest a particular text, but I Corinthians 13 would be suitable here.)

Minister: _____ and_____ have come here together today for a special reason and with a particular intention. Their coming marks the end of a precious relationship between them. *(At this point the minister may add, if appropriate, 'one which began with a solemn pledge undertaken before God,' or some suitable phrase.)* They share a common burden of promises broken, hopes left unfulfilled, and trust betrayed. They ask God's forgiveness for all these things. At the same time, however, they want to thank him for many blessings bestowed on them together and particularly, for a new kind of love which he is fostering between them—different perhaps, but no less real. This is the love which exists between friends. Such a love lays no claim to total involvement with the other person. Nevertheless it is a love which often gives more than it owes. We ask God to bless them both.

HYMN #358 PrH "Help Us Accept Each Other"
(At the end of the hymn, _____ and _____ move to the front of the church, side by side but without touching each other or holding hands. They kneel down facing one another.)

Minister: Let us all kneel in silence and confess our sins to God.

(After a pause, the minister moves to the altar, where there is a bowl of water.)

Minister: God our Father, your gift of water is always bringing new life to the earth. We ask you to bless this water as a symbol of your cleansing grace. Accept the prayers we offer in Christ Jesus' name and send your Holy Spirit to sanctify a new relationship between these two people.

(He takes the water and sprinkles a few drops over them. Others in the congregation may come forward and kneel down with them to be sprinkled with the water.)

Minister: The God of all grace who called you to his eternal glory in Christ Jesus, establish, strengthen and settle you in faith; and the blessing of God Almighty, the Father, the Son, and the Holy Spirit, be among you and remain with you always.

All: Amen.

(During the singing of the hymn, those kneeling return to their seats.)

HYMN   #318   PrH   "Gracious Spirit, Holy Ghost"

Minister: _____ and _____ have made a solemn act of penitence. They have brought their new relationship before God. As fellow members of Christ's Body, we have asked God to bless them in both these things.

Lord God Almighty, in your Son Jesus Christ you have redeemed the life we live towards one another. There is no shadow of turning in you. Hold our variable natures within your everlasting embrace. Give us stability and constancy, so that we may accept each other as we are, and go forward in the new way you open before us. Through Jesus Christ our Lord.

All: Amen.

PSALM 121

THE LORD'S PRAYER

Minister: Bow to him who is able to do immeasurably more than all we can ask or conceive, by the power which is at work amongst us, to him be glory in the Church and in Christ Jesus throughout all ages.

All: Amen.

HYMN   #322   PrH   "Spirit of the Living God"

Minister: Let us depart in peace.

All: In the name of the Lord. Amen.

END OF A MARRIAGE[72]
(Anglican)

THE GATHERING OF THE COMMUNITY

Leader: The grace of our Lord Jesus Christ
and the love of God,
and the fellowship of the Holy Spirit
be with you all.

People: And also with you.

Leader: Dear friends in Christ,
we have come here today with *N*,
to acknowledge before God
that *his/her* marriage has ended.

Marriage is intended as a lifelong commitment,
in which husband and wife
give themselves to each other,
to care for each other in good times and bad.
They are linked to each other's families,
and they begin a new life together
in the community.

Sometimes, however, despite good efforts,
human frailty destroys marriage,
changing mutual comfort and help
into brokenness and pain.

When a marriage ends in this way,
memories are tarnished,
and hopes and dreams are dashed.
Many people are affected,
family relationships may end,
friends are saddened,
and a time of mourning ensues.
It is to acknowledge this,
and to pray for healing and wholeness,
that we gather here with *N* today.

Let us pray.

Almighty God, you enlighten every heart.
Give comfort and healing
to your people gathered here today.
Enable us, with *N*,
to acknowledge what has been lost,
and to turn to you in faith and hope,
trusting in the new life that lies ahead,
through Jesus Christ our Lord.

All: Amen.

CONFESSION OF SIN

Leader: Dear friends in Christ,
God is steadfast in love and infinite in mercy.
Let us confess our sins,
confident in God's forgiveness.

Most merciful God,

**All: we confess that we have sinned against you
in thought, word, and deed,
by what we have done,**

>and by what we have left undone.
**We have not loved you with our whole heart;
we have not loved our neighbors as ourselves.
We are truly sorry and we humbly repent.
For the sake of your Son Jesus Christ,
have mercy on us and forgive us,
that we may delight in your will,
and walk in your ways,
to the glory of your name. Amen.**

ABSOLUTION

> **Leader:** Almighty God have mercy upon you,
> pardon and deliver you from all your sins,
> confirm and strengthen you in all goodness,
> and keep you in eternal life;
> through Jesus Christ our Lord.

> **People:** **Amen.**

(A deacon or layperson using the preceding form substitutes us *for* you *and* our *for* yours.)

(The divorced person may say in these or similar words,)

> **Person:** God of infinite comfort and wisdom,
> the marriage I once entered has now ended.
> I give thanks for all that was good,
> and ask to learn from all that was not.
> Help me to let go of all resentment.
> By the power of your Holy Spirit,
> give me new life in your service,
> through Jesus Christ our Lord.

> **People:** **Amen.**

> **Leader:** N, *(couple's names)*

> **People:** **We share your sorrow,
> we rejoice in your hope,
> we pray for your new life.
> May God strengthen you,
> preserve, shelter, and keep you,
> now and always. Amen.**

THE PEACE
(The Peace is exchanged. If the eucharist is to be celebrated the service continues with the preparation of the gifts. If the eucharist is not to be celebrated the service continues as follows.)

Leader: Gathering our prayers and praises into one,
Let us pray as our Savior taught us.

THE LORD'S PRAYER

BLESSING
(The leader dismisses the congregation with this blessing.)

Leader: God of care and mercy,
be now and evermore our healing and our hope.
In your great compassion, enable *N* the blessing of your love;
equip *him/her* with everything good
that *he/she* may do you will,
through Jesus Christ our Lord.

People: Amen.

AFTER DIVORCE[73]
(Ecumenical)

THE GATHERING OF THE PEOPLE

Dearly beloved: We have come together in the presence of God to witness and bless the separation of this man and this woman who have been bonded in the covenant of marriage. The courts have acknowledged their divorce and we, this day, gather to support them as they give their blessing to one another as each seeks a new life.

In creation, God made the cycle of life to be birth, life, and death; and God has given us the hope of new life through the Resurrection of Jesus Christ, our Savior. The Church recognizes that relationships follow this pattern. While the couple have promised in good faith to love until parted by death, in some marriages the love between a wife and a husband comes to an end sooner. Love dies, and when that happens we recognize that the bonds of marriage, based on love, also may be ended.

God calls us to right relationships based on love, compassion, mutuality, and justice. Whenever any of these elements is absent from a marital relationship, then that partnership no longer reflects the intentionality of God.

The Good News of the Gospel of Jesus Christ is that we are forgiven our sins and our failures, we are raised from the dead and restored to a new life. The death of love, like the death of the grave, has no power to rob us of the life that is intended for the people of God.

Thus Father we ask you this day to support and bless _____ and _____ as they confess their brokenness, forgive one another for their transgressions, receive God's blessing, celebrate the new growth that has occurred in each of them, and make commitments for a new life.

THE DECLARATION OF CONSENT

Celebrant: *(to the man)* _____, do you enter into this parting of your own free will; do you confess before God, ____, and the Church that you repent your brokenness that kept you in a destructive relationship? Do you seek forgiveness for the mutual respect and justice that you have failed to give and set your spouse free of this relationship, that you and she may receive from God and from one another the gift of new life and move toward health and wholeness once again?

Man: I do.

Celebrant: *(to the woman)*_____, do you enter into this parting of your own free will; do you confess before God, _____, and the Church that you repent your brokenness that kept you in a destructive relationship? Do you seek forgiveness for the mutual respect and justice that you have failed to give and set your spouse free of this relationship, that you and he may receive from God and from one another the gift of new life and move toward health and wholeness once again?

Woman: I do.

THE MINISTRY OF THE WORD

Celebrant: The Lord be with you.

People: And also with you.

Celebrant: Let us pray.

O gracious and ever-living God, you have created us male and female in your image: Look mercifully upon _____ and _____, who come to you seeking your blessing. Forgive them for forsaking their vows, and for the pain that they have caused each other. Restore each of them by your grace to a new life of hope, renewal, and growth, and keep them ever in the love of your mercy, through Jesus Christ our Savior.

People: **Amen.**

A READING FROM SCRIPTURE

Luke 15:1–7	(Repentance and forgiveness)
Luke 9:42b–48	(Your faith has made you well)
Ps. 55:12–23	(Women who feel rejected)

(The choice of a reading depends upon the individuals' need, whether for forgiveness or wholeness, or both.)

THE UNDOING OF THE VOWS
(The man faces the woman, takes her right hand, and says:)

In the name of God, I _____, release you, _____, from your vow to be my wife. I thank you for the love and support you have given me. I ask your forgiveness for my part in the failure of our marriage.

(The woman faces the man, takes his right hand, and says:)

In the name of God, I _____, release you, _____, from your vow to be my husband. I thank you for the love and support you have given me. I ask your forgiveness for my part in the failure of our marriage.

(The celebrant asks each in turn to return their rings:*)

_____, I give you this ring, which you gave me as a symbol of our marriage. In returning it, I set you free. I pray you will find peace and joy in your new life.

(The rings are given to the celebrant, who places them upon the altar, or the man and woman may place the rings there themselves.)

(The celebrant says:)

I place these rings upon the altar to symbolize that your lives are lived in the mercy and love of God.

(Or, if the couple choose to place their own rings on the altar, the celebrant may say:)

These rings are placed upon the altar to symbolize that your lives are lived in the mercy and love of God.

THE PRAYERS

THE LORD'S PRAYER

Let us pray.

Eternal God, creator and preserver of all life, author of salvation and giver of grace: Look with favor upon the world you have made and for which your Son gave his life, and especially upon _____ and _____, who come to you seeking your blessing. Grant unto them grace in moving from the old ways and wisdom in the ordering of their new lives. **Amen.**

Grant that each may know the power of your love to transform death into life and to bring forth the discovery of new identity out of pain. Teach them to trust once again and restore their hope, that once more they may view the world through love-filled eyes. **Amen.**

Bestow on them your Spirit, that _____ and _____ may be guided and sustained by you in the choices they individually make. Inspire the service they offer to the world that it may be distinguished by compassion for all. By your grace, may each become a witness to

---

*A determination should be made beforehand of the destination of these rings after the service.

your forgiving and healing love as they reach out to care for the needs of others. **Amen.**

Make their individual lives a sign of Christ's love to this sinful and broken world, that forgiveness may heal guilt, joy conquer despair, and trust be forever placed in you. **Amen.**

(The man and woman kneel.)

Most gracious God, we give you thanks for your tender love in sending Jesus Christ to come among us, to be born of a human mother and to make the way of the cross to be the way of life. Defend _____ and _____ from every enemy. Lead them both into all peace to a renewal of life, and the hope of wholeness and love. Bless them in their separate lives, in their work, in their rest, and in their play, in their joys and in their sorrows, in their life and in their death. Finally, in your mercy, bring each to that table where your saints feast forever in the blessing of your presence and love, through Jesus Christ, who with you and the Holy Spirit, lives and reigns, One God, forever and ever. **Amen.**

BENEDICTION

> The blessing of God whose breath gives life
> be with you always.
>
> The blessing of God whose
> love is forgiving
> set you free from guilt and despair.
>
> The blessing of God
> who sanctifies your living
> be with you this day,
> to lead you to a new life
> of hope, peace, love, and service.
>
> May God be praised and glorified through your lives,
> now and forever. **Amen.**

"Now that I am old . . ."
(Ps. 71:18)

Chapter 3

Late Adulthood/Elderly

INTRODUCTION

The thesis for this chapter is that we should give "double honor to our elders," based on the New Testament claim "Let the elders who rule well be considered worthy of double honor" (1 Tim. 5:17). In our youth-oriented society, what we need is a radical change in the way that we regard older people without going to the other extreme of disregarding our youth—the byword is mutual respect, as articulated in Proverbs, "The glory of youths is their strength, but the beauty of the aged is their gray hair" (Prov. 20:29). One of the reasons for the youth cult in our society is a fear of death and a sign of age as the end of anything that is meaningful to us. This may be because meaning has been defined more in terms of profession, work, or productivity than by relationships and character. It is a flaw in our society, not in older people, that they are not valued and respected. As Carl Jung averred, "The afternoon of life must also have significance of its own and cannot be merely a pitiful appendage to life's morning."[1] The other reality of this season of life is that the divisions between late adulthood and the elderly are not sharply drawn. Some seventy-year-olds are skiing, jogging, and starting new careers, while others at fifty-five consider life over.

DISESTEEM FOR OLD AGE IN AMERICA

Disesteem for old age in American culture reflects some of our sense of loss of honoring others. Barbara Myerhoff, renowned scholar, asserts that from the time of the Social Security Act of 1935, willingness to deal with old age as a problem solidified the perception of old age as just that—a problem. In 2000 there were 35 million people over sixty-five in the United States, equal to 12.4 percent of the population. By the year 2030, the older population will more than double to about 70 million people over sixty-five.[2] While in 1800 the life expectancy was thirty-eight years, and in 1900 forty-seven years, today it is seventy-five years plus. We need to find ways to celebrate, not decry, this trend through our worship. This is why I have included a liturgy to celebrate aging.

Most people over sixty-five think of themselves as the same people they were at forty and fifty—perhaps with diminished physical powers but not ceasing to be themselves. We may not wish to grow old—"Everyone desires to live long, but no one would be old."[3] Who willingly describes him- or herself as elderly? The elderly have contributed to society—its schools, highways, hospitals, churches, and battles to ensure freedom. Now they should receive in their venerable status benefits from society. The irony of modern times is that as we find better and better technologies to sustain and prolong life, we have less regard for the very persons whom our technologies support. Downsizing by corporations and changes in technology have forced many into early retirement, and the liturgy on retirement affirms both the sense of displacement and opportunity for new experiences.

We categorize the elderly in different ways. Sixty-five to seventy-four years of age are the elderly; seventy-five to eighty-four years are the aged; and eighty-five and over the "very old." The implication in this categorization is that if you are part of the last group, you are beyond the pale. One's degree of health may be a better criterion for determining one's age; being over sixty-five is not an automatic index of poor health. "The American Association of Retired Persons (AARP) reports that ninety-four percent of all retired persons are 'hale and hearty,' not 'feeble and frail.' Moreover, despite gloomy assertions to the contrary, it is important to emphasize only five percent of the US population over sixty-five is institutionalized at any one time. That is, only twenty-two percent of adults aged eighty-five or more, which means that seventy-eight percent of the 'oldest old' are out and about."[4] I have not attached ages to any of the seasons of life in this book, since they have less and less relevance.

RESPECT FOR ELDERLY

The question we often ask is, what has happened to the respect accorded to the elderly in the past, which still is accorded in some traditional societies? One possible answer concerns the presence or absence of writing technologies. In literate societies, books and microfiche replace human memory. Nevertheless, some literate societies still hold the aged in esteem. Korea and other Asian cultures still honor and value the old and wise in their societies, though their strong authority is sometimes resented by their children.

Another reason why the elderly may not receive the same respect as in the past is that mechanized technologies are replacing craftspeople's skills, so compulsory retirement is a way of substituting machines for people. Devaluing the elderly is viewed as a necessary part of the new knowledge, new workplace relations, and sheer physical endurance that constitute today's working world.

The importance of honoring the elderly is clearly reflected in the many positive images of the elderly in Scripture. The classic Greek words for "old" first signified older in relation to others and later indicated a measure of importance. In fact, the word *presbyteros* was translated "important" and finally meant "more honored." In Plato's writing it referred to rank or dignity. In the Dorian world the preeminence that went with age led not only to a representative function abroad but also to an advisory one within the political community.

The use of these words in the Bible reflects the attitudes toward the various seasons of a person's life; the fact that *presbyteros* in its root meant "older" and then was expanded to connote "rule," "authority," and "ambassador" reflects a point of view toward the young versus the old.

One might even say that the biblical perspective on aging shows a decided preference for elders over youth. Although Jesus said that we must become like little children to enter the kingdom of heaven, this was connected not with chronological age but with faith and openness to the future and new realities. This youthful attitude we may possess at any chronological time in our life.

Despite the strong biblical and theological reasons for revering the elderly, present-day religious communities, unfortunately, have not always responded adequately to the needs of their aging congregants (who represent 25 percent of membership in our churches and synagogues—twice their percentage in the general population) or used their gifts and experiences to the fullest extent possible. When we realize that 26 million Americans over sixty-five years of age are church or synagogue members, while all Christian adherents plus the Jewish population over sixty-five equal 137 million worldwide, faith communities need to be responsive to the elderly.[5]

Our definition of worth has been tied to physical prowess and mental capabilities. The questions we need to ask from a religious faith perspective are: How do we value and involve people at all stages of life? What do we do to value, respect, and minister to the elderly? One of the ways of honoring this season of life is to celebrate the elderly and comfort those in need in the worship life of the church.

REFRAMING OLDER ADULTHOOD

Gail Sheehy has chosen a felicitous phrase from Erik Erikson for older adulthood: "passage to the age of integrity." She observes that "as we grow older, we become less and less alike. The consequences of genes, gender, race, class, marital status, income, and preventive health care (or carelessness) all pile up. But while our genes largely determine our health status and longevity, this holds true only until we reach 60 or 65. After that, if we have escaped catastrophic illness during the critical middle life period from 45 to 65, it is our psychological attitude and behavior that more likely determine the quality and duration of our third age."[6]

Some experts in the field of aging contend that "the relationship between health and mental health is greatest in later life. Data keep accumulating to show that in the face of chronic depression or stress, biological changes occur that have a negative effect on the immune system and render people more vulnerable to disease."[7] Sheehy cites the work of Margaret Kemeny, research psychologist at UCLA, who predicts, "We're on the frontier of a really fine-tuned understanding of how psychological changes relate to very specific changes in physiology." Kemeny's study demonstrates that "feeling happy or depressed even for twenty minutes affects the number and activity of natural 'good' killer cells in the bloodstream."[8]

Attention to our health is always important, but especially in the later years. Physical exercise and engaging in mental challenges to keep the intellect keen have become popular habits as a result of many studies that underscore their health-giving benefits in the aging process.

A balanced view of our personal health also includes using our minds. We need to keep our minds active. A recent study in Mankato, Minnesota, of nuns past the age of one hundred asked why these nuns stayed so mentally alert. The answer was that they were doing crossword puzzles and learning new languages and other skills. The researchers found these nuns had no Alzheimer's or loss of mental acumen because of their mental activity. One sister taught till age ninety-seven. Now she helps ailing nuns exercise their brains by quizzing them on vocabulary or playing a card game with them called Skip-Bo, at which she deliberately loses. Sister Mary Esther Boor, ninety-nine, is a former catechism teacher who keeps alert by doing puzzles and volunteering to work the front desk.[9] Of course, not everyone is free from the tragedy of Alzheimer's disease, so I have included a worship service for those with early Alzheimer's.

Sheehy finds, "The word researchers apply most frequently to centenarians is *adaptable*.

All have suffered losses and setbacks. But even the most intense loss, such as that of a spouse after fifty or sixty years of marriage, was mourned, and then the person moved on."[10] This perspective, however, should be balanced by the fact that not infrequently spouses die within one year of each other. Sheehy also indicates that adaptability is linked to a lack of high ambition.[11]

PARAMOUNT FEAR: LOSS OF CONTROL

I want to be careful not to deny that there are certain losses and challenges as we age. "There are many forms of suffering: physical, psychological, spiritual, financial, social, and loss of autonomy," notes Coda Alliance, the Silicon Valley Community Coalition for End-of-Life Care.[12] These forms of suffering have led an increasing number of Americans at the very end of their life to seek suicide as a solution to their problem. Note, for example, that between one-quarter and one-third of all suicides in America are committed by people over sixty-five.[13] The loss of one's home of many years, moving into a retirement community, can create a shrinking of one's world that is difficult to face. Liturgies to mark these passages, such as "Welcome to a Retirement Community," may at least help acknowledge these losses.

In a multiple-choice question posed to clergy at an End-of-Life-Care Education Conference in October 2002 in San Jose, California, Coda Alliance asked, "Based on the Oregon experience, the most common reasons patients choose physician-assisted suicide are: (1) uncontrolled physical pain; (2) depression; (3) fear of loss of control; and (4) desire to save their money for their heirs." What would your answer be? You might be surprised to learn that "3" is the answer. "Fear of loss of control—the right and ability to choose one's own destiny—is perhaps the most common fear among those who seek to choose their destiny one last time by orchestrating their own death."[14] The conclusion we must draw is that "unrelieved psychosocial and mental suffering, not pain, are the most common reasons for patients to seek suicide," a phenomenon we can recognize as a "cry for help." What can we do to help? "Identifying the fears and naming the suffering will go a long way towards palliation and even personal growth at the end of life."[15] This is precisely what the liturgies in this section are designed to do: identify the fears and name the suffering in the context of faith and community, thereby empowering people in the last stages of life to delve deeply into their spiritual nature and, yes, grow.

What about the caregivers of the very old? Can they experience personal growth in the process of watching their loved one die? For many, such a concept is a luxury when faced with the hard reality of a larger aging population. One in four workers in America provides care for an aging relative, averaging twelve to thirty-five hours per week. This, linked with the fact that 6.6 million people over age sixty-five need some form of assistance from others, produces the "sandwich generation," that is, middle-age workers "caught" between caring for their children and for their parents. Resentment and guilt are common responses to shouldering the burden of aging parents, whose aging somehow threatens our own sense of mortality; "fear" instead of "respect" is the word we frequently use for the aging process.[16] Indeed, we can set ourselves up to be haunted by the same fear as our parents—loss of control—if we fail to identify our own buried emotions and thereby move toward wholeness. Hence I have included a liturgy for families of the terminally ill in chapter 6 on "Death and Dying." Healing liturgies within the community of the faithful give us the sacred space to begin emotionally "unpacking" our fears, sorrow, and pain so we can move to a deeper understanding of our life—and inevitable death.

General Services

"Show respect for old people." (Lev. 19:32)

CELEBRATION OF AGING[17]
(African Methodist Episcopal and Ecumenical)

A SERVICE OF AFRICAN AMERICAN WOMEN AND AGING

This service has been created for African-American women of any denomination. However, it also includes optional hymns, formats and wording so that it can be used by Latinas and Anglo sisters as well. These options will be underlined throughout the text.

THE CALL TO WORSHIP

Worship leader: We come today as women who are moving forward in life, women who are using the years that God has so graciously allotted us. We come with generations of praise, through ages of struggle, triumph and transformation. We come in thanksgiving to the one who has given us grace throughout every step of our journey. *We come united as sisters who have lived as Hagar, cleaning and cooking and caring for the children and household of the "master and his family."* We come having offered up our bodies as living sacrifices to the evils of *slavery* and gender violence. We come united as sisters, who have lived as Esther, determined, alone, and responsible for the welfare of our people.

We come united as sisters, who have lived as Naomi, displaced and defenseless, finding love and support in the company of our sisters. We come as Leah, not favored among men, yet highly favored by God. We come in the wisdom and strength of Deborah, singing the songs of Mary and Miriam, leaving the legacies of Eunice and Lois. We come in audacity and determination crying out—"If I perish, I perish, but I am going to see the king!" And we are joyous today because we have the testimony that through it all—God has beset us behind and before. We gather to worship today because we recognize that the grace that has been within us has also been behind us as a motivational force and strength. We gather in worship today because we recognize that his grace has also gone before us, giving us vision and allowing us to walk by faith and not by sight. For these and all other blessings we praise you O Lord.

(The underlined portion may be omitted for non-African-American gatherings.)

CONGREGATIONAL HYMN   #271   AAHH   "Amazing Grace"

INVOCATIONAL PRAYER
(African-American services do not typically utilize written prayers. It is important that prayers be spontaneous. The following prayer is an example of the type of prayer that could be prayed, and may be used for non-African-American services.)

O God, our help in ages past, our hope for years to come: Our shelter from the stormy blast, and our eternal home. *(first stanza of Hymn #170 AAHH "O God Our Help in Ages Past")*

We come into your presence today confessing you as the strength that has kept us these many years.

We come into your presence today awed by your power, but touched by your love;

Aware of your majesty, but grateful for your grace.

We come today acknowledging you as "God the Father, Maker of Heaven and Earth"; but we come as your daughters confessing that in our lives you have been the mother to the mother-less, a friend that sticks closer than a sister.

We invite your presence into our worship.

Come Holy One be present in our midst.

Come Holy One strengthen the areas that are tired, the back that is bent, and the knees that are weak.

Come Holy One, in fullness of power—into this place we pray.   **Amen.**

SCRIPTURE READING   Ps. 139:1–18

> **Worship**
> **leader:** David encourages us to bless the Lord at all times and in every way. We are told to praise God with every kind of musical instrument, with dance and hymns and spiritual songs. Everything that has breath is to praise the Lord. Today we honor the true spirit of worship, and offer our sacrifice of praise in solidarity with our sisters who can no longer stand to offer praise.

MUSICAL SELECTION
(This selection will be a song by the choir who are seated, regardless of their ability to stand.)

THE LIBATION

(This ritual will require a table in the center of the sanctuary, covered by an appropriate eth-nic cloth: Kente, Ikat, etc. A ceremonial bowl filled with water is placed in the center of the table.)

**Worship
  leader:** The cultures of African, Indigenous and Asian people include rituals for venerating, remembering, and giving thanks for our ancestors—those who have gone before us paving our way. The Old Testament speaks of the pour-ing out of a "drink offering" (Exod. 29:40; 30:9). In the New Testament, Hebrews 11 lists story after story of our spiritual ancestors whose trials and faith "enable us to run with patience the race that is set before us." In the tradition of our ancestors we will pause to give thanks for the mothers, the grandmothers, the aunts, the Sunday School teachers, the sister-friends who taught us and encouraged us and corrected us and loved us into woman-hood. We will pause now to thank God for their witness and their memory. They have indeed been our "great cloud of witnesses" (Heb. 12:1).

Today we honor our ancestors by calling out their names, and as we call each one's names let us be reminded of God's goodness to us.

I will begin the ritual by saying the names of those female ancestors whom I wish to remember. After the saying of each name you will support me by responding with this African word, *ase* (pronounced *Ah Shay*). Its meaning is equivalent to saying "**Amen.**" *(In Latin America, the word* presente *rep-resents the ones who have been killed, martyred, or have disappeared. Per-sons from either background may merely respond with the word* Amen.*)*

**Worship
  leader:** I honor the name of my _____ (insert the relationship of the ancestor), _____ (state the full name of the deceased).

(After the speaking of each name the worship leader dips her hand into the libation bowl and sprinkles water onto the floor. She waits each time for the response from the congregation. Once she has finished she takes her place on the floor holding the bowl in front of the first per-son in the congregation or assembly. She announces that the sisters may either choose to par-ticipate in the ceremony by dipping their hand into the bowl and speaking the names of their ancestors, or shake their heads so that they will be passed over. If the room is not configured in a large circle, it may be necessary for the leader to call for the women to form lines of two or three and come up to the bowl. She will then have to come out to those unable to come for-ward.)

(The ceremony ends by the leader raising the bowl, lowering it and sprinkling water as she says:)

We honor the names of all the unnamed women of history who have given much and have now gone on.

(The worship leader begins a chorus of the song "Somebody Prayed for Me.")[18]

TIME OF TESTIMONY
(In lieu of a sermon, the women will minister to each other through the giving of personal testimonies about God's working in their lives. This can either be done by soliciting general testimonies of God's grace, or by specifically calling for testimonies of what God did for you in your childhood, in your teens, in your adult life, in your senior years. In those communities where spontaneous testimony time is not traditional, speakers may be chosen and prepared ahead of time and listed on the program.

Testimony time is ended by the worship leader beginning a chorus of the song "I Don't Feel No Ways Tired," recorded by James Cleveland on Rev. James Cleveland 1991 Malaco, Record, Inc., a tribute to the King. Chorus: "I don't feel noways (sic) *tired. I've come too far from where I started from. Nobody told me—that the road would be easy. But I don't believe he brought me this far to leave me." Alternative song may be "I Have Decided to Follow Jesus.")*

ALTAR CALL PRAYER
(Three ushers take their places in the center holding baskets of stones. The stones are three colors: black, white, and earth-tone.)

Worship leader: It's prayer time. Time to reflect on everything that God has done for us. Altar Call time is a time when we can bring our burdens to the Lord and leave them there at the altar.

During this altar call we have selected three areas for special prayer and reflection. A different color stone signifies each of the three areas of our life's journey.

The black stone symbolizes the struggles we have had with ourselves. It represents the struggle we have had to learn to accept and love ourselves as African-American women (insert here the name of the appropriate ethnic group).

It represents the struggles we have had to learn to love our hair, and our skin—its darkness or its lightness, our weaknesses and our strengths. It represents the struggle to accept a changing body, changing health and changing status. If you remember deliverances in these areas, victories you have won or struggles you continue to fight—take a black stone as the basket passes your way.

(Here the basket is passed so that all women have an opportunity to take out a stone.)

The white stone signifies the struggles we have had developing and maintaining relationships. It signifies our making peace with our mothers, our ex-husbands, or sisterfriends. It reminds us of our struggles to overcome the break-up of relationships that were important to us, the loss of a child through miscarriage, or abortion; the losses of friends through death. It signifies the struggles of learning to love, and to trust, and to set limits and to share and to ask for help when we were in need. If you remember how God has helped you in these areas, or if you know that there are some things yet to be done in order to make your peace with someone else—take a white stone when the basket passes by.

(Here the basket is passed so that all women have an opportunity to take out a stone.)

The earth-toned stone. Lastly, the earth-toned stones signify the trials and triumphs we have had in our spiritual life. They remind us of how God has graced us to have a closer walk, a better vision, a little more strength, and patience, and love for the law of the Lord. These stones remind us of our struggles to learn to pray, to pray without ceasing, to pray in public, to pray for our family, for our loved ones, and for those who "spitefully use us." These stones remind us of the times when we were called by God, used by God, chastised, and comforted by God; of the times when God turned our "mourning into dancing," and gave us "beauty for ashes . . . and the garment of praise for the spirit of weariness." If you remember how the Lord has worked in your life through the years to give you a deeper faith, and a clearer vision, and a straighter walk—take a stone when the basket comes your way.

(Here the basket is passed so that all women have an opportunity to take out a stone).

(Once everyone has taken their stones the worship leader announces a time of silence during which we can reflect prayerfully on those areas which these stones represent.)

Worship leader: Now that we have reflected on our past and laid claim to our future, let us come one by one to the altar and cast our stones. Let us cast them in joy, because of all that God has done in our lives. Let us cast them in faithful expectation of those burdens that will yet be lifted.

(The women are directed to come to the altar and cast their stones around the libation bowl on the table. Ushers go out to gather the stones of those unable to come for themselves; it is important that each woman's stones are cast on the altar one by one by the usher, not the stones of several women simultaneously, in order to maintain the sense of individual offering time.

Once all stones have been cast the worship leader begins the fist stanza of the hymn, "If When You Give the Best of Your Service" (AAHH). In non-African-American congregations, "Rock of Ages" or "Be Thou My Vision" may be substituted.)[19]

Worship leader: God's transforming, redeeming grace, cleanses us from our past and clears a path through the future. Let us join hands in sisterhood and sing together "Bless Be the Tie That Binds."

(After the singing of the hymn, the worship leader will lift a basket of clear stones saying this Benediction:)

Bless these stones that as we carry them we will be reminded of your presence and grace in our lives. Bless these your daughters that they may live out the rest of their days as faithful carriers of your word. Fit them for your kingdom; bless them with a never-ending sense of your presence we pray in Jesus' name. **Amen.**

(Following the benediction each woman takes a clear stone as she departs).

ANOINTING OF THE ELDERLY[20]
(Anglican)

(This service is intended to minister specifically to the elderly within the Christian community, and may be held in the church, in an individual family home, or in a hospital, nursing home, or other long-term care facility. It recognizes that while many of the elderly enjoy good health into advanced years, others experience the physical, mental and emotional pain of debilitating infirmities, with probable attendant limitation, fragmentation, or separation. This anointing seeks the healing of the whole person: spirit, mind, emotions, body, and relationships. It is meant to be communal, with family members, friends, and caregivers invited to attend and participate in the liturgy. The service need not be somber, and may include a celebration of Holy Communion. If it does not include the Eucharist, then the service may be conducted throughout by laypersons. There is no need of a bulletin, and the people may simply be invited to respond with "Thanks be to God" following the scripture readings, and with "Amen" following the prayers.)

OPENING WORDS

> **Leader:** The love and fellowship of God are with us here, as we gather for a celebration of our life in Christ Jesus, and for the anointing with oil and the laying on of hands for healing into wholeness.
>
> Hear the words of Jesus (Matt. 11:28–30).

HYMN OF PRAISE   #279   PrH   "Lord of Our Growing Years"

PRAYER OF CONFESSION

> **Leader:** Gracious God, we confess our sins before you. We confess our failure to give you heartfelt thanks for the blessings of our lives, for the joys and the sorrows, for all the ways you have guided, supported and strengthened us in times of trouble and weakness. We confess the doubts and fears that even now threaten to undermine faith in your constancy and provision. Forgive

us for all our words or actions that have failed to show through us the nature of Jesus to others. It is in his name that we pray.

People: Amen.

ASSURANCE OF PARDON

Leader: God does not hold our sins against us, but forgives us all that is past. Our sins are blotted out; God remembers them no more. We are assured that in Christ Jesus we are forgiven and freed from all guilt.

People: Thanks be to God!

SERVICE OF HOLY COMMUNION *(optional)*

PRAYERS OF THANKSGIVING AND PETITION

Leader: Let us pray. We give you thanks, O God, for your presence, your power, and your everlasting love. We give you special thanks this day for the witness of faith of the elderly among us. We are blessed with the joy of their friendship, the companionship of their lives, and the example of their obedience to you. We pray that through the anointing and laying on of hands today, they may be strengthened to continue to witness the saving power of your Son's death and resurrection which heals us and draws us to you. Prepare us who are to give and receive this ministry, and open us now to hear your word through Scripture. In the name of the risen Christ we pray.

People: Amen.

(One of the readings to follow may be done by a family member or friends.)

FIRST READING   1 Pet. 1:3–9

Leader: This is a word of living hope.

People: Thanks be to God!

MEDITATIVE HYMN *(sung or played on tape)*   #390   PrH   "O Savior, in This Quiet Place"

SECOND READING   Matt. 5:1–10

Leader: This is the word of Christ Jesus.

People: Thanks be to God!

LEADER'S WORDS FOR MEDITATION
(A very brief homily may be given on this passage. Poverty of spirit, gentleness, patience, mercy, etc. may be especially evidenced in the lives of the elderly as their identification with the suffering of Christ has become more visible in their lives.)

As children of God, we all come to God with childlikeness, openness and simplicity. We trust that God who has blessed us all the days of our lives, continues to bless us with the fruit of the Spirit abiding within and that love and power strengthens us for the living out of these in our relationships.

INVITATION
(The leader will alter the invitation such that it is suitable for the situation.)

Following our prayer, let those who desire anointing and laying on of hands for renewing of strength and healing into wholeness, come forward one by one if able, or be brought by another, or remain in their seat for ministry to be received by indicating their desire in the raising of a hand or nodding of their head.

PRAYER BEFORE ANOINTING

> **Leader:** Let us pray. O God, you are a strong tower to all who put their trust in you. Grant to these who now receive anointing, deliverance from all disease of body, mind, or spirit. In your love, and by the power of your Holy Spirit, touch them with your healing, and restore them to the wholeness of everlasting life in you. In Christ's name we pray.
>
> **People:** Amen.

(As each one receives anointing and the laying-on of hands, words such as the following may be spoken.)

> **Leader:** (Name), you are anointed in the name of God, Father, Son, and Holy Spirit, and as these hands are laid upon you, may our Lord Jesus minister the blessing of healing to you, that restored to balance of spirit, soul, and body you may rejoice in wholeness, and be at peace in Christ's love. Amen.

(At the conclusion of the ministry, the leader may extend arms toward all in blessing.)

> **Leader:** Let us pray in the words of the Psalmist *(Ps. 71:17–19 Jerusalem Bible)*.
>
> **People:** Amen.

CLOSING HYMN   #402   PrH   "Now Praise the Hidden God of Love"

BENEDICTION

> **Leader:** The love of God enfolds us, the peace of Christ fills us, and the companionship of the Holy Spirit remains with us always.
>
> **People:** Amen.

TIME TO REMEMBER (FOR THOSE WITH ALZHEIMER'S)[21]
(Methodist)

This is a special worship service for persons with Alzheimer's disease and their families. Persons with many types of dementia continue to retain strong recollections of early religious experiences. Attention should be paid to the degree of Alzheimer's of those in attendance as well as focus on the needs of the family if that emphasis is desired. As part of the service, as appropriate, recognition could be given to the challenges of Alzheimer's.

GREETING AND CALL TO WORSHIP

HYMN   #64   UMH   "Holy, Holy, Holy"

THE LITURGY OF RECONCILIATION

CALL TO CONFESSION

PRAYER OF CONFESSION

Gracious God, you love us, but we do not always love you; you call to us, but we do not always listen. Help us, Dear God, to face ourselves, turn from our sin, and walk with you. Through Christ Jesus, our Lord. **Amen.**

DECLARATION OF FORGIVENESS

HYMN   #70   UMH   "Glory Be to the Father" (one verse)

RESPONSIVE PSALM   Ps. 40:1–8

HYMN   #378   UMH   "Amazing Grace!" (verses 1, 2, & 4)

SCRIPTURE LESSON   1 Cor. 1:1–9

MEDITATION   "God Called; We Answered"

CLOSING HYMN   #557   UMH   "Blest Be the Tie" (verses 1 & 4)

REMEMBERING GOD:
A LITURGY OF NAMING FOR THOSE WITH ALZHEIMER'S, THEIR LOVED ONES, AND CAREGIVERS[22]
(Presbyterian)

(As the congregation enters, quiet strains of "Precious Lord, Take My Hand" are heard from the organ or another instrument [e.g. guitar]. On the communion table, there is a colorful vase filled with water.)

HYMN   #404   PrH   "Precious Lord, Take My Hand"

CALL TO WORSHIP

Leader: Alzheimer's disease, one of the two major causes of dementia, is the loss of mental functions—such as thinking, memory, and reasoning.

People: All who hate me think that a deadly thing has fastened on me, that I will not rise again from where I lie. (Ps. 41:8)

Leader: In severe cases, Alzheimer's interferes with a person's daily functioning.

People: I am weary with my moaning; every night I flood my bed with tears; I drench my couch with my weeping. (Ps. 6:6)

Leader: Alzheimer's progressively impairs all aspects of brain function.

People: My God, my God, why have you forsaken me? Why are you so far from helping me, from the words of my groaning? (Ps. 22:1)

Leader: Some of the symptoms of Alzheimer's include progressive loss of memory, inability to concentrate, severe confusion . . .

People: You keep my eyelids from closing; I am so troubled that I cannot speak. (Ps. 77:4)

Leader: . . . motor system impairment, disorientation, memory deficit . . .

People: Turn, O Lord, save my life; deliver me for the sake of your steadfast love. For in death there is no remembrance of you; in Sheol who can give you praise? (Ps. 6:4, 5)

Leader: . . . absent or impaired language ability, personality changes, and lack of spontaneity.[23]

People: My companions see my calamity, and are afraid. (Job 6:21)

Caregiver: Part of our fear of aging is our own fear of death—we lose hope in the existence of a future.[24]

People: But now, be pleased to look at me; for I will not lie to your face! (Job 6:28)

Leader: *(praying)* O God, our God, why have you forsaken us? We search for you, we yearn for you, but to no avail. We are alone. You have left us with forgetfulness, so that we do not even know our own families. You have left us with emptiness, so that we do not even know our own desires. Come, Lord Jesus, come! Show us your face, so that we may remember your divine love.

SILENCE

HYMN   #404   PrH   "Precious Lord, Take My Hand"

THE WORD

**Person with
Alzheimer's:** In those days Jesus came from Nazareth of Galilee and was baptized by John in the Jordan. And just as he was coming up out of the water, he saw the heavens torn apart and the Spirit descending like a dove on him. And a voice came from heaven: "You are my Son, the Beloved; with you I am well pleased." (Mark 1:9–11)

Minister: Today we are going to meet God at that place where God first named us: today we are going to meet God by remembering the baptismal waters.

I am going to come around to each of you. When I get to you, I am going to dip my hand in this water *(shows vase of water)* and lay my hand on your head. I will then ask you your name.

(Minister takes vase and "anoints" everyone with the water, saying to each one, "You are God's Beloved Son/Daughter, N.; with you God is well pleased." Strains of "Shall We Gather at the River?" are heard from the organ, guitar, etc.)

HYMN   #518   BH   "Shall We Gather at the River"

RESPONSE TO THE WORD

Caregiver: Today, we know that God has *named* us.

People: And God will never forget.

Caregiver: Today, we know God has heard our lonely calls.

People: And God will never forget.

Caregiver: Today, we know that God has *named* us.

People: And God will never forget.

Caregiver: Today, we know that God has heard our whispered pain.

People: And God will never forget.

Caregiver: Today, we know that God has *named* us.

People: And God will never forget.

Caregiver: Today, we know that life, not death, is the last word.

People: **And God will never forget.**

Caregiver: Today, we know that God has *named* us.

People: **And God will never forget.**

HYMN   #276   PrH   "Great Is Thy Faithfulness"

BENEDICTION

Youth: Today, and all the days, be gentle with your loved ones.

Person with Alzheimer's: Listen to them.

Caregiver: Hear their whispered pain.

Leader: Touch them.

Youth: Include them in activities meaningful to them.

Person with Alzheimer's: Help them stay in touch with God.

Caregiver: Let them draw from your strength.[25]

People: **And God will never forget. Amen.**

(Strains of "Great Is Thy Faithfulness" are heard as people leave.)

SERVICE FOR THE AGED[26]
(Presbyterian)

CALL TO WORSHIP

PRAYER

For the Aged[27]

O Lord God, look with mercy on all for whom increasing years bring isolation and distress. Give them understanding helpers and the willingness to accept help; and as their strength diminishes, increase their faith and their assurance of your love.[28]

Eternal God, whose years extend through all generations, we have but a short span of life and we wear out as a garment. May old age bring us wisdom, contentment and a deep longing to be with thee for all eternity.[29]

God of the unknown,
as age draws in on us, irresistible as the tide,
make our life's last quarter the best that there has been.

As our strength ebbs, release our inner vitality,
all you have taught us over the years;
as our energy diminishes
increase our compassion, and educate our prayer.
You have made us human to share your divine life;
grant us the first-fruits.[30]

Through Jesus Christ our Lord. **Amen.**

HYMN   #475   NCH   "God's Eye Is on the Sparrow"

SCRIPTURE   1 Tim. 5:17
            Ps. 103

UNISON PRAYER

Great God: your mercy is an unexpected miracle. Help us to believe and obey, so that we may be free of worry and filled with new life. Remind us daily of your promise always to be with us, through Christ Jesus, our Savior, who taught disciples to pray, saying:

THE LORD'S PRAYER

HYMN   #433   W&R   "O Christ the Same"

BENEDICTION

Retirement

"I run straight toward the goal." (Phil. 3:14)

RETIREMENT RITUAL[31]
(Roman Catholic)

OPENING SONG   #556   WIII   "Lord of Our Growing Years"

READING   Eccles. 3:1–8

HONORING OF THE GIFTS OF THE ONE RETIRING

We are gathered here to show our appreciation for the gifts our friend has given us and others through *her/his* years of work. Let us now share these fruits with *her/him.*

(Those present express their gratitude, and may bring a symbol of their appreciation, e.g., a song or a diploma.)

REFLECTIONS ON THE WORKING YEARS
(The person retiring shares reflections on all or some of the following:)

> The experiences I have cherished.
> The things I regret.
> The persons and things I will miss.
> The unfulfilled dreams and desires I hope to turn to in retirement.

BLESSING WITH OIL
(The person retiring is anointed.)

May the God of Exodus and Emmaus, the God of our seasons and turning points, be with you in this time of transition.

May she who is the midwife of change teach you to be gentle with yourself as you let go of the old and wait the birth of the new.

May she who is the womb of time strengthen you with this oil of wisdom and gladness.

OFFERING OF SPIRITUAL GIFTS
(Those present offer the person who is retiring a prayer, a blessing, a wish, a promise of support.)

CLOSING SONG   #507   WIII   "God Is Working His Purpose Out"

REFRESHMENTS AND CELEBRATION

MOVING AWAY FROM A HOME[32]
(Roman Catholic)

Gather in the entry to the house. The person or persons moving from the home or someone designated by them carries a lighted candle. Another person brings a basket or scrapbook in which to store memories from each room. You may also wish to use an audio- or videotape to record memories.

OPENING REFRAIN

SCRIPTURE   Lev. 26:11–13

(The group moves from room to room in the home. The following ritual is repeated in each:)

- *Upon entering each room light a candle which has been placed there.*
- *Share stories of the happy and sad times experienced in that room.*
- *The person leaving the home is given a symbol of this room to take to her next home, e.g., pictures for a scrapbook, a small memento which is placed in her basket of memories, written memories of special times there.*
- *The person taking leave blows out the candle. While leaving the room all recite together,* **I will set up my dwelling with you, and I will not desert you. I will live in your midst; I will be your God and you shall be my people.**

PRAYER

You, O God, have been our dwelling place from age to age. We ask you to heal the sad and painful events that took place in this house. Bring to us the winnowing fan of your mercy that separated wheat from chaff. Show us how to save what can be saved and let the rest go.

You, who meet us in the places and people with whom we live, we give thanks for the growth and joy we have found in this home. We know we stand on holy ground. As we say goodbye, may we carry with us the blessing lived in every room.

WELCOME TO A RETIREMENT COMMUNITY[33]
(Roman Catholic)

Note: If the new resident is not able to assume an active role in this ritual a family member or staff member could pray those sections with some minor adaptation. Follow this "Welcome Ritual" with a special luncheon or tea in honor of the new resident. Include family members, other residents, and staff members. Consider printing the "Blessing Prayers" for appropriate display in the resident's room.

MATERIALS NEEDED
Holy water, an evergreen branch for sprinkling

PREPARATION AND ENVIRONMENT
Gather in the new resident's room with staff, family members of the new resident, and residents from neighboring rooms.

INTRODUCTION
Introductions of leader and participants

GREETING

It is with joy that today we welcome N. to our community, and so we gather here in her/his room to bless N.'s new home and to bless N.

PRAYER FOR A NEW STAGE OF LIFE

New resident: God, as I begin this new stage of life,
Let me retain strength of spirit.
May my life maintain its sense of purpose;
may it continue as an example of
faith, hope, love, and courage
to my family and friends.

ROOM BLESSING

Leader: Let us pray:
Good and Gracious God,
this room is to be N.'s new home.
We pray that you furnish it in peace
and decorate it with holiness,
so that your Sacred Presence will abide here, too.

New resident: Lord, it is not large or grand,
but it is to be my new home,
a place for living, sleeping, and praying.

May I also find within it
refreshment, serenity, and healing.

Leader: Loving God, may peace, love, and beauty
flow out from this room in all four directions
and up and down as well.

**New
resident:** May this room of mine
be blessed by you, my God,
as a home for me
and for you as well. **Amen.**

(A sign of the cross may be traced on the four walls and on the door of the room.)

BLESSING OF NEW RESIDENT

Leader: N., may God grant you peace and rest while you live with us.
May your family and friends always feel welcome.
May the time you live with us
be filled with joy, comfort, and special warm feelings
of friendship and care.
May each day be filled with fond memories,
for we treasure the gift that you are.
May you trust in the beauty of tomorrow
as you continue on life's journey.
And may you succeed in enjoying the rarest gem of all,
the making of beautiful days worth remembering.

(Invite participants to lay their hands on the head and shoulders of the new resident and/or extend a hand in blessing.)

May God bless you and keep you.
May God's face shine upon you
and be gracious to you.
May God look upon you with kindness
and give you peace.
And may God always hold you
in the palm of his hand.
Amen.

(Sprinkle the room and the new resident with holy water.)

BIRTHDAY CELEBRATION IN A RETIREMENT HOME[34]
(Roman Catholic)

This ritual can be adapted and used for the celebration of a couple's anniversary.

MATERIAL NEEDED
Table for participants to gather around with a specially decorated place for the celebrant, a decorated birthday cake, a candle, party hats for everyone.

PREPARATION AND ENVIRONMENT
Gather participants around the table. If necessary help them put on the party hats.

INTRODUCTION
Greetings and introduction of the resident who is celebrating a birthday. Explain that this gathering is to pray with and for the celebrant and bestow a special blessing upon him/her.

OPENING PRAYER

> **Leader:** Lord of Life,
> we gather today to celebrate the day
> when N. was born
> and became a gift to her/his parents
> and to the world.
> We thank you for giving us N.
> for she/he is a gift to us as well.
> And we thank you for her/his ____ years of life.
> Thank you, Lord, for giving us N.

> **All: Thank you, Lord, for giving us N.**

SCRIPTURE   Isa. 43

RITUAL ACTION
(The celebrant is invited to light the birthday candle and share with the group her/his story of life. Note: Some residents may need prompting questions. When the story is finished, the leader says:)

> **Leader:** Thank you, Lord, for giving us N.

> **All: Thank you, Lord, for giving us N.**

BLESSING
(Invite more mobile residents, family members, and staff to gather around the celebrant and place their hands on her/his head, shoulders, arms and hands.)

> **Leader:** Lord of Birthdays and Festivals,
> Send your blessing on N. today.
> May she/he grow younger with each birthday.

May the gifts of this day
be the blessing of good health,
peaceful days,
and the joys of family and friends.
Happy birthday, N.
May God bless you today
and all the days of your life.

GESTURE OF FRIENDSHIP
(All sing "Happy Birthday" and enjoy cake and ice cream.)

BLESSING OF RETIREMENT COMMUNITY RESIDENTS[35]
(Ecumenical)

CALL TO WORSHIP

Leader: God's mercies never come to an end.

INVOCATION

O God of all the seasons, we give you thanks that while the earth remains, seedtime and harvest, cold and heat, summer and winter, day and night shall not cease just as your love for us will never end. **Amen.**

OPENING HYMN   #473   PrH   "For the Beauty of the Earth"

PSALM READING   Lam. 3

RESPONSE

Leader: God's mercies never come to an end.

All: **The steadfast love of the Lord never ceases;**
God's mercies never come to an end;
They are new every morning; your faithfulness, O Lord is great.
You are all that I have and therefore I will wait for you;
You O Lord are good to those who wait for you; to all who seek you.
It is good to wait in patience; for the salvation of the Lord.
Glory be to God the Creator, to Christ our Redeemer and to the Holy
  Spirit;
As it was in the beginning is now and shall be ever more. Amen.

HYMN   #359   PrH   "More Love to Thee, O Christ"

SCRIPTURE READING   Gen. 5:6–9, 14, 17–19, 22, 32; 7:11–13; 8:13–15

RESPONSE

> **Celebrant:** This is the word of the Lord.
>
> **All: Thanks be to God.**

HOMILY   "The Elderly in the Bible"

INTRODUCTION TO THE BLESSING WITH OIL

I recognize that growing old is hard. One does not have to spend much time with you to hear the aggravation of fingers which don't work as they once did, the frustration of poor eyesight, and the loneliness of having family who live too far away to visit frequently, just to name a few. I hear in your voices and see in your eyes that the process of growing old is not always pleasant. So I have brought some scented oil with which I would like to give each of you a blessing while I make the sign of the cross on your forehead. Growing old is hard, but with God's help it can also be a rich experience of grace.

BLESSING WITH OIL

May God be your light and hope. May God be your strength and comfort this day and in all the days to come. **Amen.** (*Adapted from a benediction from the* New Zealand Prayer Book.)

HYMN   #210   PrH   "O God, Our Help in Ages Past"

BENEDICTION   #438   PrH   "Blessed Be the Tie That Binds"

PASSING OF THE PEACE

May the peace of Christ be with you.

Seasons of Crisis

"The comfort you give is only torment."
(Job 16:1)

"Come to me all of you who are tired."
(Matt. 11:28)

Chapter 4

Illness: As Life-Altering

Lord
you are
a present
help in trouble.
Come revive. Redeem.
Restore. In our darkness come
as light. In our sadness come as joy
In our troubles come as peace. In our
weakness come as strength. Come Lord
to our aid. Revive. Redeem. Restore us. O
Lord, Open our eyes to your presence. Open
our minds to your grace. Open our lips to your
praises. Open our hearts to your love. Open our lives
to your
healing
And be
found among us.
—David Adam, "Help
in Trouble," in Tides
and Seasons"[1]

INTRODUCTION

THEOLOGY OF HEALTH AND SICKNESS

Our response to people in crisis needs to be based on a Judeo-Christian theology of health, healing, and healers. We begin with health in order to understand illness. We should not conduct healing services, especially with those with physical illness, without a clear theology of sickness and health. This chapter refers to life-altering illness because of the chronic nature of the illnesses. Included here are liturgies treating addiction, mental illness, and disabilities, as well as services for victims of domestic violence and sexual abuse. In the case of the latter, the perpetrators are also ill, but the focus in these liturgies is on the victims, who suffer psychological and physical harm. While it is true that any serious illness alters who we are even if we recover, conditions such as addiction, mental illness, and disabilities by their very nature are

147

rarely "cured." In one sense, remission is possible, but "recovering" is used to describe the ongoing nature, for instance, of addiction. Success in the treatment of serious mental illness has been tremendous with the advent of targeted medications, but for many, such as those with schizophrenia, without the drugs the worst symptoms of the disease may reappear.

As a church plans health ministry programs with those suffering from life-altering illness, it is important to recognize these facts. In the conducting of healing services, the inclusion of the support and advocacy by others is as important a part of the service as prayers for healing.

The major points of this Christian reconstructionist view are as follows:

- Man/woman is an integrated whole—body, mind, and spirit created to live in community.
- Health and salvation are twin concepts signifying wholeness.
- Sin and sickness interrelate as a reflection of brokenness—individual and global—but not always in a causal way.
- Healing includes a wide variety of resources, activities, and attitudes that move us toward wholeness in all seasons of life. It may include suffering and is more than curing. It is communal as well as individual.
- Christ's healing ministry is a paradigm for healing, where all resources, including prayer, faith, and medicine, are vehicles used by God, the source of all healing.
- "Miraculous" healing is not contrary to nature but a fuller revelation of God's Word.
- Healers are those persons who move us toward wholeness; all Christians are called to be healers.
- The church, both past and present, is a corporate expression of an individual Christian's calling to a healing ministry.

The unique contributions of the biblical definition of health are: (1) its doctrine of man/woman as a unity—both within himself/herself and with the environment and community; (2) its definition of health as wholeness which includes a spiritual dimension; (3) its orientation to health instead of sickness; and (4) its primary goal of others' health, not just our own.

The Judeo-Christian framework shifts the focus from my health to that of others as the driving force in the pursuit of health. Health is viewed in terms of the ultimate purpose of humankind and the implied concern for social justice and service for others. He/she only is whole who is joined to the suffering of others. In other words, we cannot be in full health without sharing the burden of others' sickness. Wholeness is not an individual achievement but a joint adventure.

People are made to be in relationship, to experience acceptance by others, and to find a meaning and purpose in life outside of themselves. This orientation toward others is an important part of what it means to be healthy. The communal dimension to our nature is reflected in the image of the church as the body of Christ. The church, then, is especially suited to participate in this communal dimension to healing by its liturgies and ministry. We have a responsibility to offer God's healing power in the midst of great suffering and sickness in a variety of ways, which includes prayers and services.

Wholeness depends on one's relationship with God and one's relationship with others (freedom from a state of sin) and on physical reconstruction (well-being). The biblical view is that physical well-being is only one aspect of health, that bodily health supplies but one part of salvation. "For [God] wounds, but [God] binds up; [God] strikes, but [God's] hands heal" (Job 5:18). The Hebrew word *raphâ* means "heal," "repair," "mend." In the Greek language of the Christian Scriptures, what is often translated as *sōzō*, "to save," and, secondarily, "to be saved, well," originally was more inclusive. "If I only touch his cloak, I will be made well [whole]" (Matt. 9:21). In the biblical tradition, health and salvation are integrally connected, and Jesus' title, Savior, also means healer.[2]

Not only health but also sickness needs to be viewed holistically. A holistic view of sickness is contained in the definition of sickness as brokenness. There are four ways of understanding brokenness: (1) internal brokenness of a person's spirit and mind; (2) illnesses of one's body; (3) alienation from one's neighbor; and (4) estrangement from God. Brokenness is an apt metaphor for defining sickness as the malfunction of all creation.[3] A family, a community, a nation, or even the physical world, in the instance of pollution, can be sick. Medically, reference is made to torn ligaments, ruptured blood vessels, or dislocated bones. More popularly, we refer to splitting headaches and split personalities—people "cracking up" or "going to pieces." All these expressions connote brokenness, separation, and division. Societal terms, such as fragmented communities, racial divisions, and schisms, describe this same brokenness. So sickness may manifest itself in different forms at different levels, but all sickness is derived from a brokenness that pervades every level of human existence.[4]

Sickness as brokenness describes an ongoing state, not merely the experience of episodic events. It involves the whole person at every level of life, though at any given moment it may present itself specifically in the physical, emotional, mental, or spiritual dimension. A person may experience broken relationships or an alienation from the world. This brokenness from a theological perspective is called sin.[5]

While personal sin is one's own fault, sickness is not always a consequence of an individual's own thought or actions. As part of the human race we suffer the consequences of fallen human nature, as well as experience the joys of being human. As we enjoy the gifts of life that we may not directly create or warrant, so we suffer the liabilities of life—epidemics, tornadoes, wars for which we may not be directly responsible.

A number of scriptural passages attribute sickness and even death to sin or view sickness as a direct punishment from God. For example, "I will continue to punish you sevenfold for your sins. . . . Your strength shall be spent to no purpose. . . . I will send pestilence among you" (Lev. 26:18–25). In order to appreciate what the Old Testament writers were saying about the relation of sin and sickness, it is necessary to understand the attitudes prevalent at the time the Old Testament was written.

The inclusion of the story of Job in the Jewish canon is extremely important as a corrective to the oversimplified view that all sickness was the direct result of a particular person's sin. One eagerly awaits God's resolution of the conflict between Job and his friends about the connection between sickness and sin. We are left with the mystery of suffering.

This complexity in the relationship between sin and sickness carries forward into the New Testament. On the one hand, Jesus implies that sickness is the work of demons (Matt. 8:16). On the other hand, after healing the paralytic, Jesus tells him to sin no more lest a worse thing befall him (Luke 5:17–26). There are cases mentioned in the New Testament where sickness or even death was seen as a direct punishment from God. Ananias and Sapphira were struck dead because they lied about the purchase of property (Acts 5:1–11). Herod Agrippa I was eaten by worms because he did not give God the glory in his reign (Acts 12:23).

Paul, reflecting the Deuteronomic point of view, appears to correlate a person's sin and sickness in relation to the incorrect eating of the Lord's Supper (1 Cor. 11:29–30). In James 5:15, we read that "the prayer of faith will save the sick, and the Lord will raise them up; and anyone who has committed sins will be forgiven [healed]." Sickness here is regarded as a special opportunity to take stock, to examine oneself concerning the reasons for illness.

In the midst of these stories that connect sin and sickness comes the account of the man born blind. "As he walked along, he saw a man blind from birth. His disciples asked him, 'Rabbi, who sinned, this man or his parents, that he was born blind?' Jesus answered, 'Neither this man nor his parents sinned; he was born blind so that God's works might be revealed in him" (John 9:1–3). This story disturbs the pat answers, just as the story of Job questioned the Hebrew's correlation of sin and sickness. The story addresses the question of whether sickness is always God's will and a punishment for sin. Everyone operates with a different set of presuppositions. Jesus upsets everyone's stereotypes and restores physical sight and gives spiritual insight to one man, but he is unable to restore spiritual sight to the others, that is, the Pharisees.

As we reflect on sickness and suffering, it is also important to remember our times of health. Furthermore, we should relate to people as persons, not principally as patients. Illness, whether chronic or episodic, is part of the reality of being human. However, God wills our health, not our illness. Jesus' short ministry included forty healing miracles of all sorts of illnesses.

Four emphases in Jesus' healing ministry illumine the Christian perspective on the nature and process of healing: "(1) Jesus affirms health as an important goal, desired by God; (2) he addresses the whole person while respecting his or her autonomy; (3) he meets people's voiced needs; and (4) he addresses what is behind a person's sickness. These emphases in Christ's healing ministry provide insight into the Christian ministry of healing."[6]

What difference does it make to our present understanding to have examined the concepts of health and sickness from the Judeo-Christian perspective? Just this: conceiving health as wholeness expands the understanding of healing. Healing is any activity or attitude that moves one toward wholeness—a wholeness greater than the sum of its parts. It restores harmony with oneself, God, and the world—akin to the Hebrew understanding of *shalom*.[7] In participating in healing services, this wholistic view of health helps us accept that healing may not be physical but spiritual or psychological, which is equally important.

HEALING FOR ALL PEOPLE

It is important to note that the inclusion of liturgies for healing of people with a variety of illnesses is to acknowledge that all our conditions and frailties can be healed by God's power, whether physical disabilities, cancer, addiction, or mental illness. There are not acceptable and unacceptable illnesses. Furthermore, healing, as mentioned in the Introduction, comes in a variety of ways—physical, mental, emotional, social, or spiritual. The healing may be different from what we pray for as God meets us at unexpected places and in unforeseen ways.

One of the principal goals of these services is the inclusion of all God's people—no matter what their condition. Too often the church has been a place of guilt and judgment for those suffering from socially controversial illnesses. Even worse, there has been a silent rejection of those with mental illness or disabilities, where they are made to feel either invisible or odd. Serving as a pastor and then a consultant to churches about health ministries, I found not only architectural but attitudinal barriers for inclusion of those with mental and physical challenges.

Hopefully, the conducting of these healing liturgies for people of all conditions will assure not only their healing but also the healing of the church of its prejudice and segregation.

DISABILITIES

When ministering with those with disabilities, understanding on the part of the leaders and participants in a service is crucial. William Gaventa, director of the Boggs Center on Developmental Disabilities of Robert Wood Johnson Medical School, New Brunswick, New Jersey, has written a very helpful piece about ministry with persons with disabilities.[8] One of the challenging features of this ministry that I discovered while working in this field in Washington, D.C. was the question of definitions. "What does 'disability' mean? The World Health Organization's threefold definition of disability is very helpful. There are three levels to the definition: a disability is first of all an impairment; that impairment causes some level of disability; what do we think about the impairment and disability? What is the value judgment placed on that difference? That is the 'handicap.'"[9]

Most Americans define disability in relation to work—whether it limits or inhibits their ability to do it.[10] "An 'impairment' involves psychological, physiological, or anatomical loss and abnormality of function. The condition may be permanent or transitory, involving, for example, an amputated limb, diabetes, a limited hearing capacity, or mental retardation."[11]

"A 'disability' results from an impairment. It restricts or prevents the performance of an activity within the range considered normal for a given age level. Examples are in walking, reading, or communication which limit one's abilities."[12]

"A handicap is simply the social disadvantage that results from a disability. For example, one who uses a wheelchair is handicapped when all entrances to a church building have stairs. A child born with impaired vision is handicapped in a society wherein the culture (buildings, attitudes, and schooling) are all geared to those with normal vision."[13]

The International Center for the Disabled (ICD) has defined a person with disability as follows:

- Had a disability or health problem that prevented him or her from participating fully in work, school, or other activities.
- Said that he or she had a physical disability; a seeing, hearing, or speech impairment; an emotional or mental disability; or a learning disability.
- Considered himself or herself disabled, or said that other people would consider him or her disabled.[14]

In the church, as we consider ministry with persons with disabilities, our starting point is our mutual humanity. We are linked by the fact that we are all broken and in need of God. "In other words, while the basic premise that all human beings are created in God's image is an extremely important issue, and must be discussed, the place where we as Christians must operate is from within liturgy, the 'work of the people.' How is it that we carry the symbols of Christ and his church into the world? How is it that we live out those ethical acts that we claim within the liturgy of our church?"[15] We must learn through all acts of worship how to include those with mental and physical disabilities. Unfortunately, the church has often failed to be inclusive, hence risking becoming unhealthy itself. We can only become the true church when all are included.

DOMESTIC VIOLENCE

Domestic violence is widespread in our society. Nearly one-third of American women (31 percent) report being physically or sexually abused by a husband or boyfriend at some point in their lives, according to a 1998 Commonwealth Fund survey.[16] From 1992 to 1996, victimization by an intimate accounted for about 21 percent of the violence experienced by females. It accounted for about 2 percent of the violent crime sustained by males.[17] About half of all female victims of intimate violence report an injury of some type, and about 20 percent of them seek medical assistance.[18] In a national survey of more than two thousand American families, approximately 50 percent of the men who frequently assaulted their wives also frequently abused their children.[19] Three in four women (76 percent) who reported they had been raped and/or physically assaulted since age eighteen said that a current or former husband, cohabiting partner, or date committed the assault.[20] As one of our liturgies indicates, domestic violence does not precisely fit in the category of illness except in the sense of the perpetrator's addiction to power and violence. Of course, the victim not only suffers bodily but also incurs psychic injury that takes years to heal. Posting signs in the women's restroom about stopping domestic violence, literature on a fellowship hall table, and adult education classes on the subject all give evidence of a church that cares. This creates a climate where victims and, perhaps by some miracle, perpetrators would participate in a service.

As was mentioned in the introductory chapter, it is essential that church leadership and members prepare by educating everyone for these services. In the area of domestic violence, the understanding of its nature as not about sex but addiction to power and control will help address the problem.[21] The complex profile of the perpetrator and the innocence of the victim are central, for too often a pastor has sent a wife back to her abuser under the guise of the obedience of a wife to her husband, no matter what.

ADDICTION

Recognizing addiction as an illness, not a sin, is perhaps one of the most important contributions of the church in the area of health ministry. Addiction includes both substance and behavioral addictions such as stress and workaholism. Addiction is a multidimensional illness that includes physiological, psychological, sociological, and spiritual aspects. "All addictions have in common a search for pleasure, on the one hand, and an escape from life, on the other; they seek the object rather than its Creator, God. Often it is a form of self-medication used to cope with emotional conflicts and shortcomings. Gerald May defines addiction as 'any compulsive, habitual behavior that limits the freedom of human desire.'[22] It is caused by the attachment, or nailing, of desire to specific objects. The word 'behavior' is especially important in this definition, for it indicates that action is essential to addiction. May describes five essential characteristics of addiction: tolerance, denial, withdrawal symptoms, loss of willpower, and distortion of attention."[23] Diagnosis and treatment need to include all these areas. Anne Schaef, feminist and psychotherapist, describes two categories of addiction—substance addictions and process addictions.[24]

I have discussed in my book *The Healing Church* a number of strategies for church involvement in addiction prevention—to preach, teach, and practice a theology of health, hope, and healing; to create a caring community of acceptance and a ministry of presence; to provide values that encourage healthy lifestyles and positive virtues in our society; to develop a systemic understanding of the nature and process of addiction; to work toward changing economic, social, and racial injustice, and false values in society, which create a climate for substance abuse and other addictions; to offer educational programs in prevention for children, youth, adults, and pastors through churches, seminaries, and presbyteries; to train intervention teams; to develop a congregational, regional, or judicatory policy on substance abuse; to advocate laws, policies, and advertising that deglamorize alcohol and other drugs and harmful substances; to organize a referral and resource network with community and government agencies and a clearinghouse for materials; and to organize and participate in ecumenical coalitions to combat substance abuse, domestic violence, and other addictions, including international information networks on production, distribution, and use.[25] Although these health ministries areas—educational, support/advocacy, and direct health care—are crucial to addressing addiction problems, the liturgical response is also important. The healing services here are structured to recognize this reality.

MENTAL ILLNESS

There was a seismic change in the treatment of mental illness with the introduction of antipsychotic drugs in the 1950s and the subsequent deinstitutionalization, which led to group homes and many returning to their homes, in the 1970s and 1980s and beyond. Yet one observer had concluded this plan was the greatest failure, a sort of launching of a "psychiatric Titanic."[26] The support structures were simply not in place, including the church community.

We must confess a lack of understanding and readiness as a church to deal with persons with mental illness. Our society has had a history of figuratively stuffing people into closets, whether alcoholics, gays, the mentally ill, the disabled—whomever we judge as different. The church has not been much better. However, I think there are some hopeful signs that things are changing.

Religious communities more than any others need to speak out in support and advocacy as well as being a presence, standing alongside those who are suffering in whatever ways. According to Lewis Judd of the National Institute of Mental Health, one in every five Americans will have a mental disorder at some time in life; and one person in every hundred in all societies and cultures worldwide will experience schizophrenia.[27]

The church needs to be involved, to educate people about mental illness, to incorporate persons with mental illness and their families into the life of the church, to celebrate gifts while recognizing challenges, and to collaborate with religious communities and agencies. Studies have shown the importance of religion and mental health. Some have concentrated only on the stigma and misunderstanding of religious communities and mental illness, but there are also positive sides.

Pastoral Presence in Addressing Mental Illness

A 1990 D.Min. project of Fred Cloud at Vanderbilt, which surveyed pastors, mental health care professionals, families with mentally ill members, and congregational members without mental illness, found the most important need was for pastors to participate in community programs on mental illness and congregations in order to help overcome the stereotypes, stigma, isolation, and alienation that persons who have mental illness often experience in both church and community. In this survey of four groups, clergy had the lowest rating of the healing professions, and 40 percent of those surveyed reported negative experiences with pastors in the area.[28]

Seminaries do not adequately train future pastors in this area, so ignorance often leads to avoiding those with serious mental illness. Pastors who preach on the subject of mental illness can make a big difference, because then it becomes an appropriate subject to discuss openly. As well, pastors can share their own struggles with mental illness when that is the case for them. Susan Gregg-Schroeder, a Methodist pastor in San Diego, California, recounts her own struggles with clinical depression and her decision to share them with her congregation. She writes, "I am speaking out to help erase the stigma of mental illness. Depression is an illness, like diabetes or cancer, that is caused by a chemical imbalance in the brain. The good news is that there are many effective treatments available. The bad news is that shame, guilt, and fear prevent many persons from seeking the help they need."[29] The outcome of her risk taking was an outpouring of stories from others who suffered with mental illness and the formation of a church support group for them. In moving out of the shadows, Gregg-Schroeder found time for rejoicing and a deepening of life, an awareness and intensifying of relationships.

The offering of worship services that highlight the needs of those with mental illness, such as the services on "Solidarity with the Mentally Ill" (p. 162) and "We are the Church Together: Those with Mental Illness" (p. 167), may help healing. In the Introduction, I discussed the role of rituals and their importance in our spiritual life. "Our souls need daily nourishment; ritual, ceremony, and symbol bring us closer to ourselves, to one another, and to God."[30]

Church Strategies to Address Mental Health Issues

Of course, there are many more important ministries besides worship for reaching people with mental illness. Pathways to Promise, founded in 1987, was established to link religious communities with those with mental illness. One of the first organizations to provide support and advocacy was the Presbyterian Serious Mental Illness Network in 1987.[31] Mennonites started the Mennonite Mutual Aid program, which helps congregations minister to those with mental illness.

Robert Anderson, director of Pastoral Services, Connecticut Mental Health Center, New Haven, Connecticut, which was founded in 1947, started collaborative aftercare programs with Connecticut Mental Health Center and seven community churches. They, in turn, have provided twenty-five local mental health agencies and affiliated faith communities across the United States with training.[32] These and hundreds of other programs provide a foundation and framework in which these special liturgies take place.

Disabilities

"Let him down on his bed into the middle of the group." (Luke 5:19)

ENCOURAGING PERSONS WITH DISABILITIES[33]
(Anglican)

A celebration of the love of God, from whom we have strength and assurance.

'Blessed art thou, O Lord our God, King of the universe, who variest The forms of thy creatures'

Those in wheelchairs are placed where all can see as well as hear.

The deaf are seated with their 'interpreter' from the Diocesan Mission to the Hard of Hearing, who has been provided previously with a script of the service and the address.

The 'mechanics' of the service are explained by the vicar, particularly in regard to standing and sitting.

The organ has played quietly as the congregation assembles.

PRAISE
(When all are in their places, the vicar says:)

Hear the comforting words of the Prophet Isaiah: *(Isa. 40:25–end)*

To whom then will you liken me . . . they will march on and never grow faint.

(The reading ended, the congregation standing or sitting, as is convenient, all sing the hymn:)

HYMN #192 HAM (#365 AMR) "Praise, My Soul, the King of Heaven" (verse 3 unaccompanied)

(At the end of the hymn there is a moment of silence.)

RESPONSORIAL PSALM

Psalm 121   (ASB p. 1264)
I lift up my eyes to the hills:
But where shall I find help?

(Now, as all remain seated, on the organ is announced the chant for a psalm to be sung.)
(All join in singing:)

Psalm 150   (ASB p. 1289)
Praise the Lord.
O praise God in his sanctuary:
Praise him in the firmament of his power.

(pointed for the congregation if possible)

WORDS OF STRENGTH AND ASSURANCE
(Now as all remain seated, there is a reading from the lectern:)

READING   Isa. 35

The prophet tells of the love of God which can give peace in place of anxiety and can change sorrow into joy.

(The lesson ended, and the reader returning to his or her seat, a silence follows. Then, a voice:)

GOD SPEAKS

My child, it is not necessary to know much to please me; it is sufficient to love much. Speak to me as thou wouldst to a father if he drew near. Are there any for whom thou wouldst pray to me? Repeat to me the names of thy relations, thy friends; after each name add what thou wouldst have me do for them. Ask much, ask much; I love generous souls who forget themselves for others.

Tell me of the poor thou wouldst relieve, the sick whom thou hast seen suffer, the sinners thou wouldst have converted, those who are alienated from thee, whose affection thou wouldst regain. Are there graces thou wouldst ask for thyself? Write, if thou wilt, a long list of what thou desirest, of all the needs of thy soul, and come and read it to me.

Tell me simply how proud thou art, how sensitive, egotistical, mean and indolent. Poor child, do not blush; there are in heaven many saints who had their faults; they prayed to me, and little by little their faults were corrected.

Do not hesitate to ask me for blessings for the body and mind; for health, memory and success. I can give you all things, and I always give, when my blessings are needed to render souls more holy.

Today what wilt thou have, my child? If thou knowest how I long to do thee good! Hast thou plans that occupy thee? Lay them all before me.

Dost thou wish to give pleasure to thy mother, to thy family, to those on whom thou dost depend? What wouldst thou do for them?

And for me? Hast thou no zealous thought for me? Dost thou not wish to do a little good to the souls of thy friends who have perhaps forgotten me?

Bring me all thy failures, and I will show thee the cause of them. Hast thou not troubles? Who has caused thee pain? Tell me all. And wilt thou not end by adding that thou wilt pardon and forget?—and I will bless thee.

Dost thou dread something painful? Is there in thy heart a vain fear which is not reasonable, but which is tormenting thee? Trust thyself wholly to my care. I am here. I see everything.

I will not leave thee.

Hast thou not joys to be made known to me? Why dost thou not let me share thy happiness? Tell me what has happened since yesterday to cheer and console thee. An unexpected visit which did thee good; a fear suddenly dissipated; a success that thou thoughtest thou wouldst not reach; a mark of affection, a letter, a gift which thou hast received? I have prepared it all for thee.

Thou canst show thy gratitude and give me thanks.

Art thou resolved no longer to expose thyself to this temptation? Not to finish this book which excites thy imagination? No longer to give thy friendship to a person who is not godly and whose presence disturbs the peace of thy soul? Wilt thou go at once to do a kindness to this companion who has hurt thee?

Well, my child, go now; take up thy work; be silent, humble, submissive and kind; and come back tomorrow, and bring me a heart still more devout and loving. Tomorrow I shall have more blessings for thee. (—From *God of a Hundred Names,* Barbara Greene and Victor Gollancz)

(After a moment of silence, there is a musical interlude.)

MUSICAL INTERLUDE   Chopin: *Valse No. 9 in A flat major, Op. 69, No. 1 Lento*

(or quietly meditative organ music)

(Now at the lectern is read:)

READING   Acts 3:1–16

St. Luke tells how the spirit of the love of Christ is always at work to make us whole.

(The reading ended, a silence falls. For a moment, only quiet organ music. Immediately on the piano is played:)

MUSICAL INTERLUDE   Chopin: *Valse No. 16 in A flat major, Op. posth.*

(The music ended, all sing the hymn:)

HYMN   #565   HAM   "Songs of Praise"   (Jan Struther, Tune: Slane)
        #394   HAM   "Lord of All Hopefulness, Lord of All Joy"

THE ADDRESS
(This must be straightforward, essentially brief, and a simple declaration that the love of God is the source of all comfort, strength, assurance and hope.)

(The address ended, all sing the hymn:)

HYMN   #426   HAM   "The Lord's My Shepherd, I'll Not Want"

THE THANKSGIVINGS AND THE PRAYERS
(The hymn ended, the vicar says:)

> Let us pray.

(An act of penitence)

> **Vicar:** Let us confess our sins to almighty God.
>
> **All:** **Almighty God, our heavenly Father,**
> **we have sinned against you and against our fellow men,**
> **in thought and word and deed,**
> **through negligence, through weakness,**
> **through our own deliberate fault.**
> **We are truly sorry and repent of all our sins.**
> **For the sake of your Son Jesus Christ, who died for us,**
> **forgive us all that is past; and grant that we may serve you in newness**
> **of life; to the glory of your name. Amen.**

(ASB p. 127)

> **Response: Amen.**

(After a space the vicar says:)

Words like 'handicapped' or 'disabled' are unfortunate. They set people apart as different, when in fact they are just ordinary people who have a certain problem.

(Silence)

> **Vicar:** Let us thank God for his love for you and me.
>
> Let us thank God for the strength he gives to triumph over every difficulty, and the courage he gives to overcome every kind of handicap.
>
> Let us thank God for that love which brings its daily gifts of joy and hope to every changing circumstance of life.
>
> Lord, in thy mercy:
>
> **People: Hear our prayer.**

Vicar: Let us pray for a sensitive ear, and a watchful eye to all who need our encouragement in love: for those who suffer any kind of physical or mental disability, that we may accord them consideration and concern.

Let us pray for patience, thoughtfulness and regard in love, for all who are disabled, that we give to them that dignity which belongs by right to every child of God.

O Loving Father, we pray for all who are handicapped in the race of life: the blind, the delicate, those worn with sickness, and all who are permanently injured. May they learn the mystery of the road of suffering which Christ has trodden and saints have followed, and bring thee this gift which angels cannot bring, a heart that trusts thee even in the dark; and this we ask in the name of him who himself took our infirmities upon him, even the same Jesus Christ, our Savior.

—A.S.T. Fisher
(from *Parish Prayers*)

Response: Amen.

Vicar: God grant me
Serenity to accept the things I cannot change,
Courage to change the things I can,
And wisdom to know the difference.

(All say together:)

THE LORD'S PRAYER

(Then all sing the hymn:)

HYMN #205 HAM (#379 AMR) "Now Thank We All Our God"
(Alternative:) #179 NCH "We Yearn, O Christ, for Wholeness"

(After the hymn, a profound silence falls.)

(Then the vicar reads from the writings of Julian of Norwich:)

HE KEEPS ALL THAT IS MADE

He showed me a little thing, the size of a hazelnut, in the palm of my hand, and it was as round as a ball. I looked at it with my mind's eye and I thought, 'What can this be?' and answer came, 'It is all that is made.' I marveled that it could last, for I thought it might have crumbled to nothing, it was so small. And the answer came into my mind, 'It lasts and ever shall because God loves it.' And all things have being through the love of God.

In this little thing I saw three truths. The first is that God made it. The second is that God loves it. The third is that God looks after it.

What is he indeed that is maker and lover and keeper? I cannot find words to tell. For until I am one with him I can never have true rest nor peace. I can never know it until I am held so close to him that there is nothing in between.

THE BLESSING

>**Vicar:** Give to me, O Lord, a steadfast heart, which no unworthy affection may drag downwards; give me an unconquered heart, which no tribulation can wear out; give me an upright heart, which no unworthy purpose may tempt aside. Grant me also, O Lord my God, understanding to know thee, diligence to seek thee, wisdom to find thee, and a faithfulness that may finally embrace thee.

>And the blessing of God Almighty, the Father, the Son and the Holy Spirit, be with you now and evermore.

Response: Amen.

THE WITHDRAWAL
(As the clergy withdraw to shake hands and to say goodbye to the people, on the organ is played:)

POSTLUDE   Karg-Elert *'Chorale-Improvisation on Nun danket alle Gott' Opus 65 no. 59* (1909)[34]

FRIENDSHIP SERVICE WITH THOSE WITH MENTAL IMPAIRMENTS[35]
(Reformed Church)

CALL TO WORSHIP

CONGREGATION'S STATEMENT OF INTENT   #250   PsH   "I've Come to Tell"

THE GREETING TO GOD

>**Leader:** The Lord is our God.

>**People: He made us, and we belong to him.**

>**Leader:** We are God's children and God's people.

>**People: God's love and care for us will go on forever.**

>**Leader:** Grace to you and peace from our triune God; Father, Son and Holy Spirit.

>**People: Amen.**

(God's people greet each other.)

SONGS OF PRAISE   #241   PsH   "This is the Day"
#264   PsH   "Lord, I Want to Be a Christian"

READING FROM SCRIPTURE   John 14:1–11

OFFERING OF MUSIC

READING FROM SCRIPTURE   John 20:30–31

MEDITATION   "Jesus Who Does Miracles"

PRAYER *(concluded with "Open Our Eyes, Lord")*

SONG OF PRAISE   #462   PsH   "Amazing Grace"

OFFERING

SONGS OF PRAISE   #228   PsH   "Rejoice in the Lord Always"
#152   PsH   "I Will Sing Unto the Lord"
#457   PsH   "He's Got the Whole World"

BENEDICTION AND CHORAL AMEN

Mental Illness

"David would get his harp and play it."
(1 Sam. 16:23)

SOLIDARITY WITH THE MENTALLY ILL[36]
(Interfaith)

GATHERING MUSIC

LIGHTING OF THE PEACE CANDLE
(As we light the candle that indicates our intention to be builders of peace in our world, we pray for all who yearn for the sense of being calmed and affirmed by the Creator God.)

PASSING OF THE PEACE
(We say to one another, "The Peace of God be with you." As you say this, enfold the hands of the ones to whom you speak and gather their names so we worship as people who call each other by name, affirming the personhood of all.)

WHY ARE WE GATHERED HERE?

> **Leader:** From east and west, north and south, we come to this safe place and holy time as people of faith.
>
> **People:** **We come because the Spirit of God invites us here.**
>
> **Leader:** We bring tired bodies and weary spirits, hoping to find some sense of release from our burdens.
>
> **People:** **We yearn to be free of that which weighs us down.**
>
> **Leader:** We bring our doubts and our questions about who God is and who God created us to be.
>
> **People:** **We dare to admit that our faith sometimes falters.**

Leader: We come with voices to sing praise, arms to embrace, feet to dance, lives to celebrate.

People: We come to cry and to laugh, to say "Yes" and to say "No," to listen and to speak.

Leader: May our worship bring glory to God and empower us to know life in its fullness.

OPENING HYMN
(Please stand, as able, for all hymns.)

(Hymns will be played through once.) "O God of Mercy"   Words: Margee Iddings   Tune: #618   H82   "Ye Watchers and Ye Holy Ones"

O God of mercy, God of grace, O God of every age and race,
      We praise You, Alleluia!
O grant to all who worship here
      Your Spirit's presence strong and clear
            As we bring You all our sorrow,
            All our hopes for each tomorrow—
            Alleluia!

O God of justice, hear our sigh.
Sometimes with angry voice we cry:
      "Why, oh why, God, Why such suffering?"
The chaos rages 'round about.
Yet even in the midst of doubt—
      Still You seek us and You lead us
      Toward the goal of all that's righteous—
      Alleluia!

O God of love that knows no end;
We feel love's power in family, friend,
      Colleague, neighbor. Alleluia!
Words spoken, gestures freely given,
Affirming acts compassion driven—
      These sustain us, give life meaning,
      So great God hear our thanksgiving.
      Alleluia!

O God of life: we trust in You
To daily prompt faith's growth anew
      Through each season. Alleluia!
Bring wind to blow away our fears.
Send love to dry up all our tears.
      O refresh us, breathing with us,
      As we work for healing justice.
      Alleluia!

FIRST READING   Isa. 58:6–12

THE PRAYER OF DOCTORS AND NURSES

O Great Healing Force: Strengthen all who spend their lives as channels of this healing energy for all who have mental illness. Be a discerning power in our decision-making. Be a guiding power as we use our skill. Enable us always to be sensitive to the person whom we are treating. Stir up in us a great well of compassion and courage, we pray.

People: O Great Healing Force: Hear this prayer.

THE PRAYER OF SOCIAL WORKER, THERAPIST, CASE MANAGER

O Creator of us all: You have called us into partnership with You in caring for those who are poor, sick, neglected, on the margins of our society. How easy it is to forget these persons, God, though they are precious to You. Help us to bring light where there is confusion, healing where there is pain, and confidence where there is self-doubt.

Grant us the energy and commitment to be a champion for adequate resources, facilities and services for all who suffer from serious mental illness, we pray.

People: O Creator of us all: Hear this prayer.   Amen.

SECOND READING   Ps. 123

THE PRAYER OF THE CONSUMER

O Comforter and Sustaining Presence: I call out to You for You have promised to always be within me and around me. You cause healing power to be at work in me. You give my spirit courage and strength. These gifts enable me to move from a place where fear reigns to a place of confidence and calm. Grant me, not only the assurance of your graciousness, but the love of family, the support of friends, the hope of advocates, the kinship with other consumers.

People: O Comforter and Sustaining Presence: Hear this prayer.

THE PRAYER OF FAMILIES AND FRIENDS

O Nurturing One: When we feel empty, frustrated, depressed, alone, it is a great comfort to know that there is nothing that can separate us from Your love. When we get to the breaking point, You are there with encouragement. When we find ourselves battling societal forces that seem overwhelming and defeating, even there we experience your empowerment. When energy seems to wane and we want to give up, Your Spirit revives us.

You are present in the scientist who removes our guilt. You are there in the support group where we are held in compassion. You are there in legislators who fight for basic human rights of our loved one. You are there in friends who are not afraid to ask how things are going. Thanksgiving we offer for all such signs of Your accompanying presence.

People: O Nurturing One: Hear this prayer.   Amen.

SPECIAL MUSIC   "Litany"   Words: Langston Hughes   Music: John Musto

THIRD READING   Ps. 142

THE PRAYER OF CLERGY

O Holy God: Our congregations are filled with persons who are challenged by mental illness and families who struggle to meet the ongoing medical and physical, emotional and spiritual needs of their loved ones.

Create in us an openness to their gifts, a commitment to their struggle for justice, and a tenderness to their need.

Take away our fears and timidness, replacing them with courage and advocacy.

As people of faith, rooted in Your love and guided by Your grace, make us strong to serve Your will that all creation may know fullness and satisfaction in life.

People: O Holy God: Hear this prayer.

THE PRAYER OF ADVOCATES

O God of Justice and Truth: Especially tonight, we pray for those people who have no one to stand with them as they live with mental illness—those who are homeless, immigrants, people recently deinstitutionalized, people in prison. In Your mercy, defend them from those who would neglect, exploit and stigmatize them.

For all who cannot advocate for themselves, cause Your power to stir up in us a voice that will not be silenced, a vision that will not be clouded, a determination that will not be dampened, a sense of righteousness that can only be triumphant.

People: O God of Justice and Truth: Hear this prayer.   Amen.

HYMN OF HOPE   "God of All Hopefulness"   Words: Jan Struther, as edited by Margee Iddings   Music: #339   PrH   "Be Thou My Vision"

God of all hopefulness, God of all joy,
Whose trust ever child-like, no cares could destroy:
Be there at our waking, and give us, we pray,
Your bliss in our hearts, God, at the break of the day.

God of all eagerness, God of all faith,
Your strong hands hold each of us firm in our place:
Be there in our working and give us, we pray,
Your strength in our hearts, God, at the noon of the day.

God of all kindliness, God of all grace,
Your love swift to welcome, Your arms to embrace:
Be there at our homecoming, give us, we pray,
Your love in our hearts, God, at the eve of the day.

THE OFFERING

THE OFFERTORY

A STORY AND REFLECTION   Josh., Chapter 4   "Out of the Wilderness, into the Promise"

A PROCESSION—LIVING STONES

> **Leader:** —for all who need a word of promise and hope
> —for all who suffer the ambiguities and agonies of serious mental illness
> —for families and friends of sufferers who suffer their own exquisite suffering
> —for caregivers
> —for the health care system
> —for faith communities
> —for all in the world locked up by oppressive systems
> —for all who have died from mental illness
> —for all who mourn their death, who grieve their absence
> —for all the signs of hope around us
> —for all whom we experience as healing agents
> —for all who gather for this conference

DISTRIBUTION OF POLISHED STONES TO THE CONGREGATION

PRAYER OF THANKSGIVING

> **Leader:** Like our faith ancestors did centuries ago, the living stones of our age and circumstance have been brought forward to become a memorial. As God commanded such a piling of remembering stones in the promised land, and, as Joshua set up such a piling of remembering stones in the Jordan River, so we, too, make witness to God's power among us. Let us pray:

> **People: O God of yesterday, today, and tomorrow: Your greatness is seen in all the world around us. It is in remembering in Your presence with us through past difficulties. It is treasured in Your guiding hand in the present. It is hoped for as we envision the future. The polished stone we receive serves to remind us that there is nothing that can separate us from Your love. We trust in Your grace as we move from the wilderness areas of our own lives into the lands of promise. So be it! Amen.**

HYMN OF ASSURANCE   "You Are Before Me, Lord"   Words: A setting of Ps. 139   Tune: #543   PrH   "Abide with Me"

You are before me, Lord, You are behind,
And over me You have spread out Your hand;
Such knowledge is too wonderful for me,
Too high to grasp, too great to understand.

Then from Your Spirit where, Lord, shall I go;
And from Your presence where, Lord, shall I fly?
If I ascend to heaven, You are there,
And still are with me if in hell I lie.

If I should take my flight into the dawn,
If I should dwell on ocean's farthest shore,
Your mighty hand will rest upon me still,
And Your right hand will guard me evermore.

If I should say, "Let darkness cover me,
And I shall hide within the veil of night,"
Surely the darkness is not dark to You:
The night is as the day, the darkness light.

Search me, O God, search me and know my heart;
Try me, O God, my mind and spirit try;
Keep me from any path which gives you pain,
And lead me in the everlasting way.
                    —Ian Pitt Watson, 1973, 1989

BENEDICTION

RECESSIONAL WITH CANDLES

> People: **We take the light of God's presence with us, symbolically,
> as we move from this place into the streets, from wilderness
> to promise, from despair to hope.**
>
> **Each candle will be lit from the light of the peace candle
> which was lit at the beginning of the service.**

WE ARE THE CHURCH TOGETHER: THOSE WITH MENTAL ILLNESS[37]
(Presbyterian)

CALL TO WORSHIP

Let us worship God who loves us all;
    whether we're old or young,
    educated or uneducated, healthy or ill,
    dark-skinned or light-skinned,
    rich or poor, conservative or liberal.

Let us worship God who wants us to
    love our neighbor as ourselves;
    the one who is weak and the one who is strong,
    the one we understand and the one we don't,
    the one who is like us and the one who is different.

Let us worship the God who desires our love;
    whether we are confused or together,
    happy or sad, smart or delayed,

trusting or fearful, ugly or beautiful,
successful or a failure.

Let us worship God with our thoughts, prayers and songs.

PRAYER

O God who cares about your children, grant us the gift of acceptance that we might find the courage to cope with the disease of mental illness. Teach us the patience and understanding our brothers and sisters with mental illness so deserve. Help us not to victimize with uninformed and uncaring attitudes, but show us the ways to give and receive love. Give us wisdom to be instruments of your grace and peace.

In your holy name, **Amen.**

RESPONSIVE READING

> **Leader:** O God, we pray for all who suffer in mind or spirit.
> Grant them your peace.
>
> **People: Hear our prayer, O Lord.**
>
> **Leader:** As David ministered to Saul with kindness and understanding,
> enable us to care for our brothers and sisters who have a
> mental illness.
>
> **People: Hear our prayer, O Lord.**
>
> **Leader:** Grant that we may identify mental illness as the disease it is,
> and without fear, reach out with compassion to be instruments
> of your grace and peace.
>
> **People: Hear our prayer, O Lord.**
>
> **Leader:** Grant us courage and wisdom to remove the stigma of mental illness.
> Open our eyes to the need all around us. Enable us to recognize
> those who hurt and welcome them with open arms of your love into
> the fellowship of faith so that we might receive your grace and peace
> through them.
>
> **People: Hear our prayer, O Lord.**
>
> **Leader:** Strengthen us with wisdom and guidance, empower us with love,
> patience and understanding.
>
> **People: Hear our prayer, O Lord.**
>
> **Leader:** Grant us this ministry of service, nurture and witness in your holy name.
>
> **People: Amen.**

SERMON   Unconditional Love

READING   Matt. 5:43–48; 26:6–13 *(optional)*

CLOSING HYMN   #69   SNC   "We Cannot Measure How You Heal"

BENEDICTION

MOVING TOWARD WHOLENESS
FOR THOSE WITH MENTAL ILLNESS[38]
(Presbyterian)

OPENING SENTENCES
(The people are called to worship in these [Ps. 124:8] or similar words from Scripture.)

(One of the following, or another verse from Scripture, is said:)

VERSE   2 Cor. 1:4–5

PSALM, HYMN, OR SPIRITUAL   #392   PrH   "Take Thou Our Minds, Dear Lord"

CONFESSION AND PARDON

CALL TO CONFESSION
(The people are called to confession with sentences of Scripture that promise God's forgiveness.)

Friends in Christ, God knows our needs before we ask,
and in our asking prepares us to receive the gift of grace.
Let us open our lives to God's healing presence,
forsaking all that separates us from God and neighbor.
Let us be mindful not only of personal evil
but also of the communal sins in which we play a part.
Let us confess to God whatever has wounded us or brought injury to others,
that we may receive mercy and become for each other ministers of God's grace.

CONFESSION OF SIN
(A brief silence may be observed for examination of conscience.)

Let us confess our sins together.

(All confess their sin, using one of the following, or another prayer of confession:)

> **Leader:** We confess that we are still not fully informed about mental illness and how
> it impacts persons and their families.

People: **At times, because of our lack of knowledge and understanding we find ourselves separated from our sisters and brothers with mental illness, their families and ourselves.**

Leader: There are lines drawn between us because we may define wholeness and normality with different words, but not a different spirit.

People: **Because of our lack of knowledge we live cut off from sources of strength and power that would help us be present to all people, including those with mental illness. This lack often makes us feel that we cannot act.**

Leader: So many events, meetings, and needs call to us, grabbing for our attention, that we find ourselves stretched to a fine, thin line.

People: **In the face of all this, we continue to seek knowledge and understanding of mental illness that will bring liberation and shalom to us and those we serve.**

All: **O God, our liberation and shalom, we seek the power of your Spirit, that we may live in fuller union with you, ourselves, and all our sisters and brothers, including those with mental illness. Also that we may gain courage to love and understand each other. Amen.**

DECLARATION OF FORGIVENESS

Leader: God created the world and all that is in it.
God has the power to transform this world and each of our lives.
Christ died for us, Christ rose for us, Christ reigns in power for us, Christ prays for us.
Anyone who is in Christ is a new creation.
The old life has gone; a new life has begun.
Be at peace, believe the good news of the Gospel.

All: **In Jesus Christ we are forgiven.**

HYMN   #380   PrH "O, Christ the Healer"

READINGS FROM SCRIPTURE
(Before the Scriptures are read, a prayer for illumination may be said by the reader. Appropriate selections from the Scripture are read.)

SERMON
(A sermon follows: It is appropriate for this to draw out dimensions of healing and mental health from the texts.)

OFFERING OF OUR LIVES TO GOD

I appeal to you therefore,
brothers and sisters,
by the mercies of God,
to present your bodies as a living sacrifice,
holy and acceptable to God,
which is your spiritual worship.

(Here, acknowledging all the wholeness and apparent brokenness in their lives, all present may ponder in silence all that is happening in their lives, and may, with renewed commitment, offer themselves and their gifts for ministry to the service of Jesus Christ in the world. This commitment may be expressed in some form such as the following prayer of commitment:)

Leader: O God, we pray for all those with mental illness and their families. In your mercy, shield them from those who would neglect, exploit and stigmatize them. Your Son has told us repeatedly that it is Your will to guide and protect. Help us to believe and understand that this is always true.

People: **For all who cannot advocate for themselves, cause Your power to awaken in us a voice that will not be silenced, a vision that will not be clouded, a determination that will not be dampened, a sense of righteousness that can only be triumphant. The rejection and frustration that we may experience is never a product of Your Holy hand. The lifting of the mantle of ignorance, fear and injustice is Your intent. The word which is Yours inspires each of us to direct our energy and creativity to bring hope and healing, acceptance and empowerment to those with mental illness and their loved ones. Amen.**

INTERCESSION FOR HEALING
(One of the following, or a similar prayer of intercession, is said:)

Almighty God, Creator, Redeemer and Sustainer of Life, we invoke your presence and guidance this day. For those who suffer from mental illness and are deeply troubled by their lives and by the storms they experience, we pray. May they feel your loving hand and your sustaining and nurturing power. May they, whether in the hospital, a community facility, at home, or homeless, find us eager to be supportive to them in the midst of their illness. May we always encourage them to grasp hold of an identity of worth and value despite the community and self-condemnation. Save us from our ignorance, Lord, that we may not see persons as equal to the illness they have, but rather see persons as having an illness and also possessing much more richness in life.

For the many contributions persons with mental illness make to our lives in teaching us about ourselves, and for the many creative insights, ideas, and works of art which emerge from times of despair and struggle, we give thanks.

For families and neighbors of persons with mental illness, we pray. Fill us, O Lord, with a sense of compassion and openness. Educate us to overcome the fears and stereotypes we have of persons with mental illness. Lead us as we open our hearts and homes, our communities and job opportunities, our houses of worship and communities of faith; and include people living with mental illness in our everyday lives.

For our own mental health also we pray. Help us, O Lord, not to be ashamed of our own difficulties in life—to take the "medicine" we so readily prescribe to others, to not cower in shame and secrecy but with courage share our own struggles betwixt illness and health so that the stigma of mental illness may be shattered.

Lastly, O Lord, help us to develop our spiritual selves, that we may know both how to hold on and how to move on in faith. **Amen.**

(Or:)

In the power of the Spirit, who aids us in our weakness and teaches us to pray, let us offer to God our intercessions for those who, through mental illness, have lost their health and freedom.

Raise up in us a greater awareness of the burden of those who suffer from mental illness. Help us in that awareness to share these burdens.

Lord, in your mercy, **hear our prayer.**

For all who suffer from mental illness, that in seeking help, they may call upon you. Give us, your servants, the courage to respond with open hearts.

Lord, in your mercy, **hear our prayer.**

For all caregivers, that they may be sustained by your patience, understanding and persevering love.

Lord, in your mercy, **hear our prayer.**

For scientists and researchers in health disciplines, as they seek to understand the causes of mental illness; may they work together in an atmosphere of love and mutual respect. Reveal to them the connectedness of body, mind and spirit.

Lord, in your mercy, **hear our prayer.**

For the families, friends and loved ones of those who suffer, that they may find comfort and understanding in the Christian community.

Lord, in your mercy, **hear our prayer.**

That all may be freed from the fears and prejudices about mental illness that limit access to treatment and care.

Lord, in your mercy, **hear our prayer.**

(Or, especially if the service has a focus broader than mental illness:)

Leader: God, our creator,
your will for us and for all your people
is health and salvation:

People: Have mercy on us.

Leader: Jesus Christ, Son of God,
you came that we might have life
and have it in abundance:

People: **Have mercy on us.**

Leader: Holy Spirit,
dwelling within us,
you make us your temples of your presence:

People: **Have mercy on us.**

Leader: To the triune God,
the source of all love and all life,
let us offer our prayers.

For all who are in need of healing . . .

People: **Lord, in your mercy, hear our prayer.**

Leader: For all who are living with mental illness . . .

People: **Lord, in your mercy, hear our prayer.**

Leader: For all who are affected by another person's mental illness . . .

People: **Lord, in your mercy, hear our prayer.**

Leader: For all who are disabled by injury or illness . . .

People: **Lord, in your mercy, hear our prayer.**

Leader: For all who are troubled by confusion or pain . . .

People: **Lord, in your mercy, hear our prayer.**

Leader: For all whose increasing years bring weariness . . .

People: **Lord, in your mercy, hear our prayer.**

Leader: For all about to undergo surgery or other major procedures . . .

People: **Lord, in your mercy, hear our prayer.**

Leader: For all who cannot sleep . . .

People: **Lord, in your mercy, hear our prayer.**

Leader: For all who practice the healing arts . . .

People: **Lord, in your mercy, hear our prayer.**

(Here petitions for specific needs may be offered by the people, if they were not already lifted up in the above litany.)

Leader: Into your hands, O God,
we commend all for whom we pray,

                    trusting in your mercy;
                    through Jesus Christ our Lord.

People: **Amen.**

Leader: O Creator, we pray for all who suffer in mind or spirit. Grant them your peace.

People: **Help us identify mental illness as the disease it is. Help us share our knowledge with others.**

Leader: Grant us the courage and wisdom to help remove the stigma of mental illness from those who suffer.

People: **Give us understanding and openness that we might reach out in love to persons who are ill and their families.**

Leader: Make us channels of care, communicating the needs of those living with mental illness to our faith communities, helping them respond with compassion.

People: **Strengthen us in our efforts, empower us for our task, unite us for action.**

Leader: Let us join in asking:

All: **Lord, in your mercy, hear our prayer. Amen.**

Laying-on of Hands and Anointing with Oil

(Those desiring laying-on of hands and anointing with oil come forward, and bow or kneel. Each may make her or his request known to the minister[s] and/or the elder[s].)

Thanksgiving and Invocation
(One of the following is said. The last is only appropriate if at least some of the people are to be anointed.)

Gracious God, source of all healing,
in Jesus Christ you heal the sick and mend the broken.
By your Spirit,
come upon all who receive the laying-on of hands,
that they might receive your healing touch
and be made whole,
to the glory of Jesus Christ our Redeemer.
Amen.

    (Or:)

Lord and giver of life,

as by your power
the apostles anointed the sick,
and they were healed,
so come, Creator Spirit,
and heal those who now receive the laying on of hands.
Amen.

(Or:)

Gracious God, source of all healing,
in Jesus Christ you heal the sick and mend the broken.
We bless you for this oil pressed from the fruits of the earth,
given to us as a sign of healing and forgiveness,
and of the fullness of life you give.
By your Spirit,
come upon all who receive this ministry of compassion,
that they may receive your healing touch and be made whole,
to the glory of Jesus Christ our Redeemer.
Amen.

LAYING-ON OF HANDS
*(The minister, and/or elders, lay both hands on the head of each individual and, after a brief
silence, say one of the following prayers. During the laying on of hands and anointing, the
congregation may sing a hymn, psalm, or refrain.)*

N., may the Lord Christ grant you and your community healing.

Amen.

(Or:)

N., may the God of all mercy
forgive you your sins,
release you from suffering,
and restore you to wholeness and strength.
Amen.

(Or:)

Spirit of the living God, present with us now,
enter N., in body, mind, and spirit,
and heal *him/her* of all that harms *him/her*.

ANOINTING WITH OIL
*(If the person is also to be anointed, the minister or elder dips her or his thumb in the oil and
makes the sign of the cross on the person's forehead, adding these words:)*

I anoint you with oil,
in the name of the Father,
and of the Son,

and of the Holy Spirit.
Amen.

(Or:)

As you are anointed with this oil,
so may God grant you the anointing of the Holy Spirit.
Amen.

LORD'S PRAYER OR PRAYER

And now, with the confidence of the children of God, let us pray:

(All pray together the Lord's Prayer in the form that is the local custom.)

(Then, those who have received the laying-on of hands [and anointing] are dismissed with these or similar words.)

Go in peace to love and serve the Lord.

HYMN, PSALM, CANTICLE OR SPIRITUAL

BLESSING
(A blessing, such as one of the following, is given, or one of the Benedictions.)

The Lord bless you and keep you.
The Lord be kind and gracious to you.
The Lord look upon you with favor
and give you peace.
Amen.

(Or:)

May the God of hope
fill you with all joy and peace in believing,
so that you may abound in hope
by the power of the Holy Spirit.
Amen.

(Or:)

Lord, God, you are the Alpha and Omega, the beginning and the end. Bless all of us with the gift of your love enabling us gathered here today to be truly signs of that love. Send us, your servants, out from this place. Be our constant companion so that all our efforts to better serve our neighbors, people with mental illness and their families, may be sustained by your presence. May we realize the life-giving power of your love. May it bring us profound peace and unfailing trust and enable us to rely on you. In the silence of our hearts we promise to do all we possibly can do to be truly signs of your love to people with mental illness among us and to their families. **Amen.**

(Or:)

Lord, grant courage and faith to those with mental illness and their families. Grant love and strength to us and all who love them. Grant empathy and insight to those who bring healing.

Grant openness and compassion to our congregation as we reach out to those who are ill and their families. Grant us the perseverance to fight against ignorance and injustice. May we continue to find within ourselves the will to reach out to those in need. And in the love of others, may we know the blessing of community, and the blessing of renewed faith. **Amen.**

(Or:)

All-merciful and loving God, you spoke to us through the prophet Isaiah, saying, "The Spirit of God is upon us because we have been anointed to bring good news to the oppressed, to heal the broken-hearted, to proclaim liberty to the captives, and comfort to all who mourn." We thank you, God, for the opportunity to provide care and comfort for your people in need of healing. Help us to remain strong in our desire to be caring, to seize each opportunity to bring comfort, to never lose our capacity to show concern, to educate ourselves so we can overcome the fear and misunderstanding that comes from ignorance. Help us to live by the words of the beatitude, "Happy are the merciful for they shall obtain mercy." We ask this through your Son, Our Lord, Jesus Christ. **Amen.**

Addictions

"He broke the ropes around his arms."
(Judg. 15:14)

ALCOHOL AND DRUG AWARENESS[39]
(Methodist)

A CALL TO WORSHIP

> **Leader:** O come, let us draw near to Christ our Savior.
>
> **People: That we may touch the hem of his garment and be healed.**
>
> **Leader:** Let us bow down before the giver of life.
>
> **People: That we may share in the truly abundant life.**

A PRAYER OF PREPARATION

Dear Lord, help us recognize that our bodies are temples of your Holy Spirit. Help us to face the reality that abuse of tobacco products, alcohol, prescription drugs, and illicit substances such as heroin, cocaine, marijuana, crack cocaine, PCP, and angel dust is harmful to our health. Help us see that both societal factors and our personal habits contribute to and promote substance abuse. In Christ's name we pray. **Amen.**

A PRAYER FOR HEALING

We beseech thee, O Lord, to seek ways to bring healing and reconciliation to the affluent, oppressed, and disenfranchised people who use and abuse substances. Open our minds and our hearts to see that none of us can escape addressing this issue, whether we live in rural hamlets, comfortable suburbs, quiet towns, or bustling cities. Help us not to blame drug-producing nations for our problems of addiction in drug-consuming nations. Help us seek a more humane and just global society in terms of economics, foreign affairs, and health. We ask that you move us to act with faith and guide us with truth. In the spirit of compassion and unconditional love, we ask your healing grace for the health and well-being of your human family. We ask this in the name of Jesus Christ our Lord. **Amen.**

A Litany for Substance Abuse Awareness

Leader: Drug trafficking, use, and abuse is a global plague that threatens the health and survival of the human race.

People: In the beginning, God created the heavens and earth.

Leader: Drug trafficking is a 500 billion dollar business per year.

People: The eyes of the Lord are everywhere, keeping watch on the wicked and the good.

Leader: The market for illicit drugs in the United States is 50 to 100 billion dollars a year.

People: We wrestle not against flesh and blood, but against principalities, against powers, against the rulers of the darkness of this world, against spiritual wickedness in high places.

Leader: In 1996, 316 tons of cocaine were seized worldwide.[40]

People: Rescue us, O God, from the hand of the wicked, from the grasp of the unjust and cruel.

Leader: In 1998, 1,160 tons of cocaine were seized in the United States.[41]

People: Blessed is the nation whose God is the Lord, the people whom the Lord has chosen as a heritage.

Leader: In the United States, 60 million people are addicted to cigarettes, 13.4 million to alcohol, and 4 million to prescription drugs which are *legal* substances.[42]

People: Happy are those who take refuge in God "instead of things of this world."

Leader: In the United States, 16.6 million people are known to be addicted to *illegal* substances such as marijuana, heroin, cocaine, and pain relievers.[43]

People: The Lord looks down from heaven and sees all peoples; the Lord sits enthroned and looks forth on all inhabitants of the earth, fashioning the hearts of them all and observing all their deeds.

Leader: Over 5 million of the 60 million women 15 to 44 years of age, the child-bearing years, have used an illicit drug. There are few facilities that treat addicted pregnant women.

People: And Jesus said: "Daughters of Jerusalem, do not weep for me; weep for yourselves and for your children. For the time will come when you will say, 'Blessed are the barren women, the wombs that never bore and breasts that never nursed!'"

Leader: 375,000 newborn babies may be damaged by maternal drug addiction.

People: **These are they who have come out of the great tribulation. . . . Never again will they hunger or thirst, and God will wipe away every tear from their eyes.**

Leader: Drug-exposed babies are more likely to be born prematurely, with an increased risk of infant mortality and childhood disabilities.

People: **And Jesus said, "Whoever welcomes a little child like this in my name welcomes me."**

Leader: AIDS and HIV (human immunodeficiency virus) infection in babies is linked to drug abuse in adults.

People: **Suffer the little children to come unto me and do not hinder them, for the Kingdom of God belongs to such as these. . . . And he took the children in his arms, put his hands on them, and blessed them.**

Leader: The third-highest death rate in the United States is alcohol-related.

People: **Wine is a mocker and beer a brawler. Whoever is led astray by them is not wise.**

Leader: Tobacco products cause more health-related problems and deaths than all other substances used in the United States.

People: **We know that our bodies are God's temple and that God's spirit lives in us. If anyone destroys God's temple, God will destroy them; for God's temple is sacred, and we are that temple.**

Leader: Drug use and abuse occur more often in highly intelligent, well-educated, middle to upper income individuals and families.

People: **Rich and poor have this in common: the Lord is the Maker of them all.**

Leader: Drug use and abuse occur in all professions, in all ethnic groups, in all social classes, and in all neighborhoods.

People: **Who can say, "I have kept my heart pure; I am clean and without sin?"**

Leader: Persons who abuse harmful substances are among both regular churchgoers and those who do not go to church.

People: **In Jesus' spirit and name, we are ready to accept the challenge of social holiness. We will make this a high priority in our lives. Lord, we stand before you ready. Help our unreadiness. _Amen_.**[44]

A PRAYER OF COMMITMENT

Lord, you are calling us as Christians to walk around the walls of Jericho to help create drug-free environments. Give us strength, Lord. As Jesus challenged his disciples to "interpret the signs of the times," we, too, must interpret the signs of these times as a call for action. Help us share our brothers' and sisters' disease. We all are recovering from something, especially from denial that addiction affects each and every one of us. As we face one day at a time, we ask for your blessings in recovering our spiritual health and well-being. Thank you for your healing grace, in the name of Jesus, our Guardian and Protector. **Amen.**

LEAVING ADDICTION[45]
(Presbyterian)

ONE: ADMIT . . . GET READY

GATHERING

REFLECTION

> God, grant me the serenity to accept the things I cannot change,
>> the courage to change the things I can,
>> and the wisdom to know the difference.

> (*Open yourself again to the power of the beginning . . .*
>> *the new beginning, the first step . . . new life,*
>>> *new wisdom and new direction. . . .*)

WELCOME

PRAY TOGETHER

God, I offer myself to you—to build with me and to do with me as you will, as a part of whatever families you give me to be in. . . .
Bring me to a fuller awareness of my inner wisdom which comes to me from you through those I've come to know. Help me to learn what it would teach me about my limitations and my attempts to control things. Turn me to a clearer understanding of the richness of the spiritual wells you have created deep within me . . . in order to find there the new life I crave so much and that you have promised through your servants before me. In the power of your name, I pray, Amen.

SING TOGETHER   #525   PrH   "Here I Am, Lord"

PASSAGES

(*Reflections on growth and limitations, on gains and losses, on victories and struggles; closing, in unison, with:*)

. . . My Creator, I am now willing that you should have all of me—good and bad. I pray that you now remove from me every single defect of character which stands in the way

of my usefulness to you and those around me. Grant me strength, as I continue to grow in your grace . . . to keep myself humble in the management of my own affairs and in my opinions of others; to be ever ready to admit my limitations; and to use those limitations as my lifeline to your love, your grace and your power. Amen.

SING TOGETHER   #316   PrH   "Breathe On Me, Breath of God"

READINGS AND REFLECTIONS   Rom. 7:15; 8:34–39
"A Moment of Clarity"

RESPONSE   #280   PrH   "Amazing Grace" (verse three only)

COMMITMENT
"Lord, make me a channel of thy peace . . ."
St. Francis of Assisi Prayer

SING TOGETHER   #572   UMH   "Pass It On"

BLESSING, CLOSING, AND RESPONSE
(Forming a circle, we join hands, say the Lord's Prayer and then sing together:)

God be with you till we meet again.
Loving counsels guide, uphold you,
With a Shepherd's care enfold you.
God be with you till we meet again.

FELLOWSHIP . . . DEPARTURE . . . TO GATHER AGAIN

TWO: THERE IS HELP

GATHERING

(Quiet time for reflection)

God, grant me the serenity to accept the things I cannot change,
the courage to change the things I can,
and the wisdom to know the difference.

(Recall . . . the feeling you had when someone affirmed your inner wisdom and sense—learning that you could have confidence in your inner voice.)

WELCOME

CALL TO WORSHIP
(in unison)

God, I offer myself to you—to build with me and to do with me as you will. Relieve me of the bondage of self that I may better do your will. Help me to grow through my diffi-

culties, that overcoming them I may bear witness to those I would help of your power, your love, and your way of life. May I do your will always! Amen.

SONG OF PRAISE   #469   PrH   "Morning Has Broken"

PRAYER OF PASSAGE

(closing, in unison, with:)

... My Creator, I am now willing that you should have all of me—good and bad. I pray that you now remove from me every single defect of character which stands in the way of my usefulness to you and those around me. Grant me strength, as I go from here, to do your bidding. Amen.

SONG OF MEDITATION   #38   PrH   "Troubled Souls Go Free"   Words by Tom Walsh
Tune: "It Came Upon a Midnight Clear"

It came to me one night alone,
That I was a troubled soul.
But a light turned on inside
And touched my worried soul.

I heard this voice inside me say
"If you are a troubled soul,
just look for me and trust in me,
and I will set you free."

Peace on the earth good will to all
Who have a troubled soul.
For it's God's light that's touched your soul,
So walk alone no more.

Thank God for all undying light
That's touched our troubled souls.
For now we're free to love and see
All life's abundant love.

READINGS AND REFLECTIONS   From Matt. 11, Ps. 62   *"Learning to trust beyond ourselves
. . . Wholeness"*

RESPONSE   #280   PrH   "Amazing Grace" (one verse)

DISCOVERIES AND JOURNEYS

(discussion and sharing)

(Close in unison with:)   The Prayer of St. Francis

SONG OF COMMITMENT   #525   PrH   "Here I Am, Lord"

CLOSING BLESSING AND RESPONSE

(Forming a circle, we join hands, say the Lord's Prayer, and then sing together:)

God be with you till we meet again.
Loving counsels guide, uphold you,
With a Shepherd's care enfold you.
God be with you till we meet again.

THREE: WE'LL TAKE HELP

GATHERING

(Quiet time for reflection)

> God, grant me the serenity to accept the things I cannot change,
>   the courage to change the things I can,
>   and the wisdom to know the difference.

*(**Picture** . . . Someone leaning hard, struggling before a fierce wind . . . squared off against it, buffeted, bent into it, each step a tremendous effort. . . . There are at least three options: Continue to struggle into the wind; Go limp and be blown wherever the wind takes one; Stop. Turn sideways and wait for the wind to blow by. . . .)*

WELCOME

CALL TO WORSHIP
(in unison)

God, I offer myself to you—to build with me and to do with me as you will. Relieve me of the bondage of self that I may better do your will. Help me to grow through my difficulties, that overcoming them I may bear witness to those I would help of your power, your love, and your way of life. May I do your will always! Amen.

PRAISE   #544   PrH   "Day Is Done"

PRAYER OF PASSAGE
(closing, in unison, with:)

. . . My Creator, I am now willing that you should have all of me—good and bad. I pray that you now remove from me every single defect of character which stands in the way of my usefulness to you and those around me. Grant me strength, as I go from here, to do your bidding. Amen.

MEDITATION SONG   #319   PrH   "Spirit"

READINGS, REFLECTIONS   From Psalm 111, John 15   *"Fullness of Joy . . . Letting Go"*

RESPONSE   #280   PrH   "Amazing Grace" (one verse)

DISCOVERIES, JOURNEYS

(discussion and sharing)

(Close in unison with:)   The Prayer of St. Francis

COMMITMENT   #525   PrH   "Here I Am, Lord"

BLESSING AND RESPONSE
(Forming a circle, we join hands, say the Lord's Prayer, and then sing together:)

> **God be with you till we meet again.**
> **Loving counsels guide, uphold you,**
> **With a Shepherd's care enfold you.**
> **God be with you till we meet again.**

CELEBRATING THE MIRACLE OF RECOVERY[46]
(Presbyterian)

ADDICTION AWARENESS WORSHIP SERVICE

SILENT MEDITATION

Perhaps one of the greatest rewards of meditation and prayer is the sense of belonging that comes to us. We no longer live in a completely hostile world. We are no longer lost and frightened and purposeless. The moment we catch even a glimpse of God's will, the moment we begin to see truth, justice, and love as the real and eternal things in life, we are no longer deeply disturbed by all the seeming evidence to the contrary that surrounds us in purely human affairs. We know that God lovingly watches over us. We know that when we turn to (God), all will be well with us, here and hereafter.[47]

PRELUDE

GREETING

Welcome to worship this Sunday as we gather to celebrate the miracles of recovery. The Presbyterian Church has set aside a Sunday for congregations to intentionally focus on the issue of addictions. Friends, we have all been touched in one way or another by alcoholism, drug use or other addictions. We know many people who have found help through 12 step programs. Some of these programs use our building. We want to be a support to people in recovery and the programs that help them. We as a worshiping community hope to be a part of the spiritual solution of recovery. Our service today uses many of the phrases and readings familiar to people in recovery groups. We pray there will be a special blessing for each one of us as we share in this hour of worship.

So expect a miracle and let us worship God!

INVOCATION

God, as humans, Christians, Presbyterians, people of recovery, help us realize that we are all becoming who you would have us be. It is a process of progress, not perfection. Open our hearts and minds to your will for us. Open our hearts and minds to each other, that through the community of faith, your love will be perfected, through Jesus Christ our Lord. **Amen.**

(Or:)

God, we offer ourselves to you to build with us and to do with us as you will. Relieve us of the bondage of self, that we may better do your will. Take away our difficulties, that victory over them may bear witness to those we would help of your power, your love and your way of life. May we do your will always. **Amen.**[48]

CALL TO WORSHIP
(Pulpit/lectern sides of sanctuary or a "Greek Chorus" of participants at front of sanctuary.)

Pulpit: We admitted we were powerless, that our lives were unmanageable.

Lectern: God is our refuge and strength, a very present help in trouble.

Pulpit: We came to believe that a power greater than ourselves could restore us to sanity.

Lectern: Therefore, we will not fear though the earth should change, though the mountains shake in the heart of the sea; though its waters roar and foam, though the mountains tremble with its tumult.

Pulpit: We made a decision to turn our will and our lives over to the care of God, as we understand God.

Lectern: There is a river whose streams make glad the city of God, the holy habitation of the Most High. God is in the midst of it, it shall not be moved; God will help right early.

Pulpit: We made a searching and fearless inventory of ourselves, admitted to God, ourselves and another human being the exact nature of our wrongs.

Lectern: Come, behold the works of the Lord; how God has wrought desolations in the earth. God makes wars cease to the end of the earth; God breaks the bow and shatters the spear; God burns the chariots with fire!

**All: Be still, and know that I am God.
I am exalted among the nations,
I am exalted in the earth!**[49]

(Or:)

**God, we offer ourselves to you,
And ask that You guide us and build us
To serve Your will.
Relieve us all of the bondage of self will,**

> **That we may do Your will and live as witnesses**
> **of Your power and Your love.**[50]

CONFESSION
(unison)
God, we confess that we have not always believed your promises to us. We have failed to realize how much you love us. We have been unable to receive your love. If we will stand still for just a short time, it happens. We experience the beauty of the creation, the warmth of the sunshine, the loving presence of family and friends. God, slow us down, so that we might feel your Presence. We want to experience life and love anew. We want to participate fully in your creation. We begin again now in the silence.

(Or:)

God, we confess our lack of power. We sometimes feel helpless, alone and weak. We realize that we know only a little, and each time we try to do everything on our own, we fail. We need your power. We want to rely on you daily to guide us to do the things that are necessary for our life. We want your power to be ours, so that we can stand strong in your world. We need to be reassured that death to our old ways need not be feared and that true life is found in YOU.

(A time for silent prayer and reflection.)

ASSURANCE

In creation, we see God's power and majesty. In Jesus Christ, we see ultimate love for us in action. In the Holy Spirit, we see ongoing encouragement and power every day. Our God is a great God! Jesus has forgiven our sins and made a right relationship between us, once and for all. God has given us all the gifts necessary to do the work of a believer and experience life fully. Praise God for love and healing!

RESPONSIVE HYMN #191 PrH "God Is Our Refuge and Our Strength"

SHARING THE PEACE

RESPONSORIAL PSALM OR ANTHEM

PRAYER OF ILLUMINATION

SCRIPTURE READING   First Lesson: Ruth 3:1–5; 4:13–17
                      Second Lesson: Heb. 9:24–28
                      Gospel: Mark 12:38–44

SERMON
(The following are notes to aid in preparing the sermon.)

In view of the social impact of substance abuse, we as Presbyterians accept the challenges of conscience and informed responsibility, for ourselves and others in faith and action.

Individuals are asked to prayerfully explore their substance use behaviors and make decisions about personal substance use based on our church's confessions and teachings.

We will spend time this week in prayer, individually and with members of our households, asking for guidance and support for our family, our congregation and our denomination.

The General Assembly urges the following guide: Abstinence from manufacture, sale, purchase, possession, or use of illicit drugs. Restraint in use of over-the-counter drug preparations, caffeine, and the emotional use of food.

We will reflect on the use of substances in our life and in our household.

Study and reaffirmation of General Assembly positions on abstinence and appropriate use of alcohol, as well as the abstinence from tobacco products, are encouraged.

We will share our faith decisions and reflections on substance abuse with others in relationships of trust and respect. The elements of healing include honesty, confession, repentance, forgiveness and faithful action.

Recognizing our responsibility to the wider community, we are prepared to confront, challenge and report substance abuse, manufacture, sale, purchase, possession.

During this week, our prayers will be directed to all who suffer from addictions. We will ask for guidance and direction and we will review our own behavior.

In honesty and humility, have you responded to God's love and wisdom for yourself and others regarding the use of alcohol, tobacco and other substances?

Minister: Let us pray: God, we give you thanks for this day. For the opportunity to gather in this place to celebrate the miracles of grace and healing through recovery and talk honestly about addictions.

We give thanks for the many people who work with alcoholics and addicts; their service has made relief from the effects of these spiritual diseases possible for so many. We pray that this church along with community agencies and 12–step programs can be a part of the spiritual solution in freedom from substance abuse and compulsive behaviors.

Each one of us has a particular need in this area. Some of us are recovering from addictions or the effects of parental and generational addictions. Some of us struggle with our behaviors or with family members and friends who still suffer. Some of us are interested, concerned, curious. We care about our family, our congregation, our community, our church, our society.

Hear now as we offer prayers of concern for ourselves and others. . . .

God, open our hearts and minds to new awareness, new understanding, new action, that we might experience our own healing more deeply and grow in compassion as we serve others in your world.

All: **To heal the hurt of substance abuse, its pain, violence, alienation and despair, we pledge our help to speak aloud the words of grace.   Amen.**

CALL FOR THE OFFERING

THE LORD'S SUPPER
(optional)

HYMN   #505   PrH   "Be Known to Us in Breaking Bread"

CHARGE AND BENEDICTION

God will show us how to create fellowships that support us spiritually. We only need to rely on God.[51]

Abandon yourself to God, as you understand God. Admit your faults to (God) and your friends. Give freely of what you find and join us. We shall be with you in the Fellowship of the Spirit. May God bless you and keep you—until then.[52]

(Or:)

God has shown you what is good.
What does the Lord require of you
but to do justice, and to love kindness,
and to walk humbly with your God?
                              Mic. 6:8

The Lord look upon you with favor
and give you peace. Amen
                    Num. 6:24–26

POSTLUDE

Domestic Violence and Sexual Abuse

"It was by accident that he killed a man."
(Deut. 19:6)

STRIKING TERROR NO MORE[53]
(Ecumenical)

SERMON THEMES[54]

BREAKING THE SILENCE OF ABUSE

As Christians we have often been reluctant to acknowledge that abuse happens in our homes and our churches. These Scriptures illustrate that God's people have always struggled with sexual and domestic violence. These biblical stories assist us in naming violence in our own lives.

Biblical Texts   Judg. 11:29–40; 2 Sam. 13:1–19; Ps. 55:1–15, 20–21; John 8:31–32

SUFFERING, ABANDONMENT, HOPE

These texts demonstrate the range of emotions that survivors may feel. The journey toward healing involves intense pain and intense feelings, including feelings of being abandoned by God. Caring church people can become a source of hope when they provide safe places for pain and a whole range of feelings to be expressed.

Biblical Texts   Ps. 22; Ps. 27; Isa. 25:4–5; Rom. 8:31–39

CHURCH'S RESPONSE TO SURVIVORS

Sometimes our tendency is to blame the "victim" for the abuse they have suffered. These passages demonstrate that Jesus honors people's pain and suffering. Jesus' healing power is demonstrated by his compassionate nonjudgmental response to suffering.

Biblical Texts   John 9:1–7; John 4:7–14; Luke 8:40–48; Luke 10:29–37

CHURCH'S RESPONSE TO PERPETRATORS

Responding to perpetrators in our midst may be one of the most difficult challenges we face. Our tendency might be to avoid or to "shun" offenders. These biblical texts emphasize naming offenses as sin, holding offenders accountable for their actions, and challenging them to repent, to turn away from evil.

Biblical Texts   Matt. 18:15–18; Gal. 6:1–2

Calls to Worship

God of compassion, you feel our pain and cry with us in our passion. God of justice, you rage with us against the injustice of our experience. Be with us today.

We gather today in sadness to remember all victims of violence, but especially those women and children who have been victims of violence in their own homes.

We come together because there is so much violence experienced every day by the vulnerable ones in our world: countless women, children, and men.[55]

> **Leader:** We are gathered in the presence of God, who asks us to choose between life and death, blessing and cursing.
>
> **People:** **We are gathered like the people of Israel, who were challenged to choose the way of life.**
>
> **Leader:** Like them, we often follow the ways of death.
>
> **People:** **Yet, like them, we have the freedom each day to begin anew by the grace of God.**
>
> **Leader:** By our presence here, we are saying that we want to choose life one more time.
>
> **All:** **Let us praise the God of love and life who has called us to this place. Amen.**[56]

Come to Christ, the living bread, who satisfies those who hunger and thirst for what is right. Come to Christ, who gives living water, that you may never thirst again.

Come to Christ, that being filled yourself, you may minister to the hunger and thirst of others. Come to God, in worship and praise, through Jesus Christ who gives us life.[57]

We gather today to worship a living God, a God who hears our cries, shares our tears, knows our anger, and is steadfast now and always.

We gather today to be in each other's presence as we remember, confess, name, and respond to the violence in our lives, in our families, our churches and our communities.

Let us walk this way together.[58]

> **One:** Come, all who are weary and heavy-laden; come, all who seek God's rest and peace.

People: **We come with reluctance, knowing the pain and suffering and fear of our lives, fearing that they may be revealed.**

One: Come before our God, who knows the hidden depths of each heart, and knowing, loves us completely.

People: **We come with expectation, seeking out of our confusion and fear the light and hope of God's love.**

One: Come, all who seek transformation. Let us worship our God who offers us new life.[59]

INVITATION TO CONFESSION

Dear Friends, God knows and understands the heart of each one of us. In that understanding, God reaches out lovingly to call us to repent of all our wrongdoing and to seek new ways of living with one another. When we confess our sins as a community, we do not usually separate anyone from the whole body, but make our confession as one unit. Today, however, we want to be especially sensitive to the fact that the body of Christ is divided, for some are abused, some are abusers, and some condone the abuse by looking away. As the community of faith, let us join with God and with one another in making our confession before God.

A LITANY OF CONFESSION

All: **God of wisdom and mercy, you have created a world of beauty, a world where each one has a special and honored place in your love. Forgive us that some of us have not honored one another as you have honored each of us. O God, in your mercy, forgive us.**

One: O God, for all the times when some of us have not valued ourselves as people created in your image . . .

People: **O God, in your mercy, forgive us.**

One: O God, for all the times when we have known of the suffering of others but turned away from it . . .

People: **O God, in your mercy, forgive us.**

One: O God, for all the times when some of us have seen pain and blamed it on those who suffer . . .

People: **O God, in your mercy, forgive us.**

One: O God, for all the times when some of us have cried out in pain but blamed ourselves, for the times when we burdened ourselves with guilt when we suffered injustice at another's hand . . .

People: **O God, in your mercy, help us, befriend us, hear our cry, comfort us, send us a friend, let someone see . . .**

One: O God, for all the times when some of us have heard cries of pain and not believed them . . .

People: **O God, in your mercy, forgive us.**

One: O God, for all the times when we alone, or as a church, have not sought to end pain and bring about your justice . . .

People: **O God, in your mercy, forgive us.**

One: O God, for all the times when we ourselves have been the cause of human suffering . . .

People: **O God, in your mercy, forgive us.**

One: Loving God, you alone know how these burdens weigh on our souls. Forgive us, free us, and show us the paths of love you would have us choose. **Amen.**[60]

A LITANY OF CONFESSION

Leader: Estimates range from 960,000 incidents of violence against a current or former spouse, boyfriend, or girlfriend per year to 3.9 million women who are physically abused by their husbands or live-in partners per year.[61]

All: **"There is a balm in Gilead to make the wounded whole, there is a balm in Gilead to heal the sin-sick soul."**

Leader: Thirty-five to forty percent of battered women attempt suicide. Wife abuse accounts for 25 percent of suicides by all U.S. women and 50 percent of suicides by African American women.

All: **"There is a balm in Gilead to make the wounded whole, there is a balm in Gilead to heal the sin-sick soul."**

Leader: One in five women is raped in her lifetime. Seventy-eight percent of rapes are committed by relatives, friends, or neighbors. During the 1996–1997 school year, there were an estimated 4,000 incidents of rape or other types of sexual assault in public schools across the country.[62]

All: **"There is a balm in Gilead to make the wounded whole, there is a balm in Gilead to heal the sin-sick soul."**

Leader: Eighty-four to ninety percent of child sexual abuse cases are never reported to law enforcement or protective services agencies. In over 80 percent of reported cases, the perpetrator is someone known to the family.

All: **"There is a balm in Gilead to make the wounded whole, there is a balm in Gilead to heal the sin-sick soul."**

Leader: Over one million older adults are physically, financially, and emotionally abused by relatives or loved ones annually.

All: **"There is a balm in Gilead to make the wounded whole, there is a balm in Gilead to heal the sin-sick soul."**

Leader: The likelihood of a case [of elder abuse] being reported depends on state laws, local police practices, Social Services assistance levels, court-related activities, and the people involved. . . . One thing is certain: the vast majority of cases in all likelihood don't come to public attention.

All: **"There is a balm in Gilead to make the wounded whole, there is a balm in Gilead to heal the sin-sick soul."**

Leader: Disabled children are two to three times more likely than their nondisabled peers to be sexually abused.

All: **"There is a balm in Gilead to make the wounded whole, there is a balm in Gilead to heal the sin-sick soul."**

Leader: One child is killed each day in the U.S. by a family member, and 90 percent of these children are under five. Half of the children killed are infants in homes where their mothers are being battered. Children themselves are at great risk for abuse and serious neglect.

All: **"There is a balm in Gilead to make the wounded whole, there is a balm in Gilead to heal the sin-sick soul."**[63]

PRAYERS OF CONFESSION

O God, You know our hearts, our minds, our feelings, and our thoughts, You know the heavy stones that weigh down our spirits. We cry for all that cannot be saved. Comfort us as we mourn the loss of women's lives to violence. Strengthen us as we break the silence, confront evil, and cry out for justice. Help us see the chains that bind us and the chains that we place around others. Set us free to walk in the fullness of life that is promised to all people. Let us live into that promise with every moment of our lives. **Amen.**[64]

O merciful one, we confess that by our silence and inaction we have passed by on the other side, leaving a sister suffering by the side of the road. We confess that in our fear, we have hesitated and turned away from life, adding to the pain and suffering.
Bring us to repentance.
O Holy One,
Open our eyes to see the violence in our lives, within us and among us.
Open our mouths to name what we see and to acknowledge our own pain.
Open our hearts to let in the pain and suffering of family members, friends, child victims, adult survivors, and our neighbors.
Open our mouths to call to account those who have harmed others.
Be merciful and bring us back to life in Christ. **Amen.**[65]

Assurance of Pardon

Sisters and brothers, hear the good news! There is no sin so large, no shortcoming so great that can separate us from the love of God. For all who truly desire new life, God offers forgiveness and new opportunities for healing and wholeness in our lives. Accept God's grace and live![66]

Prayers of the People

Prayer of Dedication

We offer ourselves to you, O God our Creator. We offer our hands.
Use healing touch to comfort sisters, brothers, and children who are afraid.
We offer our eyes and ears. May we see and hear the signs and stories of violence so
    that all may have someone with them in their pain and confusion.
We offer our hearts and our tears as their hurt and sorrow echo within us.
We offer our own stories of violence.
May we be healed as we embrace each other.
We offer our anger. Make it a passion for justice.
We offer our faith, our hope, our love. May our encounters with violence bring us closer
    to you and to each other.
All this we ask through Jesus Christ who knows the pain of violence. **Amen.**[67]

God of Love and Justice

God of love and justice,
    we long for peace within and peace without.
We long for harmony in our families,
    for serenity in the midst of struggle.
We long for the day when our homes
    will be a dwelling place for your love.
Yet we confess that we are often anxious;
    we do not trust each other,
And we harbor violence.
    We are not willing to take the risks
And make the sacrifices that love requires.
    Look upon us with kindness and grace.
Rule in our homes and in all the world;
    show us how to walk in your paths,
    through the mercy of our Savior. **Amen.**[68]

God of Peace and Comfort

God of peace and comfort,
we pray for those who are not safe in their own homes
or with people they care about because of domestic violence.
Give strength and courage to those who are abused and battered.
Grant repentance to those who abuse the ones they love.

Help all of us to nurture one another in the spirit of love and peace proclaimed by Jesus Christ, in whose name we pray. **Amen.**[69]

CHARGES AND BENEDICTIONS

Now, go and breathe deeply, for each breath is from God;
go and serve gently, for the earth and its people are fragile;
go with energy and strength, for God knows your every need, and God's Spirit will grant
   you peace.[70]

Stay with us, O God,
for the day is far spent
and we have not yet recognized Your face
in each of our brothers and sisters.
   Stay with us, O God,
   for the day is far spent
   and we have not yet shared Your bread
   in grace with our brothers and sisters.
Stay with us, O God,
for the day is far spent
and we have not listened to Your Word
in the words of our brothers and sisters.
   Stay with us, O God,
   for the day is far spent
   and our hearts are still so slow to believe
   that you had to die in order to rise again.
Stay with us, O God,
because our very night becomes day
when you are there.[71]

LITANIES

Let Love Be Genuine

Group One: Society says, "Don't worry about taking advantage of others."

Group Two: But the Scripture says, "Let love be genuine."

Group One: Our culture says, "Being male is an asset; being female is a liability."

Group Two: But the Scripture says, "Hate what is evil, hold fast to what is good."

Group One: Society says, "Look out for Number One."

Group Two: But the Scripture says, "Love one another with mutual affection."

Group One: Our culture says, "Turn your head the other way; someone else will eventually help."

Group Two: But the Scripture says, "Outdo one another in showing honor."

All: **O God, open our ears to hear clearly your words of Scripture. Give us a strong resolve to live our lives as the people you desire us to be—people of loving and peace-filled ways.** *(Litany based on Rom 12:9–10)*[72]

A Litany of Courage

Leader: Paul writes, "So then, putting away falsehood, let all of us speak the truth to our neighbors." O God in whom there is no falsehood, teach us how to express our feelings in healthy ways. Help us to find our voices to name and confront domestic violence, especially when it is happening to those we know—or even to ourselves. With boldness we pray.

All: **Give us courage to speak the truth, O God.**

Leader: Paul writes that we are members of one another. O God of community, help us to remember that we are not alone. Thank you for the persons in our lives with whom we can share our joys as well as our pains. With boldness we pray.

All: **Give us courage to speak the truth, O God.**

Leader: Paul writes, "Be angry but do not sin; do not let the sun go down on your anger." O Source of Justice, help us to remember that you—not we—are God. Show us how to live in right relationship with all of your children. Grant that we may never take for granted those about whom we care the most. With boldness we pray.

All: **Give us courage to speak the truth, O God.**

Leader: So be it. Go in peace and safety.[73]

Remembering

Leader 1: O God of compassion, you feel our pain and cry with us in our passion.

All: **God of justice, you rage with us against the injustice of our experiences of violence and abuse. Be with us today.**

Leader 1: As sisters of faith and hope, gathered here today, we remember:

Left Side: Our mothers, who had few choices; who did what they had to; who resisted sometimes quietly, sometimes loudly; who carried the secrets of their abuse silently in their hearts.

Right Side: Our sisters, who were made the scapegoat; who said, "No!" but to no avail; who thought they were protecting us; who were given tranquilizers to quiet their rage; who carried the secrets of their abuse silently in their hearts.

Left Side: Our neighbors, whose cries we heard in the night, whose bruises we saw in the day, who fought back and paid the price, who carried the secret of their abuse silently in their hearts.

Right Side: Our girlfriends, who spent so much time at our house, not wanting to go home; whom everyone thought were just shy and quiet; who carried the secrets of their abuse silently in their hearts.

Left Side: Ourselves, who may have tried to tell but were ignored; who were not protected by anyone; who were not believed; who carry the secrets of our abuse silently in our hearts.

Right Side: We remember and mourn the loss of childhood; the loss of creativity; the loss of vocation; the loss of relationships; the loss of time; the cost of resources required for healing; the enormous waste of humanity caused by sexual and domestic violence.

All: **We remember and mourn those who have not survived; whose lives were taken by someone's violence; who died in despair never knowing justice.**[74]

TOWARD HEALING SEXUAL WOUNDS[75]
(Nondenominational)

PREPARATION
(Silent meditation while instrumental music plays in candlelit sanctuary.)

INVITATION

This is an opportunity to reflect on the healing of sexual wounds. Join with me for this brief time together on these difficult issues.

Leader: Some thoughts towards the healing of sexual wounds,
and towards freedom from compulsive behavior:

Remember the occasion of your wounding,
how you were hurt by another or by yourself.

Remember the person who used you, abused you,
or the person you yourself used.

Remember when sexual desire took you over
and you became less than human,
when force blotted out care.
Remember when you were overpowered by another's desire.

Let your feelings rise—grief, anger, fear,
and express them with noise and movement.
Ask somebody to be with you as you do this,
a person who will simply receive you
and your feelings together, without comment.

Lay quietly on one side the spirit of possessiveness,
of the unmet ancient needs for comfort,
for recognition, for affirmation.
Lay aside too the spirit of violence,
the desire for revenge;
turn to self-acceptance, a sense of inner worth,
a willingness to stand and to be and to affirm.

Let thoughts drop into the heart,
let desires rise through the heart.
Let love spread through the heart.

Cherish your flesh-body.

Breathe into your loneliness and go deep,
and then move gently into what you choose to do next.

Be thankful for athletic beauty
(even if the psalmist said
that God takes no delight in any man's legs).

Laugh at yourself long and out loud.

All these will never be enough
to assuage all the pain.
Simply bear whatever pain that will not shift.
There may be no meaning yet.[76]

HYMN   #171   PrH   "The King of Love My Shepherd Is"

Leader: Now we invite those who wish to come forward for anointing, saying

N, through faith in the power and the will
of our Savior Jesus Christ
to make you whole and holy,
to consecrate you with joy
for ever deeper service and friendship,
to give you courage
to go through the narrow gates of your journey,
I anoint you with oil
in the name of God,
who gives you life,
bears your pain,
and makes you whole.
Amen.[77]

HYMN   #394   PrH   "There Is a Balm in Gilead"
(*Sung meditatively while people come forward.*)

BENEDICTION

FROM VICTIM TO VICTORY[78]
(Christian Reformed Church)

(See explanatory notes on pp. 201–206.)

ENTERING GOD'S PRESENCE[a]

SONGS   #1005   CMP   "AWESOME GOD"
         #398   CMP   "King of Kings"

GOD GREETS US[b]

WE PRAISE GOD FOR HIS PRESENCE[c]

HYMN   #244   PsH   "God Himself Is with Us" (stanza 1)

WE CONFESS WHO WE ARE

LITANY OF CONFESSION AND PARDON

WE PASS THE PEACE OF GOD TO EACH OTHER[d]

> The peace of God be with you.
> **And also with you.**

GOD SPEAKS TO US OF HIS WILL

PRAYER FOR ILLUMINATION   #278   PsH   "Holy Spirit, Mighty God"[e]

SCRIPTURE   Matthew 18:15–35

SERMON   From Victim to Victory, a New Healing[f]

WE RESPOND TO GOD'S WORD

HYMN   #261   PsH   "LORD, WE CRY TO YOU FOR HELP"[g]

CONFESSION OF FAITH   "OUR WORLD BELONGS TO GOD"[h]

PRAYERS OF INTERCESSION[i]

OFFERING[j]

GOD SENDS US OUT[k]

HYMN   #489   PsH   "WHEN LIKE A RIVER"

BLESSING

POSTLUDE

WORSHIP NOTES

a. A music worship leader other than the pastor will ask the congregation to stand. An over-head projector may be used since the songs are sung as a medley. The medley begins with "King of Kings" twice through, each time a little faster. Then "Awesome God" is sung three times through, with the tempo picking up slightly. The medley is closed with a return to "King of Kings," sung twice through, the last time very fast. Percussion and clapping are important. In addition, instruments such as guitar, piano, and maybe a bass could be used. Note that these are upbeat songs in a minor key. The intent is to create the feeling of antici-pation that the Jews might have experienced while heading to the temple.

b. Second worship leader leads in the greeting:

> God greets us as he did Israel, centuries ago. In Jeremiah God says: I have loved you with an everlasting love; I have drawn you with loving kindness. I will build you up again and you will be rebuilt (Jer. 31:3–4).

c. Second worship leader:

> That God who loves us enough to rebuild our lives is here! Sing praise to his presence by turning with me to "God Himself Is with Us," the first stanza.

LITANY OF CONFESSION AND PARDON

A JOURNEY FROM EARTHLY REALITY TO HEAVENLY LIGHT

Based on Psalm 130

Leader: O Lord, we come into this place singing praise.
Yet there is darkness in our hearts.
Come to us in that dark loneliness.
Hear us as we are:
afraid of your light,
afraid of your blinding honesty.
Hear us Lord, as we cry:

People: Lord, have mercy.

Leader: Lord, we come to this place washed with soap,
perfumed with deodorants,
hiding behind our clothes and jewelry.
But your light is piercing.
You know our sins.
How can we stand so naked?

People: Lord of light, have mercy.

Leader: Lord, the world says "get even."
But you tell us to feel our pain and forgive seventy-seven times.
That is scary, Lord.
We do not want to be vulnerable.
We fear the honesty of your forgiveness.

People: Lord of the universe, have mercy.

Leader: Lord, our only hope is your unfailing love.
The world is naked and empty without it.
Cover our nakedness with the cloth of your love.
Shine your light into our darkness.
Redeem us from our fears and loneliness.
Lord Jesus, your blood can make us cleaner than any soap.
Wash our sins from our naked frames.

People: Lord Jesus Christ, have mercy.

(A brief silence)

Leader: Lord Jesus, as we look at your empty tomb;

People: We remember

Leader: the light of your love.

People: We remember

Leader: the brightness of your light.

People: We remember

Leader: the forgiving power of your bright spirit.

People: We remember

Leader: the love of your bloody act of forgiveness.

People: We remember,

Leader: and our darkness,
loneliness,
vengeful spirit,

> and sins
> cease to exist.

People: **We praise you Lord Jesus,**

Leader: for your unfailing love.

People: **We praise you Lord Jesus,**

Leader: for remembering us.

People: **We praise you Lord Jesus,**

Leader: for hearing our cry.

People: **We praise you**

Leader: that through your name,
we can come to you.

People: **Thank you, Jesus.**

     Amen.

d. After the Prayer of Confession, the second leader will say:

> "Since we have been pardoned by God through the work of his Son, we can
> greet each other with the peace that comes only from him and his gift.
> Please turn to your neighbors to pass the peace."

e. After passing the peace, the music leader will ask the congregation to pray for the illumination of God's Word in Scripture by singing "Holy Spirit, Mighty God."

During the singing of this song, a reader or group of readers will arise from the congregation, since the Word belongs to us all. This passage could be read by a narrator reading the part of Jesus, and others taking the parts of Peter, the servants, and the master. It could also be read by one reader.

f. Sermon Ideas

The sermon's intent is to move people to own the process of healing that exists in forgiveness—to take the stance of victory, leaving behind the identity of survivor. The Scripture passage (Matt. 18:15–35) outlines a process of forgiveness that leads to healing. In contrast, the typical starting point of "becoming survivors instead of remaining victims" used in many self-help groups does not lead to complete healing. "Becoming a survivor" means our identity is that of "survivor," instead of "image-bearer of God." The process of healing outlined in the passage is as follows:

a. We must acknowledge our pain in order to start the process of forgiveness. (This is implicit in verse 15. We cannot face our perpetrator if we do not recognize our feelings of being the victim.)

b. We must reframe the perpetrator. (In verse 27, the master takes pity, which is God reframing us.) Most perpetrators were once abused.

c. We must face the one who hurt us (back to verse 15 and following). Make special note of the fact that we do not have to face the perpetrator alone if there is danger of denial.

d. Then we must forgive. The difficulty of forgiveness is brought out in verses 21–22. Not seventy-seven sins, but seventy-seven times. Jesus knows that we will have to go through it over and over again. He knows our limits.

The sermon closes by recognizing the difficulty we have in following the process and reminding us that the power of the Holy Spirit can give us the strength we need.

g. The sermon ends with a song rather than a spoken prayer. The pastor makes the transition to the sung prayer in the sermon.

h. The pastor will introduce the Confession of Faith:

"As a people seeking forgiveness and learning how to forgive, we confess our faith in what God is doing among us. Please rise and in unison say with me:"

CONFESSION OF FAITH
(portions may be selected or all used)

37. In our world, bent under the weight of sin,
    Christ gathers a new community.
    Satan and his evil forces
    seek whom they may confuse and swallow;
    but Jesus builds his church,
    his Spirit guides,
    and grace abounds.

41. The Spirit empowers each member
    to take part in the ministry of all,
    so that hurts are healed
    and all may rejoice
    in the life and growth of the fellowship.

42. The church is a gathering
    of forgiven sinners,
    called to be holy,
    dedicated to service.
    Saved by the patient grace of God,
    we deal patiently with others.
    Knowing our own weakness and failures,
    we bring good news to all sinners
    with understanding of their condition,
    and with hope in God.

43. We grieve that the church
    which shares one Spirit, one faith, one hope,
    and spans all time, place, race, and language

has become a broken communion in a broken world.
When we struggle for the purity of the church
and for the righteousness God demands,
we pray for saintly courage.
When our pride or blindness blocks
the unity of God's household,
we seek forgiveness.
We marvel that the Lord gathers the broken pieces
to do his work,
and that he blesses us still
with joy, new members,
and surprising evidences of unity.
We commit ourselves to seeking and expressing
the oneness of all who follow Jesus.

i. Suggestions for Intercessory Prayer based on the Lord's Prayer:

Our Father in heaven, hallowed be your name.
(Remind God and us of his name of Loving Parent, like no earthly parent.)

Thy kingdom come, thy will be done, on earth as it is in heaven.
(Pray for God's will in the injustice of abuse, personal and social. Include prayers for justice to the perpetrators of personal abuse. Pray for the injustice of hunger and war in the world and nation.)

Give us this day our daily bread.
(Thank God for caring for us and supplying all of our needs. Pray for those who have extra needs, such as emotional or physical healing.)

Forgive us our trespasses as we forgive those who trespass against us.
*(Repent of our lack of forgiveness and our trespassing against others. **Silence could be used here for reflection on personal failures and sins.**)*

Lead us not into temptation.
Deliver us from the evil one.
*(Bind the demons that encourage or cause abuse. Bind the forces of evil that cause injustice. Protect us from continuing the patterns of abuse in our lives. We are dealing with principalities and powers. **Use that concept here.**)*

For thine is the kingdom and the power and the glory forever. Amen.

j. The pastor announces the offerings. They should be for a cause that has to do with abuse, such as a shelter for women. The announcement should relate to the sermon and the theme: healing the wounds of abuse. Music to be played during the offering should also reflect the theme.

When presenting the offerings, a deacon should pray, "Jesus, your grace to us is great. Though you were rich, yet for our sake you became poor, so that by your poverty you might become rich. Bless those who need your healing riches in *(insert name of cause)*. Use us and our gifts to bring your grace to the many persons who suffer abuse in our society. **Amen.**"

k. Suggested parting words by the pastor:

"Jesus' words to us today bring the victory of true healing. Jesus comes to all of us in our helpless state. Such healing brings us peace that passes all understanding. Let us go out with this song on our heart, with this assurance in our soul. Please rise and sing 'When Peace Like a River.' "

The pastor gives the blessing:

Receive God's blessing:
May the God of hope fill you with all joy and peace in believing, so that you may abound in hope by the power of the Holy Spirit. **Amen.**

HEALING AFTER RAPE[79]
(Presbyterian)

(Women assemble in a circle, with the woman who has been raped inside the circle and others facing her. Someone says:)

We are here because our sister *(name)* has been violated. Her body, her feelings, and her spirit have all been gravely injured. We are here to mourn with her and also to cry out in anger with her. We are outraged—outraged at the hostility to women and the distortion of sexuality into violence that are all around us in patriarchal society, taking the most extreme form in rape. We are filled with grief because we don't know when the violence will end and how we can repair the damage that has been done. But we refuse to give up. We will not be defeated. We will not be intimidated and turned into fearful people, unable to claim our freedom to go where we please and do what we wish.

(A second person says:)

We love and affirm our sister *(name)* who has been hurt. Although she has been injured, she is not destroyed. Although she has been demeaned, yet she has not lost her integrity. Although she has been subjected to ugliness, yet she is still beautiful. Although evil has gripped her, yet she is still good. Although lies may seek to impugn her, yet she is still truthful. We affirm her wholeness, her goodness, her truthfulness, her integrity, her beauty. We dispel the forces of destruction, of ugliness, of violence, and of lies, which seek to make her their victim.

(The woman may now choose to say something about her experience, or she may prefer to remain silent or express herself in nonverbal ways.)

(The group now leads the woman to a ritual bath. The bath is filled with herbs and sweet-smelling flower petals. Her body is immersed and massaged with sprays of warm water. She is dried and anointed with fragrant oils and clothed in a festive dress with a crown of sage leaves and a bouquet of flowers and herbs. Reassembling in a circle around the woman, one woman facing her says:)

- *(With hands on abdomen)* From violence to your body, be healed. *(Others repeat)* Be healed.
- *(With hands on breast)* From violence to your feelings, be healed. . . . Be healed.
- *(With hands on forehead)* From violence to your mind and spirit, be healed. . . . Be healed.
- *(All together)* **The Mother-Spirit of Original Blessing surrounds you, upholds you on all sides, flows round about you, caresses you, loves you, and wills you to be whole. Be whole, sister, be whole.**

(If the rape has taken place in the woman's home, her house or apartment should be purified and rededicated, with special attention to the room where the rape took place, and the door or window by which the rapist entered.)

A SONG OF HEALING   #394   PrH   "There Is a Balm in Gilead"

CIRCLE OF PRAYER

Most gracious God, mother and father to us, fill this your daughter with the presence of your Healing Holy Spirit. Help her to rediscover her body as the temple of the Holy Spirit, to love and cherish it, to feel cleansed and renewed. Now hear our individual prayers on her behalf.

(Each person present offers a prayer as they feel led, all closing with the Lord's Prayer.)

FINAL BLESSING

SOLIDARITY WITH THE VIOLATED[80]
(Nondenominational)

Where violence has been done to the boundary between public and private life, particular care needs to be taken with any healing ritual and prayer that there is a secure boundary which cannot be intruded upon. Where that is so, there can be a measure of healing when a particular deep emotional wound can be exposed for acceptance and binding. Even though a group may be entirely supportive, parts of this process of healing may well need to be undertaken by the person alone or at most with one trusted other. There needs to be sufficient sense of privacy for acknowledgement of the violation and sufficient openness so that the violation may be held and to a degree healed.

The person may already have shared the painful story in a counseling setting. It may be that some of the detail is still too painful to tell out loud. But it may be that the story can be told as part of the ritual, or that it can be written down and presented to the group.

In preparation for the ritual the person may wish to take a cleansing bath and be gently massaged all over the body.

What follows are but suggestions, not experienced by the author directly but entrusted to him by those who have and who believe them to be of help. And such prayer seems, alas, all too sorely needed.

THE TRUTH OF OUR FEELINGS

Voice 1: The blood that flows cries for revenge.

Voice 2: Cursed be the violence of the strong.

Voice 1: The child howls in the lonely night.

Voice 2: Cursed be the hand that bruised.

Voice 1: The woman/man lies sobbing on the floor.

Voice 2: Cursed be the hard eyes and the unyielding stone.

Voice 1: The body that trusted lies rigid in shock.

Voice 2: Cursed be the relishing of pain.

Voice 1: The weak are intimidated and afraid.

Voice 2: Cursed be our arrogance and lust for power.

Voice 1: The abused shrink away in silent shame.

Voice 2: Cursed be the evil power of secrecy.

Voice 1: The abusers protest their innocence.

Voice 2: Cursed be those who deny their responsibility.

Voice 1: The comfortable turn away, refusing to see.

Voice 2: Cursed be our collusion and cowardice.

All: **Just and holy God,**
receive our fear and shame,
our grief and anger,
and channel these strong energies
in the service of truth and healing.

THE GREETING OF LOVE AND THE TELLING OF THE STORY

N, we love you, we affirm you, we recognize you.
We hear and see your wounding;
We touch your pain.
Tell us, if you will, your story.

(N may wish to tell the story or present a written version of it, perhaps with such words as: This is my story. I am wounded and I hurt. If the story has already been told to someone in the group, perhaps such words as these could be used: I have shared my story with X, who has received it with care. I am wounded by what happened to me, and I hurt and seek healing.)

N, you have been harmed but you have not lost your capacity for healing.
You have been helpless but you have not lost your ability to act.

You have been humiliated but you have not lost your integrity.
You have been violated but you have not lost your strength for love.

By the sweep of our arms *(a gesture here of wide dismissal)*
and in the power of the Holy Spirit,
we dispel the forces of violence and abuse,
of harm and humiliation.

By the gathering of our arms *(a gesture here of embrace)*
and in the presence of the Holy Spirit,
we affirm the ultimate power of love and truth and healing.

*(It may be appropriate for the piece of paper to be burned, and some such words used as these:
May the evil and the harm wither away and be consumed.)*

LIGHT IN THE DARK PLACES

N, let the light of this candle be for you the light of God,
as you meet the darkness in the deep places of your being.
See the hidden things, the creatures of your dreams,
the storehouse of forgotten memories,
the gifts you never knew you had been given.
Touch the wellspring of your life,
and hear your own true nature and your own true name.
Take the freedom to grow into that self
the seed of which was planted at your making.

Listen to the language of your wounds.
Do not pine away in the pain of them,
but seek to live from the depths of them.
Make the extent of your desolation
the extent of your realm.

Take into your arms your wounded frightened child within.
Give her/him your adult caring strength,
for your child has protected your gifts
until the time they can be given and not be betrayed.

May your only wounds be these:
the wound we cannot avoid because we belong to one another
and feel and hear the murmur of the world's pain;
the wound of a sense of compassion for others;
the wound of a sense of longing for God,
the source of life and love deep within us and beyond us.

THE ANOINTING
*(A small empty bowl can be passed round the group, together with a small jug of oil from which
each person can pour a little into the bowl. A prayer of blessing can be used, and different*

members of the group can anoint different parts of the body. The details need to be worked out as appropriate to the person concerned. For example:)

> *(At the anointing of the throat)*
> From violence to your voice, be healed.

> *(At the anointing of hands and feet)*
> From violence to your body, be healed.

> *(At the anointing of the breast)*
> From violence to your feelings, be healed.

> *(At the anointing of the forehead)*
> From violence to your mind, be healed.

> *(At the anointing of the lower stomach)*
> From violence to your sexuality, be healed.

THE PRAYING

> The Creator Spirit surrounds you,
> upholds you on all sides,
> flows round you, caresses you, loves you,
> and wills you to be whole.

> N, be healed.
> Be well again.
> Live from your scars with compassion.

> > Love your flesh-body,
> > You are a body,
> > not a no-body,
> > not just any-body,
> > but some-body.

> And we are a body,
> the Body of Christ.
> The body is the dwelling place
> of the healing Holy Spirit.
> You are body in the Spirit.

Be in love with life,
wrestle with the chaos and the pain,
with yourself and with others,
spirit echoing Spirit,
trusting in the victory of the vulnerable,
glimpsing the peace and wholeness, the justice and freedom,
that comes from following the Pioneer
made perfect in suffering,
striving and yearning and crying out
from the very depths and heights

of the world's anguish and the world's bliss,
and so becoming friends and partners of God
in the divine creating.

> The God who gives healing to the violated
> and power to the powerless,
> fill you with the spirit of a strong love,
> that you may flow with grace and truth and beauty.

HEARING THE UNHEARD WOMAN—
WALK, WEEP, AND DANCE WITH GOD[81]
(Ecumenical)

CALL TO WORSHIP

I was glad when they said to me let us go to the house of the Lord (Ps. 122). This house, as the Psalmists understood it, is a place where we go to walk with God, to pray with God, to plead with God, to weep and to dance with God (Ps. 30). And who is this God? Our God is gracious and merciful, slow to anger, and abounding in steadfast love (Ps. 86). Let us worship God!

OPENING PRAYER

Our creator who is in heaven
we revere your name.
Your kingdom come,
your will be done
on earth as it is in heaven.
Let us all share our daily bread
with all who are in need.
And forgive us our shame
as we forgive those who have shamed us.
Lead us not into complacency
but deliver us with your redeeming love.
For yours is the kingdom,
and the Power,
and the Glory forever.
Amen.

HYMN #172 PrH "My Shepherd Will Supply My Need"

ANTHEM "Hammer and a Nail" or a setting of Psalm 86 or #172

READINGS

> **Reader 1:** Let us begin with the words of Ruth to Naomi. Ruth 1:16–17
>
> And how do Sarah and Hagar walk with God?

Reader 2: Painfully . . . for Sarah is jealous of Abraham and Hagar.   Exod. 16:5–6

And how does Esther walk with God?

Reader 3: Eloquently . . . listen as Esther petitions the king.   Esth. 7:3–4

And how does Miriam walk with God?

Reader 4: Joyfully! She dances with God . . . listen as Miriam celebrates.   Exod. 15:20–21

And how does Lot's wife walk with God?

Reader 5: She couldn't walk, she was told "it's not too late, you can look back still . . ."

Her eyes that were still turning when as a bolt
Of pain shot through them, were instantly blind;
Her body turned into transparent salt,
And her swift legs were rooted to the ground.

Who mourns one woman in a holocaust?
Surely her death has no significance?
Yet in my heart she will never be lost,
She who gave up her life to steal one glance.[82]

And how does Rebekah walk with God?

Reader 6: Bravely . . . She walks away from all that she knew.   Gen. 24:60

And how does Judith walk with God?

Reader 7: Triumphantly! She also dances . . . listen to how they celebrate Judith.
Judith 15:12–13

And how does Tamar walk with God?

Reader 8: Sadly—she weeps, for she is raped by her brother.   2 Sam. 13:11–14

And how does Shug (short for "sugar") walk with God?

Reader 9: Confidently—she lifts up a new God for us: Here the thing, say Shug. The thing I believe. God is inside you and inside everybody else. You come into the world with God. But only them that search for it inside find it . . . yeah, it. God ain't a he or a she, but a it . . . you have to get man off your eyeball, before you can see anyting a'tall. Man corrupt everything. He on your box of grits, in your head, and all over the radio. He try to make you think he everywhere. Soon as you think he everywhere, you think he God. But he ain't. Whenever you trying to pray, and man plop himself on the other end of it, tell him to git lost, say Shug. Conjure up flowers, wind, water, a big rock.[83]

And how does Lydia walk with God?

Reader 10: Graciously . . . she welcomes all. Listen as Lydia opens her heart and home.
Acts 16:14–15

And how do Martha and Mary walk with God?

Reader 11: Differently . . . listen as Martha and Mary welcome Jesus.   Luke 10:38–41

And how do the women at the tomb walk with God?

Reader 12: Courageously—women are the first witness to a risen Christ.   Mark 16:1–4

And how does Phoebe walk with God?

DIALOGUE *(Select several dialoguers and readers.)*
Dialoguer: Although I am wondering about Phoebe I need to take a breather. Y'all have thrown out a lot of good readings, but can we take some time to reflect? Take the first reading about Ruth telling Naomi "where you go I will go," "where you lodge I will lodge," and all of that. It could be an example of woman as dependent, woman as follower.

Dialoguer: Or it could be an example of dedication. When you really love someone you open your heart to everything, including moving to a strange land. It could be seen as sacrificing positively—giving up something for another as a road to growth. Ruth as well as Rebekah were taking charge of their lives. They left all that they knew because they saw opportunity . . . plus, they completely trusted their travel companions to lead them on a just path. And Rebekah knows her family loves her and wants the best for her. What exactly do they say?

Reader: May you, our sister, become thousands of myriads.

Dialoguer: Yes, thousands of myriads, so Rebekah is made strong for her journey because her family believes in her. Ruth has a harder time in convincing Naomi, but in the end she is able to show her strength. In Naomi, Ruth saw an old, wise woman who would be a good advisor, a nurturing ear, and a woman who would let Ruth talk "until all the parts fitted together." Naomi's reluctance to travel with Ruth is tempered by Ruth's energy and determination. It's intergenerational bonding at its best.

Dialoguer: Ruth and Rebekah were "big girls." They knew some of what they were getting into, but I'm more worried about Lot's wife. Like Jephthah's daughter she has no name, and like Eve who ate of the tree, she too does what we all would want to do. Yet Lot's wife pays for her "stolen glance" with her life. There is no grace, no second chance for this nameless woman . . . remind me again of the loneliness and isolation of Lot's wife?

Reader: Who mourns one woman in a holocaust?

Dialoguer: Yes, "who mourns one woman in a holocaust?" We do not often think of Lot's wife, or Eve for that matter, because we are reminded of times when we stumbled, when we were wounded because of our curiosity. And we rarely mourn one woman in a holocaust because we ache with personal loss;

we look for our lost mothers in the empty spaces of our homes and hearts. And we feel this personal loss constantly, although we do not always name it. We leave home, dreams are lost or forgotten, friendships fade, relationships break, and people we love die. But these losses happen like gusts of wind and perhaps that is why we don't concern ourselves with holocausts—because we do not always know how to cope with what is no longer a part of our lives.

Dialoguer: Yet we usually continue to open our hearts, or we come in contact with people who show us how to love and be loved. Take Lydia, for instance—by day she deals in purple cloth and by night she welcomes the stranger into her home. What, again, exactly was so compelling about Lydia?

Reader: God opened Lydia's heart to listen eagerly to what was said.

Dialoguer: So Lydia isn't just providing space for her guests, she is also a joyous listener and is willing to be taught and cannot wait to give back to her teachers. Because she opens her ears, she finds that her gifts are recognized too, and her hospitality is welcome. Lydia shows us that so much of love is listening, and is giving and receiving out of our strengths and gifts. And Mary further illustrates this in her attention to Jesus' words. Tell me again the tension between Martha and Mary?

Reader: Mary sat at Jesus' feet and listened to what he was saying. But Martha was distracted by her many tasks.

Dialoguer: So while Martha is up and about, Mary is willing to sit and hear the words.

Dialoguer: There are listeners and doers. Mary's a listener, Martha's a doer (or I guess you could say Martha's a task-master and Mary takes the backseat). Clearly, Martha and Mary could probably both learn a lot from each other. So often women of action do not take the time to stop and reflect, for there is always more to do. And women with good ears often cocoon themselves in this talent, never venturing out in words or action, for fear of offending someone. And then there are women like Judith—Judith's definitely a doer. She simply slices off a man's head because he refuses to listen. Women of action sometimes throw great parties—Judith and Miriam certainly know how to celebrate. Again, what did Judith do to celebrate?

Reader: Judith went before all the people in the dance, leading all the women.

Dialoguer: Yes. And Miriam?

Reader: Miriam took a tambourine in her hand; and all the women went out after her with tambourines and with dancing.

Dialoguer: Yes, yes. Miriam and Judith surely had the power to uplift. We admire them and turn to them because we want to be a part of their dance. Although we rarely allow ourselves to be in the role of a conquering Judith or a prophet Miriam, we still feel the joy of women's triumphs. When women are elected or appointed, given tenure or ordained, when women survive and prosper, or when they are praised and honored our hearts grow a little larger, we hold our heads a little higher, and we wish we had a tambourine nearby to shake.

Dialoguer: And like Miriam and Judith, Esther is also able to ascend somewhat to a position of power. Esther saves a people the only way she knows how—with words. Remind me of her words again.

Reader: Let my life be given me—that is my petition—and the lives of my people—that is my request.

Dialoguer: Esther's impassioned and ultimately persuasive words show us that women's meditation and dialoguing skills have a rich history indeed. But women are not always saving a people or throwing big parties. Just look at Sarah and Hagar. These two are the antithesis of Ruth and Naomi. We don't want to celebrate with Sarah and Hagar; we want to shut our ears to their painful connection because we see how it can apply to our relationships with our bosses, mothers, sisters, employees, or friends. In Sarah and Hagar we are reminded of how we forsake other women and forsake God. Ruth and Naomi met because of a man and they stay connected forever, but it's not always like that. Where was the sisterhood with Sarah and Hagar? One was the married lady, one was the slave and each one wanted God only on her side. So they were jealous and scornful of one another and when Hagar got some of the attention from Sarah's husband, Sarah flew off the handle. What exactly did she do?

Reader: Then Sarah dealt harshly with Hagar, and she ran away from Sarah.

Dialoguer: Then she dealt harshly with her and she ran away from her. So when it comes right down to it, Sarah threw Hagar out on the street! Because they refused to hear and listen to one another, Sarah and Hagar could not and would not reconcile.

Dialoguer: And it seems clear that scriptural relationships between women and men are also often especially hard to reflect upon. Please read again of Tamar and her brother.

Reader: But he would not listen to Tamar, and being stronger than she, he forced her and lay with her.

Dialoguer: He forced her and lay with her. Broken and battered, Tamar is left to weep alone, for there is no rape crisis center to call. Tamar is the woman in all of us whose cries for compassion we abandon and ignore because we refuse to expose our own aching Woundedness. Our spirit crushed, we simply turn to survival, not uncovering or caring to uncover the hidden atrocities in our midst.

Dialoguer: But the women at the tomb do not abandon anyone. The two Marys and Salome are fearless of political reprisals, though they are fearful of what they saw. They are the first to preach the gospel that Christ was risen. They are also continuing on in the great preaching tradition of women, seen also with the Samaritan woman at the well. The Samaritan woman really understood what Jesus was trying to say and the three women at the tomb really understood what Christ was about. These great preaching women show us what a combination of fear, joy, reflection, and action can bring to the community. Because they were unafraid to show that God was alive in them and through them, we are all able to see God walk and talk with women. No longer is there an excuse to ignore and abandon women's voices, no longer is there an excuse to hear and not listen, and no longer is there an excuse to see and not do.

Dialoguer: But let's face it, the pickings are awfully slim for women in Scripture. It's such an odd struggle to integrate a faithfulness to texts, to appropriate new and inclusive images, and to develop symbolic trajectories out of the few instances that women appear in the texts.

Dialoguer: That's probably why Shug's words are so important. Instead of celebrating women, we cannot "get man off our eyeballs." That man is everywhere has made many of us believe that woman is nowhere. And because man is everywhere in Hebrew and Christian Scriptures, we often gender divinity accordingly. Instead, every morning as we praise, every evening as we give thanks, EVERYDAY we should repeat Ntozake Shange's words "I found god in myself & i loved her/i loved her fiercely."[84]

Dialoguer: i found god in myself & i loved her/i loved her fiercely.
i found god in myself & i loved her/i loved her fiercely.
i found god in myself & i loved her/i loved her fiercely.
i found god in myself & i loved her/i loved her fiercely.

Reader: i found god in myself & i loved her/i loved her fiercely.

All readers and dialoguers together: i found god in myself & i loved her/i loved her fiercely.

Congregation: i found god in myself & i loved her/i loved her fiercely.

PRELUDE TO KYRIE

Sisters and brothers, all who are led by the Spirit of God are children of God. We know that the whole creation has been groaning in labor pains until now, and not only the creation but we ourselves. We do not know how to pray as we ought, but the Spirit intercedes for us with sighs too deep for words. So then, let us pray (Rom. 8).

KYRIE

One: Lord, we pray for women, poor, overpowered in the marketplace and in their homes, women suffering, beaten, and raped. We pray for women who live on the edge, who live in fear. We pray for a world in which we stand back and watch, and for the strength to stand up and speak out, to work for a different kind of world.

All: **Lord, O Lord, have mercy.**

One: Women are poor and they and their children are getting poorer. Two out of three poor adults are women. Three-quarters of people over the age of 65 who live in poverty are women. Women still earn only two-thirds of men's pay.

All: **Lord, O Lord, have mercy.**

One: Women head one-third of the world's households, but own only one percent of the world's property. Women put in 60 percent of the hours worked and earn only 10 percent of the world's income.

All: **Lord, O Lord, have mercy.**

One: Every three minutes a woman is beaten. Every five minutes a woman is raped. Every ten minutes a little girl is molested. Every three minutes. Every five minutes. Every ten minutes. Every day.

All: **Lord, O Lord, have mercy.**

One: Violence against women occurs in at least two-thirds of all marriages at least once. Seventy percent of assault victims in emergency rooms are women who have been attacked in their own home. Ninety-five percent of all assaults on spouses are committed by men. Every three minutes a woman is beaten. Every three minutes. Every day.

All: **Lord, O Lord, have mercy.**

One: Rape happens to women of all ages, races and economic levels. Fifty percent of women who are raped are raped in their own home. Seventy percent of rapes are perpetrated by a man known to the woman. Every five minutes a woman is raped. Every five minutes. Every day.

All: **Lord, O Lord, have mercy.**

One: Over ninety-nine percent of sexual abuse of children is committed by men. Sexual abuse happens more than twice as often to girls than boys. Fifty percent of sexual abuse cases against girls are committed by a family member. Every ten minutes a little girl is molested. Every ten minutes. Every day.

All: **Lord, O Lord have mercy. Every three minutes. Every five minutes. Every ten minutes. Every day. Lord, have mercy.**[85]

SENDING FORTH

Now we appeal to you, sisters and brothers, to respect those who labor among you, and have charge of you in the Lord and admonish you. Be at peace among yourselves. And we urge you, beloved, to admonish the complacent, encourage the fainthearted, help the weak, and be patient with all of them. See that none of you repays evil for evil, but always seek to do good to one another and to all (1 Thess. 5). Now go in peace and serve God!

POSTLUDE

"His heart was filled with pity."
(Luke 10:33)

Chapter 5

Illness: As Life-Threatening

INTRODUCTION

This chapter contains liturgies and prayers for the major illnesses facing Americans—cancer, heart disease, and AIDS—as well as general healing services for all illnesses and times of hospitalization and surgery.

Serious illness permanently changes who we are. As Eric Cassell, oncologist and ethicist, suggested, it is not like a knapsack we carry and take off; even after we are cured or recovered, our sense of vulnerability and nagging fears are there.[1] The church has long recognized the importance of ministry to sick people and bringing the care, concern, and prayers to the bedside.

As a guide for the church's response to those with life-threatening illnesses, Galatians 6 provides an injunction—bearing one another's burdens. This means being with one another, helping one another. We cannot stand by and say, "Look at that poor person with AIDS, cancer, heart disease, or whatever else. What will become of him or her?" We have to be with that person, caring for him or her, or we are worse off than the sick person. The passage that refers to "bearing one another's burdens" (Gal. 6:1–5) arises in the context of those who have brought misfortune on themselves, so we are to help people, not blame them.

We are in no position to condemn, but only to assist, to respond to others' needs. Bearing one another's burdens involves being with people where they are and, whenever possible, changing the circumstances that put them there in the first place. It means to lighten the burden of physical pain, fear of death, ostracization, and loneliness of the seriously ill person. Unless we stand with our brother or sister, how can we bear the name of Jesus Christ? However, the patient also must be responsible. The second half of this passage is "carry your own load." We are accountable. In this setting, patients must follow treatment, cultivate a hopeful attitude, and marshal all the resources to combat their illness. Resignation is not the only response. Patients work with others in their movement toward wholeness. In light of the suffering from serious illness, the church is challenged to respond to patients' needs on a variety of levels. Our focus here is on the liturgical response to a variety of illnesses.

AIDS

AIDS is a pandemic in the twenty-first century. Statistics are frightening, though because of available miracle drugs, we have become somewhat complacent. As of the end of 2002, an estimated 42 million people worldwide were living with HIV/AIDS. Approximately 50 percent of adults living with HIV/AIDS worldwide are women. The Centers for Disease Control and Prevention (CDC) estimate that 850,000 to 950,000 U.S. residents are living with HIV infection, one-quarter of whom are unaware of their infection. Approximately forty thousand new HIV infections occur each year in the U.S., about 70 percent among men and 30 percent among women. Of these newly infected people, half are younger than twenty-five years of age.[2]

It is important initially to provide some perspective on AIDS, as it is the modern-day equivalent of leprosy. An appropriate response to AIDS entails an examination of theological, pastoral, ethical, medical, educational, and governmental issues. AIDS, even more than other illnesses, raises for us basic questions about the relationship between sin and sickness, health and salvation, evil and a God of love, the existence of suffering, punishment and innocence, community responsibility and individual accountability, forgiveness, and restoration. Stemming from these fundamental issues are concerns about sexual ethics and education, confidentiality versus public safety, health care practices and protection, access to miracle drugs, and so forth.

The AIDS crisis confronts the church with the need to examine the relationship of God to human sickness and suffering and our response to it. The question is not simply one of sexual ethics or lifestyle but one that strikes at the heart of our theology. As one married church member dying of AIDS asked me, "Why should I have contracted AIDS from one sexual encounter with the wrong person when thousands of other sexually promiscuous people are disease free?"

What is the church's ministry to the person with AIDS? Initially, AIDS was put in a very special category of infectious diseases, based on the prevalence of this disease among homosexuals, bisexuals, and intravenous drug users. Now the fastest-growing group of AIDS patients are women. Many persons see AIDS as a sickness resulting from sin, especially those from certain theological positions who claim AIDS is God's punishment for sinful behavior.

While the Old and New Testaments frequently correlate sin and sickness, they usually do so in the context of a warning, an admonition to avoid certain acts (sins) in order to prevent undesirable consequences. Although there is relevance to warnings in the context of AIDS and acts that can lead to its infection and transmission, the issue here is one of response, after and not before the infection. AIDS should be viewed not as some special sickness singled out by God as a judgment on certain people but rather as a further reflection of the broken world in which we live. It, like other forms of suffering, is a mystery and a tragedy, the result of a mixture of our imperfect world, our own culpability, and the tragic sense of life.

We should be guided by Christ's response to illness, which was one of healing and not of judgment. We should examine how the church can best minister to the person with AIDS, to heal, if possible, or make the best of the remainder of their days if physical healing is not possible. Compassion, not judgment, should be our response. We cannot stand over against others, since we also experience brokenness in our lives.[3]

In light of these perspectives, the church has an important role to perform—to be a community of acceptance. Because of the gospel mandate to bear one another's burdens, the church's response to persons with AIDS should be to create a community of acceptance, to practice a personal ethic of compassion, and to bring healing wherever possible.

In responding to the AIDS crisis, one of the key tests for the religious community, and specifically the Christian church, is how seriously they take the church as the body of Christ. This image of the church reflects the view that if one member suffers, we all suffer—it is not *we* versus *they* but *us*. As Robert Lambourne expressed it, one only is whole who shares in the brokenness of others.[4] The AIDS crisis should produce not simply anxieties of self-protection but compassion for those with AIDS. Furthermore, the church is not immune to this tragedy. As we conduct healing liturgies for persons with AIDS, we proclaim the inclusion of all God's people.

Initially, some in the church rejected those with AIDS, but now an ethic of acceptance for persons with AIDS has put the church at the vanguard of such a ministry. Just as Jesus walked among the lepers and the medieval church set up the first hospitals for sick strangers, we welcome the person with AIDS as our neighbor, that is, as the person in need. Judgment in the face of sickness simply does not have a place; we cannot care for the lung cancer patient who smoked for twenty years, the liver-damaged alcoholic, or the high-speed car accident driver on the one hand, and on the other hand judge the person with AIDS as not deserving care.

CANCER

Cancer is the number-two cause of death in the United States.[5] In 2002, 1,284,900 people died from cancer.[6] Like AIDS, the diagnosis of cancer sends a chill through people. In this last decade great strides have been made in treatment and recovery, but a lot of the success is tied to early detection. Treatments are still very debilitating, and cure is not always the outcome.

Compared with AIDS, cancer is considered an acceptable disease. Few people hesitate to tell of their struggles with cancer. Even breast cancer, which was not openly discussed twenty years ago, is acknowledged by famous personalities as well as average women who join support groups. However, mammograms and pap smears still produce anxiety until the results are negative.

Melvyn Thompson, in *Cancer and God of Love,* describes the types of feelings that surface with the diagnosis of cancer: (1) the unreality of illness compared to the normalcy of life; (2) the challenge of trusting and believing the medical staff (do they know the truth about my illness and will they tell it?); and (3) willingness to accept that what happens to others can happen to me.[7] Christians have the opportunity to bear the symbols of hope and healing even in the midst of suffering and pain.

HEART DISEASE

Perhaps the heart, more than any other organ of the body, has special significance. We think of it as the seat of our emotions and even identify it with our personality. It is for this reason that the first heart transplant by Christian Barnard in 1967 met with a fair degree of resistance. For some, having the heart of a person of another race or gender strikes us as strange. The "Baby Fae" case in the 1980s, where the medical team at Loma Linda Medical Center transplanted a baboon's heart into a newborn with a fatal heart condition, brought a hue and cry from bioethicists around the world (though this was as much in response to the experimental nature of the surgery as from the fear of creating a chimera, that is, part animal, part person).

The fact is, however, that heart disease is the top killer of North Americans. About 600,000 people suffer a stroke per year[8] and in 2002 over 515,000 people died of heart attacks.[9] There has been a tremendous public health campaign to follow measures to lower blood pressure and cholesterol as preventive measures from having heart disease. The church has been part of these preventive health initiatives. One such program is John Hatch's blood pressure reduction program, which is cosponsored by the North Carolina Black Baptist Convention and the School of Public Health at the University of North Carolina. This program trained church members how to be blood pressure measurement specialists and created support groups within the church to encourage healthy diets and, where needed, the taking of medication by those with high blood pressure. Elijah Saunders at Provident Hospital in Baltimore started a similar program in the 1980s. Recently, a church in California began a support group, facilitated by a cardiologist, for people who recovered from heart attacks and strokes. It is hoped that the church in its general healing services will recognize the special needs of those with heart disease.

HOSPITALIZATION AND SURGERY

All the above illnesses may require hospitalization and surgery. Physical illness can alter our self-perception, while hospitalization can be traumatic. Hospitalization is not only a physical crisis but also a psychological assault to our identity. "The concept of initiation, specifically the rites of passage, has been applied to the hospital experience by John Katonah as a way to understand the crisis of hospitalization. He designates the stripping process as the rite of separation. The liminal period takes place in the hospital. The final stage of incorporation, or what Katonah refers to as 'transformation,' does not occur in the hospital. For Katonah, the rite of passage experienced in a hospital is not an initiation of person to patient, but occurs on a spiritual level where the person experiences a deeper purpose for life."[10] Hence liturgies are offered in this section to name communally the epiphanies wrought so privately in physical illness, and to restore the identity of the patient through a rite of transition.

While Michael Aune and Valerie DeMarinis, authors of *Religious and Social Ritual,* claim that hospitalization is itself ritual—a rite of passage from illness to health—I believe we need liturgy to give meaning to that rite.[11] Surgery can be daunting without rituals that promise meaning and safety.[12] When we reflect on illness, one of the most frightening aspects is the need for surgery and hospitalization. "Along with divorce, career changes, and menopause, surgery can be a physical and symbolic transitional experience that challenges individuals to create personal rites of passage."[13] The special prayers and rituals for hospitalization and surgery remind us of God's presence at all seasons of crisis.

Theologians and pastoral counselors are discovering the importance of ministry during these harrowing times. "The experience of surgery merits the need for a rite of passage to help patients cope with the predicament of surgery."[14] Such a rite can serve the purposes of restoring one's identity. Often, too, time later is needed to process the events.

For some, a certain ritualization of the hospital experience is possible with removing of one's clothes, storing them away, and receiving the hospital gown in order to protect oneself from the clinical gaze of the medical establishment. After the ordeal of surgery, personal mnemonic artifacts can be used to recover one's sense of self.[15]

What we discover in these experiences is that ritual can help us. Now Aune and DeMarinis are referring to rituals in a very broad sense, but I believe that worship, especially these healing liturgies, can help people interpret and confront their fears and anxieties, hence assisting in the healing process. As important as health ministries programs and hospital chaplaincy are, the church as well has responded liturgically through the centuries to the needs of ill persons. We are rediscovering the rich tradition of the liturgical resources of the church, especially the rite/sacrament of healing.

RITE/SACRAMENT OF HEALING

When I wrote of the history of the church's health ministry, I suggested that the history of the sacrament of healing forms an important part of ministry to the sick. In James 5, from which we trace the sacrament/rite of healing ("sacrament" for Roman Catholics, "rite" for Protestants), the elders are summoned as the representatives of the community, not as *thaumatourgoi* ("wonder-workers"), nor even as *sacerdotes* (priests able to perform sacrifices). Their function, according to Thomas Talley, is "not to heal nor is it yet to administer last rites, but to protect the sick member from dereliction and separation from the ecclesial body."[16] In the traditions where anointing is a sacrament, then, there is a special incarnational dimension to this rite. In other Christian denominations, communion is brought by elders to the bedside so not only the terminally ill person but others may celebrate the sacrament together.

I have placed general healing services here rather than in chapter 6 on "Death and Dying" to reflect the contemporary understanding of this sacrament. Historically, the transition from the sacrament of healing, as instituted in James 5, to extreme unction reflected a shift in the church's theology that occurred in the eighth and ninth centuries. Some attributed this change to the separation of sin and sickness and to the church's interest in salvation rather than health. "Unction at that time focused on the remission of sins as its principal benefit and was regarded as a sacrament of the dying because of its association with deathbed penance."[17] The emphasis on repentance of the sick derived from a theology that equated sin and sickness. However, "the majority of Anglican scholars believe that the James passage does not support the late medieval theory that unction was primarily ordained for the remission of sins; rather, they believe that it was for the healing of the whole person."[18] The change from healing to extreme unction, formalized at the Council of Trent in 1535, did not reverse until Vatican II of the Roman Catholic Church in 1963.[19]

The rite of healing is used for those who have declared their need in advance and have been prepared for this ministry. It is not a solo ministry but one where the congregation joins in the prayers for the one who is sick with laying-on of hands and anointing. In some traditions, links are made between confession and healing, which are followed by the Peace as an assurance of the corporate undergirding of sick persons.[20]

Several general healing services included in this section are similar in focus. However, they reflect the diversity of denominations or settings and often include unusual elements. For example, the healing service at Westminster Presbyterian Church in San Diego, California, included among its leadership a healing touch therapist to whom people could go at one of the healing stations in the church chancel.

Burrswood Health and Healing Centre in Tunbridge Wells, England, has a hospital, counseling center, chapel, and respite care ministry. The service there is part of a wholistic treatment plan for patients. The laying-on of hands and anointing with oil are understood as an extension of the health practices of the physician, nurse, and counselor.

Shorter versions of the rite of healing are held at the bedside at home or in the hospital. Although hospital stays are considerably briefer since the development of DRGs (diagnostic-related groups), where hospital stays are determined by approved categories of illness that are assigned length of hospitalization and costs covered. However, hospital ministry is still very important.

FAMILIES OF PATIENTS

Illness affects not only the patients but also their families and loved ones. There is a growing recognition of the needs of families of the sick and dying. We have too often concentrated solely on the patient, but with the advent of family systems theory, we see that the well-being of each person in the family ultimately affects the health of the patient in the broadest sense, and vice versa. Some of these liturgies are for people whose loved ones are poised between lingering life to approaching death. Mary Frances Duffy's book *Rituals of Healing for Families of the Terminally Ill* helps fill that gap, describing pastoral care to family members, who are often left in the shadows with no resources. Pastoral care also includes rituals. "These rituals," notes Duffy, "provide the Christian community with an opportunity to engage in a ministry of presence and support, perhaps simply 'being there' to a group of people who are all too often left standing alone, keeping solitary vigil at home, in hospitals, or in nursing homes."[21] Liturgical ritual helps bring those who intimately cosuffer with a dying person together with the whole body of Christ in the embrace of prayer.[22]

General Prayers

"Take this cup of suffering from me!"
(Matt. 26:39)

REFLECTION ON HEALING[23]
(Nondenominational)

The whole of me, the whole person,
physical, mental, emotional, spiritual,
is in need of being healed,
of being made whole.
The curing of physical symptoms
is but one part of this process:
the absence of cure need not hinder it.

Illness is not an unfortunate incident,
but a phase of life with its own time and meaning.

The words 'healing' and 'salvation' are close:
they derive from the same Greek root, '*sozein.*'
We experience moments of salvation,
the gift and the grace of freedom,
of breathing again in wide open spaces,
of being sprung from the trap,
released from confinement or oppression.

My own healing is bound up with that of others.
I need to pray and work
for the healing of the nations,
for food for the hungry,
for justice for the downtrodden,
for my neighbors in a global village.
Without their well-being
I cannot be completely well.

Everything that I am and do
contributes to the making of my soul-body,
and the making of the soul-bodies of others,
and the coming to glory of the whole universe.
The eye of faith looks to a transfiguration
of everything that is of agony or ecstasy
in the life of my flesh-body,
of the flesh-bodies of others,
of the material stuff of this earth and beyond.

Through grace and in faith
I receive the gift of eternal life,
abiding close to the self-giving love of God,
the love that is not destroyed by death.

PRAYERS FOR THE SICK AND ANXIOUS[24]
(Anglican)

Spoken prayers can be extremely helpful but we do not need to fill every space with them. Just being there is important. Silence can be upholding.

A GENERAL INTERCESSION

Minister: Let us beseech the Lord, mighty and pitiful,
for all who in this transitory life are in
trouble, sorrow, need, sickness, or any other adversity:

For the bereaved and sorrowful;
for widows and orphans;
for the lonely and unloved;

All We beseech thee, O Lord.

Minister: For women in labor;
for suffering children;
for the naked and hungry;

All We beseech thee, O Lord.

Minister: For those who face danger;
for those who travel by land or sea or in the air;
for the anxious and uncertain;

All We beseech thee, O Lord.

Minister: For the aged and weak;
for the disabled and handicapped;
for the blind, the deaf, and those unable to speak;

All We beseech thee, O Lord.

Minister: For the sleepless and fevered;
for the injured and wounded;
for those in great pain;

All We beseech thee, O Lord.

Minister: For those weary with suffering;
for the bedridden and housebound;
for those sick unto death;

All We beseech thee, O Lord.

Minister: For the ministries of healing;
for doctors and nurses;
for pastors and priests;

All We beseech thee, O Lord.

(This litany may be concluded with a prayer drawn from this section.)

O Lord Jesus Christ, who by the power of thy word didst heal all who were brought unto thee in the days of thy flesh, mercifully help thy servant in *his/her* hour of need: grant, if it be thy will, that by the same power *he/she* may be delivered from sickness and restored to health, and may forever hereafter serve thee in newness of life to the glory of thy name; who livest and reignest with the Father and the Holy Ghost, ever one God, world without end. **Amen.**[25]

O almighty Father, who dost heal both the bodies and souls of men, who didst send thine only-begotten Son, our Lord Jesus Christ, to heal every sickness and disease, and to redeem us from death, deliver this thy servant, we humbly beseech thee, from all infirmities, both of body and soul, which do hinder *him/her*, and quicken *him/her* by the grace of thy Christ; for thou art the fountain of healing, O our God, and unto thee do we give the glory with thine only-begotten Son, who with thee and the Holy Ghost liveth and reigneth ever one God, world without end. **Amen.**[26]

O holy Lord, almighty Father, everlasting God, who dost confirm the frailty of our nature by pouring upon it thine exceeding goodness, that our limbs and bodies may be strengthened by the healthful medicine of thy mercy: look graciously upon this thy servant, that *he/she* may be freed from the hands of all bodily infirmity, and by thy merciful favor *his/her* former health may be renewed; through Jesus Christ our Lord. **Amen.**[27]

Sovereign Lord, our God, Almighty, we beseech thee save us all,
thou only Physician of souls and bodies.
Sanctify us all, thou that healest every disease; and heal especially this thy servant.
Raise *him/her* up from the bed of pain by thy tender loving-kindness;
visit *him/her* in mercy and compassion;
drive away from *him/her* all sickness and infirmity;
that, being raised up by thy mighty hand, *he/she* may serve thee with all thankfulness;
and that we, being made partakers of thy goodness,
may praise and glorify thee,

who doest great works and wonderful and worthy to be praised.
For it is thine to pity and to save; and to thee we ascribe glory,
Father, Son, and Holy Spirit, now and for evermore. **Amen.**[28]

A PRAYER FOR ONE WHO IS GOING BLIND[29]
(Anglican)

O God,
It is hard to think of a world
in which I cannot see the sun and the flowers,
and the faces of those I love.
It is hard to think of a life
in which I cannot read or watch things,
or see lovely things anymore.
But even in the dark there will be something left.
I can still have memory,
and I can still see things again
with my mind's eye.
I thank you for all that skill and kindness
do for people like me.
I thank you for Braille, which keeps the world of books
from being altogether closed to me.
I thank you that I will still be able
to hear the voices that I know
and to touch the things and the people I love.
Lord Jesus you are the Light of Life;
Be with me in the dark.

Let me remember what Jesus said:
I am the light of the world; he who follows me will not
walk in darkness, but will have the light of life.

John 8:12

A PRAYER FOR ONE WHO HAS LOST THE POWER TO SPEAK[30]
(Anglican)

O God,
I cannot speak to you in words,
but I can still send my thoughts to you;
and, although I can't say the words out loud,
I know that you will hear.
Life can be very difficult
when you can't speak.

Not to be able to tell people what I want;
Not to be able to ask or answer a question;
Not to be able to talk to friends and dear ones;
To have the barrier of silence on my lips—
It is very difficult.
Thank you, O God, for what is left—
for writing;
for the language of signs;
for those who have learned to read my lips.
Help me to bear this that has happened to me,
and to accept it and not to feel frustrated.
Thank you
for the people who are kind to me;
Thank you
for making me sure
that you can hear the words
that I can't speak,
and the things I can think
but cannot say.

Let me remember that words are unnecessary with God, for,
as the Psalmist said to God:
Thou discernest my thoughts from afar.

Ps. 139:2

A PRAYER FOR ONE WHO IS GOING DEAF[31]
(Anglican)

O God,
The trouble about being deaf is that most people
find deaf people just a nuisance.
They sympathize with people
who are blind and lame;
but they just get irritated and annoyed
with people who are deaf.
And the result of this is
that deaf people are apt to avoid company,
and so get more and more lonely,
and more and more shut in.
Help me now that my hearing has begun to go.
Help me
to face the situation
and to realize that there is no good trying to hide it,
for that will only make it worse and worse.

Help me
to be grateful for all that can be done
for deaf people like me.
If I have got to wear a hearing aid,
help me to do it quite naturally,
and not be shy or embarrassed about it.
Give the perseverance
not to let this trouble get me down,
and not to let it cut me off from others.
And help me to remember
that, whatever happens,
there is nothing which can stop me from hearing your voice.

Even if I cannot hear the voices of men, let me remember
Samuel and say: Speak, for thy servant hears.

1 Sam. 3:10

During Hospitalization

"But God's spirit entered me and raised me to my feet." (Ezek. 3:24)

A PRAYER OF ST. CHRYSOSTOM
(Anglican)

Almighty God, who hast given us grace at this time with one accord to make our common supplications unto thee; and dost promise, that when two or three are gathered together in thy Name thou wilt grant their requests; Fulfill now, O Lord, the desires and petitions of thy servants, as may be most expedient for them; granting us in this world knowledge of thy truth, and in the world to come life everlasting. **Amen.**[32]

DAILY MORNING PRAYER
(Anglican)

O Lord, look down from heaven, behold, visit, and relieve these thy servants *in this Hospital (especially* _____*)*. Look upon them with the eyes of thy mercy; give them comfort and sure confidence in thee; defend them from the danger of the enemy, and keep them in perpetual peace and safety; through Jesus Christ our Lord. **Amen.**

Hear us, Almighty and most merciful God and Savior; extend thy accustomed goodness to these thy servants who are grieved with sickness. *(Bless the means used for their recovery; assuage the pains of those who suffer; comfort their distress.)* Sanctify, we beseech thee, this thy fatherly correction to them; that the sense of their weakness may add strength to their faith, and seriousness to their repentance: That, if it shall be thy good pleasure to restore them to their former health, they may lead the residue of their lives in thy fear, and to thy glory: or else, give them grace so to take thy visitation, that, after this painful life has ended, they may dwell with thee in life everlasting; through Jesus Christ our Lord. **Amen.**[33]

Most gracious God, we give thee hearty thanks for the blessing of health which thou art bestowing upon thy servants in the different Wards of this Hospital (*especially* _____);

and we humbly pray thee to continue this thy good towards each one of them. Prepare them by thy blessing in this life for the enjoyment of eternal happiness in the life to come; through Jesus Christ our Lord. **Amen.**"[34]

A PRAYER FOR A SICK CHILD
(Anglican)

O Almighty God, and merciful Father, to whom alone belong the issues of life and death; Look down from heaven, we humbly beseech thee, with the eyes of mercy upon this child (_____) now lying upon the bed of sickness; Visit *him/her*, O Lord, with thy salvation; deliver *him/her* in thy good appointed time from *his/her* bodily pain, and save *his/her* soul for thy mercies' sake: That, if it shall be thy pleasure to prolong *his/her* days here on earth, *he/she* may live to thee, and be an instrument of thy glory, be serving thee faithfully, and doing good in *his/her* day and generation; or else receive *him/her* into those heavenly habitations, where the souls of them that sleep in the Lord Jesus enjoy perpetual rest and felicity. Grant this, O Lord, for thy mercies' sake, in the name of thy Son our Lord Jesus Christ, who liveth and reigneth with thee and the Holy Ghost, ever one God, world without end. **Amen.**[35]

A PRAYER FOR RESTORING HEALTH[36]
(Methodist)

O God,
the strength of the weak and the comfort of sufferers,
hear our prayers for those who are in need of healing and wholeness
Grant to them your compassion
Use our hands to show your care.
Strengthen us in the healing work of Jesus Christ
Our Lord and Savior.   **Amen.**

A PRAYER FOR HOSPITAL STAFFS[37]
(Anglican)

Father,
your Son Jesus Christ healed all kinds of sickness
as he went among the crowds
proclaiming the gospel of your kingdom.

Take all that is done in this hospital
in medical and nursing care,
in training and research,
in physiotherapy and psychiatry,

and in other practical ways,
and make it a continuation of his gracious ministry among us.

May the members of the staff,
whom you have equipped for this work,
come to know Jesus as their only Doctor and Savior.
I ask this in his name.

A PRAYER FOR DOCTORS, NURSES, AND HOSPITAL STAFF[38]
(Anglican)

O God,
I ask you to bless
All those who care for me in this hospital.
Bless the surgeons and the physicians.
I thank you
For the knowledge and for the skill
Which you have given to them.
Bless the nurses.
I thank you
For their cheerfulness and their patience and their watchfulness
All through the day and night.
Bless those who cook the meals
And who clean the wards,
And carry out the endless administrative duties that a place like this needs.
Give to all who care for the sick,
Not only here but in all hospitals and infirmaries and nursing homes,
Joy and satisfaction in their work.
And when they get tired of their work,
And a bit fed up with people like me,
Help them to remember how great a thing it is to ease the pains
And heal the bodies of suffering men and women.
And help them never to forget
Jesus who healed all those who had need of healing.

Let me remember what the Gospel tells me about Jesus: Matt. 8:16–17

A PRAYER FOR OPERATION DAY[39]
(Anglican)

O God,
This is the day
when operations are carried out.
Help those who have to go to the operating theatre today

not to be too nervous or anxious or frightened.
Help them to trust
in the kindness and the efficiency of the nurses,
the wisdom of the anesthetist,
the skill and the knowledge of the doctors and the surgeons.
And help them to remember
that you are just as near them in an operating theatre
as you are in any church.
Help the rest of us who have already been through things
to help those who have to go through them.
Help them to know that it is worth anything to be well again,
and to remember that nothing in life or in death
can separate them from you.
Help those at home
not to worry too much.
We cannot help being anxious
when our loved ones are ill.
But help us in confidence and in calmness
to leave everything
to the healing skill of men,
and to your love.

Let me say what the Psalmist said:
When I am afraid,
I put my trust in thee.

Ps. 56:3

A PRAYER FOR ONE INJURED IN AN ACCIDENT[40]
(Anglican)

O God,
I never thought when I went out that morning
that I would finish up here in this hospital.
Now I really know
that life is an uncertain business,
and that you never know
what is going to happen.
I don't really know whether the whole thing was my fault,
or whether someone else was to blame.
Don't let me start wondering about that.
Just let me accept this,
and do everything I can
to help my own progress.
Help those who love me

to get over the shock
that this must have been to them.
Help them not to worry,
but to be sure
that I'm in good hands here.
And when I get out of here
help me to remember to be a lot more careful,
so that I won't get involved in an accident
and so that I won't be the cause of an accident
to anyone else.
I am very grateful that I am still alive,
and that things are no worse than they are.
Help me to be a good patient
so that I will soon be on my feet again.

The Sage was right when he said:
You do not know what a day may bring forth.

Prov. 27:1

A PRAYER FOR ONE WHO KNOWS HE WILL NEVER BE FULLY WELL AGAIN[41]
(Anglican)

O God,
I know that when I get back home
life is never going to be quite the same again.
I know
that I will always have to take care;
and that I will have to go much slower;
and that I will not be able to make the efforts
that I used to make.
Help me to be glad that I am as I am,
and that I have got what I have.
I am still alive, and I can still work;
I can still move about;
I can still meet my friends,
and see the beauty of the world.
I can see now
that I was living at far too fast a pace,
and at far too great a pressure.
So help me from now on
to accept life as it is,
and to make the best of it.
And help me to be sure that,

if I go about it in the right way,
life is not finished,
but that the best is yet to be.

Let me remember what Paul said:
I have learned, in whatever state I am, to be content.

Phil. 4:11

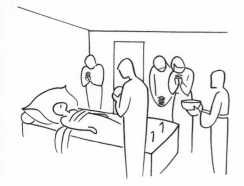

General Healing Services

"This prayer, made in faith, will heal the sick man." (James 5:15)

INTERFAITH HEALING SERVICE[42]
(Interfaith)

GATHER IN SILENCE

CENTERING CHANTS (TAIZÉ)   #857   or   #473   WIII   "Veni Sancte Spiritus" (Come, Holy Spirit)

SILENCE

SCRIPTURE READINGS

In the Tradition of Hinduism, a Reading from Atharva Veda *19.9.14*

Peace be to earth and to airy spaces!
Peace be to heaven, peace to the waters,
peace to the plants and peace to the trees!
May God grant me peace!
By this invocation of peace may peace be diffused!
By this invocation of peace may peace bring peace!
With this peace the dreadful I appease,
with this peace the cruel I appease,
with this peace all evil I appease,
so that peace may prevail, happiness prevail!
May everything for us be peaceful!

In the Tradition of Judaism and Christianity, a Reading from Isaiah 35:5–6

In the Tradition of Islam, a Reading from the Qur'an 10.57

O Humanity! There has come to you an exhortation from your Lord, a balm for that which is in the breasts, a guidance and mercy for believers.

In the Tradition of Sikhism, a Reading from Adi Granth, Bilaval, *M.5*

Under shelter of the Supreme Being, not a
    whiff of hot air touches us—
All around us is drawn the mystic circle of
    divine protection,
Keeping away suffering.
We have met the holy Preceptor, perfection
    incarnate,
Who has established this state.
He has administered medicine of the divine
    Name,
And attached our devotion to the Sole Lord.
The divine Preserver has preserved us, and all
    maladies removed.
In His grace has the Lord come to
    succor us.

In the Christian Tradition, a Reading from Mark 5:24–34

SILENCE

GATHERING OF HEALERS

BLESSING OF OIL

O God who sanctifies this oil, as You grant unto all who are anointed and receive of it the hallowing with which you anointed the kings and priests and prophets, so grant that it may give strength to all that partake of its mystery this night and health to all who seek Your Holy blessing from it. In the Power of your many names we pray, **Amen.**

COMMISSIONING OF HEALERS
(A prayer will be offered in the spirit of helping the healing teams open themselves as vessels of God; to be available to the people who will come to them and share their hearts; and to be in Covenant with God and with their prayer partner to hold space for the joys and concerns for which they will be privileged to pray.

    Healers depart to Healing Stations; all individuals in the congregation are invited to go to the station nearest them for a blessing. Participants are invited to ask for a blessing or prayer for an issue that is in need of healing attention. You are welcome to bring a joy or a concern— please keep in mind the number of participants and the need to share your thoughts in a brief sentence or two.)

CHANTING (TAIZÉ)   #21   PTWS   "O Lord, Hear My Prayer"
                   #24   PTWS   "Stay with Us"

DECOMMISSIONING OF HEALERS
(The intent of this prayer is to allow the healers to lift from their hearts to God's ears the prayers and concerns that have just been offered up to them.)

SILENCE

CLOSING CHANTS (TAIZÉ)   #604   WIII   *or*   #28   PTWS   "Ubi Caritas" (Where charity and love are found, God is there.)

BENEDICTION

May the God of Peace, Hope and Love,
Grant that we may have good health
And be enriched by the Holy Spirit's blessings. **Amen.**

DEPART IN SILENCE

MODERN LANGUAGE ANOINTING RITE[43]
(Anglican)

(This preparatory prayer may be said.)

Holy Spirit, come and be with us,
guide and inspire us,
let us know your power.
Power to heal,
power to comfort,
power to console.
Holy Spirit, come and be with us.
               —Martin Dudley

ANTIPHON

Savior of the world, by your cross and precious blood you have redeemed us; save us and help us, we humbly beseech you, O Lord.

(This psalm [121] may be said, or else another psalm, especially 23, 27, 43, 71 [verses 1–17], 77, 86, 103, 130, 142 or 146.)

PSALM 121

ANTIPHON

Savior of the world, by your cross and precious blood you have redeemed us; save us and help us, we humbly beseech you, O Lord.

NEW TESTAMENT LESSON   Jas. 5:14–16

LAYING-ON OF HANDS
(The minister then lays hands upon the sick person, and says one of the following:)

N, I lay my hands upon you in the name of the Father, and of the Son, and of the Holy Spirit, beseeching our Lord Jesus Christ to sustain you with his presence, to drive away all sickness of body and spirit, and to give you that victory of life and peace which will enable you to serve him both now and evermore. **Amen.**[44]

(Or:)

N, I lay my hands upon you in the name of our Lord and Savior Jesus Christ, beseeching him to uphold you and fill you with his grace, that you may know the healing power of his love. **Amen.**[45]

ANOINTING
(If the person is to be anointed, the minister dips a thumb in the holy oil, and makes the sign of the cross on the sick person's forehead and, if desired, on their hands, saying:)

N, I anoint you with oil in the name of the Father, and of the Son, and of the Holy Spirit. **Amen.**

(The minister may add:)

As you are outwardly anointed with this holy oil, so may our heavenly Father grant you the inward anointing of the Holy Spirit. Of his great mercy, may he forgive you your sins, release you from suffering, and restore you to wholeness and strength. May he deliver you from all evil, preserve you in all goodness, and bring you to everlasting life; through Jesus Christ our Lord. **Amen.**[46]

(After the anointing, the minister may say one of these prayers:)

God our healer,
keep us aware of your presence,
support us with your power,
comfort us with your protection,
give us strength
and establish us in your peace.[47]

(Or:)

God of mercy, source of all healing,
we give you thanks for your gifts of strength and life,

and especially for the gift of your Son, Jesus Christ,
through whom we have health and salvation.
Help us by your Holy Spirit to feel your power in our lives
and to know your eternal love;
through Jesus Christ our Lord. **Amen.**[48]

   Minister: As our Savior has taught us, so we pray:

THE LORD'S PRAYER

UNISON READING

Three in One[49]

> **O mighty God of every place,**
> **O Holy Son of kindly face,**
> **O Spirit God of inner grace,**
>   *Have mercy upon us.*
>
> **Creator God on You we rely,**
> **Savior God let us not die,**
> **Spirit God come from on high,**
>   *Have mercy upon us.*
>
> **Three in One of you we are blessed,**
> **One in Three give us your rest,**
> **Trinity God by us confessed,**
>   *Have mercy upon us.*
>
> **Holy God, make us holy,**
> **Wholesome God make us whole,**
> **Healthy God make us healthy,**
> **Holy, Strong One, God Almighty.**

(The minister may conclude with these words:)

The almighty Lord, who is a strong tower to all who put their trust in him, to whom all things in heaven, on earth, and under the earth bow and obey, be now and evermore your defense, and make you know and feel that the only name under heaven to give for health and salvation is the name of our Lord Jesus Christ. **Amen.**[50]

(The minister may say this or another blessing:)

The blessing of God Almighty, the Father, and Son, and the Holy Spirit be upon you and remain with you always. **Amen.**

BURRSWOOD HEALING SERVICE[51]
(Anglican)

BURRSWOOD CHRISTIAN COMMUNITY, TUNBRIDGE WELLS, ENGLAND

PREPARATION

(A hymn or song of praise is sung.)

HYMN   #192   HAM   (#365   AMR)   "Praise my Soul the King of Heaven"

(A welcome and a call to recollection and worship may be given, and the theme of the service set.)

> **Leader:** You are worthy, our Lord and God:
>
> **All: to receive glory and honor and power.**
>
> **Leader:** For you created all things:
>
> **All: and through your will they have their being.**
>
> **Leader:** You are worthy, Jesus our Lord, for you were slain:
>
> **All: and by your blood you ransomed us for God.**
>
> **Leader:** From every tribe and people and nation:
>
> **All: you made us a kingdom of priests to serve our God.**
>
> **Leader:** To you, O Lord our God, upon the throne of heaven
>
> **All: be blessing and honor, glory and might,**
>
> **Forever and ever. Amen.**

(In conclusion, all pray,)
> **Merciful God,**
> **You have prepared for all who love you,**
> **Such good things as pass our understanding.**
> **Pour into our hearts such love towards you**
> **That we, loving you in all things**
>   **and above all things,**
> **May obtain your promises**
>   **which exceed all that we can desire,**
> **Through Jesus Christ our Lord.   Amen.**

TEACHING

THE MINISTRY OF THE WORD
(A lesson will be read, and an address may be given.)

(Silence may be kept or music played.)

PRAYER OF INTERCESSION   Begin with Phil. 4:5b, 6–7
(During the offering of the intercessions the leader may invite a response:)

> **Leader:** Father, by your Spirit,
>
> **All: bring in your kingdom, we pray.**

THE LORD'S PRAYER

APPROACH

HYMN   #175   NCH   "O Christ the Healer We Have Come"

Let us be still and reflect upon what the presence of the Lord reveals. Christ the Light of the World has come to dispel the darkness of our hearts. In His light let us examine ourselves: preparing to confess our sins, and to lay before Him our burdens or hurt memories, and offering Him all our sorrows.

(A silence may be kept.)

> **All: Father eternal, source of all mercy:**
> **We are heavy laden and confess to you now,**
> **deep wounds from times past**
> **the griefs of today, and fears for the future.**
> **Loose and deliver us, setting us free:**
> **Father, in Jesus' name, hear our prayer.**
>
> **Leader:** Jesus said, "Come to me all who labor and are heavy laden, and I will give you rest."
>
> **All: Father eternal, source of all mercy:**
> **By our many sins we have spurned your love,**
> **and spoiled your image in us.**
> **We are ashamed and repent in sorrow.**
> **Forgive us and cleanse us of our sins;**
> **Father, in Jesus' name, hear our prayer.**
>
> **Priest:** May Almighty God, who is loving and merciful
> forgive you your sins, and free you from guilt;
> deliver you from evil, lifting away your burdens;

>to strengthen you in His service,
>and keep you in life, abundant and eternal,
>through Jesus Christ our Lord.   **Amen.**

INVOCATION

>**Leader:** Like the first disciples
>before the coming of God's power at Pentecost
>we wait in faith and pray.

(Silence.)

>**Leader:** Be with us, Holy Spirit:
>
>**All: nothing can separate us from your love.**

>**Leader:** Breathe on us, breath of God:
>
>**All: fill us with your saving power.**

>**Leader:** Speak in us, Spirit of God:
>Bring comfort, healing and peace.
>
>Spirit of the living God, fall afresh on us,
>Spirit of the living God, meet our need today,
>Touch us, hold us, heal us, make us,
>Spirit of the living God, fill us with your love.

(The minister may explain the way in which the laying-on of hands will be ministered.)

MINISTRY OF THE LAYING-ON OF HANDS

Jer. 17:14

(A hymn will be sung, which can be the Veni Creator.)

(Those ministering will go before the altar, to minister to each other that God may use their service, and also to pray for those whose names are written in the Altar Book.)

(After the hymn the leader will pray:)

>**Leader:** O God of peace and Lord of love, help us to be quiet,
>trusting and receptive today, accepting the inpouring
>of yourself; so that in the depths of our nature and being,
>your healing grace may take from us any anxious
>cares, any unworthy thoughts, and all ingratitude:
>
>**All: Thus Lord, may your healing love
>fill us in body, mind and spirit
>and our hearts be at rest in you.**

(The ministry of the laying-on of hands is available to all. First the ministers come to those unable to go to the altar rail. Stewards will indicate to you when and where to come forward.

You may stand at the rail, instead of kneeling, if you wish. Although there is not time to give long explanations, you may ask the minister for prayer for a particular need, for yourself or for someone else. Music may play softly during the ministry.)

Leader: (Titus 2:11)

**All: Eternal God, comfort of the afflicted,
and healer of the broken,
we thank you that you have met us
at our point of need.
Grant that we, who are being made whole,
may channel your healing love
to your damaged and broken world,
in the name of Jesus Christ our Lord. Amen.**

THE BLESSING

HYMN #224 HAM (#311 AMR) "Lead Us Heavenly Father"

EPISCOPAL SERVICE OF HEALING[52]
(Episcopal)

SAINT ANDREW'S EPISCOPAL CHURCH, SARATOGA, CA

Invite those who desire the laying-on of hands to come to the altar rail. They may kneel or stand. This service follows the regular Communion service.

OPENING SENTENCE

Grace and peace be with you, from God our Father and the Lord Jesus Christ.

Let us pray.

Almighty God, giver of life and health, send your blessing on all who are ill, and upon those who minister to them, that wellness may triumph through the risen Christ, who lives and reigns forever and ever. **Amen.**

(A prayer may be offered for each person individually according to that person's need, with laying on of hands [and anointing].)

(The Officiant then lays hands on each person [or if the person is to be anointed, the Priest dips a thumb into the holy oil and makes the sign of the cross on the person's forehead], saying one of the following:)

I lay my hands upon you (and anoint you with oil) in the name of the Father, and of the Son, and of the Holy Spirit, beseeching our Lord Jesus Christ to sustain you with his presence, to drive away all sickness of body and spirit, and to give you that victory of life and peace which will enable you to serve him both now and evermore. **Amen.**

(Or this:)

I lay my hands upon you (and anoint you with oil) in the name of our Lord and Savior Jesus Christ, beseeching him to uphold you and fill you with grace, that you may know the healing power of his love. **Amen.**

(In cases of necessity, a deacon or layperson may perform the anointing, using oil blessed by a bishop or priest.)

(Or this:)

The Almighty Lord, who is a strong tower to all who put their trust in Him, to whom all things in heaven, on earth, and under the earth bow and obey: be now and evermore your defense, and make you know and feel that the only Name under heaven given for health and salvation is the Name of our Lord and Savior Jesus Christ. **Amen.**

Officiant: Let us bless the Lord.

Response: Thanks be to God.

SCRIPTURE READINGS

OLD TESTAMENT

Exod. 16:13–15	(Manna in the wilderness)
1 Kgs. 17:17–24	(Elijah restores the widow's son to life)
2 Kgs. 4:9–14	(Healing of Naaman)
2 Kgs. 20:1–5	(I have heard your prayer . . . I will heal you)
Isa. 11:1–32	(Gifts of the Spirit)
Isa. 42:1–7	(The suffering servant)
Isa. 53:3–5	(With his stripes are we healed)
Isa. 61:1–3	(Good tidings to the afflicted)

PSALMS

Ps. 13	(My heart is joyful because of your saving help)
Ps. 20:1–6	(May the Lord answer you in the day of trouble)
Ps. 23	(You have anointed my head with oil)
Ps. 27 *or* 27:1–7, 9, 18	(The Lord is the strength of my life)
Ps. 91	(He will give his angels charge over you)
Ps. 103	(He forgives all your sins)
Ps. 121	(My soul waits for the Lord)
Ps. 139:1–17	(Where can I go from your Spirit?)
Ps. 145:14–22	(The eyes of all wait on you, O Lord)
Ps. 146	(Happy are they who have the God of . . .)

THE GOSPEL

Matt. 9:2–8	(Your sins are forgiven)
Matt. 26:26–30, 36–39	(The Last Supper: Not as I will)
Mark 1:21–28	(Jesus heals the man with the unclean spirit)
Mark 1:29–34a	(Jesus heals Peter's mother-in-law and others)
Mark 5:1–20	(Healing of Gerasene demoniac)
Mark 5:22–24	(Healing of Jairus's daughter)
Mark 6:7, 12–13	(They anointed with oil many that were sick)
Luke 17:11–19	(Your faith has made you well)
John 5:1b–9	(Do you want to be healed?)
John 6:47–51	(I am the bread of life)
John 9:1–11	(Healing of the man born blind)

NEW TESTAMENT

Acts 3:1–10	(Peter and John heal the lame man)
Acts 5:12–16	(Healings in Jerusalem; Peter's shadow)
Acts 10:36–43	(Apostolic preaching: He went about . . . healing)
Acts 16:16–18	(Slave girl with the spirit of divination)
Rom. 8:18–23	(We await the redemption of our bodies)
Rom. 8:31–39	(Nothing can separate us . . . the love of God)
2 Cor. 1:3–5	(God comforts us in affliction)
Col. 1:11–20	(May you be strengthened with all our power)
Heb. 12:1–2	(Looking to Jesus, the perfecter of our faith)
Jas. 5:13–16	(Is any among you sick?)
1 John 5:13–15	(. . . know that you have eternal life)

LUTHERAN SERVICE FOR THE SICK[53]
(Lutheran)

(This order is for use in a hospital or home with individuals who are unable to attend a corporate service of the Word for healing.

Confession and Forgiveness; Psalms, Lessons, and Prayers; Laying-on of Hands and Anointing the Sick; and Holy Communion are components of a ministry of healing.

Anointing normally is done by a pastor.)

(The minister says these or similar words:)

Minister: Peace to you from our Lord Jesus Christ.

All: Amen.

(Or:)

Minister: The peace of the Lord be with you always.

All: And also with you.

(P) We are here in the name of our Lord Jesus Christ, who restored the sick to health and who himself suffered for our sake. He is present among us still to heal and to make whole. We entrust our *brother/sister*, _____, to the grace and power of Jesus Christ, that the Lord may ease *his/her* suffering and grant *him/her* health and salvation.

(Confession and Forgiveness may follow.)

(One or more of the following lessons are read: Luke 4:40; Matt. 10:1,5,7–8a; Mark 6:12–13; James 5:14–16a.)

(The minister lays both hands on the person's head and, following a brief silence, says:)

(P) I lay my hands upon you in the name of our Lord and Savior Jesus Christ, beseeching him to uphold you and fill you with grace, that you may know the healing power of his love. **Amen.**

(If the person is to be anointed, the minister dips a thumb in the oil and makes the sign of the cross on the sick person's forehead, saying:)

(P) _____, I anoint you with oil in the name of the Father, and of the Son, and of the Holy Spirit. **Amen.**

(The prayer is said.)

(P) God of mercy, source of all healing, we give you thanks for your gifts of strength and life, and especially for the gift of your Son, Jesus Christ, through whom we have health and salvation. Help us by your Holy Spirit to feel your power in our lives and to know your eternal love; through Jesus Christ our Lord. **Amen.**

(The blessing concludes the service.)

(P) Almighty God, Father, Son, and Holy Spirit, give you strength and bless you with peace, now and forever. **Amen.**

NOTES ON THE SERVICE

Our Lord in his ministry performed many different acts of healing—forgiving sins, casting out demons, curing physical disease. His disciples also performed similar acts. These practices continued as part of the Church's ministry of healing. The laying-on of hands was associated with prayers for the work of the Holy Spirit. Anointing with oil was also associated with the activity of the Holy Spirit, but was especially related to the healing of sickness or infirmity.

In recent decades, many have rediscovered the value of the laying-on of hands and anointing with oil, both in the visitation of the sick and in public services of healing.

The oil used for anointing is olive oil, to which an aromatic ingredient such as synthetic oil of cinnamon or oil of bergamot may be added. This prayer may be said when the oil has been prepared:

(P) Lord God, you bring healing to the sick through your Son, Jesus Christ our Lord. May your blessings come upon all who are anointed with this oil, that they may be freed from pain and illness and be made whole. **Amen.**

The oil may be kept in a stock (a small metal cylinder) with a securely fitting lid. To prevent spillage, cotton may be put in the stock and only enough oil poured in to moisten the cotton.

INDIVIDUAL CONFESSION AND FORGIVENESS

The confession made by a penitent is protected from disclosure. The pastor is obligated to respect at all times the confidential nature of a confession.
The pastor greets the penitent. Then the penitent may kneel. The pastor asks:

> **Pastor:** Are you prepared to make your confession?

> **Penitent:** I am.

The pastor and penitent say the psalm together. Ps. 51:1–2, 16–18.

(P) You have come to make confession before God. In Christ, you are free to confess before me, a pastor in his Church, the sins of which you are aware and the sins which trouble you.

I confess before God that I am guilty of many sins. Especially I confess before you that
. . .

The penitent confesses those sins which are known and those which disturb or grieve him/her.

For all this I am sorry and I pray for forgiveness. I want to do better.

The pastor may then engage the penitent in pastoral conversation, offering admonition and comfort from the Holy Scriptures. Then they say together: Ps. 51:1, 11–13.

The pastor faces the penitent.

> **Pastor:** Do you believe that the word of forgiveness I speak to you comes from God himself?

> **Penitent:** Yes, I believe.

The pastor lays both hands on the head of the penitent.

> **Pastor:** God is merciful and blesses you. By the command of our Lord Jesus Christ, I, a called and ordained servant of the Word, forgive you your sins in the name of the Father, and of the Son, and of the Holy Spirit. **Amen.**

The penitent may pray silently in thanksgiving, or may pray together with the pastor.

> **Pastor/**
> **Penitent:** Ps. 103:8–13.

> **Pastor:** Glory to the Father, and to the Son, and to the Holy Spirit, as it was in the beginning, is now, and will be forever. **Amen.**

> **Penitent:** Blessed are those whose sins have been forgiven, whose evil deeds have been forgotten.

Pastor: Rejoice in the Lord, and go in peace.

The penitent may exchange the peace with the pastor.

PSALMS, LESSONS, AND PRAYERS

SICKNESS

Jer. 14:9b; Ps. 27; Ps. 42:1–3; Ps. 91; Matt. 11:28–30; Luke 4:38–44; John 14:27; Rom. 8:38–39; 1 Pet. 5:6–9a

Other lessons: 2 Kings 5:1–14; Matt. 8:1–13; Matt. 9:2–8, 18–26; Matt. 15:21–28; Mark 6:7, 12–13; Mark 7:31–37; Luke 6:6–10; Luke 17:11–19; John 4:46–53; James 5:10–20

PRAYERS

O Lord, visit and restore your servant for whom we offer our prayers. Look upon *him/her* in your mercy; give *him/her* comfort and sure confidence in you; defend *him/her* from danger and harm; and keep *him/her* in perpetual peace and safety; through your Son, Jesus Christ our Lord.

O God, the strength of the weak and the comfort of sufferers: Mercifully hear our prayers and grant to your servant, _____, the help of your power, that *his/her* sickness may be turned into health and our anxiety into joy; through Jesus Christ our Lord.

O God of power and love, be present with _____, that *his/her* weakness may be overcome and *his/her* strength restored; and that, *his/her* health being renewed, *he/she* may bless your holy name; through Jesus Christ our Lord.

Heavenly Father, giver of life and health: Comfort and relieve your servant, _____, and give your power of healing to those who minister to *his/her* needs, that *he/she* may be strengthened in *his/her* weakness and have confidence in your loving care; through Jesus Christ our Lord.

O Lord, look upon your servant, _____. Touch *him/her* with your healing hand and let your life-giving power flow into every cell of *his/her* body and into the depths of *his/her* soul, restoring *him/her* to wholeness and strength for service in your kingdom; through Jesus Christ our Lord.

GRATITUDE

Ps. 103:1–5, 19–22

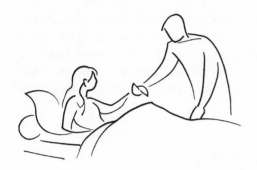

Diminished Physical Health

"He . . . took her by the hand, and . . . the fever left her." (Mark 1:31)

LAMENT FOR PHYSICAL OR MENTAL LOSS[54]
(Roman Catholic)

OPENING CHANT OR INSTRUMENTAL MUSIC

READING   MARK 15:33–34

LAMENTATIONS   PS. 44:17–19

SILENT MEDITATION

CLOSING PRAYER

Hidden God,
You are midwife who works with those in pain to bring
about the new creation. May your healing support us
in our struggle.
You are mothering bird who shelters those in difficulty
under the protective shadow of your wings. Hover over
our troubled hearts.
Come to our help. Bear us up. Be with us in our confusion
and sorrow. Deepen our sense of what remains to us amid
our losses. Strengthen our faith that your divine
compassion is present in ways we cannot see or understand.
We count on your love and mercy. Amen.

ANOINTING THE SERIOUSLY ILL[55]
(Roman Catholic)

This ritual is designed as a communal celebration of the sacrament of the anointing to take place within the context of a Eucharistic liturgy. Family, friends, and, if possible, caregivers are invited to gather with the seriously ill in a place suitable for worship. The primary community of worship, however, remains the ill persons themselves. Care should be taken that the liturgy not be celebrated in such a way that the sick persons become passive observers because of a pace set by the healthy. Care should be taken too that the sick persons gathered achieve some sense of relationship among themselves, and not simply with the cluster of their family and friends.

INTRODUCTORY RITES

GATHERING
(As the people gather in the space set aside for worship, music which is soft and inviting and yet which proclaims the presence and comfort of God should be playing. It may be recorded music or music sung by a small group of singers.)

(As the people gather, the presiding celebrant greets each of the sick in a personal manner and also welcomes the accompanying families and friends.)

CALL TO WORSHIP

> **Presider:** My brothers and sisters,
> welcome to God's house.
> I wish you peace and healing
> and the deep strength of our common faith
> in God and in Jesus Christ.
>
> You who are sick especially
> are honored guests in God's house.
> And we who join you in prayer
> are honored to be with you.
>
> May the peace and blessing of God our Father
> and the Lord Jesus Christ be with you.

> **All:** **And also with you.**

(The presider goes now to each of the sick and asks in these or similar words:)

> **Presider:** *N.,* as you come into God's presence this day,
> what special prayer do you bring to God?

(Each of the sick is invited to name a special prayer. When all have been given an opportunity to do so, the presider addresses all the sick:)

Presider: You have each named a special prayer of your own,
And have heard each other's special prayers.
Will you pray for each other
That God may bless you all?

(Some word or gesture of assent is invited, for example:)

The Sick: We will.

(The presider then addresses all who are gathered:)

Presider: And you who gather in love
With this blessed community of faith and hope,
Will you join in prayer for all the sick
That God will heal them and give them peace?

All: We will.

OPENING PRAYER

Presider: Then let us now pray:
Good and gracious God,
in your Son Jesus Christ,
you reach out to the sick
and touch them with your healing power.
Be with us now with this same healing power.
You hear the desires of our brothers and sisters
who come before you in hope and in trust.
You see us all
gathered in love before you.
Show yourself once more
a God who blesses and cares and gives peace.
We ask this through Christ our Lord.

All: Amen.

LITURGY OF THE WORD

Presider: And now let us listen and take comfort
in the word God speaks to us.

READING   Isa. 43:1–4a

RESPONSORIAL PSALM   Ps. 3

R. My soul is thirsting for you, O Lord my God.

GOSPEL ACCLAMATION   Cf. James 1:12

> **Alleluia.**
> **Blessed are they who stand firm when trials come;**
> **when they have stood the test,**
> **they will win the crown of life.**
> **Alleluia.**

GOSPEL   Matt. 11:25–30
(Other appropriate readings, psalms and verses may be chosen from among those offered in Pastoral Care of the Sick, *Part III,* Liturgy Documentary Series, *Volume 3: Pastoral Care of the Sick [Washington, D.C.: United States Catholic Conference]).*

HOMILY

INTERCESSIONS
(These may be composed by the presider or by some other minister, or they may be taken from Pastoral Care of the Sick *#122, 138.)*

LITURGY OF ANOINTING

INSTRUCTION

> **Presider:**   My brothers and sisters,
> we come now to the time of special grace,
> the time of anointing.
>
> The apostle James asked:
> "Are there people sick among you?
> Let them send for the priests of the Church,
> and let the priests pray over them,
> anointing them with oil in the name of the Lord.
> The prayer of faith will save the sick
> and the Lord will raise them up.
> If they have committed any sins,
> their sins will be forgiven them."
>
> My brothers and sisters
> who are sick among us,
> it is our privilege as a priestly people
> to pray God's healing and anointing upon you.
>
> Know that it is in your power
> to offer even your sickness
> as a gift of worship to God.
>
> In God's power may you be healed.

LAYING-ON OF HANDS
(Joined by some of the friends and family, the presider goes to the sick one by one, places hands on each of them, and prays silently.)

ANOINTING
(The presider then anoints the sick on the forehead and hands, saying:)

(anointing the forehead)

Presider: Through this holy anointing
May the Lord in his love and mercy help you
With the grace of the Holy Spirit.

All: Amen.

(anointing the hands)

Presider: May the Lord who frees you from sin
Save you and raise you up.

All: Amen.

(Pastoral Care of the Sick #124, 141)

PRAYER AFTER ANOINTING
(When all have been anointed, the presider invites the sick to join hands, if this is possible, during the following prayer:)

Presider: Good and gracious God,
God of love, ever-caring,
we give you praise and thanks
through your Son, Jesus Christ.

In him you show us how much you love us.
In him you have tasted
the beauty and the pain of all human life.

Those who were sick came to him
and found healing.
Those who had sinned asked of him
And found your forgiveness.

With oil that is blessed
and hearts that are humbled
we have anointed our sisters and brothers
here present.

With us at their side
they offer to you
their fears and their doubts,
their suffering and pain,
their human lives, fragile and broken.

Send your own Spirit of love upon them.
Speak the healing words of your Son to them.
Give them the grace of your loving presence.

Keep their eyes fixed firmly upon you
in the eager hope and expectation
that with you, and with you alone,
their lives will be transformed.

Where sin and death will be no more,
where sickness and sorrow will be overcome,
there may we know together
that you are our God,
and we the people you call your own.

All glory be to you, Father,
and to your Son,
and to your Holy Spirit,
now and forever.

All: Amen.

(If this service of anointing takes place apart from the Eucharist, the Lord's Prayer and a final blessing follow. If it takes place during the celebration of the Eucharist, the liturgy continues as usual:)

LITURGY OF THE EUCHARIST

(If possible, while the gifts are brought to the altar, some personal effect of each of the sick is also to be brought forward. This serves to unite their own sickness and suffering symbolically with the offering of Christ enacted in the Eucharist.)

(At the sign of peace, where it is possible, the sick extend the greeting to each other.)

(The following orations are suggested:)

PRAYER OVER THE GIFTS

Presider: Lord our God, giver of all good gifts,
from among the many you have given us
we bring bread and wine to give you thanks and praise.
In simple gifts we bring all that we are
and all that we hope for.

Look with special kindness
on our brothers and sisters who are sick among us.
Give them healing and peace.

Be pleased with us and the offering of our lives.
Unite us to Christ
and his own sacrifice of praise.

We ask this through Christ, our Lord.

All: Amen.

CONCLUDING PRAYER

Presider: Lord Jesus Christ,
you are the beginning and the end
of all God's creation.

You have gone before us to prepare the way.
Yet you remain among us as companion and friend.

As you have nourished us with your own food of life,
help us to be strong in faith,
a source of courage to each other,
and a gift of praise
to the God you have revealed.

We ask this in your name,
for you live and reign forever and ever.

All: Amen.

PASTORAL NOTE

There will, of course, be some who will not be able to participate in this communal form of anointing. For the long-term ill, the regular enactment of this anointing will serve as the context, the "world remembered," when they no longer can participate with the others. For these, it would be helpful if some of the "community of the sick" join in the prayer of the anointing. For others too it would be helpful if some continuity with this communal celebration could be established so that the witness it represents may be a ministry to all who are anointed in whatever circumstances it proves necessary to anoint them. It might be helpful to conclude the communal service with a "dismissal" that sends those who have been anointed to minister in some way to those who were not able to attend. The anointing of these others would then be held as part of the communal celebration itself.

HEALING AND WHOLENESS[56]
(Presbyterian)

NATIONAL PRESBYTERIAN CHURCH, WASHINGTON, D.C.

WE ASSEMBLE IN GOD'S NAME

PRELUDE   "Benediction"   Karg-Elert

CALL TO WORSHIP

SUNG PRAYER OF ADORATION   #482   PrH   "Praise Ye the Lord the Almighty"

> **Leader:** God, whom we gather to worship,
> knows the masks we so often wear:
> tolerance, when we feel hate;
> acceptance, when we feel disdain;
> calmness, when storms rage within;

> **People: Praise to God for continuing love for us,
> sinners that we are!**

> **Leader:** Praise to God for continuing acceptance of us,
> even when we disfigure the image in which we were created.

> **People: Praise to God for the Holy Spirit
> who consoles the faint-hearted.**

> **Leader:** Come, let us worship God, and to God let us sing!

PRAYER OF CONFESSION (UNISON)

Christ our Lord, You have graced our lives with love lavished beyond measure. Emptied of any selfish ambition, You poured yourself out for us with a resolution that shames our pale commitments. The depth and breadth of Your love should inspire us to a ministry knowing no barriers and no limits in its kindness. Our response has hardly been generous.

And our love for You, far from being whole-hearted, is undermined by fickle enthusiasms. Christ our Savior, have mercy upon us. Cleanse our hearts. And through Your loving Spirit, empower us to love as You have loved us. Amen.

DECLARATION OF FORGIVENESS

> **Leader:** The mercy of the Lord is from everlasting to everlasting. I declare to you in the name of Jesus Christ, you are forgiven!

People: May the God of mercy, who forgives all our sins, strengthen us with all goodness, and by the power of the Holy Spirit, keep us in eternal life.

WE PROCLAIM GOD'S WORD

OLD TESTAMENT READING   Jer. 18:1–11

HYMN   #382   UMH   "Have Thine Own Way"

CONTEMPLATION ON   Matt. 26:36–46

Centering
Listening
Imagining
Journaling
Experiencing

WE OFFER OUR LIVES TO GOD

INTERCESSION FOR HEALING

Leader: God, our Creator, Your will for us and for all Your people is health and salvation:

All: Have mercy on us.

Leader: Jesus Christ, Son of God, You came that we might have life and have it in abundance:

All: Have mercy on us.

Leader: Holy Spirit, Your dwelling within us makes us the temples of Your presence:

All: Have mercy on us.

Leader: To the triune God, the source of all love and all life, let us offer our prayers for healing and wholeness.

(Silence)

Lord in Your mercy,

All: Hear our prayer.

Leader: For all who are disabled by injury or illness,

(Silence)

Lord in Your mercy,

All: Hear our prayer.

Leader: For those who grieve,

(Silence)

Lord in Your mercy,

All: Hear our prayer.

Leader: For all who are troubled by confusion or pain,

(Silence)

Lord in Your mercy,

All: Hear our prayer.

Leader: For the Presbyterian Church, broken and divided,

(Silence)

Lord, in Your mercy,

All: Hear our prayer.

Leader: For all who work for healing and wholeness,

(Silence)

Lord, in Your mercy,

All: Hear our prayer.

Leader: Into Your hands, O God, we commend all for whom we pray, trusting in Your mercy; through Jesus Christ, our Lord.

All: Amen.

LAYING-ON OF HANDS AND ANOINTING WITH OIL
(Those wishing to be anointed and/or desiring special prayers for healing for the church, themselves, or others, are invited to approach one of the eight prayer stations in the sanctuary. Others are asked to remain seated and are invited to continue in silent prayer.)

UNISON PRAYER

Holy God, we pray that we may be comforted in our suffering and made whole. When we are afraid, give us courage; when we feel weak, grant us strength; when we are afflicted, afford us patience; when we are lost, offer us hope; when we are alone, move us to each other's side. This we pray in the name of the one who heals us by His Passion. Amen.

GO IN GOD'S NAME

HYMN   #535   PrH   "Go with Us Lord"

BLESSING

POSTLUDE   "Mass for the Parishes"   Couperin

BENEDICTION
(Worshipers are asked to be seated until the conclusion of the Postlude as we continue to worship through the language of music.)

(Please leave the Sanctuary in silence.)

GOD'S HEALING TOUCH[57]
(Presbyterian)

WESTMINSTER PRESBYTERIAN CHURCH, SAN DIEGO, CA

LISTEN TO THE SILENCE
(Open your heart and mind and soul to God's presence.)

PSALM OR HYMN   "The Long Way Home"   #61   PrH   to the tune of UNE JEUNE
PUCELLE, words by George R. Pasley
or
#380   PrH   "O Christ the Healer"

THE LONG WAY HOME[58]

There was a man who could not walk
And neither could he run—
But four good friends did carry him
To the house where Jesus was.
But when they came upon the door
They found they could not enter there.

Refrain:
We have not seen before,
Never, before.
In excelsis Gloria!

The crowd was great where Jesus was
They could not use the door.
So on the roof the four friends climbed
Determined to get in,
And through a hole they lowered him
Into the place where Jesus was.

Refrain

When Jesus saw their faith was great,
He said unto the man—
All sins that you have done 'til now
Are wiped away this day.
That made the scribes and Pharisees
Cry blaspheme and grumble angry.

Refrain

But Jesus was not finished yet,
He had more grace to give.
And looking at the man, he said:
Take up your mat and live!
And so the man whose sins were gone
Stood, and walked the long way home.

Refrain

PRAYER FOR ILLUMINATION

SCRIPTURE READING AND REFLECTION

OFFERING OF LIVES TO GOD

Rom. 12:1–2

PERSONAL PRAYER FOR HEALING AND WHOLENESS

THANKSGIVING FOR GOD'S HEALING TOUCH

LORD'S PRAYER

BLESSING

GUIDANCE

For Personal Prayer
1. *When you wish personal prayer, please go to an available prayer team. You may ask for specific prayer, general prayer or simply sit with the prayer team in the presence of God. A Healing Touch practitioner is at one of the stations.*
2. *You may express your preferences for prayer and anointing or prayer only.*
3. *Return to your seat when the prayer is completed.*
4. *You are welcome to stay and continue in prayer to the close of the service or to leave as your needs require.*

AIDS

"Help carry one another's burdens." (Gal. 6:2)

HEALING AND ANOINTING FOR PERSONS WITH AIDS[59]
(Methodist)

GATHERING

Informal greetings, conversation, and fellowship
Announcement and welcoming

The gathering can include any of the information from the following statements of explanation. In this brief time before worship, the leader can explain the worship service to the congregation. It is best if the leader simply puts the announcement into words which express personal feelings and understanding of the service.

ANNOUNCEMENT AND WELCOME

Welcome to this service of worship! It is part of our Christian tradition to come together, united in Jesus Christ, particularly in times of stress and trouble. Today we gather because the impact of AIDS has touched the life of our human community.

We gather because our lives have been impacted in various ways. Some of us have experienced first-hand the illness or death of a loved one. Some of us have HIV infection and are living with AIDS. All of us are imprinted with the pain and fear surrounding this international epidemic.

So we come together in worship, united in knowing that not AIDS, but God is the Alpha and the Omega, the beginning and the end. Let us pray and sing the songs of faith, confident in a God who stands by us, affirms us, and gives us the strength to be sustained and to live today fully.

(Or:)

ANNOUNCEMENT

As a worshiping community, we have been challenged by such a moment as this!
A moment when we know we are living with AIDS and that we are loved and affirmed.
A moment in which we can offer compassion to those with AIDS and those who are HIV positive.
A moment where we can sit and comfort those who suffer illness or grieve loss.
A moment when we stand in solidarity with the care partners, health care workers, and researchers as they continue their diligent labor.
A moment and an opportunity to be with all those who are ill with any disease. Those worried, fearful or weary. Those carrying others in prayer.

In this moment:
We *all* stand in need of God's healing.

GREETING AND HYMN

HYMN   #205   SNC   "Healer of Our Every Ill"
(This is a more formal greeting in the Lord's name. It declares that the Lord is present and empowers our worship.)

GREETING

Welcome to the Body of Christ gathering to pray, sing, and give one another words of encouragement. We come to seek strength, courage, and hope. Come, Lord Jesus. Strengthen our spirits, reinforce our courage, and renew our hope.

(or:)

RESPONSIVE ACT

> **Leader:** Come Lord Jesus, and empower our worship:
>
> **People:** **So our community can be a sign,**
> **among other signs, of God's gracious love.**
>
> **Leader:** Come Lord Jesus, and guide our worship:
>
> **People:** **So we can be a symbol of hope**
> **and compassion for the world.**
>
> **Leader:** Come Lord Jesus, and move our worship:
>
> **People:** **So we can be a vision of wholeness**
> **and partners in healing.**
>
> **Leader:** Great Physician, healer of body, mind and spirit:

People: **Make us a sign, a symbol, and an**
embodiment of the vision. Refresh us with
the healing balm of your presence.

(or:)

Greeting

Leader: We come to worship, seeking healing and hope.

In this time together we will offer prayers and songs to God and words for each other, but especially friends, family, care partners, and persons with AIDS. Let us call upon God's power and presence in this time of worship.

(or:)

Opening Scripture Sentence

Leader: Be comforted, knowing that the sufferings of this present time will be surpassed by the glory about to be revealed to us. For the creation waits with eager longing for the revealing of the children of God.

(Based on Rom. 8:18–19)

Leader: Let us worship our Creator.

Hymns

(These listed hymns from the United Methodist Hymnal *can be used anywhere appropriate in the service. The selections were chosen because they express the concerns and needs of the people in worship. The hymn may precede or follow the greeting.)*

#128 "He Leadeth Me"
#138 "The King of Love My Shepherd Is"
#262 "Heal Me, Hands of Jesus"
#265 "O Christ, the Healer"
#266 "Heal Us, Emmanuel, Hear Our Prayer"
#377 "It Is Well with My Soul"
#476 "Lonely the Boat"
#505 "When Our Confidence Is Shaken"
#512 "Stand by Me"
#521 "I Want Jesus to Walk with Me"
#523 "Saranam, Saranam" (Refuge)
#549 "Where Charity and Love Prevail"
#561 "Jesus, United by Thy Grace"

Opening Prayers and Praise

(Prayer of the day, such as a collect. In addition a prayer of confession and act of pardon may be placed here.)

PRAYER OF THE DAY

> **Leader:** Loving God, you are the source of our courage each day. You hold each of us in your care and you know our deepest needs. We stand firm in the hope of your presence which sustains us. **Amen.**

(or:)

RESPONSIVE LITANY

> **Leader:** We thank you, God for inviting us to pray.
>
> We pray for your presence
> and the power of the Holy Spirit.
>
> **People:** **Fill us with your healing power
> and grace-full love.**
>
> **Leader:** We pray for courage to live with AIDS
> and walk with those living with HIV infection.
>
> **People:** **Encourage us to open our arms and hearts.**
>
> **Leader:** We pray for all care partners, family members,
> and friends.
>
> **People:** **Give us perseverance and patience.**
>
> **Leader:** We pray for the lonely, frightened, and despairing.
>
> **People:** **Grant us relief and gentleness of spirit.**
>
> **Leader:** We pray for others and for ourselves.
>
> **People:** **Fill us, encourage us,
> grant us your enduring love. Amen.**

(or:)

PRAYER OF THE DAY

> **Leader:** Gracious God, we give you thanks that our time of living can be both holy and healing. We gather here to seek your presence among us. Fill us with your healing power that we may be channels of your love.
>
> **People:** **Amen.**

PRAYER OF CONFESSION AND ACT OF PARDON

(When a Prayer of Confession and Act of Pardon are used, the tone should be one of assurance, acceptance, and hope. The emphasis should be on the confession of all the sin of all the

people present. The confession or pardon should not insinuate in any way that AIDS is either the result of sin or a punishing judgment from God.)

A LITANY OF CONFESSION

> **Leader:** He was dying of AIDS.
> He said to me, "No one touches me."
>
> **People: I did not touch him.**
>
> **Leader:** Her face was old and worn before its time.
> She told me "I'm sick and tired
> of being sick and tired."
>
> **People: I had no time to stop.**
>
> **Leader:** His dreams for the future were dimmed.
> He asked: "Where is the welcome I once enjoyed?"
>
> **People: I remained silent.**
>
> **Leader:** She was angry, with feelings of resentment
> and the unfairness of life.
> She implored: "Where were you
> when I needed you?"
>
> **People: I turned away from her.**
>
> **Leader:** In these and in many ways, O God, we are caught in fear, confusion, and anger. We have not loved our neighbors or heard their needs. Forgive us, we pray, as we reach out with hearts to respond, hands to help, and ears to hear.
>
> **People: Amen.**

(or:)

PRAYER OF CONFESSION

> **People: We confess, O God, that we long to be**
> **faithful disciples of Jesus Christ:**
> > **To be loving as he was loving,**
> > **To show mercy and compassion as he did.**
> > **To give generously and sacrificially of ourselves as he did in his life.**
> > **We have acted in self-serving ways.**
> > **We have hurt others with our words.**
> > **We have ignored persons who need us and turned instead to those**
> > **from whom we find favor and admiration.**
> **As you have so graciously promised,**
> **Forgive us our sin.**
> **Be generous with your compassion and mercy,**

> **And grant us new opportunities to serve and to love.**
> **We pray in the name of the loving**
> **And compassionate one, Jesus Christ. Amen.**

ACT OF PARDON

Leader: Hear the Good News of forgiveness! God grants new life to those who turn and seek it. In the name of Jesus Christ, you are forgiven.

People: Amen.

(or:)

ACT OF PARDON

Leader: And Jesus said:
> "For I was hungry
>   and you gave me food,
> I was thirsty and
>   you gave me something to drink,
> I was a stranger and
>   you welcomed me."

"Come, you who are blessed, inherit the kingdom prepared for you from the foundation of the world."

People: Amen.

Based on Matt. 25:34–35

(or:)

PRAYER OF CONFESSION

Leader: Merciful God, you who know us as we are and still love us, we confess that we are afraid to admit the fear that lies in the depths of our souls. Help us to face that which we want to hide even from ourselves.

Forgive us: The walls around our hearts,
     —Our apathy in the face of need,
     —Our indifference to oppression,
     —Our dry eyes in the midst of sorrow.

Forgive us: The loss of FAITH
     in your steadfastness,
Our loss of HOPE
     in your faithfulness,
Our loss of LOVE,
     for each other,
Our numbness to the loss.

Instill in us a sense of active compassion. Humble us to see and name our inadequacy and call upon your presence in the midst of this perplexing need. Give us the courage to find ways of being faithful disciples. Awaken us to your presence and support in affliction so that we do not judge illness as a sign of your absence. May your piercing knowledge of us lead us to healing. Break down barriers we have built. Forgive our sins.

People: **Lead us to be people of FAITH, channels of HOPE, and vessels of your LOVE. Amen.**

ACT OF PARDON

Leader: Hear the Good News:
God gives us the courage we need to keep FAITH,
the support we need in affliction to HOPE,
and the compassion we need to LOVE.
In the name of Jesus Christ, you are forgiven!

People: **In the name of Jesus Christ, we are forgiven!**
Glory to God. Amen.

PROCLAMATION AND RESPONSE

PRAYER FOR ILLUMINATION
(The blessing of the Holy Spirit is invoked upon the reading, preaching, hearing, and doing of the Word. See the United Methodist Hymnal *for appropriate prayers. One, from page 6, is printed here for you.)*

BLESSING OF THE HOLY SPIRIT

Leader: Lord, open our hearts and minds
by the power of your Holy Spirit,
that, as the Scriptures are read
and your Word proclaimed,
we may hear with joy what you say to us today.

People: **Amen.**

RESPONSIVE PRAYER

Leader: As we listen to the Scriptures read this day,

People: **Open our minds by the strength**
of your Holy Spirit, Lord.

Leader: As we hear the Word proclaimed in your name,

People: **Open our hearts by the power**
of your Holy Spirit, Lord.

Leader: As we who have ears, hear,

> **People: Change us, and lead us to new life, through
> the vitality of your everflowing Spirit. Amen.**

SCRIPTURE
(Choose from the following Psalms—13, 23, 27, 30, 46, 90, 91, 107, 116.)

SERMON
(Suggested texts—Ruth 1:1–19a; Isa. 40:28–31; Mark 2:2–12; Mark 4:35–41; Luke 10:30–37; John 13:1–20; 1 Thess. 1:1–10.)

RESPONSE TO THE WORD
(An invitation to Christian discipleship, followed by a hymn of invitation or of response, or a baptism or confirmation hymn or affirmation of faith can be found on pages 880–889 in the UMH. Suggested affirmation: #887 "Affirmation from Romans" 8:35, 37–39.)

CONCERNS AND PRAYERS
(Joys and concerns to be included in the prayers may be expressed. Suggested prayers from the UMH are "For the Sick" [#457], "The Serenity Prayer" [#459], and "In Time of Illness" [#460].)

PASTORAL PRAYER

(or:)

RESPONSIVE PRAYER

> **Leader:** O Great Physician:
>
> We who are surrounded by your love thank you for your healing power. We lift our hearts in thanksgiving for your presence as we struggle with the mystery of suffering and pain.
>
> **People: O God of love, heal your people.**
>
> **Leader:** Our lives have been set off balance by the impact of AIDS: the scare of headlines, the stretching of budgets, unpaid medical bills, soaring prices of saving medicines.
>
> **People: O God of love, mend your people.**
>
> **Leader:** We cry, "How many more will be lost before this health crisis is over?" We fear further loss of our sons and daughters from this disease.
>
> **People: O God of love, cure your people.**
>
> **Leader:** We've become a fearful people living in the midst of fearful people. We fear the possibility of our own illness or an illness of those we love.
>
> **People: O God of love, comfort your people.**

Leader: For you, O Lord, have the power to transform our illness of body, mind, and spirit. Bless us now. Give us comfort and healing, wholeness and peace, strength, hope, and fullness of life.

People: Our Great Physician, God of love, you are the source of healing. Mend us, cure us, and comfort us. Amen.

(or:)

PETITION PRAYER
(Following each petition there may be a period of silence in which the congregation is invited to name aloud or silently those persons or situations they wish to remember.)

Leader: God of mercy we thank you today that we are invited to be in this holy space to bear witness to the sacredness of all human life. We are all children of your creation and ask now for your blessing.

(Silence)

We pray and bring before you our pain, anger, grief, and tears. We seek your guidance to comfort one another and find comfort for ourselves.

(Silence)

We pray and set before you our hope, courage, wholeness, and peace. We lift these up as signs of your presence among us.

(Silence)

We name before you those who have been affected by the crisis of AIDS. We pray for any others in grief or trouble, that they may call upon you for help.

(Silence)

We pray and release all these concerns into your sustaining power. Bless us, heal us, make us whole. Through Jesus Christ our Lord, who lives and reigns with you and the Holy Spirit, one God, now and forever. **Amen.**

CONFESSION, PARDON, AND PEACE

THE PEACE
(We believe this is a necessary part of the worship service. It is an opportunity to offer signs of reconciliation and love. The congregation may stand and greet one another in the peace of our Lord Jesus Christ. The leader may use these words or other words which reflect the purpose of the Peace:)

Leader: We are not to fear one another but embrace one another. Christ seeks to heal brokenness, wherever it is found in life, and offers us peace.

The peace of the Lord be with you all.

People: And also with you.

OFFERING

CLOSING HYMN   #377   UMH   "It Is Well with My Soul"

BENEDICTION

PRAYER OF ENTREATY (FOR THOSE WITH AIDS)[60]
(Interfaith)

Leader: We cry aloud.
Wounded, body and spirit,
darkness come upon us,
we wait.
Crying out from the depths,
we wait; we pray.

**People: How much longer will you
forget us God:
how much longer will you
hide your face from us?**

Leader: We wait; we pray
for those struck down,
brought low,
deprived of the
rest of their years,
for all who have died of AIDS.
We shake our fists,
we wrestle with pain.
Why? How can this be?
We call to mind and
hand over to your care,
the ones who suffer now.
We wait; we pray.

**People: How much longer
must we endure
grief in our souls and
sorrow in our hearts,
by day and by night?**

Leader: We wait; we pray.
We beg your healing power
on those who suffer:

the families faced with death,
the loved one bowed in grief;
on all who struggle
to give comfort,
on all who seek
to ease the dying.
We wait; we pray.

People: **How much longer**
must our foes
face the upper hand of us?
Look, answer, God our God.

Leader: We wait; we pray
for those unable to reach out,
for those who are apart,
for the evil in our world
which scorns the weak,
the sin in each of us
that leads us to reject.
For we acknowledge that
we fear
the loneliness of life
without your spirit,
the surrender required
to live in relationship,
the hesitation, the uncertainties,
we fear these;
the more that you love,
we wait, we pray.

People: **Give light to our eyes or**
we shall sleep in death.

Leader: We wait; we pray;
in need of your presence.
Let our prayer, your work in us,
be healing;
renew and strengthen us,
that we may go our way in joy, and
be led forth in peace.

People: **But we, for our part, rely on**
your love, O God.
Let our hearts rejoice
in your saving help.

**Let us sing to God
for goodness shown.**

AIDS: PRAYER AND HEALING[61]
(Interfaith)

OLD PINE STREET PRESBYTERIAN CHURCH, PHILADELPHIA, PA

(As we come together as a community of prayer and healing let us take time to greet those people we know and those we do not.)

"We Gather Together" *(a Netherlands folk song as adapted by Ruth Duck)*

"The God of Prophets Praise" *(revised version of the Yigdal adapted and copyrighted in 1974 by the Ecumenical Women's Center, further adapted by Grace Moore)*

(We sit as we experience the Voice of ISOLATION.)

READING

I was alone, frightened, and confused. I desperately needed help in coping with the emotional turmoil of facing this unknown. Was I going to die? *(Stephen Morin & Walter Batchelor, Public Health Reports, Jan.–Feb. 1984)*

> **One:** Where there is despair in life,
>
> **Many: Let us bring hope,**
>
> **One:** Where there is no light,
>
> **Many: Let us bring only light,**
>
> **One:** And where there is sadness,
>
> **Many: Ever joy.**
>
> **One:** Grant that we may not so much seek to be consoled,
>
> **Many: As to console:**
>
> **One:** To be understood,
>
> **Many: As to understand: For it is in giving that we receive, it is in pardoning that we are pardoned, and it is in dying that we are born to Eternal Life. God, make us instruments of Your peace.**

READING

What is needed? . . . Everything needs to be done: people with AIDS need money (many become unemployable), shelter, clothing, food. They need friends and support groups and medical care and professional counseling and prayer groups and spiritual direction. They need friends to assure them. . . . They need to be surrounded by the mantra that saw me through my one dreadful night. ("I am safe in the palm of God's hand.") There need to be healing services and vigils, the right kinds of funerals and memorials, generosity for research, and hospice care. And prayer. Lots and lots of prayer. *(John Fortunato,* The Witness, *September 1985)*

(Please be seated)

SOLO   "I Know That My Redeemer Liveth"   Handel (from the "Messiah")

SILENT REFLECTION
(We sit as we experience the Voice of FEAR.)

READING

A Georgia couple, in a four-page letter to the New Orleans Chamber of Commerce this summer, recounted how they panicked by what they considered the large percentage of gay waiters in French Quarter restaurants. After their first night on the town, fearing they would get AIDS, they bought all their food at a downtown supermarket and ate in the hotel rooms. (Wall Street Journal, *October 10, 1985)*

THE HOMILY   Luke 13:10–13

SILENT REFLECTION
(We stand as we give Voice to HEALING.)

HYMN   "Be Not Afraid" based on Isa. 43:2–3 and Luke 6:20 by Robert J. Dufford

READING   1 John 4
Ps. 34

A TIME OF HEALING

Let us be of one mind in a spirit of prayer and meditation claiming wholeness for ourselves and others. Let us remember the sick, the worried well, those who are caring for the sick, and our society in its and our fear. All are invited to come forward to receive personal prayer for healing of body, mind or spirit. A Jewish person will be at the Left station to pray the blessing *"Me Shebayrach"* with those for whom that would be a helpful ministry. The two Center stations will make available the Christian rite of Anointing for Healing for those for whom that would be helpful. The station to the Right is available for those who might wish a moment of meditation rather than prayer.

CHORAL MUSIC   "May Thy Blessed Spirit"   (unknown)

A TIME OF PRAYER

(We pray or meditate as we are called and led to do.)

(Please respond to each petition with:)

God, Hear us and make us whole.

WE PASS THE PEACE

(Moving beyond ourselves, we reach out to one another with a healing touch. Be open to one another. Do not intrude.)

Cancer and Stroke

"I will give you what I have." (Acts 3:6)

BLESSING RITUAL AROUND THERAPY FOR A DISEASE[62]
(Evangelical Lutheran Church in America)

"EMBRACING WHOLENESS"

COMMENTS

A man was diagnosed with cancer in the fall. Although relatively healthy throughout most of his life, the diagnosis was a shock but not a surprise. His family history was rife with the disease, and as he shared with me, "It was only a matter of time." Having had intimate knowledge of the courses of treatment available and the effects of that treatment made this particular situation easier to discuss, but all of the emotions of the less knowledgeable were still evident. As we created this ritual, we talked at length about the burgeoning research data available regarding the positive attitude of cancer patients, and how prayer and hope were critical to the therapeutic process.

ITEMS NEEDED

Prepare for this ritual with some type of planting items. Since this diagnosis came in the fall of the year, bulbs were readily available, and should be even throughout the winter in indoor varieties such as the paperwhite narcissus. In the spring and summer months, fast-growing seeds could be used. If indoors, have a pot, soil, trowel, and bulb/seed on hand, as well as a place prepared for the actual planting. If weather permits, you may wish to plant outside. Location may be the church's own garden or a site of the counselee's choice.

Pastor: We begin in the strong name of God our Creator, who planted for us a goodly garden in which to live, and still sustains us through the water of our Baptism and the nourishment of his Holy Supper.

_____, you have come here to give your grieving into God's care, and to ask for God's blessing as you begin the battle against the disease which has invaded your body.

Let us pray: O God, your precious child is calling on you today, and in faith and trust is asking for your presence in a powerful way in his life. We believe in your promise of abundant life, we thank you for the health that _____ has enjoyed for so many years, and we are confident that you will be with us as we begin a new journey together.

Take all of his anger and grief, his fear and his pain, and wrap them in your loving arms of health. Keep him secure in the love of his family and this community, and bring him courage and strength to face each day focused only on you.

As we plant this bulb/seed in the ground that you yourself created, we ask that you might use this growth as a symbol to _____ of the miracle of life and health. Allow him to ponder the cycle of growing on his journey: first the dark coolness of the surrounding earth, the stretching and reaching in that darkness for the source, you his light and his life. Let him feel the waters of Baptism bathing his whole body and soothing his pain, and nourish him often on your own body and blood, for the growth of his spirit and his very health. And, finally, bring him through the night and the darkness into the brilliance of your own light, that he might continue to grow and bring forth fruit among your faithful people in the world. *(The bulb/seed is planted.)*

Bless _____ as you bless the growth of this wondrous example of your creation. We pray in the name of the Great Physician, your Son, Jesus Christ, our Lord. **Amen.**

BLESSING OF MARROW[63]
(Ecumenical)

Leader: We come today to celebrate a new beginning.
We come to bless a marvelous gift.
Any new beginning stirs up many feelings within us.

All: **We feel afraid and anxious about the unknown,
but at the same time we feel excited and hopeful
as we look forward to new possibilities.**

Leader: The marrow we bless today offers new possibilities of healing.
This marrow is an amazing gift from the Creator of all life,
and a magnanimous gift from the donor.

All: **Thank you, Great Creator, for this gift of life and for the compassion
and generosity of the one who donated it.**

Leader: Absolute Love, our Understanding Friend,
we come bringing all our fears and hopes to you
as we bless this marrow for (*marrow recipient's*) healing.

Marrow
Recipient: I receive this marrow with profound hope and
faith. I come bringing all my feelings, for "when I kept
silent, my bones wasted away in my groaning all the day.
For day and night Thy hand was heavy upon me;
my marrow dried up as in a summer draught" (Ps. 32:3–4).

Family/
Friends: *(Recipient)*, may you feel our love surrounding you
and nurturing you, bringing you renewed energy and hope.
And may Divine Love and Wisdom "be healing to your flesh
And marrow to your bones" (Prov. 3:8).

Leader: Gracious Creator, Absolute Love, and Healing Spirit,
bless this marrow for *(recipient's)* healing according to
(his/her) deepest needs of body, mind, and spirit.
May *(recipient)* feel your resurrection power embracing *(him/her)*
and flowing through *(him/her)*, bringing a new day
of health and joy and creative energy.

Marrow
Recipient: (Ps. 63: 3–8)

Family/
Friends: Great Creator of all life, we praise you. (*Then* Isa. 25:1, 4, 6, 8.)

All: **Gracious Creator, Resurrected Friend, and Caring Spirit,**
come with us now on our journey into the new.
Lead us forward with your vision of abundant life,
and help us to continue to become all you created us to be
in your divine image, now and forever. Amen.

HEALING TOUCH FOR THOSE IN CANCER TREATMENT[64]
(Methodist)

One: We are here because our sister/brother, ____, is preparing again for the
regime of chemotherapy and stem cell transplant. Her/his body is being
threatened by a cancer.

All: **_____ *(name)*, we come to this ritual of healing tonight as your fam-**
ily. You are part of our life and we cherish you. We rejoice in your
laughter, we celebrate your determination, and we marvel at your
courage.

One: As your companions, we are also willing to hear your fear, and to be with
you in your pain, and to honor your right to make your own decisions about
your treatment and your health care.

> **All: We are committed to walking with you as you struggle against this disease.**

(Two matching candles are lighted. One will remain in our sanctuary and be lighted each day as part of a prayer vigil. The other will go with _____ to remind her/him s/he is being held in prayer.)

> **One:** Tonight, _____, we give thanks for your presence in our midst, and we pray with our whole hearts for the success of your treatment. Some of us will travel with you to the hospital; some will care for your home, your pets, your business. Some of us will encourage you with cards and letters and calls; some of us will hold you in prayer each and every day.

> **All: All of us will hope with God for your healing.**

(The community is invited forward to lay hands on the person desiring healing and pray together the following prayer of support and hope.)

May the life-giving spirit of God which first breathed life into you, now surround you, uphold you, and flow through you. May God's tender compassion heal your wounded body and renew your weary spirit. May Her "fierce tenderness" surround with the assurance of support and care and His gentle peace be a safe retreat for your fear.[65] May our courage encourage you in times of fear or loneliness, and our strength be a resource when the way is long and hard. May the light of Christ be faithfully present with you and give you hope as your body struggles toward healing. Amen.

CANCER PRAYER GROUP[66]
(Roman Catholic)

OPENING SONG

OPENING PRAYERS
(Prayers to invoke God's favor through the intercession of St. Peregrine, Patron of Cancer and to St. John Neumann.)

O good St. Peregrine, patron of those suffering from foot ailments, cancer, and incurable diseases, grant, we beseech you, relief from suffering to . . . *(silently mention the names of persons for whom you are praying)*. In your compassion, we beg you to intercede with our Lord Jesus Christ that mankind may soon find a cure for the dread disease of physical cancer as well as for the moral cancer which grips so much of our world today.[67]

Oh, my God, I adore your infinite majesty with all the powers of my soul. I thank you for the graces and gifts which you bestowed upon your faithful servant, St. John Neumann. I ask you to glorify him also on earth. For this end I beseech you to grant me the favor . . . *(silently mention the favor desired)*, which I humbly ask from your fatherly mercy.[68]

PRAYERS OF COMFORT, HOPE, AND HEALING

1.   Dear Jesus, healer of the sick, we turn to you in this time of illness. Alleviate our worry and sorrow with your gentle love and grant us the grace and strength to accept this burden. We place our worries in your hands. We place ourselves in your care and humbly ask that you restore us to health again. Above all grant us the grace to acknowledge your holy will and know that you love us, and are with us in this our most difficult time. **Amen.**[69]

2.   Christ Jesus, we desire a positive attitude in facing our cancer. Lord, we know full well how the mind and emotions can determine what happens in the body. For this reason, we affirm a future full of hope because we see your hand in our past as well as in our present. We believe with all our heart that you are with us always.

Touch all those who share this cancer with us and may your blessing upon their lives make their journey easier. As Divine Physician, lead our doctors and caregivers to make the best possible decisions. Help them choose the most effective methods of treatment for our cancers.

May we experience you this day and in the days to come, working in our life for our recovery and our complete healing. **Amen!**[70]

3.   O kind and merciful Son of God, come to us now as we pray for each other. Wrap us in your blanket of love, ease the anguish that this sickness brings and fill our hearts with serenity and peace.

Jesus, you were always compassionate to those who knew suffering and pain. You know the frailty of the human spirit when faced with the difficult challenge of living with an affliction beyond control.

Let your healing love bring endurance and your power overcome despair that our faith in you may not weaken. Lord, we rely on your promise of eternal love, on this day and all days to come. **Amen!**[71]

4.   Heavenly Father, I call on you right now in a special way. It is through your power that I was created. Every breath I take, every morning I wake, and every moment of every hour, I live under your power.

Father, I ask you now to touch me with that same power. For if you created me from nothing, you can certainly recreate me. Fill me with the healing power of your spirit. Cast out anything that should not be in me. Mend what is broken. Root out any unproductive cells. Open any blocked arteries or veins and rebuild any damaged areas. Remove all inflammation and cleanse any infection.

Let the warmth of your healing love pass through my body to make new any unhealthy areas so that my body will function the way you created it to function.

And Father, restore me to full health in mind and body so that I may serve you the rest of my life. I ask this through Christ our Lord. **Amen.**[72]

WITNESS

INFORMAL SHARING

PETITIONS

Response: Lord Jesus, healer of the sick and suffering, hear our prayer.

THE LORD'S PRAYER

CLOSING PRAYER

LIGHTING OF CANDLES

SPIRITUAL REFLECTION AND QUIET MEDITATION

MIRACLE PRAYER

Lord Jesus, I come before you just as I am. I am sorry for my sins. I repent of my sins. Please forgive me. In your name I forgive all others for what they have done against me. I renounce Satan, the evil spirits, and all their works. I give you my entire self, Lord Jesus, now and forever. I invite you into my life, Jesus. I accept you as my Lord, God, and Savior. Heal me, change me, and strengthen me in body, soul, and spirit. Come, Lord Jesus! Cover me with your precious blood and fill me with your Holy Spirit. I love you, Lord Jesus! I praise you Jesus! I thank you, Jesus! I shall follow you every day of my life. **Amen!**

Mary, my mother, queen of peace; St. Peregrine, the cancer saint, all you angels and saints, please help me. **Amen!**[73]

PRAYER FOR A STROKE PATIENT[74]
(Ecumenical)

This prayer was written by a physician.

(The physician discerns whether the individual is open to prayer and, if so, asks permission. After a moment of quiet, so as to come into the presence of the Lord, hands are placed upon the individual and silently the Lord is asked to speak through the physician. During the acute phase of the attack, the person having just been admitted to the hospital and the medical workup underway, with the curtains drawn allowing for some privacy, the prayer might be something like the following:)

Dear Father, ever-present with us, we thank you for this precious child of yours and for *already* starting the healing process. Trusting in your healing power, we see him/her healed in mind, body, and spirit—walking through the fields and being as active as before. For all of this we give you our praise and thanksgiving as we pray in Jesus' name. Amen.

(For those who have recovered, *a prayer might be:)*

Thank you, O God, for completely healing your servant, N., who once again enjoys the wholeness in mind, body, and spirit that you have so graciously bestowed. Your love and grace are always with us; our prayers are always heard. Be our Guide and Protector as we continue our journey as your disciples. We ask this in Jesus' precious name.

BLESSING BEFORE SURGERY[75]
(Roman Catholic)

In her book Kitchen Table Wisdom, *Dr. Rachel Naomi Remen describes how she asks her patients to bring a stone (small enough to fit in the palm of one's hand) to the hospital when they come in for surgery. She asks the patient to invite a small group of family members and/or friends who have a "heart bond" with him or her to come the night before surgery. That evening they gather around the bedside and each tells a story of a significant time when he or she needed strength and found it. As each one concludes her or his story, she or he names a quality from that life event and says something like, "I put encouragement into this stone," or "I put hope into this stone." The stone is then passed on to the next person who continues the process. The stone then becomes the patient's "courage stone." This ritual incorporates the "courage stone" into a blessing.*

(As the patient holds the stone, the leader begins by asking those gathered to repeat the words of Psalm 18:2.)

Leader: *(the patient continues to hold the stone)* This stone has been a part of the universe for untold years. It is a symbol of strength and endurance. As each of us here holds this stone, we will bless it as a courage stone for you while we tell you stories of strength from our lives. Let us each pause to think about a time in our life when we longed for strength and found it in our time of need.

(The leader then holds the stone and tells his or her story of strength, ending with a statement such as:)

And so, _____ *(name of patient)*, I bless this stone with the gift of courage *(or another quality, such as hope, humor, faith, peace).*

(Then the leader hands the stone to the next person with the invitation to continue the storytelling and the blessing.)

(After each one around the bedside has held the stone, told their story, and blessed the stone, it is then placed in the patient's hand. All those around the bedside now place their hands on some part of the patient while the leader prays the following blessing:)

Leader: May the divine Spirit give attentiveness and guidance to the surgical staff.

May you trust in your body's ability to heal.

May you have compassion for any part of your body that experiences pain or discomfort.

May you befriend your fears and be freed from all anxiety.

May you be at peace.

We send our love and our vitality to you. Receive this loving energy from our hearts to yours and be strengthened for your journey toward healing.

(Conclude by each one present extending some gesture of love to the patient [a hug, kiss, gentle bow, sign of cross on forehead, a gentle touch of the hand on the very frail, etc.].)

"Praise the Lord, who carries our burdens day after day . . . who rescues us from death."
(Ps. 68:19–20)

Chapter 6

Death and Dying

When our days are at their longest
When our life is at its strongest
Kyrie eleison.   Lord have mercy

At the first coming of the dawn
On the life that's newly born
Kyrie eleison.   Lord have mercy

At the turning of each tide
On life's ocean deep and wide
Kyrie eleison.   Lord have mercy

At the ending of the way
At the closing of the day
Kyrie eleison.   Lord have mercy

When our powers are nearly done
At the going down of the sun
Kyrie eleison.   Lord have mercy

When we come to breathe our last
When the gates of death are passed
Kyrie eleison.   Lord have mercy
                    —David Adam, "Sixfold
                    Kyries," in Tides
                    and Seasons[1]

INTRODUCTION

Death is the final leveler of all people—the last enemy, which was conquered by Jesus Christ.

"Where, O death, is your victory?
Where, O death, is your sting?" . . .
But thanks be to God who gives us the victory through our Lord Jesus Christ.
                                        (1 Cor. 15:55–57)

If ever there is a time that people turn to the church, it is when they or their loved ones are dying. But if the church's only comfort to them is to bury the dead, we fall far short of Christ's call to ministry. Before we conduct any healing liturgies, it is essential to educate our congregations about a theology of death that makes clear the issues at stake. We must give our congregations the opportunity to ponder, "The meaning of every illness is dying and every healing is resurrection"[2]—hence accomplishing the church's mission to make whole what is broken, to gather what is scattered, to do more than simply bury the dead. We must also recognize that to face death, we must first understand life. There are many definitions of life that influence our views of death and the fundamental questions about death and dying that frame our analysis.

VIEWS OF LIFE

"The great use of life," notes William James, "is to spend it for something that outlasts it."[3] Some believe that life is an intrinsic good, like happiness, truth, freedom, or justice; an absolute value above all others. Others believe that it is simply an instrumental value, a means to an end.[4] For others, life is a relative value. As ethicist Lewis Smedes observes, "In moments of joy, when we are glad to be alive, we experience life as a gift. Now and then we feel the reality of being held up in life by a power beyond our control and we feel gratitude, which is the essence of joy."[5] We are thankful for God's gift of life, which we cannot earn.

However, there are paradoxes in the notion of life as a gift. On the one hand, we have to accept it, as we did not choose not to be born. "What is given is not ours to dispose of as if we created it, not ours . . . to mutilate, wantonly destroy, and to deprive others of," Smedes writes in *Respect for Human Life*. "Rather, if life is given in grace . . . we are to care for it and share it graciously." On the other hand, the "gift" of life can become an almost unbearable burden. A seriously ill person may be more than ready to let God have God's gift back again; indeed, he or she may give it to God with respectful resignation. "Others, whose job it is to care for such a person, may feel bound to force him to bear the gift of life beyond the time when nature calls for release. Are we scorning the gift of life when we let nature release the person who has to bear it? To feel life as a gift is a power to rejoice in it and nourish it. But when we sense that life is a terrible burden, do others have the duty to force us to bear it beyond the span that nature itself dictates?"[6] It is at this point of allowing a disease to take its course where treatment prolongs the dying instead of enhancing the living that the liturgy for removing life supports is appropriate. This liturgy is best done with medical personnel present, but if this is not possible, then it should be conducted immediately before life supports are withdrawn.

NEGOTIATED DEATH

Debates about death and dying are often framed by certain fundamental questions. The question "Who is dying?" makes a difference for some in the case of a newborn, comatose, incompetent, or "normal" person. Of course, our view of death also impacts how we approach our dying: Is death a friend, an enemy? Does it lead to resurrection, immortality, or nothing at all? An important distinction exists between the process of dying and the state of death itself. Dying well or choosing when we die or death itself affects how "in charge" people feel. The manner in which death occurs especially impacts on the family and friends of the patient. Whether death is the result of natural causes or is caused by someone else (such as homicide or suicide) can deeply affect those left behind.

A new phenomenon, what I call "negotiated death," has arisen due to the medical interventions and treatments that are now possible. The issues referred to here involve the ethical questions surrounding death and dying. Yet the terms used in these new choices about death and dying are often misunderstood. For some, euthanasia is a reaction to the burden of dying; they want to get the dying out of the way, be rid of the pain and suffering, not think about death. Yet, literally translated, *euthanasia* means a good death; fully engaging the dying process rather than escaping it is the real concern.

There are parallel distinctions made between passive/active and direct/indirect euthanasia. *Direct/active euthanasia* is bringing about another person's death against one's desire (active, involuntary euthanasia), without one's consent, or at one's request (voluntary euthanasia). For some, this is killing. *Indirect/passive euthanasia* is letting die, the failure to prevent death, an omission, a failure to perform certain acts. *Suicide* is noncoerced death by one's own hand, where the primary intent is to end one's physical life. *Heroic self-sacrifice* is giving up one's life, other-regarding, involving a principle or another person. *Physician-assisted suicide* is arranged death by mutual agreement between a patient and physician. *Treatment* may involve withdrawal of treatment; withholding treatment; ordinary versus extraordinary treatment, which is defined by the illness or individual patient (reasonable/unreasonable); and refusal of treatment. Treatment includes the patient's right of self-determination, proxy decision where consent is not possible, or presumed consent for infants or the mentally incompetent. *Advanced directive* is a DPA (Durable Power of Attorney) or DNR (Do Not Resuscitate) or a living will, where autonomous individuals express their wishes now in the future event that they are no longer competent.

In addition, there are psychological and spiritual aspects of death and dying in these ethical dilemmas. In her book *On Death and Dying*,[7] Elisabeth Kübler-Ross speaks of the five stages through which the dying patient passes—denial, anger, bargaining, depression, and acceptance. If we already have a serious illness, then our bargaining with death may take the form of "Just let me live 'til my son is married, or my daughter finishes college, or I can visit my home once more." Or when we think about death in the future, we might dicker, "Just let it be fast when my time comes, or don't let me have a lingering, painful illness." We do not necessarily pass through these stages in sequence, but they are pieces of our experience.

We are never ready for death—life's concerns are too absorbing, and we cannot bear to leave those we love. We have to face this mystery alone. No one can die for someone else. Death may come today, or tomorrow, or in a decade. The thread between life and death is fragile. One minute a friend is in the prime of health and another minute is struck down dead by a drunk driver. These realities cry for liturgical and pastoral responses.

A CULTURE OF DENIAL

Despite the fear of death, many people in both the medical and psychiatric professions believe that dying people really want very much to talk about their impending death and are rarely given an opportunity to do this. However, people in the United States today have tried to remove death from their minds. We are a death-denying society. Since half of the patients today die in hospitals, with transfusions and strangers, rather than (as was the case forty or fifty years ago) at home, with chicken soup and families, it has become easier for us to wipe death from our minds. The funeral homes reflect the American's desire to hide death by cosmetic wonders performed on cadavers, so they look better than they did in life. Flowers and saccharine music complete the picture, and an elaborate vocabulary of euphemisms is developed to circumvent the fact that a death has even taken place.

We mask real death because we are afraid we are not immortal and this could be the end, so let's not admit it. It seems as if death has replaced sex as a taboo in drawing-room conversation. When it does invade our lives, we are not granted the time or the space to mourn, which could be a release and catharsis for our sorrow. In Latin America and other countries, death is out in the open, with unfettered wailing at funerals. First there is a viewing of the body, often in the home—and in a three-room house this is very much in sight—and then the procession down the main street to the cemetery.

Perhaps as a substitute to facing our deaths or those of our loved ones, Americans portray the most violent deaths imaginable in books, television, and films, and people line up for blocks to see *The Gladiator* or the *Terminator* movies, with death in all its gore. Could this fictionalized death at its most terrifying be remote enough for us?

Martin Marty, Evangelical Lutheran Church of America clergy member and theologian par excellence, in *A Cry of Absence* lifts up the importance of accepting suffering and death.[8] No one can escape the winter of the heart, and acknowledging that reality is at the core of the believer's struggle. Summer-style believers seem to shun the doubter and offer a Christianity of cool comfort. Winter Christians often find themselves alongside the atheists, living on the edges of doubt but still struggling to include a yes to God. Sometimes we never leave winter; all of life seems meaningless. Marty draws heavily on Karl Rahner, the great twentieth-century German scholar, agreeing with him that we need not eliminate a summer Christianity, but neither should it be allowed to be the only season. I agree that we need to pass through winter, which leads us to spring, in the same way we move from Good Friday to Easter. Yes, death is inevitable, the final enemy; but thanks be to Jesus Christ who gives the victory.

CHRISTIAN VIEWS OF DEATH

We move from winter to spring as we examine Christian perspectives on death. There is a paradox at the heart of the Christian faith—life is a gift and a trust to be enjoyed, and yet in death we are free from pain and suffering and enter fully into the joy of God. This is the tension to which Paul referred (Phil. 1:23–24). In his own life, Jesus asked God several times if he could forgo his own death: "Now my soul is troubled. And what should I say—'Father, save me from this hour'?" (John 12:27); " 'Father, if you are willing, remove this cup from me. . . .' In his anguish he prayed more earnestly, and his sweat became like great drops of blood falling down on the ground" (Luke 22:42–44). His final words in the Markan account are " 'Eloi, eloi, lema sabachthani? . . . My God, my God, why have you forsaken me?' " (Mark 15:34).

In the Johannine account of Jesus going to the tomb of his friend Lazarus, we are told that Jesus was deeply moved in spirit and troubled; he wept on learning of Lazurus's death. But it was precisely at this moment of greatest sorrow that Jesus turned the situation around completely by his words and his actions; he said, " 'Did I not tell you that if you believed, you would see the glory of God?' " (John 11:40). Then Jesus raised Lazarus from the dead to show forth his power over death and to foreshadow his own resurrection.

No doubt 1 Corinthians 15 is the *locus classicus* of the Christian faith regarding eschatology. In fact, so much theology is concentrated in this fifteenth chapter that Karl Barth wrote a whole volume on it. In 1 Corinthians 15, we are told that Jesus' resurrection was an act by the ever-creating God. "Christ . . . was raised on the third day" (15:3–4). "We testified of God that he raised Christ—whom he did not raise if it is true that the dead are not raised. For if the dead are not raised, then Christ has not been raised" (15:15–16). Paul's thoughts remind us of the *Eighteen Benedictions,* a version of which he may have known and recited in the synagogue.[9] There are five main points that Paul makes here concerning the last things: (1) Christianity without resurrection is a lie; (2) because Christ rose, we will overcome death; (3) how we live is affected by our understanding of death; (4) at our resurrection we will have new bodies; and (5) our victory over death calls forth thanksgiving to God. These points provide a Christian theological framework for understanding death and resurrection.

When we die, we fall into the hands of the Living One. Death cannot separate us from the love of Jesus Christ. We have no fellowship with death but community with God. When we believe that Jesus Christ died and was raised for us, the opposite of death is not physical life but eternal life. When we weep here and say goodbye to a loved one, God answers, "Hello, welcome into my presence." The assurance of this truth forms the bedrock for the liturgies in this section.

THE CHURCH'S MINISTRY TO THE DYING

The formal rite of healing discussed in chapter 5 reflects a broader number of important liturgies that surround serious illness and death. Often rituals related to death contain three phases in these "rites of passage"—separation, transition, and reincorporation. Rituals can help people enter the mainstream of life as well as enter into their dying, notes William Willimon in *Worship as Pastoral Care.*[10] Rituals, adds Mary Frances Duffy, ideally arise from within the context of a broader and more comprehensive lived experience of the persons involved, which extends far beyond the fragile boundaries of the ritual itself.[11] Rituals should be an integral part of the pastoral ministry to the dying and reflect the symbols of life and hope in the midst of death and dying. Additionally important is the presence of the Christian community with those who are facing death.

In his foreword to *A Manual for Ministry to the Sick,* Martin Dudley writes, "Christians are called to serve Christ in their neighbors. When we stand by a sick bed or attend the dying, we are to be there with the respect and the tenderness which is appropriate to being in the presence of Christ. There should be no room for any kind of exploitation of a person's vulnerability at such moments, but rather a note of gentleness and attention."[12]

PASTORAL RESPONSE TO THE DYING

The previous Christian theological perspective on dying, death, and resurrection provides the foundation for our pastoral response to the person who is dying and those whose loved ones have died. Grave illness separates us from all that is familiar and draws us closer to the God who calls us into being and back to God's full presence at the end of our life. Words of God's continual love and care for us in the midst of dying need to be declared. The liturgies in this chapter are for those who are dying and those who grieve and are left behind.

Death is always a sad time, but especially traumatic are the violent deaths from suicide or through terrorist attacks. The general funeral service may not be enough, so special liturgies for these occasions have been included here. They speak to the shock, anger, and, yes, fear that these deaths engender.

PASTORAL CARE OF THE BEREAVED

There is little, if any, grief more intense than that of a parent for a lost child, as one of our liturgies reflects. Mary Frances Duffy, in her work *Ritual of Healing for Families of the Terminally Ill* uses Scripture as a guide to lead us through this uniquely acute event. In Mark 5, Jesus is confronted with a grieving parent, Jairus, who pleads for him to come and lay hands on his daughter and save her life. Obediently, Jesus goes with him. While on the way, they learn that the little girl is already dead. To the grief-stricken father Jesus speaks words of comfort—"'Do not fear, only believe'" (Mark 5:36)—and he raises her from the dead.[13]

In another healing miracle cited by Duffy, a centurion pleads for Jesus to heal his servant, asking only for a word or command, believing Jesus need not be present (Matt. 8:5–13). Once again, in the face of death, faith triumphs over grief.[14] In the Gospel narratives, we learn that Jesus "felt sorry" for the widow of Nain, who had lost her only son in death. Addressing the woman in simple, direct language, Jesus tells her, "'Do not weep'" (Luke 7:13).[15] In the famous story of Lazarus, when Mary and Martha plead for Jesus to save their brother, we read of Jesus' distressed response: "'Where have you laid him?'" (John 11:34). On seeing the place, we are told, "Jesus began to weep" (John 11:35). With those words, says Duffy, "the evangelist confirms our belief, satisfies our desire, rewards our hope, and fulfills our need to know that Jesus himself experienced bereavement."[16]

General Rites and Prayers with the Terminally Ill

"Those who sleep in death will also be raised."
(1 Cor. 15:20)

RITES WITH THE DYING[17]
(Anglican)

It may be appropriate to use the rites for anointing and for giving Holy Communion in addition to this rite.

Minister: Almighty God, look on this your servant, lying in great weakness, and comfort him with the promise of life everlasting, given in the resurrection of your Son Jesus Christ our Lord. **Amen.**[18]

(The minister may sprinkle the sick person, the person's bed and those gathered, with holy water, saying:)

Minister: Sprinkle me, O Lord, with hyssop, and I shall be purified; wash me, and I shall be whiter than snow.

(The minister may present an image of Christ crucified to the sick person and may light a candle or employ other devotional aids. When possible, it is desirable that members of the family and friends come together to join in this litany.)

Minister: God the Father,

    All: Have mercy on your servant.

Minister: God the Son,

    All: Have mercy on your servant.

Minister: God the Holy Spirit,

    All: Have mercy on your servant.

Minister: Holy Trinity, one God,

> **All: Have mercy on your servant.**

Minister: Look with mercy on your servant, and in your loving mercy,

> **All: Good Lord, deliver *him*.**

Minister: From all evil, from all sin, from all tribulation,

> **All: Good Lord, deliver *him*.**

Minister: From darkness and doubt,

> **All: Good Lord, deliver *him*.**

Minister: By your holy incarnation, by your cross and passion,
by your precious death and burial,

> **All: Good Lord, deliver *him*.**

Minister: By your glorious resurrection and ascension,
and by the coming of the Holy Spirit,

> **All: Good Lord, deliver *him*.**

Minister: We sinners beseech you to hear us, Lord Christ:
that it may please you to grant *him* relief in pain.

> **All: We beseech you to hear us, good Lord.**

Minister: That it may please you to deliver the soul of your servant
from the power of evil, and from eternal death.

> **All: We beseech you to hear us, good Lord.**

Minister: That it may please you mercifully to pardon all *his* sins.

> **All: We beseech you to hear us, good Lord.**

Minister: That it may please you to grant *him* a place of refreshment
and everlasting blessedness.

> **All: We beseech you to hear us, good Lord.**

Minister: That it may please you to give *him* joy and gladness in your kingdom, with
your saints in light.

> **All: We beseech you to hear us, good Lord.**

Minister: Son of God,

All: **We beseech you to hear us, good Lord.**

Minister: Jesus, Lamb of God:

All: **Have mercy on *him*.**

Minister: Jesus, bearer of our sins:

All: **Have mercy on *him*.**

Minister: Jesus, redeemer of the world:

All: **Give *him* your peace.**

Minister: Lord, have mercy.

All: **Christ, have mercy.**

Minister: Lord, have mercy.[19]

(Either version of the Lord's Prayer may be used.)

(One of these prayers may be said.)

Minister: Let us pray.

Deliver your servant N, O Sovereign Lord Christ, from all evil, and set her free from every bond; that she may rest with all your saints in the eternal habitations; where with the Father and the Holy Spirit you live and reign, one God, for ever and ever.   **Amen.**[20]

(or:)

O Lord, your servant N has come to the end of his life.
May your holy angels now receive him;
may he come to Paradise this day;
far from pain, and struggle, and tears,
may he find peace and dwell with you for ever.   **Amen.**

(or, if it be a child who is dying)

O Lord Jesus Christ, the only-begotten Son of God,
for our sake you became a babe in Bethlehem.
We commit to your loving care this child whom you have called to yourself.
Send your holy angel to lead her gently to those heavenly dwelling places
where the souls of those who sleep in you
have perpetual peace and joy; and fold her in the
everlasting arms of your unfailing love;
for you live and reign with the Father and the Holy Spirit,
one God, for ever and ever.   **Amen.**[21]

(When the minister judges that death is near, one of the following versions of the commendation may be said:)

Minister: Depart, O Christian soul, out of this world;
in the name of God the Father Almighty who created you;
in the name of Jesus Christ who redeemed you;
in the name of the Holy Spirit who sanctifies you.
May your rest be this day in peace,
and your dwelling place in the Paradise of God.[22]

Go forth upon your journey from this world, O Christian soul,
in the name of God the Father almighty who created you;
in the name of Jesus Christ who suffered for you;
in the name of the Holy Spirit, who strengthens you;
in communion with the blessed saints,
and aided by angels and archangels, and all the armies of the heavenly host.
May your portion this day be in peace,
and your dwelling the heavenly Jerusalem.[23]

Go forth upon thy journey, Christian soul!
Go from this world! Go, in the name of God
The Omnipotent Father, who created thee!
Go, in the Name of Jesus Christ, our Lord,
Son of the living God, who bled for thee!
Go, in the Name of the Holy Spirit, who
Hath been poured out on thee! Go, in the name
Of angels and archangels; in the name
Of Thrones and Dominations; in the name
Of Princedoms and of Powers; and in the name
Of Cherubim and Seraphim, go forth!
Go, in the name of Patriarchs and Prophets;
And of Apostles and Evangelists,
Of Martyrs and Confessors; in the name
Of holy Monks and Hermits; in the name
Of holy Virgins; and all Saints of God,
Both men and women, go! Go on thy course;
And may thy dwelling today be found in peace,
And may thy dwelling be the Holy Mount
Of Zion; through the Same, through Christ our Lord.

—John Henry Newman

(When a life-support system is withdrawn, this prayer may be said:)

Minister: God of compassion and love,
you have breathed into us the breath of life
and have given us the exercise of our minds and wills.

In our frailty we surrender all life to you from whom it came,
trusting in your gracious promises;
through Jesus Christ our Lord.   **Amen.**

(The dying person may be addressed in these words:)

Minister: N, our companion in faith and sister in Christ,
we entrust you to God who created you.
May you return to him who formed you from the dust of the earth.
May the angels and the saints come to meet you
as you go forth from this life.
May Christ, who was crucified for you,
Take you into his kingdom.
May Christ, the Good Shepherd,
give you a place within his flock.
May he forgive you your sins
and keep you among his people.
May you see your Redeemer face-to-face
and delight in the vision of God forever.   **Amen.**

(Either of these versions of the Nunc Dimittis may be said:)

Minister: Lord, now lettest thou thy servant depart in peace:
according to thy word.
For mine eyes have seen thy salvation,
which thou hast prepared before the face
of all people;
To be a light to lighten the Gentiles,
and to be the glory of thy people Israel.

(or:)

Minister: Lord, now let your servant go in peace:
your word has been fulfilled.
Mine own eyes have seen the salvation
which you have prepared in the sight of every people;
A light to reveal you to the nations
and the glory of your people Israel.

(This commendatory prayer may be said:)

Minister: Into your hands, O merciful Savior, we commend your servant N. Acknowledge, we humbly beseech you, a sheep of your own fold, a lamb of your flock, a sinner of your own redeeming. Receive him into the arms of your mercy, into the blessed rest of everlasting peace, and into the glorious company of the saints in light.   **Amen.**[24]

(After death, the following may be said:)

> **Minister:** Come to her aid, O saints of God;
> come forth to meet her, angels of the Lord;
> receiving her soul,
> presenting it to the Most High.
>
> May Christ, who has called you, now receive you,
> And may the angels bring you to Abraham's bosom.
> Rest eternal grant to her, O Lord,
> and let light perpetual shine upon her.
>
> May her soul and the souls of all the departed,
> through the mercy of God, rest in peace.   **Amen.**

(This thanksgiving or something similar may be said:)

> **Minister:** We give thanks to you, Lord our God,
> For the life of your servant N,
> Who has now passed from this world.
> We thank you for . . .
> We are glad that we shared some part of his life
> And now entrust him to you,
> O God of the living and the dead.   **Amen.**

RITES WITH THE TERMINALLY ILL[25]
(Roman Catholic)

During a period of crisis and transition a ritual can play a significant role in the emergence and resolution of such a time. A ritual can be understood as a social, symbolic process which has the potential for communicating, creating, criticizing, and even transforming meaning. It is a dynamic system of symbols constituted by symbols and what they signify. Symbols can be any object, activity, relationship, word, gesture, or spatial arrangement which serves as a unit in the ritual process. The major benefit of a ritual is that new relationships may be formed and previous relationships among participants may be strengthened.[26]

The purpose of this particular ritual is for those who minister to the sick and dying to bring together the terminally ill person with family and friends at this moment of transition, so that the bond of relationship between them can be strengthened in the presence of God and one another. As a ritual symbol, family members and friends will commit themselves in both word and action to be present to the terminally ill patient throughout the remainder of his or her illness. Just as Christ showed great concern for the bodily and spiritual welfare of the sick and dying by his presence to them, so family members and friends, as fellow Christians, will commit themselves in the "Rite of Christian Commitment to the Terminally Ill" to do the same.

The following is an outline of the "Rite of Christian Commitment to the Terminally Ill":

INTRODUCTORY RITES

GREETING

> **V:** The peace of the Lord be with you always.
>
> **R: And also with you.**

INSTRUCTION

My dear brothers and sisters, the Lord Jesus, who went about doing good works and healing sickness and infirmity of every kind, commanded his disciples to lovingly care for the sick and dying, to pray for them, and to lay hands on them. In this celebration we shall entrust our sick brothers and sisters to the care of the Lord, asking that he will enable them to bear their pain and suffering in the knowledge that, if they accept their share in the pain of his passion, they will also share in its power to give comfort and strength.[27]

LITURGY OF THE WORD

SUGGESTED READINGS

Hebrew Scriptures	**Christian Scriptures**
1. Ps. 23	1. 2 Cor. 1:3–7
2. Ps. 71	2. Rom. 8:31b–35
3. Job 7:1–4, 6–11	3. Rom. 8:18–27
4. Job 7:12–21	4. Col. 1:22–29
5. Job 19:23–27	5. Matt. 5:1–12
6. Isa. 35:1–10	6. Matt. 11:28–30
7. Isa. 52:13–53:12	7. Luke 12:22–32
8. Isa. 61:1–3	8. John 6:35–40
9. Wisd. of Sol. 9:1, 9–18	9. John 6:53–58

PRAYERS OF CHRISTIAN COMMITMENT

(The Pastoral Care member will begin by introducing the individual prayers of Christian commitment with a short prayer calling upon God to give comfort and care to the person who is ill. Then each person present will present a prayer for the person who is ill stating his/her intention to be present with the person who is ill throughout the remainder of the illness.)

INTRODUCTION

Jesus came as healer of body and of spirit in order to cure our ills. He chose to be like us in all things in order to assure us of his compassion. He bore our weakness and carried our sorrows. He felt compassion for the crowd and went about doing good and healing the sick. With trust let us pray to Jesus that he will comfort *(N.)* with his grace and that he will fill *(N.)* with new hope and strength.

FAMILY AND FRIENDS

I pray that Christ will comfort you as you follow him on the path he has set before you. As your *(family member/friend),* I promise to walk with you on your journey and that I will be present to you in both word and action. Just as Jesus felt a passion for the crowd and went about doing good by caring for them, I promise that I will watch over you, that I will be there when you need me, and that I will show you the love of Christ by my very presence. *(N.),* in the presence of God and your family, I commit myself to you with the love of Jesus Christ.

PRAYER OF BLESSING

(All present will extend their hands over the person who is ill and pray the following prayer. At the conclusion of the prayer each person will trace the sign of the cross on the forehead of the person who is ill.)

Lord our God, you sent your only begotten Son into the world to bear our infirmities and to endure our sufferings. Look with compassion upon your servant *(N.).* Give *(him/her)* strength in body, courage in spirit, and patience in pain. Support *(N.)* with your grace, comfort *(him/her)* with your protection, and give *(him/her)* the strength to fight against all evil. Since you have given *(N.)* a share in the passion of your Son, help *(him/her)* to find hope and consolation in suffering, for you are Lord forever and ever. Amen.

> **All: Our Father . . .**

CONCLUDING RITE

God of mercy, look kindly on your servant *(N.)* who has grown weak under the burden of illness. Strengthen *(him/her)* by your grace and help *(him/her)* to remain close to you in prayer. Fill *(him/her)* with the strength of your Holy Spirit. Keep *(him/her)* strong in faith and serene in hope, so that *(he/she)* may give us all an example of patience and joyfully witness to the power of your love. Lord, we ask you to soothe the hearts of the family members and friends of *(N.)* gathered here today. In your loving kindness enlighten their faith, give hope to their hearts and peace to their lives. We ask this through Christ our Lord. **Amen.**

DISMISSAL

Go in the peace of Christ to serve him in the sick and in all who need your love.

WITHDRAWAL OF LIFE SUPPORT[28]
(Nondenominational)

Occasion: The decision to withdraw life-support machinery from a loved one.
Location: The bedside of the ailing individual.

CALL TO SERVICE

Leader: Let us join in prayer and open our hearts to the presence of God, the Author of Life. Let us take comfort in the promise that God is present with those who gather in faith. And let us now pray in the name of the Father and of the Son and of the Holy Spirit.

PRAYER

Lord God, you are the Creator of all life. You allow us the joy of sharing our lives with each other and experiencing your love through our families and friends. We ask you to be with us now and comfort us. We have been blessed with the company and joy of our *(relative/friend)*, *(name),* and we take comfort in the memory of those moments. We know you have promised us a greater joy, richer and more lasting than the joy we experience in this life. We wish to gather here as *(name),* our *(relative/friend),* enters into that joy. We wish to accompany *(her/him)* at the beginning of that journey to the place where all tears will be wiped away and sorrow turned to joy. In the name of Jesus Christ, our Savior and Redeemer, **Amen.**

SCRIPTURE   John 14:1–6.

This is the Word of the Lord.

PRAYER

Gracious God, look upon *(name),* whom you created in your image, and claimed as your own through baptism. Comfort *(her/him)* with the promise of life eternal, made sure in the death and resurrection of your Son, Jesus Christ our Lord. **Amen.**

RESPONSIVE READING

Leader: Let us now join in prayer. Word of God, we affirm that you are the beginning and end of all life.

Family: Risen Lord, help us to trust in your promise of life everlasting.

Leader: Lord God, you have promised that our lives will be changed and transformed.

Family: Good Shepherd, death is hard to accept, but help us to understand that life's journey leads to you.

Leader: Source of all goodness, we give you thanks for the blessing that you bestowed on *(name)* in this life.

Family: Gracious God, help us to recall the joy and warmth of our times together as we prepare to unbind *(name),* our *(friend/relative),* and let *(her/him)* go free.

Leader: Lord Jesus, we recall your command to love and care for one another.

Family: Crucified Lord, help us to understand that while we love, our love has limits and we cannot do everything we would wish to do.

Leader: God of all creation, strengthen us as we release *(name)* from the bonds that hold *(her/him)* from you.

Family: Merciful Lord, help us to accept this parting and hold us in your love until we meet again.

Leader: Now, Master, you can let your servant go in peace, just as you have promised; because my eyes have seen the salvation which you have prepared for all the nations to see, a light to enlighten the pagans and the glory of your people. Let us now unbind *(name)* and let *(her/him)* go free so that *(she/he)* may enter into the life that has been prepared for us through the resurrection of Jesus Christ.

Family: Amen. We believe in your Word and the eternal life you have promised to us. We pray that our *(mother, or other)* may now enter this life, free of the bonds that hold *(him/her)* from you, our Gracious God who awaits *(him/her)* with welcoming arms.

A MOMENT FOR FAMILY REMEMBRANCES

PRAYER

God of compassion and love, you have breathed into us the breath of life and have given us the exercise of our minds and our wills. In our frailty we surrender all life to you from whom it came, trusting in your gracious promises; through Jesus Christ our Lord. **Amen.**

POEM
(Appropriate poems may be found in Charles L. Wallis's Funeral Encyclopedia *[Grand Rapids: Baker Book House, 1991].)*

PRAYER

Lord Jesus, we wait for you to grant us your comfort and peace. We confess that we are slow to accept death as an inevitable part of life. We confess our reluctance to surrender this our *(relative/friend)* and loved one to your eternal care. You, Lord Jesus, know the depth of our sorrow; you also wept for a dead friend. Let the Holy Spirit, the Comforter you promise, come upon us now. Grant us your love and peace as we reach out to console one another. Be our companion as we live through the painful days ahead; and even as we mourn, may all we feel, think, say and do bear witness to our faith. **Amen.**

BLESSING

(Name), the Lord bless you and keep you. The Lord be kind and gracious to you. The Lord look upon you with favor and give you peace. **Amen.**

(Other possible scriptures: Prov. 3:1–6, 9; 4:7–15; Isa. 25:6–9; Ezek. 37:1–14; Matt. 11:25–30; Luke 23:33, 39–43; John 11:32–45; John 12:23–26; Rom. 8:14–23; 1 Cor. 15:51–57; 2 Cor. 4:14–5:1; Rev. 21:1–5a, 6b–7.)

LET THEM GO FREE[29]
(Roman Catholic)

A FAMILY PRAYER SERVICE TO ASSIST IN THE WITHDRAWAL OF LIFE SUPPORT SYSTEMS

Family: Come, Lord God. Be our strength in this hour, for whether we live or die, we are yours, merciful God, forever.

Minister: Lord God, you are the Creator of all life. You allow us the joy of sharing our lives with each other and experiencing your love through our families and friends. We ask you to be with us now and comfort us. We have been blessed with the company and joy of N. *(insert name)* and we take comfort in the memory of those moments. We know you have promised us a greater joy, richer and more lasting than the joy we experience in this life. We wish to gather here as N. enters into that joy. We wish to accompany *(him/her)* at the beginning of that journey to the place where all tears will be wiped away and sorrow turned to joy.

Family: Amen. We believe in you and your word, O Lord. May you bring N. to the joy of your presence.

Minister: Let us now listen to the Word of God.

(Readings from the Jewish Scriptures.)

1. Ezek. 37:1–14. I shall put my spirit in you, and you shall live.
2. Wisd. 3:1–6, 9. The souls of the virtuous are in the hands of God.
3. Wisd. 4:7–15. A blameless life is a ripe old age.
4. Isa. 25:6–9. The Lord God will destroy death forever.

Minister: This is the Word of the Lord.

Family: Thanks be to God.

Minister: Let us respond to God's Word by praying together Psalm 23.

(Readings from the Christian Scriptures. From the Letters of the Apostles.)

5. Rom. 8:14–23. We groan while we await the redemption of our bodies.
6. 1 Cor. 15:51–57. Death is swallowed up in victory.
7. 2 Cor. 4:14–5:1. There is a house built by God for us.
8. Rev. 21:1–5, 6b–7. There will be no more death.

Minister: This is the Word of the Lord.

Family: Thanks be to God.

(Readings from the Gospels.)

9. John 11:32–45. Lazarus, come out.

10. Matt. 11:25–30. Come to me . . . and I will give you rest.
11. Luke 23:33, 39–43. Today you will be with me in paradise.
12. John 12:23–26. If a grain of wheat fall on the ground and dies.
13. John 14:1–6. There are many rooms in my Father's house.

> **Minister:** This is the Gospel of our Lord Jesus Christ.
>
> **Family: Praise to you, Lord Jesus Christ.**

(Silent reflection may follow each Scripture reading. A homily may be given after the reading of the Gospel.)

> **Minister:** Let us now join in prayer. Word of God, we affirm that you are the beginning and end of all life.
>
> **Family: Risen Lord, help us to trust in your promise of life everlasting.**
>
> **Minister:** Lord God, you have promised that our lives will be changed and transformed.
>
> **Family: Gentle Shepherd, death is hard to accept, but help us to understand that life's journey leads to you.**
>
> **Minister:** Source of all goodness, we give you thanks for the blessings which you bestowed on N. in this life.
>
> **Family: Gracious God, help us to recall the joy and warmth of our times together as we prepare to unbind N. and let *(him/her)* go free.**
>
> **Minister:** Lord Jesus, we recall your command to love and care for one another.
>
> **Family: Crucified Lord, help us to understand that while we love, our love has limits and we cannot do everything we want.**
>
> **Minister:** God of all creation, strengthen us as we release N. from the bonds that hold *(him/her)* from you.
>
> **Family: Merciful Lord, help us to accept this parting and hold us in your love until we meet again.**
>
> **Minister:** Now, Master, you can let your servant go in peace,
> just as you have promised;
> because my eyes have seen the salvation
> which you have prepared for all the nations to see,
> a light to enlighten the pagans
> and the glory of your people Israel.
>
> Let us now unbind N. and let *(him/her)* go free so that *(he/she)* may enter into the life that has been prepared for us through the resurrection of Jesus Christ.
>
> **Family: Amen. We believe in your Word and the eternal life you have promised to us. We pray that N. may now enter this life, free of the bonds that**

hold *(him/her)* from you, our gracious God who awaits *(him/her)* with welcoming arms.

(The family may now wish to give a final gesture of love or affection for the individual, e.g., a kiss, an embrace, a sign of the cross on the person's forehead. The life support system may be disconnected at this time in the presence of the family while the following prayer is recited. Or the following prayers may be recited by all and then the life support system may be disconnected after the family departs.)

PRAYER OF COMMENDATION
(to be prayed as the life support system is disconnected)

Minister: I commend you, my dear *(brother/sister),* to almighty God,
and entrust you to your Creator.
May you return to him
who formed you from the dust of the earth.
May holy Mary, the angels, and all the saints
come to meet you as you go forth from this life.
May Christ who was crucified for you
bring you freedom and peace.
May Christ who died for you
admit you into his garden of paradise.
May Christ, the true Shepherd,
acknowledge you as one of his flock.
May he forgive all your sins,
and set you among those he has chosen.
May you see your Redeemer face-to-face,
and enjoy the vision of God forever.

Family: **Amen.**

(An Our Father and Hail Mary may be added.)

Minister: Loving and merciful God,
we entrust our *(brother/sister)* to your mercy.

You loved *(him/her)* greatly in this life:
now that *(he/she)* is freed from all its cares,
give *(him/her)* happiness and peace forever.

The old order has passed away:
welcome *(him/her)* now into paradise
where there will be no more sorrow,
no more weeping or pain,
but only peace and joy
with Jesus, your Son,
and the Holy Spirit
forever and ever.

Family: Amen.

A PRAYER FOR THE FAMILY AND FRIENDS

Minister: God of all consolation,
in your unending love and mercy for us
you turn the darkness of death
into the dawn of new life.
Show compassion to your people in their sorrow.

Be our refuge and our strength
to lift us from the darkness of this grief
to the peace and light of your presence.

Your Son, our Lord Jesus Christ,
by dying for us, conquered death,
and by rising again, restored life.
May we then go forward eagerly to meet him,
and after our life on earth
be reunited with our brothers and sisters
where every tear will be wiped away.

We ask this through Christ our Lord.

Family: Amen.

FINAL BLESSING

Minister: Blessed are those who have died in the Lord: let them rest from their labors,
for their good deeds go with them. Eternal rest grant unto *(him/her),* O Lord.

Family: And let perpetual light shine upon *(him/her).*

Minister: May *(he/she)* rest in peace.

Family: Amen.

Minister: May *(he/she)* soul and the souls of all the faithful departed, through the
mercy of God, rest in peace.

Family: Amen.

Minister: May the love of God
and the peace of the Lord Jesus Christ
bless and console us and gently wipe every tear from our eyes:
in the name of the Father,
and of the Son,
and of the Holy Spirit.

Family: Amen.

Grief and Bereavement

"David went on up to the Mount of Olives crying." (2 Sam. 15:30)

HEALING FOR FAMILIES OF THE TERMINALLY ILL[30]
(Roman Catholic)

CALL TO WORSHIP AND GREETING

Presider: My brothers and sisters:
In the name of our Lord Jesus Christ I welcome you.
I invite you to come to him who says
to the weary, the burdened, and the sorrowing:
"Come to me and I will give you rest."
Place yourselves now in Christ's compassionate presence.
He desires to share your pain
so that he may sorrow with you
and grant you peace.
May the Lord be with you.

All: And also with you.

OPENING SONG   #746   WIII   "Great God of Mercy"

OPENING PRAYER

Presider: Let us pray.
God of all comfort and consolation,
be with us now in our prayer.
We suffer with those who suffer;
we die with those who die.
Touch us in the deepest recesses of our grief,
in those hidden places we fear to acknowledge
or give to your keeping.

> Help us be compassionate
> toward those who are sick.
> Help us be gentle with ourselves.
> May we come to understand and accept
> the mystery of sickness and death
> which holds our loved one(s) in its grip.
> In the fullness of time and in the slowness of our hearts
> speak to us your word of comfort and your word of peace.
> We ask this in the power of the Spirit
> and in your Son, Jesus Christ, the Lord.

All: Amen.

INSTRUCTION

Presider: The journey of life brings each of us, at one time or another, to a place of pain. Without our will we are brought into life; against our will we are forced to confront the pain of sickness and the sorrow of death.

Each of you knows the pain associated with the sickness and death of those you love. Your concern is for them, and yet your own hearts are torn apart. Your own lives are disrupted.

This pain and disruption you may nobly try to deny; yet it is there. It may bring you anger, or lead you to bargain with God and with life "if only things could be different." Or it may make you very, very sad.

Yet, however you feel at this moment, the healing power of Christ seeks to touch your hearts. He seeks to lead you to accept and embrace this life with all its mystery, and to discover his love for you in the midst of this sadness and grief.

May we spend a few moments in quiet reflection before our God, and allow ourselves to experience honestly and with reverence the feelings which are uniquely our own. Let us express ourselves to God in truth, without fear or shame.

REFLECTIVE SILENCE

READING   Matt. 26:36–46

HOMILY
(The homily is usually given by the presider or by some other person invited to provide this ministry. In some situations, however, it may be appropriate to invite the participants to share their reflections on the scripture reading in the format of a dialogue homily.)

PSALMS/SONG OF HOPE AND TRUST   #750   WIII   "Your Hands O Lord in Days of Old"
(At the end of the homily, some form of common prayer or song is appropriate as both a conclusion to the Word and a transition into prayers of petition.)

PRAYER OF PETITION

Presider: My brothers and sisters,
the God to whom Jesus prayed for deliverance
invites each of us to be healed.
In Jesus we find the hope that makes us whole
and the promise that life is forever.
God is no stranger to our human pain and suffering.
In Jesus God has embraced our own human life
even to the point of suffering and death.
In Jesus God has become companion to us
in our own journey through life.
"Behold, I am with you all days";
"I make my abode with you."
Unite then your sorrow to the dying and rising of Christ.
Believe and your faith will make you whole.
In faith and in hope be companion to those
with whom you keep vigil,
your loved ones for whom we now pray:

(All in the assembly are invited to pray in their own words for their loved ones and for themselves. If it is helpful the presider may form the first several petitions. After the petitions:)

Presider: Loving God,
Lord of all health and wholeness,
you are source of our life
and fulfillment of our death.

We come to you now with varied needs.
Into your gentle care we place ourselves
and our loved ones who are ill.

Be for us now
light to brighten our darkness,
strength to transform our weakness,
and comfort in the midst of our pain.

We ask this in the power of the Spirit
through Christ, our Lord.

All: Amen.

RITE OF ANOINTING

ANOINTING

Presider: My brothers and sisters,

as a sign of our faith
and in hope for the healing embrace of God,
come forward now
to be anointed with holy oil.

May Jesus Christ
who is infinite compassion
touch you and bless you,
and give you his healing grace.

(As each member of the assembly comes forward, he/she is anointed on both forehead and hands. The presider prays the accompanying prayer:)

Presider: *(anointing the head)*
May God heal your own wounds
as you stand in hope
with N. who is ill.

(anointing the hands)
May God give you
eyes to see and ears to hear
and hands that you may touch
and bless and understand.

(When all have received the sacrament of the anointing, there follows a brief period of silence.)

COMMON PRAYER   PS. 23
(The service concludes with Psalm 23 recited or sung in common. If desired, the Lord's Prayer or a suitable prayer of praise and thanksgiving may be prayed instead.)

CONCLUDING RITES

DISMISSAL

Presider: Signed with the cross of Christ,
and touched with his healing grace,
go forth now from this place
to serve God's people
in compassion, kindness, and love.

All: Thanks be to God.

CLOSING SONG   #612   WIII   "The Living God My Shepherd Is"

MEMORY WREATH[31]
(Methodist)

Instructions: Either as a separate event or during a worship service, those who have lost a loved one bring a ribbon to tie to a wire frame wreath. After the wreath has been finished, it can be hung in an appropriate place in the church.

The multitude of colorful ribbons that make up this wreath were tied in honor of loved ones who have died. All of us together can build a powerful and colorful tribute to those we love. It is a visual testimony for all of us. Each ribbon will remind us of someone special in our lives and yours.

You might want to stop and remember the people in your life who have died. Remember a smile or the sound of laughter. Favorite things you enjoyed doing. Meaningful times shared together.

"What is lovely never dies, put passes into other loveliness"
—*Thomas Bailey Aldrich*

May you cherish your memories.
—*from your Parish Nurse*

CHRISTMAS MOURNING[32]
(Reformed Church)

A Service for the Bereaved

LIGHTING OF THE CHRIST CANDLE
(in silence)

WELCOME AND INTRODUCTION

HYMN   #493   PsH   "Precious Lord, Take My Hand"

SCRIPTURE
(Three or four brief passages focused on God's care and faithfulness [possibilities include Ps. 27, 46, 91, 121, Isa. 43, John 14, Rom. 8, Phil. 4, 1 Pet. 1].)

THE SHARING OF THE LIGHT
(The pastor invites the congregation to light a candle, using words such as the following:)

You are invited to come forward and light a candle in memory of your loss, taking the light from the Christ candle.

(While people are coming forward, quiet instrumental music is played based on hymns that will be sung later.)

THE SHARING OF GRIEFS
(The pastor invites all who lit a candle to share their loss briefly, perhaps beginning this time with a personal account.)

OUR COMFORT AND HOPE

SONGS OF COMFORT AND HOPE #494   PsH   "There Is a Balm in Gilead"
#579   PsH   "What a Friend We Have in Jesus"
#121   PsH   "To the Hills I Lift My Eyes"

PRAYER FOR THE SORROWING

MEDITATION
(No more than 5–10 minutes seems most appropriate.)

BLESSING

HYMN   #556   PsH   "Great Is Thy Faithfulness"

CONSOLATION CANDLE SERVICE[33]
(Roman Catholic)

Seven candles are placed on a stand, a platform, an altar, or any other space that allows the candles to be seen by all. Seven individuals light each of the candles in turn. Appropriate instrumental music plays as a background to the ritual, and a single voice, perhaps alternating female and male voices, reads each of the seven sections.

We light a candle for LOVE:

for the love that we have shared with those who are precious to us;
for the love that flows deep within us that will never end;
for the love that has lived through changing times and events;
for the love that grew from small seeds into great oak trees within us;
for the love that lifts up our spirits and our hearts.

We light a candle for JOY:

for the joy that gave birth to so many positive moments, days and years;
for the joy that our loved ones experienced during their time here on earth;
for the joy and smiles those near to our hearts gave and received;
for the joy that flowed from the accomplishments our loved ones performed and witnessed;
for the joy that gave encouragement to those who would follow in their footsteps.

We light a candle for MEMORIES:

for the memories of gatherings, holidays and unrepeatable special occasions;
for the memories of smells and sounds and meals together that satisfied far more than our
    appetites;
for the memories of times together that reminded us of what it means to be human;
for the memories of faces and voices that are records of our journey together with others;
for the memories of the people who not only gave us gifts, but who truly *were* gifts to us.

We light a candle for TEARS:

for the tears that flow from our eyes and down our chins at a moment's notice;
for the silent tears that arrive for no apparent reason, and those that no one else sees or hears;
for the tears of joy as we remember jokes and stories we have shared with our loved ones;
for the tears that point us toward our true feelings, and root us in time and eternity's deepest
    truths;
for tears that signal an inner release, a new freedom, a relief shared with those we mourn.

We light a candle for HOPE:

for the hopes and dreams and plans we shared with those precious to us;
for the hope and trust we place in the power to continue loving those whom we have lost in
    death;
for the hopes our loved ones carried within their hearts and spirits;
for the hope that brings forth in us a confidence to love others now without regrets;
for the hope and desire to look forward to the next stage of loving anew those who are close
    to us.

We light a candle for PEACE:

for the peace that we want for our loved ones and for ourselves;
for the peace that is even deeper than our words and feelings can express;
for the peace that focuses us for now, and helps us to claim our place in the world;
for the peace that joins time and eternity in an eternal song of love;
for the peace that helps to heal the distance that separates us one from another.

We light a candle for STRENGTH:

for the strength that comes from deep within me and sustains me;
for the strength that empowers me to live each moment and each day to the fullest;

for the strength that encourages me to live one day at a time without regrets;
for the strength that allows forgiveness to heal the unfinished parts of our relationships;
for the strength that allows us to remember those who have left their imprint on our hearts.

DEATH OF AN ADULT CHILD[34]
(Roman Catholic)

Instructions

This service is especially for use in a retirement or nursing home. Before scheduling and celebrating this service, it would be advisable to meet with the resident who has lost an adult child. Suggest the possibility of the service and get their approval. Spend some time talking with the parent about memories they have of the child who has died. This service can also be adapted for use on the occasion of the death of a spouse.

Materials Needed

Photos of the child who has died (if possible, photos from various stages of the child's life), a small green plant, a candle.

Preparation and Environment

Inform congregation/residents of person's loss and invite those who wish to join in supportive prayer. Gather the participants around a table on which the above materials have been arranged.

INTRODUCTION

Leader: Our friend N. has lost her/his son/daughter. News of this type often comes as a shock. We seldom think that our children will die before us, who are older. And so, we gather in prayer and support of N. in her/his sorrow at this time.

OPENING PRAYER

Leader: Gracious God, we have learned of the death of N., daughter/son of N. The news carries with it the shadow of sorrow and fear, for it reminds us that, someday, we, too, shall die. It also carries with it the shadow of grief, for at our age, we feel that we should die before our children. But your ways are not ours, God. And so we gather here today to remember with N. her/his child and to pray with and for her/him and the members of her/his family in their time of sorrow.

All: **Lord, may the news of this death be for us a holy message. Let us be grateful for life today. Let us not waste our days, or be unprepared for the arrival of our own death.**

STORY SHARING

> **Leader:** Lord of life and death, today we remember the death of N., child of N. We pause now to recall the good times N. and her/his child shared together.

(Invite the person who has lost a child to share pleasant stories about the child. Use the photos and your previous conversation with the parent to help trigger reminiscences. After each story, all might respond: "Glory to God for a good life.")

LITANY OF THANKS

> **Leader:** For all that has been in the life of our dearly departed N., let us pray.
>
> **All: We thank you, Lord.**

> **Leader:** In gratitude for the treasure just shared,
>
> **All: We thank you, Lord.**

> **Leader:** For all that was enjoyed by N.'s family and friends,
>
> **All: We thank you, Lord.**

> **Leader:** For affection and trust,
>
> **All: We thank you, Lord.**

> **Leader:** For memories of good times,
>
> **All: We thank you, Lord.**

> **Leader:** For love that is beyond the touch of death,
>
> **All: We thank you, Lord.**

> **Leader:** For the presence we feel of N. today,
>
> **All: We thank you, Lord.**

> **Leader:** For the support of family and friends at this time,
>
> **All: We thank you, Lord.**

> **Leader:** For our belief in resurrection,
>
> **All: We thank you, Lord.**

CONCLUDING PRAYER

> **Leader:** Mysterious Lord of Life and Death,
> a special part of N.'s life has died.

> Send to her/him your angel of consolation,
> for we know her/his sorrow is heavy and deep.
> Mary, Mother of Sorrows,
> who was also a parent who lost an adult child,
> you know the pain of such loss.
> Be a comfort to N. in this time of sorrow.
>
> Loving God and Merciful Mary, support N.,
> wrap her/him in your gentle love
> as she/he attempts to carry this bitter cross,
> just as your Son, Jesus, carried his cross.
> His cross led to Resurrection and New Life
> which is also waiting for N., child of N.

RITUAL ACTION

As a sign of our belief that N's child lives on in her/his memory and lives now with Christ, we present to N. this green plant.

(The small green plant is presented to the parent along with a copy of the above prayer signed by friends and relatives.)

HOW LONG WILL YOU FORGET ME, LORD?[35]
(Reformed Church)

A SERVICE OF LAMENT BASED ON PSALM 13

WE APPROACH GOD IN GRIEF AND SORROW

PRELUDE   "Duet No. 2 in F Major," Beethoven
Unaccompanied flute and bassoon

THE CALL TO WORSHIP

HYMN   #460   PsH   "Immortal, Invisible, God Only Wise" (Stanzas 1–3)

OUR DECLARATION OF TRUST AND GOD'S GREETING

> **Leader:** Congregation of Jesus Christ, in whom are you trusting?
>
> **People: Our help is in the name of the Lord who made heaven and earth.**
>
> **Leader:** Grace, mercy, and peace to you in the name of the Father, the Son, and the Holy Spirit. Amen.
>
> **People: Amen!**

RESPONSE   #460   PsH   "Immortal, Invisible, God Only Wise" (Stanza 4)

The Word of the Lord

SCRIPTURE   Psalm 13

SERMON   "How Long Will You Hide Your Face from Me?"

We Respond with Trust

How Long, O Lord?

READING

> Long enough, God—
> you've ignored me long enough.
> I've looked at the back of your head
> long enough. Long enough
> I've carried this ton of trouble,
> lived with a stomach full of pain.
> Long enough my arrogant enemies
> have looked down their noses at me.
> —From Ps. 13

OPENING PRAYER   #13   PsH   "How Long Will You Forget Me, Lord" (Stanza 1)

We Cry for Help

READING

> Take a good look at me, God, my God:
> I want to look life in the eye
> so no enemy can get the best of me
> or laugh when I fall on my face.
> —From Ps. 13

HYMN   #261   PsH   "Lord, We Cry to You for Help"

PRAYERS OF INTERCESSION

We lift our hearts to you, Lord God, as the mighty one who by the word of your mouth created the heavens and the earth; and as the merciful one who gives us the right to address you
in the name of Jesus Christ, your Son and our Lord. We lift our hearts to you because there is
no one else to whom we can turn, no one else who has the words of eternal life. We ask you
to come and enter the circumstances of our lives that bring such pain and confusion; to enter
the lives of our brothers and sisters who suffer; to enter the lives of those who live in darkness.

Refrain   **Hear our prayer, send your mercy now; answer in our need.**

We pray today for those within our local family who are in need of extra mercy and grace.
Some have fallen and need you to lift them again. Some sorrow and need your comfort. Some

experience broken relationships and need your grace. Some confront major diseases and need your hand for strength and healing. Still others confront their own doubt and confusion and need your Spirit to soothe their hearts. Many live with the loneliness and grief of loved ones taken away by death, and require sustaining grace daily. *Refrain*

We pray today for our community and those within it who feel such need for mercy. We hold up before you all those who have been affected by this tragic accident, for the families of those who lost a senior loved one, for those who are injured and hospitalized as well as their families. In particular we remember . . . *Refrain*

We pray for our world, such a mixture of truth and falsehood, light and darkness, and love and hate. Bring, we pray, the light of your presence into the middle of our society. Bring the healing power of justice and truth. May the leaders of our nations lead us to live together in harmony. Promote the causes of peace and reconciliation. But most of all open doors for the proclamation of the gospel of salvation in Jesus Christ, the Prince of Peace. May the light of salvation in Christ overcome the shadows of darkness, selfishness, immorality, and violence that hover over our land and threaten its future. *Refrain*

Let us pray the prayer our Lord taught us, saying, "Our Father . . ."

TRUSTING THE GOODNESS OF GOD

READING

> I've thrown myself headlong into your arms—
> I'm celebrating your rescue.
> I'm singing at the top of my lungs,
> I'm so full of answered prayers.
> > —From Ps. 13

HYMN   #27   PsH   "The Lord God Is My Light and My Salvation"

JESUS CHRIST, LOVE DIVINE

READING   John 10:11–18

HYMN   #506   W&R   "I Want Jesus to Walk with Me"

OFFERTORY

WE LEAVE WITH PEACE

THE BENEDICTION

POSTLUDE   "Lord, Dismiss Us with Your Blessing"

Violent Deaths

"Saul approved of his murder." (Acts 8:1)

AFTER A SUICIDE[36]
(Ecumenical)

This service is designed for family and friends of a young person who has committed suicide. It is not a substitute for a funeral but to be used later when people are beginning to process their grief and anger. It should be in an intimate setting.

CALL TO WORSHIP

Our help is in the name of the Lord, who made heaven and earth.

HYMN   Psalm 23   #171   PrH   "The King of Love My Shepherd Is"

SCRIPTURE   2 Sam. 18:19–33

READING

(Select a passage from Nicholas Wolsterstorff, Lament for a Son *[Grand Rapids: Wm. B. Eerdmans, 1987] or Iris Bolton,* My Son, My Son *[Atlanta: Bolton Press, 1991].)*

PRAYER

AFTER A SUICIDE[37]

> Lord Jesus Christ,
> you knew the agony of the garden and the loneliness of the cross,
> but remained in the love of your Father.
> We commend *N* to your mercy and, claiming no judgment for ourselves,
> commit *her* to you, the righteous judge of all,
> now and forever. **Amen.**

—Martin Dudley

Compassionate God, we entrust into your care *N*,
Who has died by *his/her* own hand.
Grant that the knowledge of your love and mercy may comfort those who grieve for *him*.
Strengthen our assurance of your redeeming purpose for all your children,
Through Jesus Christ your Son. **Amen.**[38]

Lord Jesus Christ,
You knew the agony of dying alone and abandoned.
We cannot know the agony which led *N* to take *his/her* own life.
We grieve that we could not meet *his/her* needs.
Console us in the face of death's seeming triumph,
forgive us for failing *N* in *his/her* time of need,
and give us the assurance that you can bring hope in our pain. **Amen.**[39]

(Sentence prayers by those present may be offered here.)

FINAL BLESSING

"Help those who have all kinds of troubles."
(1 Cor. 1:4)

Chapter 7

Broken World

In light defeating darkness,
In wisdom conquering foolishness,
In trust overcoming fearfulness,
            Jesus Lives.

In strength coming to weakness,
In health rescuing from sickness,
In hope saving from despair,
            Jesus Lives.

In love victorious over hatred,
In forgiveness dispelling anger,
In glory dispersing drabness,
            Jesus Lives.

In joy growing from sorrow,
In life rising from death,
In God giving the victory,
            Jesus Lives.

He holds the keys of love
            of peace
He holds the keys of life
            of death
He holds the keys of heaven
            of earth
He holds the keys of now
            of eternity.
            —David Adam,
            "Jesus Lives," in
            Tides and Seasons[1]

INTRODUCTION

NEED FOR RECONCILIATION

Given the individualistic understanding of healing, especially for North Americans, it is important to emphasize the need for communal and global healing. We must move from self-absorption to a place of inclusion and reconciliation with all peoples—the healing of relationships not only between races but also with the earth forms part of a healing ministry. There are both individual and corporate causes of the broken world in which we live. In theological terms, there is individual sin and ontological evil. The liturgies in this chapter prominently address enmity and discord on all levels: community need and reconciliation, prejudice and racism, criminal justice concerns, and tainted creation (discord with the earth).

In today's climate we talk not only about enmity between individuals but about an adversarialism abroad in our country, as William F. May labeled it.[2] We look on people in the workplace as competitors instead of colleagues. We view not only professionals but each other with suspicion, qualifying as one of the most litigious societies in the world.

There is no doubt that right now we need reconciliation in our country and our world. Racial tensions are reemerging in our cities; the gap between the wealthy and powerful and the homeless and marginalized continues to grow. On the international scene, just as we are experiencing a rapprochement between East and West, we see the specter of a major standoff in the Middle East.

What do we think the answer is? Economic recovery, philosophical theories, political blueprints, military victory, arms preparedness? No, we have the answer in the lives that have been transformed by reconciliation with God through Jesus Christ. If we reject that as oversimplistic, then we do not take our faith seriously.

We need reconciliation with each other because we are alienated from God—disobedient, restless, fractured, selfish, having replaced love of God with love of self. When we break God's laws, we suffer the consequences in our lives: the petty things of life overshadow the transcendent. Love is the transforming power—the love of enemies that Jesus preached, and that has been lived through the centuries by the saints of the church.

Even as Christians, we have trouble loving other Christians and constantly scrutinize one another's theology or conduct. How much more difficult it is to get along, then, with those whose religion or philosophy differs from our own. Yet reconciliation is the only way to heal a broken world, and it needs to be experienced liturgically to be realized in our lives. "Recommitment to Common Ground" is one such liturgy that recognizes our separation and mourns our brokenness, while rejoicing in our commonality.

Theological differences that divide Christians often take on an added emotional dimension that leads to labeling and sloganism, which further divide. These liturgies, it is hoped, will help bring people together before the divisions become too deep or will promote healing where there are already divisions. Even the "passing of the peace" in some services creates a discomfort for some people. Congregants, Willimon notes, do not really want to pass the peace because they do not want to be connected with anyone. They are hurting in their own lives, and it has become difficult for them to reach out to anyone else.[3]

PREJUDICE AND RACISM

Reconciliation between races and genders is central to the gospel, as it is Jesus Christ who has broken down the dividing wall of hostility. "There is no longer Jew or Greek, there is no longer slave or free, there is no longer male and female; for all of you are one in Christ Jesus" (Gal. 3:28). Understanding of each other is at the core of cooperation, but acceptance of one another as children of God and forgiveness of each other make reconciliation possible. Prejudice is the forerunner of racism.

Racism after the civil rights movement has taken on subtler forms. One of the most famous and effective approaches to racism was that of Martin Luther King Jr. The liturgy that celebrates his day gives testimony to his power. King's own journey to nonviolence provides insight into his struggle over how to confront the violence of racism.[4] His journey began with a recognition that neither liberalism's optimistic view of human nature nor neo-orthodoxy's concentration on human evil were sufficient. Existentialism, which recognized our state of estrangement, better described the human condition.[5] As his studies progressed, he came to see "that the Christian doctrine of love operating through the Gandhian method of nonviolence was one of the most potent weapons available to oppressed people in their struggle for freedom."[6]

King's "Letter from the Birmingham City Jail" was written as a defense for the protests of unjust segregation laws, declaring that freedom is not given but must be taken.[7] Unjust laws are no laws at all—as Christians from Paul to Augustine, Martin Luther, and Martin Luther King declared. However, the method King used to confront these injustices was nonviolent resistance, which proved its effectiveness first by Gandhi.

Black theology has also been influenced by Malcolm X, who directly attacked the white supremacy movement that hid behind a heretical Christian theology of "heaven on earth for whites and hell on earth for blacks."[8] The liturgies in this section "Common Ground: An Act of Witness against Racism" and "Juneteenth Celebration" reflect this theme of justice.

Empowerment is not only the language of turning racism on its head; it also grows out of the *conscientização* (bringing to awareness) mandate of Paulo Freire (1921–1997), a Brazilian sociologist.[9] It is my hope that these liturgies can contribute at least one small piece of an awareness of the plight of the poor, oppressed, and marginalized. Thus may the church have a "preferential option for the poor," as Gustavo Gutiérrez pleaded.[10]

The most radical power, however, in the face of racism and other oppressions is love of one's enemies. Howard Thurman, the African American mystic, wrote in 1949 of this love of enemies, which does not condone their actions but overwhelms with love.[11]

COMMUNITY NEED DEMANDS JUSTICE

The tragedy of racism highlights the need for justice. *Justice* is an underlying issue in many of the liturgies in this section of the book. Justice is linked to the practice of the gospel, and liturgy must be linked to conversion and the practice of the gospel, so they are tied together. In liturgy we make a public commitment to work on the issues of peace and justice, and some of these liturgies are structured to reflect this. In fact, many would argue that there is no peace without justice.[12] However, these forms are just that—a structure to lift up these emphases.

What we really need to emphasize is the message of the prophets, "Let justice roll down like thunder and righteousness as an ever rolling stream" (Amos 5:24), as Martin Luther King spoke of the universal need for justice.[13] Worship can give us the power to work on issues of justice. Justice in the criminal justice system is often absent, as seen by the disproportionate number of arrests and convictions of people of color versus Anglos who commit crimes and are not imprisoned. Justice as one of the key moral principles has many different faces.

The principle of justice recognizes that each person has his or her due based on his or her dignity as a person. It is closely tied to respect for persons but often involves a balancing between the competing legitimate claims of two persons. It demands a fairness in decision making. Some have referred to the two facets of justice as *comparative* (the balancing of competing claims) and *incomparative* (an absolute standard of justice).

In the health care area, this would be illustrated by the allocation of scarce medical resources based on comparative justice or a right to health care based on incomparative justice, that is, a minimum decent standard of life's necessities that would make health possible. In one sense, the principle of comparative justice is necessary because of the imperfect world in which we live. In other words, if someone is mentally or physically ill, no matter what their economic position, race, intellectual level, or ability to reciprocate, they are entitled to the best care their physician can provide based on justice. Furthermore, coupled with respect for persons, justice becomes the basis for appeal for protection of patient's rights. Health care is a fundamental human right of all God's people. With over 41 million people in the United States alone without health insurance, this is both a justice and an economic issue.[14] Since we spend $1.4 trillion annually for health care, there is something fundamentally wrong in our distribution system.[15]

The formal principle of justice as articulated by Aristotle—equal treatment for those equals in the respect under consideration—is not enough. Compensatory justice may demand preferential treatment for a period, to compensate for past injustices and unequal treatment. This view forms the basis for minority hiring quotas, or repayment to Native Americans for land taken long ago from their ancestors, or even for the homeless.

Compensatory justice in the area of health care would mean preferential allocation of scarce health resources to the most disadvantaged, for example, minority populations in the United States. Although few might agree to this application, the Rawlsian position of "a minimum level of primary goods in order to protect vital interests" could lead to a variation of compensatory justice by assuring a "decent minimum" of health care, housing, food, and the like for everyone.

TAINTED CREATION

Another aspect of brokenness is the injustice in our world that results in oppression, poverty, and hunger. One of the liturgies in this section, "Healing for a Hurting World," was written by members of the Bread for the World organization, which is a religious lobby group for world hunger issues with chapters in many local churches. World hunger is also linked to abuse of the land. Globalization, welcomed by the one-third "developed" world and often feared by the two-thirds world as leading to exploitation, is a fact of the twenty-first century. Peter Paris points out that a moral community should have the Aristotelian marks of appropriate appetite, free choice, wise judgment, and good habits as the basis for a free and just society.[16] The fair distribution of the world's goods and the care of God's creation are both rooted in moral virtue. Inequitable distribution of the world's goods leads to poverty and is related to exploitation of the earth; the greed of the "developed" countries depletes the two-thirds world.

The liturgy "The Joy of Water" is a good illustration of celebrating and valuing God's gift of creation. Acceptance of all God's people includes those who are homeless and indigent, and for this reason a liturgy for those who are homeless is included in this chapter. Peoples who have been uprooted from their homes due to war or unemployment or who spend more hours away than at home because of work in sweatshops also command respect.

CHRISTIAN PATH TO RECONCILIATION

In the face of these injustices, the Christian Scriptures point the way to reconciliation. Paul's letter to the Corinthians especially in several passages addresses the question of reconciliation, an important theme in a world turned upside down by views that challenged those of the Roman Empire. Corinth was a center of wealth and luxury as well as moral corruption. Paul visited there at least three times and wrote these letters in response to severe problems.

William Barclay, in his commentary on Paul's Second Letter to the Corinthians, indicates that this is the letter of reconciliation written after the severe first letter.[17] The Corinthian church was one full of factions, with members vying for leadership—'I belong to Paul,' or 'I belong to Apollos,' or 'I belong to Cephas,' or 'I belong to Christ' (1 Cor. 1:12)—and judging one another's spirituality—who could prophesy best, speak in tongues, preach or teach most brilliantly. Reconciliation was as much needed then as it is now.

Particularly in a passage in 2 Corinthians, we learn what happens when we are in Christ: (1) we become a new creation; (2) we become reconciled to God; (3) we become reconciled to one another; and (4) we become ambassadors of reconciliation (2 Cor. 5:16–21).

Reconciliation with God becomes the basis for reconciliation with other people. Christ's death satisfied God's passion for justice; hence harmony and unity with our maker are restored. Unity with God leads to harmony with others. There are several liturgies in this chapter that highlight God's reconciling love for us. "Recommitment to Common Ground" provides a very detailed and comprehensive service for forgiveness and reconciliation and then moving forward with this new understanding.

Community Need

"They all ate and had enough." (Luke 9:17)

HEALING FOR A HURTING WORLD[18]
(Ecumenical)

BACKGROUND

The Genesis stories tell us not only that Creation is "very good" (Gen. 1:31), but also that God intended to provide humankind with everything necessary for a healthy, wholesome life. Further, God's valuing the well-being of humankind is demonstrated graphically in the person of Jesus Christ who healed the diseased, mended the broken, helped the helpless and fed the hungry. God's intention for health and wholeness, though, is often frustrated. Our task, if we are faithful to Jesus Christ, is to affirm and cooperate with this intentional will of God for wholeness and harmonious functioning of the world. Thus, it is very appropriate for members of the Body of Christ to meet together to prayerfully lift up to God's healing both our own need to be healed of despair and apathy, whatever prevents us personally from affirming and participating in God's will for wholeness, and also specific social ills, such as hunger, that we recognize as frustrating God's intention for our world. In our obedience as part of the Body of Christ, we become living channels for his healing and saving touch in our world. For many, a healing service can provide the setting to open those channels.

Although this service can be used anytime during the year, Advent can be a particularly appropriate time; for during Advent we examine ourselves and our world in light of God's intent of salvation—wholeness—for all people.

Eucharist or Holy Communion may be observed within the healing service. To participate in the breaking of the bread and the drinking of the cup is to participate in the Incarnation, Atonement, Redemption and Resurrection of Jesus Christ. To become "at one" with him always promotes health and wholeness and, within this service, prepares worshipers to be God's channels for healing in our world.

This service also suggests including the ritual of anointing with oil. This ritual may be outside the normal traditions of many churches, but the practice is rooted deeply in Scripture. In Jesus' time, oil (usually olive oil) was universally considered a medicine. Anointing the sick with healing oil, such as in the Good Samaritan story, was common practice. So the physical symbol of anointing with oil that which is hurt and broken can be a powerful and dramatic communicator of God's love and healing at work in the world.

This worship experience is best done as the culmination of a study that relates the Gospel to our hurting and hungry world. Again, the four Sundays in Advent lend themselves very well to this purpose. Whether the service is held within the context of a study or a single worship experience, participants will need to be given some background to the idea of a "healing service" beforehand.

SILENT MEDITATION   Ps. 125:2
Rom. 12:2
2 Tim. 1:7

RESPONSIVE PRAISE

Leader: How manifold are your works, O Lord!

Men and Boys: In wisdom you have wrought them all—the earth is full of your creatures.

Women and Girls: The sea also, great and wide, schools without number, living things both small and great.

Leader: God looked at all Creation, and found it very good.

All: May the glory of the Lord endure forever. (Gen. 1:31; Ps. 104:24–25)

HYMN   #501   WIII   "The King of Glory"

PROPHETIC CHALLENGE

Leader: Listen, people of Israel, to this funeral song which I sing over you:
Virgin Israel has fallen,
Never to rise again!
She lies abandoned on the ground,
And no one helps her up.

Men and Boys: You people hate anyone who challenges injustice and speaks the whole truth in court.

Women and Girls: You have oppressed the poor and robbed them of their grain.

Men and Boys: And so you will not live in the fine stone houses you build or drink wine from the vineyards you plant.

Leader: I know how terrible your sins are and how many crimes you have committed. You persecute good people, take bribes and prevent the poor from getting justice in the courts.

Men and
   Boys: The Sovereign Lord says, "A city in Israel sends out a thousand soldiers,

Women and
   Girls: but only a hundred return;

Men and
   Boys: Another city sends out a hundred,

Women and
   Girls: but only ten come back."

   All: The Lord says to the people of Israel, "Come to me and you will live."
   (Amos 5:1–4, 10–12)

DIALOGUE
(Begin by having eight to ten worshipers stand one at a time to read a current news headline. These headlines should identify suffering in the world in need of God's healing. Ask all to reflect on these headlines and similar ones they themselves have read. Encourage worshipers to write on a 3x5 index card provided for them one or two sentences that reflect their thoughts and concerns. Allow time for participants to share aloud what they have written.)

CORPORATE CONFESSION

Lord, we listen to your prophets' words, knowing they are for us. We have misused your world, so perfect a Creation. Land meant to provide for all, provides for only a few. Young men dream of plows and corn, but find instead guns and warplanes. Women who want homes for their children and soup for their pots, pitch refugee tents and boil grass for dinner. Babies born with your promise die from disease and starvation. In your world of plenty, millions face impossible choices—food or heat, shoes or a coat, electricity or rent.

   Lord of Creation, move us from hardness to compassion, from guilt to forgiveness, from apathy to action, from complicity to justice. Heal our brokenness and the wounds of your creation. Amen.

WORDS OF ASSURANCE AND FORGIVENESS   Isa. 40:1–2; Amos 5:12

HOMILY OR SERMON
(Sermon Notes & Quotes from Leaven Vol. II, nos. 2 and 4, develop Scripture passages related to healing and wholeness.)

HOLY COMMUNION
(After partaking of the bread and cup according to your tradition, invite worshipers to the altar for special prayers of intercession and healing for our world.)

PERIOD OF INTERCESSION
(Gathered at the altar)

>   **Leader:**   (Mark 11:24)

ANOINTING WITH OIL AND LAYING-ON OF HANDS
(The rituals of anointing with oil and laying-on of hands should be incorporated according to your own religious tradition or as you feel appropriate. The following format is but one alternative.

As a part of the period of intercession, have a bowl of olive oil available. Those who wish may kneel, prayerfully lifting up both the concern written on their cards and their own personal requests for healing that in their lives which prevents them from being fully open channels for God's healing power. The pastor or a team of clergy and lay persons can move from worshiper to worshiper for laying-on of hands and anointing with oil. Some worshipers may wish to verbalize their petitions for healing while hands are laid on their heads and the oil is touched to their foreheads. But whether or not petitions are verbalized, repeat together these words for each individual:)
Lord of Creation, Lord of Mercy, bring your healing touch.

THE GOOD NEWS OF DELIVERANCE
(Read in unison)

>   **All: (Isa. 61:1–4)**

HYMN OF PRAISE AND VICTORY   #606   WIII   "My Shepherd Will Supply My Need"

BENEDICTION

REMEMBRANCE OF 9/11 TERRORIST ATTACKS[19]
(Episcopal)

INTRODUCTION TO SERVICE
This resource was composed for use by churches in the Episcopal Diocese of Chicago by Bishop William D. Persell to help in liturgy and homily planning in the remembrance of the September 11, 2001 terrorist attacks.

HYMN SUGGESTIONS

From The Hymnal 1982

#345	"Savior, Again to Thy Dear Name"	#598	"When Christ Was Lifted from the Earth"
#346	"O Spirit of Life"	#599	"O God of Every Nation"
#347	"God Is Love"	#600	"Jerusalem My Happy Home"
#348	"O God of Love, O King of Peace"	#636/7	"How Firm a Foundation"
#349	"Lord, Make Us Servants"	#649	"O Jesus Joy of Loving Hearts"
#594/5	"God of Grace and God of Glory"	#650	"The Lord My God My Shepherd Is"
#597	"O Day of Peace"	#680	"O God Our Help in Ages Past"
		#801	"God Be with You Till We Meet Again"

From Wonder Love and Praise
#789   "Peace Among Earth's People"
#790   "Put Peace into Each Other's Hands"
#791   "Peace before Us"
#796   "Together *Unidos*"

From Lift Every Voice and Sing
#191 "His Eye Is on the Sparrow"

THE APPOINTED EUCHARISTIC LESSONS FOR SUNDAY, SEPTEMBER 8, 2002   PROPER 18A

Ezek. 33:(1–6) 7–11

Jerusalem's final destruction by the Babylonians came in 587 B.C.E. Some time before that event, Ezekiel preached in the Holy City. The image of the watchman or sentinel would have had significant emotional impact for his hearers. For many years, the little kingdom of Judah (which had Jerusalem as its capital city) was caught between the super powers of its day; Egypt and Babylon. A watchman on the hills of Palestine could have spotted an approaching army and, through a timely warning, could have saved many lives.

In this text, Ezekiel uses the sentinel as a metaphor for the prophet's work. Only by attending to the dangers which others face can the prophet save himself. Further, there is great hope. God waits expectantly for the lost ones and waits like a parent standing behind a wandering child to whirl around and return. Hence the pleading triple repetition of the word "turn," in vs. 11; a word which also means, "repentance."

Following September 11, 2001, there are many who are attending to the dangers which face our nation. What might it look like if we were to take seriously Ezekiel's sentinel metaphor? How might we attend to the dangers which others face in order to save ourselves—individually, communally, nationally?

Ps. 119:33–48

Rom. 12:9–21

This reading is part of Paul's teaching about the character of new life in Christ. The call to love in vs. 9 is expanded and explained by a series of instructions about charitable acts. Zeal in affections, hope, patience, perseverance, hospitality, compassion, and humility is how one practices genuine love. This genuine love is not only a proper spiritual discipline for the individual but it is also a strategy for overcoming evil with good. To love in this way is to participate in Christ's redemptive work. In a time of terrorism and war, the call to overcome evil with good is easily dismissed. How do we take this message seriously today? Further, how do we remain faithful to this call while compassionately responding to the grief and anger of those who have suffered or lost loved ones because of recent evils? These are the kinds of questions which this text raises.

Matt. 18:15–20

Notice how carefully this Gospel instruction aims at reconciliation. First, a private and face-saving meeting is encouraged and then a meeting with two or three others. This is not merely for witnesses. Wounds may have been done to both parties. The person doing the confronting may be wrong. Reconciliation, not judgment, is the goal here. Finally, if necessary, the matter is taken before the entire community. The community's ability to bind or loose, to convict or acquit, is the last step. It is to be applied only when necessary and is based on the community's union with Christ. This text is concerned with conflict and sin within the Christian community. Do we limit to our own the high value it places on reconciliation? Do we believe that reconciliation needs to be practiced outside of the Church as well? What reconciliation needs do we have both locally and globally? Should we, and if so how do we, pursue reconciliation with terrorists?

SUGGESTED EUCHARISTIC LESSONS FOR WEDNESDAY, SEPTEMBER 11, 2002

Isa. 58:6–14

The possibility of being called, "the repairer of the breach the restorer of streets to live in," seems especially poignant after the clearing of the World Trade Center site. The author of this prophecy lived with his exiled people in Babylon (6th century B.C.E.). Where he usually preached comfort to his people, here he gives a clarion call of reform. This text speaks beautifully of the reward that God wishes to give those who repent and do what is right. This is not, however, the usual way to comfort people. Nevertheless there is comfort in this text. God is always ready to forgive and bless us. God will not hold our failings and sins against us.

It has become quite common to hear people say that because of the terrorist attacks on September 11, 2001, "everything has changed." This may be true. However, hand wringing about national security is not what this prophet would suggest. Instead, he would encourage those of us who need to grieve to do so. And the others of us he would encourage to comfort those who mourn. He would also challenge us to examine our own lives and see where we need to turn around. Every time any one of us practices self-examination and amendment of life, we help the whole world do the same. Repairing the breaches in our own relationships is the first step in restoring the streets of our world.

Ps. 122

Eph. 2:13–22

Verse 17 is a quote of Isaiah 57:19. The medieval Jewish scholar Rashi suggested that "the near" are persons who have been devoted to God through service. The "far off" are the people who are only now turning to God. Rashi felt those who are near and those who are far off are equal in God's eyes. Rashi's sense of this equality in the Isaiah text also fits well with this text from Ephesians.

In this text it is the Gentiles who were far off, while the Jews were near. In Christ, God has made both groups equal, thereby creating a new, united humanity. The dividing wall of vs. 14 was actually a wall between the outer and inner courts of the temple. On it were placed messages threatening death to any foreigners who might try to pass into the inner court of the temple. This wall was, for many, symbolic of the entire Jewish notion of separation and purity. Jesus Christ is the cornerstone of a new building in which Jews and Gentiles are united, not just brought near to one another. He crossed the dividing wall, died doing it, and became the new temple in which we all have access to God.

Matt. 5:38–48

We certainly heard the ancient cry, "An eye for an eye and a tooth for a tooth," following the terrorist attack of September 11, 2001. For many that cry flowed from the heart as tears flowed from the eyes. For others it burst forth with shock and anger. Emotionally the desire for retribution and revenge is entirely understandable. Even so, it is quite clear that Jesus taught nonresistance and love for enemies.

Verses 38–42 are about nonresistance. Verse 39 has to do with being humiliated in public. Perhaps this happened when Christians were slapped with the back of the hand (for being heretics) by synagogue officials. Verse 40 has to do with a law (Exod. 22:25–27) which said that a coat cannot be taken in credit overnight because it is often the only blanket a poor person has. Verse 41 references the right of Roman soldiers to make Jewish people serve as guides or porters (think of Simon of Cyrene). In all of these examples, force or power leaves one person diminished in order to meet another person's needs. Jesus asserts that adopting the style of one's opponent in these situations is to perpetuate the abuse of power.

Verses 43 to 48 have to deal with loving one's enemies. In Jesus' own day, there were some rabbis who put forward the idea that one should love all human beings. On the other hand, there were those like the Qumran community who practiced radical separation. The enemy in these cases was not any particular person but those who held different views. Jesus warns against this hatred which flows from uncompromising ideological positions. Love of neighbor cannot be limited, fenced in, or excluded.

The Father is perfect, in the sense of whole, undivided, and intact. Jesus offers us union with the Father. Because of that union, we should not craft divisions among those with whom we interact. Jesus is interested here in the wholeness of heart which attempts to love as God loves while receiving that ability to love as gift and miracle. Such love is humble enough not to take on God's role of judging and dividing. Hence the value, as both spiritual discipline and proclamation, of nonresistance and love of one's enemies.

SUGGESTED PRAYERS OF THE PEOPLE
(This form of the Prayers of the People is suggested for use at any 9/11 Anniversary Liturgy.)

Intercessor: Strength of all strength, sovereign God, your majestic grace crowns the sky with stars and keeps the planets on their ways. You (*in the daytime add:* turn our night to day and) fill the earth with life, granting the love which sustains us. Therefore we cry out to you saying, Hear us, O God of life. *(May be omitted.)*

Intercessor: We pray to you, redeeming God, for your people throughout the world; for Frank, our Presiding Bishop and for William and Victor our Bishops; (for N [and N], our priest[s] and for N [and N] our deacon[s]; and for all the people of God. We ask you to unite us in bonds of love, saying,

Assembly: Hear us, O God of life.

Intercessor: We pray to you, God of peace, for our nation and for those in civil authority; especially George our President, George our governor, and the members of our armed forces. We ask you to grant our decision-makers a desire for peace and the welfare of all peoples, saying,

Assembly: **Hear us, O God of life.**

Intercessor: We pray to you, God of justice, for the welfare of the world and ask your blessings for Kofi Annan and the work of the United Nations. Grant that all nations, races, and religions may show one another respect and live in harmony with the good earth which you have given us. We pray for global friendship, saying,

Assembly: **Hear us, O God of life.**

Intercessor: We pray to you, healing God, for the poor, the sick, the hungry, the oppressed, and those in prison; especially those whom we now name *(pause)*. We ask you to grant health and safety to those whose communities are shattered by war, terrorism, or any kind of violence, saying,

Assembly: **Hear us, O God of life.**

Intercessor: We pray to you, God of mercy, for our enemies and those who wish us harm. We ask you to help us forgive and seek forgiveness, saying,

Assembly: **Hear us, O God of life.**

Intercessor: We pray to you, Giver of life, for the departed and those who mourn; especially those whom we now name *(pause)*.

On this anniversary of national tragedy, we remember before you those who died on American Airlines Flight #11, American Airlines Flight #77, United Airlines Flight #93, and United Airlines Flight #175; for those who worked in the World Trade Center, those who worked in the Pentagon Building, the emergency workers who sacrificed their lives for others, and all those who died by acts of terrorism or retaliation for terrorism *(this paragraph may be omitted)*.

We ask you to help them grow from strength to strength in your eternal presence, saying,

Assembly: **Hear us, O God of life.**

Intercessor: God of endless blessing, a moment's pause in your creative stirring and everything would cease to be. But creation is your self-expression and loving communion is your nature. Deliver us from hardness of heart and keep us from stifling our souls' song of need for you. We ask you to clothe us in your Spirit that we may reach out to our world with Christ's arms of love, saying, *(may be omitted)*

Assembly: **Hear us, O God of life.** *(May be omitted.)*

Presider: O God, creator of all, Jesus your Word commanded us to love our enemies: Lead them and us from prejudice to truth; deliver them and us from hatred, cruelty, and revenge; and in your good time enable us all to stand reconciled before you; through Christ our Savior.

Assembly: **Amen.**[20]

HEALING OF THE CHURCH AND HER MEMBERS[21]
(Anglican)

AN ORDER OF SERVICE FOR THE LAYING-ON OF HANDS

(Stand as the Ministers enter.)

HYMN   #528   H82   "Lord You Give the Great Commission"

Minister: God is our hope and strength; a very present help in trouble.

Lift up your hearts;

Congregation: We lift them up unto the Lord.

Minister: Let us give thanks unto our Lord God;

Congregation: It is meet and right so to do.

THANKSGIVING

Minister: Let us thank God.

First let us thank Him for who He is.

(Here the Minister may use his own words.)

Let us bless the Lord.

Congregation: Thanks be to God.

Minister: For the movement of His Spirit in our time, and for the renewal of the Church's Ministry of Healing.

Let us bless the Lord.

Congregation: Thanks be to God.

Minister: For His abundant blessings in this and other places, for the growth of fellowships of prayer and healing, and for the prayers of many, especially at this time . . .

Let us bless the Lord.

Congregation: Thanks be to God.

Minister: For those many who have known His Healing Touch upon them . . .

Let us bless the Lord.

Congregation: Thanks be to God.

Minister: And for the new hope of those who have been released from fear, saved from despair, and delivered from the grip of moments past . . .

Let us bless the Lord.

Congregation: Thanks be to God.

Minister: Finally, let us give thanks for the life and prayers of all the Saints

(especially . . .) . . .

Let us bless the Lord.

Congregation: Thanks be to God.

INTERCESSIONS
(Kneel or sit)

Minister 2: Let us pray:

We pray that Christ may be known in His healing power in the life of the Church people.
Jesus, Lord of the Church:

Congregation: in your mercy, hear us.

Minister 2: You have called us into the family
of those who are the children of God.
May our love for our brothers and sisters in Christ
be strengthened by your grace.
Jesus, Lord of the Church:

Congregation: in your mercy, hear us.

Minister 2: You have called us to be a temple
where the Holy Spirit can dwell.
Give us clean hands and pure hearts
so that our lives will reflect your holiness.
Jesus, Lord of the Church:

Congregation: in your mercy, hear us.

Minister 2: You have called us to be a light to the world
so that those in darkness come to you.
May our lives shine as a witness
to the saving grace you have given for all.
Jesus, Lord of the Church:

Congregation: in your mercy, hear us.

Minister 2: You have called us to be members of your body,
so that when one suffers, all suffer together.
We ask for your comfort and healing power
to bring hope to those in distress.
Jesus, Lord of the Church:

Congregation: in your mercy, hear us.

Minister 2: You have called us to be the Bride
where you, Lord, are the Bridegroom.
Prepare us for the wedding feast
where we will be united with you forever.
Jesus, Lord of the Church:

Congregation: hear our prayer,
and make us one in heart and mind
to serve you with joy forever. Amen.

PAUSE FOR SILENT PRAYER

O God,
Who has prepared for them that love Thee
Such good things as pass man's understanding,
Pour into our hearts such love towards Thee
That we, loving Thee in all things and above all things,
May obtain Thy promises, which exceed all that we can desire,
Through Jesus Christ our Lord. **Amen.**

THE LESSON

MEDITATION

RECORDED MUSIC OR ANTHEM

Minister: As God's people, let us declare our faith:

All: There is one body and one Spirit, just as we are called to one hope; one
Lord, one faith, one baptism: one God and Father of all, who is over all,
and through all, and in all. Amen.

HYMN   #525   H82   "The Church's One Foundation"

CONFESSION

The grace of God has dawned upon the world with healing for all. Let us come to him, in sorrow for our sins, seeking healing and salvation.

(Kneel or sit)

PAUSE FOR SELF-EXAMINATION

Minister: Let us humbly confess our sins to Almighty God.

All: Almighty God, our heavenly Father, we have sinned against Thee, through our own deliberate fault, in thought and word and deed and in what we have left undone.
For Thy Son our Lord Jesus Christ's sake forgive us all that is past; and grant that we may serve Thee
in newness of life, to the glory of Thy Name. Amen.

THE ABSOLUTION

Almighty God, our heavenly Father, who of His great mercy hath promised forgiveness of sins to all them that with hearty repentance and true faith turn unto Him: Have mercy upon you, pardon and deliver you from all your sins; confirm and strengthen you in all goodness; and keep you in life eternal, through Jesus Christ our Lord. **Amen.**

Minister 3: Lord, have mercy upon us.

Congregation: Christ, have mercy upon us.

Minister 3: Lord, have mercy upon us.

THE LORD'S PRAYER (unison)

Minister 3: O Lord, save Thy servants;

Congregation: Who put their trust in Thee.

Minister 3: Send them help from Thy holy place;

Congregation: And evermore mightily defend them.

Minister 3: Help us, O God of our salvation;

Congregation: And for the glory of Thy name deliver us, and be merciful to us sinners, for Thy name's sake.

Minister 3: Lord, hear our prayer;

Congregation: And let our cry come unto Thee.

Heavenly Father, whose Son our Lord Jesus Christ said to his apostles,
"Peace I leave with you, my peace I give to you," regard not our sins but the faith of your Church, and grant it that peace, unity and healing which is agreeable to your will;
through Jesus Christ our Lord.   **Amen.**

(A member of the congregation says this prayer:)

God bless us, and grant that we upon whom Thou dost lay Thine hands may find healing and wholeness, through Jesus Christ our Lord.   **Amen.**

(These prayers may be used and the Ministers pray for one another and for those named in the Altar book:)

(Ministers together:)

And now, O God, I give myself to Thee. Empty me of all that is not of Thee, cleanse me from all unrighteousness, and according to Thy Will take my hands and use them for Thy glory. **Amen.**

"Lord, I am not worthy that Thou couldest come under my roof, but speak the word only, and Thy servant shall be healed."

(Remain kneeling or sitting.)

HYMN   #472   LH   "Come Holy Ghost"

THE LAYING-ON OF HANDS
("A Little Way of Prayer" may be used:)

Let us by an act of the will place ourselves in the presence of our Divine Lord, and with an act of faith ask that He will empty us of self and of *all* desire save that His Most Blessed Will may be done, and that it may illumine our hearts and minds. We can then gather together ourselves and all those for whom our prayers have been asked, and hold all silently up to Him. Making no special request—neither asking nor beseeching—but just resting, with them, *in* Him, desiring nothing but that Our Lord may be glorified in all.

In this most simple way of approach He does make known His Most Blessed Will for us. "For so He giveth Himself to His beloved in quietness."

—Dorothy Kerin

(The Ministers lay on hands and pray first with those unable to come to the rail. Then those wishing to receive the laying-on of hands at the rail come forward as directed.)

THANKSGIVING

> **Minister:** And now O Lord we pray Thee give us grace to tarry Thy leisure, and to await with hope the fulfilling of Thy promises: "For they that wait upon the Lord shall renew their strength."

Congregation: Thanks be to God.

> **Minister 2:** Remember, O Lord, what Thou hast wrought in us this day, and not what we deserve, and as Thou hast called us to Thy service, make us worthy of our calling, through Jesus Christ our Lord.

Congregation: Amen.

THE BLESSING

HYMN   #473   H82   "Lift High the Cross"

APOLOGY TO MY BROTHERS AND SISTERS
IN DEVELOPING COUNTRIES[22]
(Roman Catholic)

To my brothers and sisters in developing countries:

While I was deciding which oat bran cereal to eat this morning, you were searching the ground for leftover grains from the passing wheat truck.

While I was jogging at the health center, you were working in the wealthy landowner's field under a scorching sun.

While I was choosing between diet and regular soda, your parched lips were yearning for a sip of clean water.

While I complained about the poor service in the gourmet restaurant, you were gratefully eating a bowl of rice.

While I poured my "fresh and better" detergent into the washing machine, you stood in the river with your bundle of clothes.

While I watched the evening news on my wide-screen television set, you were being terrorized and taunted by a dictatorial government.

While I read the newspaper and drank my cup of steaming coffee, you walked the long, dusty miles to a crowded schoolroom to learn how to read.

While I scanned the ads for a bargain on an extra piece of clothing, you woke up and put on the same shirt and pants that you have worn for many months.

While I built a fourteen-room house for the three of us, your family of ten found shelter in a one-room hut.

While I went to church last Sunday and felt more than slightly bored, you stood on the land with those around you and felt gratitude to God for being alive for one more day.

My brothers and sisters, forgive me for my arrogance and my indifference. Forgive me for my greed of always wanting newer, bigger, and better things. Forgive me for not doing my part to change the unjust systems that keep you suffering and impoverished. I offer you my promise to become more aware of your situation and to change my lifestyle as I work for the transformation of our world.

SURVIVAL OF VULNERABLE PERSONS IN THE WORLD[23]
(Uniting Church in Australia)

For this service you will need

> • *Small candles and tapers to light them*

OPENING SENTENCES

Love has come.
Love has come among us, even us,
risking its own destruction:
God with us.
God for us all.

Grace lies here in frailty.
Grace has come among us, even us,
journeying through costly pathways:
God with us.
God for us all.

MUSIC

CONFESSION

O God, we see the things of hope, of love and justice,
of peace and truth, in ourselves and in our world,
in fearful battle with the powerful forces
which would defeat and destroy them.

(A silence is kept.)

When we hand them over to the tyrants of our day,
without much struggle:
Forgive us.

If we have given up hope in precious parts of ourselves:
Forgive us.

ASSURANCE

Hear the word of assurance:
life is stronger than death in us.
Christ is come.
Love is cherished in the hand of God.
Thanks be to God.

READING   Matt. 2:13–23

REFLECTION

AFFIRMATION

How will we believe, O God?
And yet we will,
And yet we must,
Or nothing is possible beyond what we can now see.
Let us affirm our faith together:

We believe,
against all our realities
and the lack of hope around us,
we believe in God.
We believe that Jesus Christ
and the life of this Christ will survive in the world.
We believe that the Spirit is still with us,
the Spirit of God, the Spirit of Christ.
We believe that we are eternally linked
with the love and good and courage of our God,
if we will choose to be.
And we so choose.

PRAYERS

Let us light a candle for each fragile cause,
for each vulnerable person we know
who needs to be carried to safety, cherished in the arms of God.

(Small candles are placed in the center and the people light them.)

Our hopes and our faith are like these very small lights,
flickering in the wind of life as they travel along unknown ways,
like Mary and Joseph carrying the Christchild to safety.
We pray, O God, that these people will be kept safe.
We will share in the holding of their life.
We will share in the carrying of courage and faith alongside them.
Be with us as we go, God of our journey.
In the name of the Christ,
Amen.

HYMN   #484   W&R   "O Lord Hear My Prayer"

BLESSING

Go in peace,
and may the God who protected the Holy Child
cover you and keep you,
the God who came to be with us be found beside you,

and the love within you be called into safe places
by the gentle Spirit.
Amen.

BLESSING OF A VICTIM OF CRIME OR OPPRESSION[24]
(Roman Catholic)

INTRODUCTION

*The personal experience of a crime, political oppression, or social oppression can be trau-
matic and not easily forgotten. A victim often needs the assistance of others, and no less that
of God, in dealing with this experience.*

*This blessing is intended to assist the victim and help him or her come to a state of tranquil-
lity and peace.*

*These orders may be used by a priest or a deacon, and also by a layperson, who follows the
rites and prayers designated for a lay minister.*

ORDER OF BLESSING

INTRODUCTORY RITES
*(When the community has gathered, a suitable song may be sung. After the singing, the min-
ister says:)*

In the name of the Father, and of the Son, and of the Holy Spirit.

(All make the sign of the cross and reply:)

Amen.

*(A minister who is a priest or deacon greets those present in the following or other suitable
words, taken mainly from sacred Scripture.)*

May the grace and peace of Christ be with you.

(And all reply:)

And also with you.

(A lay minister greets those present in the following words:)

May the Lord grant us peace, now and forever.
Amen.

(In the following or similar words, the minister prepares those present for the blessing.)

Throughout history God has manifested his love and care for those who have suffered from violence, hatred, and oppression. We commend N. to the healing mercy of God who binds up all our wounds and enfolds us in his gentle care.

READING OF THE WORD OF GOD

(A reader, another person present, or the minister reads a text of sacred Scripture.)

Brothers and sisters, listen to the words of the holy gospel according to Matthew (Matt. 10:28–33).

Or: Isa. 59:6b–8 (The Lord is appalled by evil and injustice); Job 3:1–26 (Lamentation of Job); Lam. 3:1–24 (I am one who knows affliction); Lam. 3:49–59 (When I called, you came to my aid); Matt. 5:1–10 (The Beatitudes); Matt. 5:43–48 (Love your enemies, pray for those who persecute you); Luke 10:25–37 (The Good Samaritan)

(As circumstances suggest, one of the following responsorial psalms may be sung, or some other suitable song.)

Ps. 140
R. **The Lord is my strength and my salvation.**

Ps. 142:2–3, 4b–5, 6–7
R. **You, O Lord, are my refuge.**

Ps. 31:2–3a, 4–5, 15–16, 24–25
R. **Into your hands I commend my spirit.**

(As circumstances suggest, the minister may give those present a brief explanation of the biblical text, so that they may understand through faith the meaning of the celebration.)

(The intercessions are then said. The minister introduces them and an assisting minister or one of those present announces the intentions. From the following those best suited to the occasion may be used or adapted, or other intentions that apply to the particular circumstances may be composed.)

(The minister says:)

Let us pray to the Lord God, the defender of the weak and powerless, who delivered our ancestors from harm.

R. **Deliver us from evil, O Lord.**

(Assisting minister:)
For N., that he/she may be freed from pain and fear, we pray to the Lord. **R.**

For all who are victims of crime/oppression, we pray to the lord. **R.**

For those who harm others, that they may change their lives and turn to God, we pray to the Lord. **R.**

(After the intercessions the minister, in the following or similar words, invites all present to sing or say the Lord's Prayer.)

The Lord heals our wounds and strengthens us in our weakness; let us pray as Christ has taught us:

THE LORD'S PRAYER *(unison)*

PRAYER OF BLESSING
(A minister who is a priest or deacon says the prayer of blessing with hands outstretched over the person to be blessed; a lay minister says the prayer with hands joined.)

Lord God,
your own Son was delivered into the hands of the wicked,
yet he prayed for his persecutors
and overcame hatred with the blood of the cross.
Relieve the suffering of N.;
grant him/her peace of mind
and a renewed faith in your protection and care.
Protect us all from the violence of others,
keep us safe from the weapons of hate,
and restore to us tranquility and peace.

We ask this through Christ our Lord.
R.   Amen.

(As circumstances suggest, the minister in silence may sprinkle the person with holy water.)

CONCLUDING RITE

(A minister who is a priest or deacon concludes the rite by saying:)

May God bless you with his mercy,
strengthen you with his love,
and enable you to walk in charity and peace.

R.   Amen.

(Then he blesses all present.)

And may almighty God bless you all,
the Father, and the Son, and the Holy Spirit.

R.   Amen.

(A lay minister concludes the rite by signing himself or herself with the sign of the cross and saying:)

May God bless us with his mercy,
strengthen us with his love,
and enable us to walk in charity and peace.

R.   Amen.

(It is preferable to end the celebration with a suitable song such as #512 CH, "When Aimless Violence Takes Those We Love.")

MISSING PERSONS[25]
(Uniting Church in Australia)

This introduction and prayer were created to close Missing Persons Week in the state of New South Wales in Australia. It was a week where the community focused its care both on those who were missing and those who suffered the loss of their disappearance.

OPENING

This has been a week when we as members of the community have been invited to remember that in our midst are a whole group of people who live with unresolved and mostly unrecognized grief because their family member or friend has disappeared.

We have been invited to realize that also in our midst is often hidden the answer to the questions that lie within that disappearance.

- Sometimes the answers are about the disappeared person living unknown and unnamed among us with all the complex reasons for that.
- Sometimes the answers are about hidden violence, abuse and destruction that have never been faced or made visible in this, our life together.

You who have lost the ones you love into a mystery of silence and emptiness face a hard journey into the future.

- How can you lay those missing loved ones to rest if it is still possible that you should be calling them more loudly towards life and love from you?
- Will you betray them and your love for them if you stop hoping to reconnect with their life?
- Was there something you should have done?
- Is there something more you should be doing now?

In the many crises and traumas in life, in the face of things that it seems we cannot change or really understand, often our best refuge and comfort is to place ourselves and those we love out into a wider community of life than our own and to respect our own small efforts as being enough.

In respecting our own efforts to live as best we can we can say to ourselves:

We are not God.
We are ordinary homely human beings and at each point in our lives we have done what we could.
We will rest with that and honor our own humble human journeys as significant.

If who we are and what we have done or not done has impacted on the life of others, we ask their forgiveness and the forgiveness of God.

We will walk into the future accepting our ordinary selves and giving all our energy into the future rather than into the past.

We will honor the past by carrying with us, very close to our hearts, our real and ongoing love for the things we have lost and the ones we have lost.

In placing our lives onto a wider space for healing and hope:

We ask that you see this grieving that we carry with us and gather around us the caring and respect that we need to journey on.

We ask you to share the burden of looking for the lost ones so that we do not feel the whole burden is ours.

We ask you to see if, in the midst of this our community, you can participate with us in creating a safer and more loving place for all people so that, if they go missing,

- you will all ask why;
- you will all assume responsibility for finding the lost;
- and you will not forget that this is happening among us.

That is why this week has been important for us all.
It is your way of inviting these things from us.
On behalf of the part of the community which cares about that, I can only say that we have heard. With great respect and concern, we honor your loss and your grieving and we share your pain now and into the future.

Let us gather the elements around us and those we have lost:

Let us hear the rain and see it creating rivers around our feet.

As we listen, let us imagine that even the heavens are joining their tears with ours as we grieve for those who are lost and that the rivers around our feet are joined with the rivers of the tears which have been shed.

Then let us remember that the very rain that we hear and see will join with the sun and produce the flowers around us in the spring, the greening of the trees and the earth—that from the tears may come new life and hope blossoming forth.

As we feel the breath of the wind, let us imagine that it blows our love towards our loved ones, wherever they are.

I have been asked to say a prayer:

Dear God, nothing is hidden from you.
You see all that is to be seen.
You know all that is to be known.
You understand all that is a mystery to us.

If those we love are still living,

search for them like you searched for the one sheep who is lost.
Call to their hearts in your voice of love,
a voice full of understanding of all difficult and complex journeys,
and bring our loved ones home to us.
Give to them a message of hope about our love and longing for them,
so that they may come to us without fear and with trust.
O God, bring them home if they can come.
O God, keep them safe and happy, if they will not come,
and give us peace in believing that we can live with their decision.

O God, if they are not now living,
gather their lives which are lost to us into the safety of your loving arms.
Take these our children, our wives and husbands,
our mothers and fathers and friends,
these our precious lost ones,
and tell them that we know they have been lost to us,
that we grieve them still,
that there are many things of love and truth that we wanted to say to them,
many acts of kindness and grace that are missing between us.
Love them, O God, as we would have gone on loving them.
Heal them if they have been hurt and cherish them if they have left us in fear and pain.

Give us your peace on this day and in all our next days.
Surround us with the care of those who know us,
and give us the wisdom, love and strength to make a place here for all people that is safe, com-passionate, just and free from violence.
Amen.

Let us go from here in peace.

FOR THE UPROOTED ONES: REMEMBERING REFUGEES[26]
(Uniting Church in Australia)

For this service you will need

- *A large map of the world*
- *Flowers or ribbons or small candles*

CALL TO WORSHIP

There is no place where you cannot reach:
God who made the heavens and the earth.

There is no journey which you have not traveled:
God who shared our life in Jesus Christ.

There are no people beyond your care:
God who is the Spirit, the Comforter.
Let us worship God!

SONG

GATHER THEM IN

Let us "gather in" to our community of faith
some of the people who are uprooted
from their homes and countries around the world.

(The names of countries where there are known to be refugees are read and flowers are placed on the communion table for them, or candles lit, or a ribbon attached to the map.)

As we gather together in this place,
we remember these people and the struggle of their lives.
We will remember them before our God.

IT IS NOT EASY TO WELCOME EVERYONE

Even when we hope we can do better,
it is not easy to welcome everyone who wants to live among us,
or needs our prayers and concerned support, O God.
There are many reasons why we find it hard.
(The people say why it is hard.)

(or:)

Voice 1:   Sometimes we feel people are very different from us,
in culture, in looks, in ways of relating, in their politics, in their religion.

Voice 2:   Or we feel as though there is not enough
to share with them in work, in houses, in schools, in money, in services.

Voice 3:   Sometimes we are tired
and cannot find the energy to give the care,
or the time that they may hope from us,
especially when they are far away.

All: **Forgive us, O God, if we have been less than generous.**
We remember your grace in relating to us
and we long to be as gracious to others.

ASSURANCE

Our prayers are heard.
We too are gathered into the love of God.
Thanks be to God!

READINGS

SONG

SERMON

AFFIRMATION OF FAITH

In response to the word, let us stand and affirm our faith:

We are all held in the hollow of God's hand,
loved children of the universe,
born from the life which flows from God,
freed to the fullness of God's creation
with all its beauty and variety.

We are all worth dying for in Christ Jesus,
all called to risen life in Christ's rising.
The way of Jesus gives us footprints for our following
and all our trials and longings are known
in the frailty of Christ's birth among us
and the courage of Christ's walking with us.

We are all called to new things in the Spirit,
in the hope that stirs in unlikely moments,
the home we find in the wastelands of our wanderings,
the warmth that we touch in the coldness of our need
and the opening of our hearts to adventures in belonging
or the gathering in of those without a home.

THE OFFERING IS RECEIVED

Dear God, receive our offering.
Guide those who use it, that it may help to bring fullness of life
to those who live in need and long for our care.
Amen.

INTERCESSION

As they face this day, O God, find those who are lost,
separated from those they love,
crossing unknown borders,
without a country or home,
not knowing where to turn:
Find them, God who always seeks for the lost,
and cover them safely as a hen covers her chickens.

As they face this day, O God,
stand among the ones in refugee camps around the world,
in the hunger and despair,
in the crowds and the emptiness,
in the wet and the thirstiness:

**Be their hope and their strength
in the crying out for justice
and open the ears of the world to hear their cries.**

As they face this day, O God,
may those who live with us, uprooted from their homelands,
find a new home where their history is respected,
their gifts and graces celebrated
and their fear departed from them.
**May we be their home,
may we be the ones who open our hearts in welcome.**

As we face this day, O God,
Sing to us your song of encouragement,
paint for us your bright pictures of a new world
where people need not flee from wars and oppression,
where no one lacks a country or a home,
and where we are all part of your new creation.
**For we long to be your people, in spirit and in truth.
We pray in the name of Jesus the Christ,
who knew the life of a refugee.
Amen.**

THE LORD'S PRAYER

SONG

BLESSING AND DISMISSAL

Go in peace and grace.
And may God lift up new possibilities before us,
the face of Christ be seen in our neighbors
and the Spirit lead us into the celebration of a new community.
Amen.

HELPING THE MARGINALIZED[27]
(Disciples of Christ)

As we gather to worship, we renew our hope in the power of the resurrection to establish a world where "Fundamental human needs are a human right, *not an earned privilege, including the* right *to adequate housing, food, health care, education, clothing, and for those able to work, employment that can supply the above, and basic security in case of unemployment or underemployment."*[28]

PRELUDE

It will be appreciated by many worshipers if we refrain from talking during the Prelude. The Prelude is the start of our worship service, a time to listen, to meditate or pray, and to prepare our minds and hearts to hear God's word.

GATHERING SONGS   #276   CH   "We Gather Together"
#93   CH   "Praise Him"

WELCOME PRAYER

SPECIAL MUSIC   "Earthen Vessels" (based on 2 Cor. 4:6)

CHILDREN'S MOMENT

INTERLUDE   #113   CH   "Jesus Loves Me! This I Know" (vs. 1)

SCRIPTURE   2 Cor. 4:7

SERMON   "Courage to Be Clay Vessels"

INVITATION FOR MEMBERSHIP

HYMN   #344   CH   "I Have Decided to Follow Jesus"

OFFERING

(Please place your prayer request card in the offering plate.)

STEWARDSHIP MOMENT

OFFERTORY

MUSICAL OFFERING

PRESENTATION OF TITHES AND OFFERINGS

DOXOLOGY

OFFERTORY PRAYER

PRAISES AND PRAYERS OF THE PEOPLE

PASTORAL PRAYER

COMMUNION

HYMN   #123   UMH   "El Shaddai"

HYMN   #546   CH   "Amazing Grace"
(as you come forward)

All who gather here are invited to come forward and receive the Holy Communion. You are then invited to join the Unity Circle that will be forming around the sanctuary. On your way to the Unity Circle you may want to light a candle to symbolize the transforming light of Christ working in your life. Or, after Communion you may want to receive a special prayer of healing from our prayer ministers standing in the wings of the church, then proceed to the Unity Circle.

CLOSING

UNITY CIRCLE

PASTORAL BLESSING

SHALOM

POSTLUDE

EMPOWERING THE HOMELESS[29]
(Ecumenical)

Community Homeless Alliance Ministry (CHAM) advocates for the creation of permanent housing for destitute individuals and the working poor in Silicon Valley, California. Most of the members of the ministry are homeless themselves. They are led by Rev. Scott Wagers, who has become known in Santa Clara County as the "maverick preacher for San Jose's homeless." Each Sunday, Rev. Wagers leads CHAM in a worship and healing service in the sanctuary of First Christian Church in downtown San Jose, California.

CONGREGATIONAL PRAYER

The congregational prayer is usually led by a member of the community and incorporates the needs of the congregation. It is designed to lead people into a more meditative place so they can be centered for the service. The prayer leader specifically asks that the congregation be led by the Holy Spirit in its practice of Ministry.

Example:

Loving Creator *(or Heavenly Father)* still our minds and hearts that we may hear your words and feel your Presence. Let us seek your will above our own and help us to understand your ways in our lives. Strengthen us as your people and help us to find the path to which each of us is called. *(Sometimes at this point, the Lord's Prayer may be spoken.)* **Amen.**

HYMNS

Traditional hymns like "Amazing Grace," "How Great Thou Art," or "What a Friend We Have in Jesus" are often used to start the service. Freedom songs like "Ain't Gonna Let Nobody Turn Me Round" or "We Shall Overcome" are also incorporated as second hymns.

SCRIPTURE READING

Texts are chosen from the prophetic books of the Old Testament, especially Isaiah, Ezekiel, and Jeremiah. New Testament texts may include Acts, 1 and 2 Corinthians, and Romans but usually are selected from the Gospel of Luke. Some favorites include Luke 6:17–49 (the Sermon on the Plain); Luke 4:1–13 (Jesus' Temptation in the Desert); Luke 1:46–55 (The Magnificat); Luke 9:46–48 (True Greatness); Luke 16:19–31 (The Rich Man and Lazarus); Luke 19:45–46 (The Cleansing of the Temple); and Luke 22:39–53 (Jesus at Gethsemane).

SERMON

Rev. Wagers often chooses topics that would resonate with the poor and homeless, connecting their plight to the difficulties of the Early Church or the Prophets. One of his frequent subjects is "Jesus Bringing Good News to the Poor," or "The Stone that the Builders Rejected Has Become the Cornerstone," or the "Last Shall Be First." For Rev. Wagers, these themes "reverse conventional ideas about the poor and oppressed and connect the listeners with the historical Jesus." In his sermons, Rev. Wagers says that he tries "to reflect God's love for all people and God's concern for the poor—not in a charitable sense, but in terms of justice." He also develops more individualized themes like the healing of the demoniac, the poor widow, the man with the withered hand, or the Good Samaritan. The goal of these sermons is to connect people with God's healing power and the power of our own faith. Examples of sermon titles are "Mustard Seed Faith," "He Touched Me," "No Burden Too Great," and "Holy Wholeness." Other sermon titles and themes include "Twenty-first Century Prophet" (on what it means to be prophetic today); "The Church of the New Millennium" (on what the church of the future looks like, and where the church has been historically); "The Great Counselor: The Holy Spirit" (on the work of the Holy Spirit in the world today and during the early church); and "Bringers of the Kingdom."

SHARING AND HANDS-ON PRAYER

Rev. Wagers asks people to give a brief testimony or prayer request from the pews. If the pastor feels led, or if congregants request, he will ask people to come to the front of the church for hands-on prayer with oil (usually frankincense). During this time, Rev. Wagers may pray for as many as thirty or forty people ("usually quickly, but hopefully in a way that meets the need"). People often fall backwards into the arms of a member of the prayer team and are sometimes "out" for as long as ten minutes. "In some ways," notes Rev. Wagers, "this resembles the 'faith healing' in different churches. I think this element of our ministry is an interesting juxtaposition with the social justice/prophetic message that CHAM delivers. I have referred to this spectrum of ministering as embracing the 'full Gospel.'"

MOMENT OF MISSION

This is a time when a member of the community asks briefly for any tithes or offerings. During this time, members are also invited to "take from the plate" a dollar or two if they need. After the plates are brought forward, the leader says a brief blessing over the offering.

UNITY CIRCLE

Rev. Wagers asks everyone in the congregation to move to the periphery of the Sanctuary and join hands in a circle. After all the hands are joined, Rev. Wagers tells everyone to raise their hands while he leads them in a concluding prayer, for example:

Loving God thank you for this gathering of your people. Lead us through the days ahead. Keep us thirsting for your living waters, keep us hungry for justice and truth, keep us ever seeking your will in our lives, keep us abiding in your everlasting love and healing, keep us as one in your Spirit, hallelujah, hallelujah, in Jesus' name, hallelujah.

CREATING A JUST HEALTH CARE SYSTEM[30]
(Ecumenical)

CALL TO WORSHIP   Mic. 6:8

HYMN   PrH   #434   "Today We All Are Called to Be Disciples"

LITANY

> **Leader:** Jesus said: "I have come that you might have life. Life in all its fullness." (John 10:10)
>
> **Group 1:** Ten million children in America are uninsured and denied health care.
>
> **Group 2:** Every day 95 babies die before their first birthdays. In the year 2001, in the State of New Jersey, 741 babies did not live to see their first birthday.
>
> **All:** **A total of over forty-one million people in our country have no health insurance and are denied all health services. People who do not receive the health care they need cannot live life in all its fullness.**
>
> **Leader:** "For the body does not consist of one member but of many. . . . If one member suffers, all suffer together; If one member is honored, all rejoice together." (1 Cor. 12:14, 26)
>
> **Group 1:** While nearly one half of the people with AIDS rely on Medicaid to pay their medical costs, changes in the Medicaid program will no longer guarantee coverage for AIDS patients.
>
> **Group 2:** In 2001, poor, elderly persons spent nearly three-fourths (71.8%) of their income for health care or had to forgo needed care; excluding nursing home costs.

All: We cannot rejoice until everyone in our country is treated equally, until health care is a right for all and not a financial burden for the many.

LIGHTING OF THE CANDLE

HYMN   PrH   #432   "Song of Hope"

MEDITATION

"A TRIBUTE TO TONIE"[31]

O death where is thy sting?
O grave where is thy victory?
The sting of death is sin;
And the strength of sin is the law
But Thanks be to God
Which giveth us the victory through our Lord Jesus Christ.
                                                    (1 Cor. 15:55–57)

Today, we come to honor my sister Tonie as we pray for the health care system of this land. We honor Tonie's steadfast determination in her battle against AIDS from 1988 to 1994. She indeed was truly a profile in courage. Praise be to God she was a fighter. For she had to fight to get medicine, fight to get hospital care, fight to be treated decently like a woman of God and not the outcast from society. She was like the woman with the issue of blood, seeking to touch the hem of the garment of healing. But the system had no virtue to come out of it. Even as it was time for her transition from this life to glory. We had to fight for her time of comfort but the hospital would not give her relief from agony and the pain. No, the hospital system did not do that . . . but alas again God saw fit to embrace my sister Tonie and translate her from the burdens, agonies, and discrimination of illness in this life to an eternal walk with Christ by the green pastures and still waters of heaven. And so on this day, we honor my sister Tonie. We celebrate the joy of her life, we repent on behalf of an insensitive health care system, and we pray for the deliverance of health care where all will be treated as God's children regardless of wealth, poverty, race, gender, and sexual orientation.

In the name of Jesus of Nazareth we pray. Amen.

CLOSING HYMN   #360   LW   "O Christ, the Healer, We Have Come"

BENEDICTION

Prejudice/Racism

"You are all one in union with Jesus Christ."
(Gal. 3:28)

MARTIN L. KING JR. SUNDAY[32]
(Afrocentric Methodist)

THE SECOND SUNDAY AFTER EPIPHANY

Isa. 49:1–7; Ps. 40:1–11; 1 Cor. 1:1–9; John 1:29–42

CALL TO WORSHIP

> **Leader:** The God of dreamers and visionaries summons us!
>
> **People: I have a dream![33]**
>
> **Leader:** The God who works in us the will and the ability to live, work, and die for justice, is in our midst.
>
> **People: I have a dream!**
>
> **Leader:** The God who speaks to us in dreams and reveals mystery to us in visions demands our attention!
>
> **People: I have a dream!**
>
> **Leader:** Before you were born, while yet in your mother's womb, God formed you and called you by name.
>
> **People: I am a dream! Thanks be to God!**

CALL TO CONFESSION

Too often we have relegated dreams to be only the source of the numbers runner or the lotto! But God speaks in the complexity of our dreaming. Let us confess our failure to respond.

CONFESSION

God of dreams and dreamers, forgive us for being so casual with your revelation knowledge. Instead of heeding your messages for our lives, we have envisioned only big cars, huge houses, and vacation escapes abroad! Trying so hard to escape our poverty, we have missed your signs and symbols of authentic life. Forgive us our sin. Help us to dream of better and different tomorrows. Help us to work diligently for justice. And help us to act justly in all of our dealings. In the name of the Vision of Hope, we pray.

WORDS OF ASSURANCE

Sisters and brothers, you know what is right and what God requires. It is that we do justice, love kindness, and walk dependent upon God. This is made possible by the Holy Spirit, who lives and reigns in you. Glory to God!

RESPONSIVE READING   Ps. 40

Leader: We have waited, sometimes not so patiently, for the Lord. Many times it has seemed as if God did not know our names, nor hear our petitions!

People: Yet, from slave ships, slavery, Jim Crow, and "unseen" lynchings we have been delivered. These were horrible and desolate pits and God was our Rock of Security.

Leader: The '60s, with civil rights, voting rights, and the death of "formal" segregation, gave us a brand new song. "We shall overcome!"[34] became our praise unto God!

People: Many around the world saw our deliverance and put their trust in our God. The people at the wall of Berlin, the students in Tiananmen Square, the workers of Poland, and our siblings in South Africa made the God of justice theirs!

Leader: Those who dare wait on divine time, who do not give over to their victim status, and who refuse to believe in the false gods of greed and oppression will be blessed!

People: Despite being treated unjustly, denied basic human rights or the agreed-upon restitution, "forty acres and a mule," God has multiplied us and brought us this far by faith.

Leader: Our God is wondrous; there is none like our Sovereign. The thoughts of God toward us are more in number than grains of sand.

People: The sacrifice of our own blood is not always required, but a willingness to follow after God with our whole heart is absolutely necessary.

Leader: Many brave sisters and brothers have sacrificed their lives on our behalf. Today, we recall the life and ministry of Dr. Martin Luther King Jr., who said to God, "Here I am! I delight to do your will. Oh, God, your law is within my heart!"

People: **When mother Rosa Parks sat down, the God in Dr. Martin Luther King Jr., stood up to tell the glad news of deliverance in the great congregation.**

Leader: The saving help of our God is continually spoken of and the steadfast love of the Lord is our salvation.

People: **God, do not withhold your mercy from us. Raise us up to do our part in the fight for justice. Let your love and faithfulness call us to greater service forever!**

OFFERTORY INVITATION

God is faithful! Through the gift of God we have been called into this fellowship with Jesus Christ. Let us share our gifts in order to spread this good news!

OFFERTORY PRAISE

Jesus called us to "Come and see." Use these, our gifts, in order that we may participate in the "go and tell" of helping others find the Christ. **Amen.**

BENEDICTION

Leader: Go! In the spirit of Dr. Martin Luther King Jr., who had a dream and lived for it.

People: **Thank God for dreams and dreamers.**

Leader: Go! In the spirit of mother Rosa Parks, who had a vision of equality and justice and lived for it.

People: **Thank the Proclaimer of Justice for visions and visionaries.**

Leader: Thank God for the spirit of justice, alive and spreading throughout the world.

People: **Thank the Redeemer of the oppressed for another opportunity to have a dream, see a vision, and be a justice seeker!**

Leader: Go! In the power of the Achievable God! Amen and amen!

JUNETEENTH OBSERVANCE[35]
(Afrocentric Methodist)

EMANCIPATION SUNDAY BETWEEN JUNE 19 AND JUNE 25

Gen. 21:8–21; Ps. 86:1–10, 16–17; Rom. 6:1b–11; Matt. 10:24–39

CALL TO WORSHIP

Leader: Welcome to Celebration Station! We have gathered to shout for the joy of freedom.

People: How did you feel when you come out the wilderness?[36]

Leader: Hagar, the Egyptian woman, was forced into the desert with her son, but there God promised them freedom!

People: How did you feel when you come out the wilderness?

Leader: For over two hundred years, we were forced to survive in the "wilderness" of slavery. But on June 19, 1865, the southern slaves found out they were free and celebrated the first Juneteenth.

People: How did you feel when you come out the wilderness?

Leader: Jesus, our Christ, spent his time in the wilderness and walked out with our freedom in his mind.

People: We have come to celebrate the wilderness. For we are leaning on the Lord!

CALL TO CONFESSION

Like Hagar, it is often that we are forced into unfriendly situations through no fault of our own. In the wilderness of our lives, we get afraid and get down on God. Let us take this opportunity to confess our sin, which keeps us stuck in the wilderness instead of allowing us to pass through to new horizons.

CONFESSION

God of the wilderness, forgive us our sin. We have become accustomed to being in the wilderness, fighting for our survival and feeling that we have to make it on our own. Help us to hear your voice and to know that your presence is near to guide us through every desert experience. In your name, we pray. **Amen.**

WORDS OF ASSURANCE

The angel of God called to Hagar when she felt most bereft and alone. She was told not to be afraid, for God had heard her cry. Then she received the same promise of Abraham, that her son would become a great nation! Our times in the wilderness always reap tremendous benefits when we wait and hear God. This is good news! **Amen.**

RESPONSIVE READING   Ps. 86:1–10, 16–17

> **Leader:** God heard the cries arise from the deltas of this land.
>
> **People: The stooped backs and heavy sacks, dragging the cotton and tobacco fields, did not prevent the whisper of prayers, which reached the ears of God.**
>
> **Leader:** Come by here, good Lord, come by here![37]
>
> **People: Way down here, all by myself, and I can't hear nobody pray!**
>
> **Leader:** But I trust in God, wherever I may be!
>
> **People: God, you is a mighty good God and you don't ever change![38]**
>
> **Leader:** Emancipation came!
>
> **People: But another crop had to be made and the news of freedom was slow in working its way south to the ears of those who never gave up hope and refused to give up praying.**
>
> **Leader:** Emancipation came!
>
> **People: The sweet taste of freedom arrived late, but arrived, nevertheless. God heard our cries.**
>
> **Leader:** God is a great God who does great and mighty things for us, whereof we are glad!
>
> **People: God seldom comes when we want, but whenever God shows up, it's right on time!**
>
> **Leader:** Some celebrate independence from England. We celebrate the day that God delivered us from the wilderness of slavery in this land! Juneteenth is a sign of God's favor towards us and a symbol of comfort to our souls.
>
> **People: The end of slavery is a gradual process and the journey out of the wilderness continues with God's help.**

OFFERTORY INVITATION

We have been raised from death to life! By the unmerited favor of new life in Christ, we have been freed from sin. Let us give in order that others might know this privilege and joy.

OFFERTORY PRAISE

Giver of Life, you died to sin, in order that we might live again. Accept our offerings of love, given so that others might come to know you and live with you throughout eternity.

Leader: A disciple is not above the teacher! And Jesus spent time wrestling in the wilderness.

People: **We leave, not afraid of the wilderness, but sustained by the voice of God.**

Leader: You have been saved and delivered from many desert places. Remember Juneteenth!

People: **God is working, even when we have not received the news! We will be faithful in difficult times.**

Leader: Do not even fear those who can kill the physical body. Take up your cross and follow the Christ.

People: **Those who find their life will lose it, and those who lose their life for the sake of Christ will find it.**

Leader: May the promises of God, the certainty of Christ, and the refreshing of the Holy Spirit sustain us until we meet again. Amen.

IT IS NOT EASY: SERVICE OF PROPHETIC WITNESS[39]
(Uniting Church in Australia)

For this service you will need

- *A many-colored cloth*
- *A long purple cloth*
- *A cross*

CALL TO WORSHIP

We are the people of dignity,
our many-colored lives stretched out before us:
with a God who sets us free.

(A many-colored cloth is placed on the table.)

We are the people with awesome choices:
with a God who walks before us on the way.

(A long purple cloth is placed across the colored cloth.)

We are the people called to live in fullness of life:
with a God who loves us to the death.

(A cross is placed at the head of the purple cloth.)

Let us worship God.

PRAYER OF INVOCATION

Be with us in every moment of this service, O God, who knows all that faces us.
Be with us in our praying, our singing and as we speak and listen to your word for us.
Be with us, God, who is like a mother hen who gathers us under her warm wings.
Be with us in Spirit and in truth.
Amen.

SONG   #465   PrH   "Here, O Lord, Your Servants Gather"

CONFESSION

How do we know what you want us to do, O God?
Sometimes there are more questions than answers
and we cannot decide what is due to you and how that is to be delivered to you.
We confess that sometimes it is easier to do what others ask of us.
In your mercy:
Forgive us, O God.

If we have listened to the loudest voices asking for our support,
or the ones which suit us best and ask least of us,
in your mercy:
Forgive us, O God.

(Silent reflection)

If we have given more loyalty to earthly rulers
than to your still small voice within us
and others have suffered because of this,
in your mercy:
Forgive us, O God.

When we crush the prophetic among us
because we do not want to hear the costly truth
and your call to give our due to you,
in your mercy:
Forgive us, O God.

For we ask this in Christ's name,
Amen.

ASSURANCE

Receive in faith the forgiveness of Jesus Christ, who was tempted
like us to bow down to the authority of the powers of ego, of

applause and of seductive evil forces.
We are forgiven!
Thanks be to God.

READINGS   Exod. 33:12–23; 1 Thess. 1:1–10; Matt. 22:15–22

SERMON

PRAYER OF INTERCESSION

O God, who has given us the dignity of free choice,
we often long for your wisdom
in discerning where the authority of Caesar and that of God begins and ends.
Life is sometimes very complicated
and we feel powerless to make a difference
when we are confronted by the power of Caesar.
Sometimes we think that the powers and principalities of our day
really do separate us from your love in Christ Jesus.

(Silent prayer)

We pray that your mind will become clearer to us,
that we will not shrink from the hard decisions
and that we will encourage each other more in doing that.

(Silent prayer)

There are many longings in our hearts as we remember the task before us.

(The people share their longings.)

Come to us, Spirit of wisdom,
be present in our midst, Spirit of truth,
rise again, life of Christ before us,
with your wounded hands outstretched
and linked with the suffering people of the world,
that we may be strengthened
to challenge all that stands between us and your will for the world.
This we pray,
for Christ's sake
Amen.

SONG   #337   PrH   "Isaiah the Prophet Has Written of Old"

COMMISSIONING AND BLESSING

Be bold in the claiming of the gospel for the whole creation.
Be brave in the lifting up of the life of God in every place.
Be firm in carrying the holy name of Jesus Christ into the

palaces of worldly power.
Be gentle in the understanding of ourselves and one another.
And may the songs of the Creator sound with love in all the earth,
the tenderness of Christ Jesus cover the wounds of the people
and the truth in the Holy Spirit rise free in every age.
Amen.

PEOPLE OF COLOR AND THE CRIMINAL JUSTICE SYSTEM[40]
(Presbyterian)

CALL TO WORSHIP

Is being alive to see this new day good and special in some way?
It is good and special to be alive, to see another day that our God has created.
But pain, suffering, oppression, sin, and chaos still exist today, as they did yesterday.
Yes, that is true, but with this day God has provided us a fresh new opportunity to work toward bringing health, wellness, and wholeness to a world full of pain, suffering, oppression, sin, and chaos.
With this awareness, let us worship God.

OPENING LITANY

The wind of the Spirit challenges us to change.
Give us courage to respond, O God.
The fire of the Spirit calls us to a passion for the kingdom.
Warm us and give us your energy, O God.
The breath of the Spirit offers us new life.
May we receive and live out the gospel in the world.
In a world where there is need and oppression, violence and alienation,
May we bring life and love, O God.
In a world where there is racism, hatred, and division,
May we bring unity and community, O God.
In a world where there is meaninglessness and emptiness,
May we bring purpose and hope, O God.
Lead us forth, Spirit of God, in joy and in faith, in truth and in freedom.
In ways known and unknown, may we follow. Amen.

CONFESSION

O God, we confess to you that we have sinned against you in many ways: not only by outward things, but by secret thoughts and desires which we cannot fully understand, but which are known to you. We know that people have felt our scorn and indifference. We know that we have ignored ghettos where people are politically and economically imprisoned. We know that our institutions have not only ignored such situations but have helped create them.

But knowing what we have done does not tell us why, and does not keep us from continuing. We look to you for strength, for understanding, for moral courage. As we do, we repent and are deeply sorry for the offenses we have committed. We ask that you will have mercy on us. In the name of Christ. **Amen.**

PRAYER *Heal Us*

> Grandfather,
> Look at our brokenness.
>
> We know that in all creation
> Only the human family
> Has strayed from the Sacred Way.
>
> We know that we are the ones
> Who are divided
> And we are the ones
> Who must come back together
> To walk in the Sacred Way.
>
> Grandfather,
> Sacred One,
> Teach us love, compassion, and honor
> That we may heal the earth
> And heal each other.[41]

LITANY OF CONFESSION

O God, you made the world and everything in it. You created the
human race of one stock and gave us the earth as the arena of our faithfulness.
Break down the walls that separate us, and make us one people.

O God, we come before you in sadness, for we have failed:
failed to be the imprint of your image, failed to be your stewards of life and time and nature, failed to reflect your love and mercy, failed to be servants of reconciliation. Break down the walls that separate us, and make us one people.

O God, you mean us to be a single people:
ruled by peace, feasting in freedom, freed from injustice, truly human women and men, responsible and responsive in the life we lead, the love we share, and the relationships we create. Break down the walls that separate us, and make us one people.

O God, renew within us the image of your Son. Give us ever-new insights into the truth and awareness of your will for all your sons and daughters. Give us courage to do what is right and persistence in challenging unjust structures until they crumble into dust. Give us, we pray, grace and creativity to exercise a common ministry of reconciliation.
Break down the walls that separate us, and make us one people.

O God, spread among us the fiery tongues of your Spirit, that we may each burn with compassion for all who hunger for freedom and humanness, that we may be doers of the Word and so speak with power about the wonderful deeds which you have done.

O God, in your mercy forgive us all that is past. Direct us, we pray, in ways we do not yet discern and equip us for the service of reconciliation and liberation in your world. Amen.

CONFESSION

Let us confess the secret sins in the hidden spaces of our lives, which hold us in fear and anguish, keeping us from God and from each other.

Let us confess the words of judgment we have withheld in our societies, the compromises we have made which allow evil to multiply, producing harvests of destruction and death.

Let us confess the complacency with which we live in disunity, the ease with which we keep our prejudices, refusing to be the one people of God for whom Jesus prayed.

God from whom nothing is hidden and who knows the motives of our hearts, forgives us our sins and declares to us the joyful truth that we are a liberated people.[42]

CONFESSION

God of all people and nations, hear our confession and forgive our sin. We make enemies of strangers when we distrust them. Fear and suspicion keep your people apart. Jesus came to reconcile our differences, yet your people do not dine at one common table. Heal our divisions and overcome our hostility. Unite us in the bond of your encompassing love. **Amen.**[43]

AFFIRMATION AND COMMITMENT

We, being many, are one in Christ Jesus.
We celebrate our diversity, given by God.

When it leads to disagreement, we will listen and we will speak with caring.
We celebrate our individuality, given by God.

Where we are strong, we will participate fully. Where we are weak, we will rejoice in the strength of our sisters and brothers.
We celebrate our responsibility, given by God.

When it leads to work, we will do it in cooperation with others.
We celebrate the wholeness of our community, given by God.

Where it is fractured, we will work for reconciliation.
We celebrate the wholeness of the earth, given by God.

Where its God-given beauty and harmony are threatened, we will be partners in restoration.
We celebrate the wholeness of persons, given by God.

Where persons are broken or their uniqueness denied, we will be agents of healing.
We, being many, are one in Christ Jesus. Therefore, we trust—and listen. We grow—and listen. We share—and listen. We love—and listen. We learn—and listen. We serve—and listen. We celebrate—and listen. We will dream, sing, pray, plan, hope—together! God be with us. Amen.

LITANY OF THANKSGIVING

We thank you, God, for who we are.
Some of us look like the people who lived here long ago, so close to this land that their arrival is not recorded.

We thank you, God, for who we are.
Some of us look like the Spanish, who came in big ships. They took the land from the Indians and thought it was theirs.

We thank you, God, for who we are.
Some of us look like the English, who also came in big ships. They took the land from the Indians and the Spanish and thought it was theirs.

We thank you, God, for who we are.
Some of us look like the Africans, who also came in big ships. They did not choose to come, and they had no land and no freedom.

We thank you, God, for who we are.
Some of us look like the Asians, who came in big ships across the other ocean. They came looking for work and freedom, and many found discrimination and injustice.

We thank you, God, for who we are.
All of us are different. No two of us look exactly alike. But we are all in the image of God, who came to earth that we might be one. We thank you, God, for who we are, and we pray that you show us what we are to be. Amen.[44]

LITANY

By God's great mercy:
We have been born anew to a living hope through the resurrection of Jesus Christ from the dead.

By God's mercy, you have been born:
To an inheritance that is imperishable, undefiled, and unfading, and is kept in heaven for us.

Once you were no people:
But now we are God's people.

Once you had not received mercy:
But now we have received mercy.

You are a chosen race, a royal priesthood, a holy nation, God's own people:
That we may declare the wonderful deeds of God who called us out of darkness into God's marvelous light.

For it is God's will that by doing right you should put to silence foolish ones.
Live as free men and women, yet without using our freedom as a pretext for evil, but live as servants of God.

Tend the flock of God that is in your charge,
Not by constraint but willingly, not for shameful gain but eagerly, not as domineering over those in our charge, but being examples to the flock.

Be sober, be watchful. Your adversary, the devil, prowls around like a roaring lion seeking someone to devour.
Resist him!

Be firm in your faith:
Knowing that the same experience of suffering is required of our brotherhood and sisterhood throughout the world.

And after you have suffered a little while, the God of all grace, who called you to eternal glory in Christ, will restore, establish, and strengthen you.
To God be the dominion forever and ever. Amen.[45]

PRAYER IN PRISON

Loving God, we are skilled at building walls. We build walls of gold that divide the rich from the poor. We build walls of stone that keep out the unwashed, unwanted. We build prison walls to hide the people we would like to forget. We create walls of fear that keep us isolated and helpless. We make walls of hatred that push people into crowded ghettos where suspicion, rage, and jealousy grow. In our lives we build walls of shame, walls of blame, walls of broken dreams and broken promises.

But you are the Master Builder. Your word is the blueprint for a world without walls, a world where all of us are your children. You tear down the walls that divide the earth's people. You tear down the walls of fear that destroy our dreams and lock us into discouragement. Your hand holds the key to unlock our full potential as creative and life-filled people.

In this place of walls and locks, O God, open my eyes to the greatness of your love, your hope, your promise. **Amen.**[46]

PRAYER

Justice-loving God, the people in the streets are crying, "No justice, no peace." It is the cry of the Old Testament prophets who pointed their fingers at injustice and asked, "How can you say 'peace' when there is no justice?" Still the ancient cry goes unheard, ignored. Our cities are in ruin. Our people are broken. The children are homeless and hungry.

God of justice and mercy, open the eyes and the ears of the decision makers, that they may find the way to a more just society. Walk with the people who are suffering so they may have hope and courage. Fill the mouths of the people that they may call, not for more violence, but for imagination, creativity, compassion, and peace.

We ask this in the name of the prophets and of Jesus who is our Prince of Peace. **Amen.**[47]

LITANY

God, we pray for all the people in the criminal justice system.
For the whole law is summed up in a single commandment, "You shall love your neighbor as yourself." (Matt. 22:39)

Forgive our self-righteousness when we judge others and ignore our own sins.
Do not speak evil against one another. . . . There is one lawgiver and judge who is able to save and to destroy. So who, then, are you to judge your neighbor? (Jas. 4:11–12)

We pray for all who are in prisons and jails.
I was in prison and you visited me. (Matt. 25:36)

We pray for all victims, for families, for all who are hurt by crimes.
If one member suffers, all suffer together with it. If one member is honored, all rejoice together with it. (1 Cor. 12:26)

We confess that we are a part of a system and a society that reflects sexism, racism, poverty, injustice.
Woe to you, scribes and Pharisees, hypocrites! For you . . . have neglected the weightier matters of the law: justice and mercy and faith. (Matt. 23:23)

Help us to look at our priorities as we build more prisons and jails instead of rebuilding lives and communities.
The Lord . . . executes justice for the oppressed. . . . The Lord sets the prisoners free. (Ps. 146:5, 7)

O Lord, we pray for strength in our commitment and courage in our service.
And what does the Lord require of you but to do justice, and to love kindness, and to walk humbly with your God? (Mic. 6:8)[48]

Closing Prayer

Mighty God, Loving Creator, we thank you again for this day. Thank you again for the Circle of Prayer in which we are presently blessed to find ourselves. Thank you for what we receive from and give to each other as we gather in the name of Jesus.

Grant that we would no longer look at each other and fail to see one of your children. Grant that we might no longer compete for your love, but be about the business of choosing and living as Christ commands.

For the world, *your* world—for the church, *your* church—for each other, *your* children—may we offer our gratitude and thanks. **Amen.**[49]

Resources for Worship

Scripture

Two of the lectionary passages are especially appropriate: Deut. 30:15–20. Other passages emphasize the unity of the body, the connectedness of the community: 1 Cor. 12:26; 1 John 4:21; Gal. 3:28. The prophet Isaiah said many things that we must hear today in a special way in this context: Isa. 58:1–12; Isa. 65:17–25. Also John 4:5–29; 1 Pet. 2:9; Rom. 8:38–39; Eph. 2:13–14, 10–20; and Ps. 146, Isa. 61 and Luke 4:16–21, Amos 5:24, and Mic. 6:6–8.

Hymns #413 "All Who Love and Serve Your City"
        #280 "Amazing Grace, How Sweet the Sound"

#354 "Guide My Feet (While I Run This Race)"
#358 "Help Us Accept Each Other"
#465 "Here, O Lord, Your Servants Gather"
#440 "In Christ There Is No East or West"
#338 "Kum ba Yah"
#563 "Lift Every Voice and Sing"
#332 "Live into Hope (of Captives Freed)"
#372 "Lord, I Want to Be a Christian"
#379 "My Hope Is Built on Nothing Less"
#386 "O for a World (Where Everyone Respects Each Other's Ways)"
#273 "O God the Creator (We're Brothers and Sisters in God's Love)"
#453 "O Holy City, Seen of John"
#404 "Precious Lord, Take My Hand"
#394 "There Is a Balm in Gilead"
#434 "Today We All Are Called to Be Disciples"
#296 "Walk On, O People of God"
#403 "What a Friend We Have in Jesus"
#334 "When Israel Was in Egypt's Land (Go Down Moses)"
#408 "Where Cross the Crowded Ways of Life"

(*References are to* The Presbyterian Hymnal.)

PRAYERS

Several of the prayers . . . are meant to be read responsively. The worship leader's portion is printed in plain text; *responses are given in* **bold**.

COMMON GROUND: AN ACT OF WITNESS AGAINST RACISM[50] (Interfaith)

This act of witness should take place with people seated in a circle or semicircle so that they can face each other with a space in the midst of them. It may be appropriate to hold it in a place that represents neutral ground for people of differing backgrounds and faiths, e.g., a school, community center, etc.

Voice 1: Listen to the words of a British Asian woman:

"We are told that human rights law is about uniting families. But Asian people see regularly that Britain's immigration laws are separating families. After three years of waiting, I am completely sickened and worn out by the delay and the worry. As British citizens, we have no right to family life. Yet women in Europe may enter Britain with husbands, children and her entire family without application, without interviews. There will be no racial justice for us until the law is changed. The politicians have failed us. People of faith must give a lead."[51]

Leader: A welcome to you all.
Some of us have strong faith. In some of us, faith falters.
But we are all here as children of God,
as inhabitants of one earth.
We bring to this place our fears and anxieties,
our visions and dreams for the future.
We bring our politics and our prayers,
our strengths and our weaknesses,
our issues and our concerns,
and we lay them out on the ground,
hoping that the middle ground may become,
not wasteground,
not battleground,
but common ground.

(People may, at this point, bring out symbols or placards representing some of their concerns, e.g., a passport, no entry signs, and lay them in the space or on a table in the middle.)

HYMN   #602   W&R   "Who Is My Mother, Who Is My Brother"

Voice 2:   Listen to these words from the World Council of Churches:
"Every human being, created in the image of God, is a person for whom Christ has died. Racism, which is the use of a person's racial origins to determine the person's value, is an assault on Christ's value and a rejection of his sacrifice."[52]

Voice 3:   Listen to these words from Matt. 23:23:

(Prayers for forgiveness)

Leader: Helder Camara said that
it is very difficult to create awareness
in the privileged.

Let us pray:

God, you call us to see and hear and understand,
to open our eyes and ears and hearts,
to be aware,
forgive us for our false pride and complacency
for our unthinking consumerism,

All: Lord have mercy upon us.

Leader: Forgive us for our insularity
For our reluctance to accept new ways,

All: Lord have mercy upon us.

Leader: Forgive us for our complaining,
for growing bitter and sorry for ourselves,
for becoming hardened and indifferent
to the pain of others,

All: Lord have mercy upon us.

Voice 1: "Why do you treat Asian people like this? Don't you understand that Jesus was an Asian? Would you do this to Jesus?"

(A Muslim woman, angry at the treatment of Asian families under UK immigration laws.)

(Silence)

Leader: God, make us aware, make us repentant,
we turn to you,
heal us of our privileged blindness,
and make us whole.

All: Amen.

SHARING STORIES
(People now have the opportunity to share their stories, in whatever form they wish to tell them, and to be heard without interruption or dismissal.)

SHARING MEMORIES
(People are now invited to share in a "collective memory-making" in which a particular theme or issue, e.g., law, family, travel, are either written on a large sheet of paper or written on small pieces and collected in a basket. By 'remembering' different aspects of the same thing, a collective memory is created which is presented for prayer, and may be printed and used later.)

(During this time there may be instrumental music or silence.)

READINGS   Isa. 58:6–12
(Passages from the Koran and the Talmud may be used, as well as the Scriptures of other faiths.)

PRAYERS OF CONCERN
(During the prayers of concern, a candle may be lit after each petition and placed in the center space, beside the symbols or placards of concern and the collective memory.)

Leader: Come God,
Listen to the calling of those with nowhere to turn
at the point where support fails,
the majority turns away,
and we/they are alone.

All: **We cannot remain silent**
because we fear the authorities
and do not want to rock the boat.[53]

Leader: We remember those who suffer
as a result of family break-up
or unjust immigration or nationality laws.

All: **We cannot remain silent**
because we fear the authorities
and do not want to rock the boat.

Leader: We remember those who suffer harassment or abuse
in the street or school or workplace
as a result of their religion or skin color

All: **We cannot remain silent**
because we fear the authorities
and do not want to rock the boat.

Leader: God of justice, give us voice, take away our fear, shake up our prejudices
and move us to a different place, to stand on common ground with those
who struggle for justice.

All: **Amen.**

COMMON GROUND STATEMENT
(People may be invited before the reading of this statement on racism to leave their places and stand in the center space as a sign of solidarity with its intention.)

Leader: Racism is a sin against God
and against fellow human beings.
It is contrary to the justice
and the love of God.
It destroys the human dignity
of both the racist and the victim.
When practiced, it denies any faith
or conviction we profess to hold.
We condemn racism in all its forms.

READING

All: (Luke 4:18–19)

SONG   #601   W&R   "Dear Christ, Uplifted from the Earth"

CLOSING PRAYER

Leader: God, lead us that we may stand firm in faith for justice.

All: **Teach us love. Teach us compassion.**
Above all, out of love and compassion,
teach us to act.
Amen.

Criminal Justice

"What must I do, sirs, to be saved?"
(Acts 16:30)

GENERAL PRAYERS FOR PRISONERS
(Roman Catholic)

APOSTLE'S PRAYER FOR PRISONERS[54]

Our Lord,

You consider as done to You, what we do to the imprisoned and the convicted.
In each of them, Your image is present, though sometimes disfigured and sad. . . .

The universal "fraternity," prevents us from excluding anyone from your love,
Believing in the recovery and social reintegration, of our unhappy brothers and sisters who fell
into temptation with attitudes they today lament and loathe. . . .

Our sense of community, responsibility for the Church in its entirety
And faith in a new life and a new humanity, lead us to this commitment
Towards our convicted brothers and sisters.

By sheltering, protecting and assisting them,
We express our faith in the value of fraternity, in the equality of human beings,
In their recovery and in their return to social coexistence,
Wished and always possible for every human being.

Give us, Lord,
An open and generous heart, to serve this cause which is also Yours.
Transform our will, leading it to good.
Enlighten our minds with your truth.
Make our feelings resemble and follow Your feelings and teachings.
May our FREEDOM be dedicated to Your service and the service
Of our brothers and sisters!

Lord,
After this pilgrimage on Earth

OPEN FOR US THE GATES OF ETERNAL HAPPINESS!
Amen!

RESTOREES' PRAYER[55]

Jesus,
You came to this world to free all sinners and the condemned,
You brought the light of truth for the victims of the shadows and mistakes,
You brought forgiveness and life for the victims of sin and death,
You brought charity, gentleness and peace for the victims of hatred, violence, war and
    remorse. . . .
You, our Lord, are leading us to the true path of goodness, justice, happiness. . . .
You show us the way, and walk with us along these new paths of honesty, respect and human
    and Christian ethics. . . .

Lord,
We know and understand that you condemn the acts of those that stubbornly continue to follow the paths of crime, vice, indifference and death. . . .

Lord,
We trust you, and we have the certainty that you will not abandon your sons and daughters
who fell into temptation, and have been condemned to suffering in prison for a seemingly endless period of time. . . .

You came,
"To find and restore the lost," to give everyone the possibility of a new life, through the gift
of Your own life, as holocaust for the forgiveness of the world. . . .

Thank You, Lord,
Because You timely came to me, through my brothers and sisters who brought me back from
damnation, giving new sense and content to my disorderly life.

Give us, Lord,
A renewed heart, a child's heart, open, simple, sincere, welcoming and fraternal.
Transform our will so that only good will attract it.
Enlighten our intelligence for us to contemplate everything in Your light. . . .
Penetrate our feelings for them to resemble Yours. . . .

Lord,
After this pilgrimage on Earth,
OPEN FOR US THE GATES OF ETERNAL HAPPINESS!
Amen!

SERVICE FOR PRISONERS[56]
(Methodist)

DO THINGS PLEASING TO GOD

BIBLE VERSE   1 John 3:22

PRAYER

O God, I want to be pleasing to you and to do your will in my life. I don't know how to do this. So far my life has not been pleasing to you because I have lived it my way rather than your way.

Forgive me, Lord, when I do things that are against your will. I repent of these actions anew, and give myself to doing your will. In Jesus' name. Amen.

THOUGHT FOR THE DAY

One-Eye, a new inmate with a glass eye, stood up at prayer meeting. We had just finished singing a song. One-Eye said, "I'll sing one." "Fine," I responded. "Come on." He came up front, cocked his head to one side, and sang a beautiful song. He had written the song himself. It was a witness to the Lord. He had pleased God by giving witness to God in the way that he could.

When we do things pleasing to God and keep God's commandments, we are doing *God's word—not just hearing it.*

A PERSON OF GOD DOES GOOD

BIBLE VERSE   3 John 11

PRAYER

God, we thank you for the example of faith that you gave us in Jesus Christ. He showed us what it is like to have faith. God, you taught us how to live our faith by becoming one of us and doing it yourself!

Lord, in the name of Jesus I pray that you will teach me how to live out my faith day by day! Grant, Lord, that I may live the word every day, right here where I am! I pray in Jesus' name. Amen.

THOUGHT FOR THE DAY

Practice the love of God! An older prisoner didn't have a towel. He asked me if I could get him one. At first I was irritated to be bothered. Then I asked myself, What would Jesus do? *I gave him my only towel. He smiled and said, "Thank you." The next morning someone else gave me a towel.*

To Hope

BIBLE VERSE   Zech. 9:12

PRAYER

Time is crawling, God. It seems never to pass. I turn to you for my hope and my strength. They come from nowhere else, Lord, but you. You are the source of all hope. The hope you give me for tomorrow gives me strength to live and to go a day at a time in here. Thank you, Lord. In the name of Jesus. **Amen.**

THOUGHT FOR THE DAY

Prison life drains your strength. You get little sleep and little nutrition from the food. Your emotions and your body are drained. In prison, you need the strength God can give you. Hope in the Lord gives you strength.

Sammy loves the Lord. One day he got a letter telling him he was being charged with another offense in another state. This charge could have added eight years to his sentence. We prayed together and God brought him new hope. Since that time, those new charges were dropped. Place your hope in the Lord. God will give you strength!

To Practice Faith

BIBLE VERSE   Rev. 2:10

PRAYER

O God, I'll be honest with you. I'm afraid. I'm scared to death. I'm afraid I will get sick in this awful place. I'm even afraid that I will die here.

But God, in the name of Jesus, I refuse to let this place destroy me. I cast out fear and bring in faith. I am no longer afraid of what might happen to me. I trust in you, Lord. I have faith in you, my God. In the name of Jesus, my Savior. **Amen.**

THOUGHT FOR THE DAY

A prison is hell on earth. It is a dwelling place for evil. You must *practice faith in prison. You* must *be a man or woman of God in the midst of this earthly hell. How? Listen to the word of God. "Be faithful to me, even if it means death, and I will give you life as your prize of victory."*

In prison, practice and keep your faith for victory in Christ.

CELEBRATING, SENDING OUT, AND BLESSING[57]
(Uniting Church in Australia)

FOR A DEPARTING COLLEAGUE OR GROUP MEMBER WHO HAS WORKED FOR JUSTICE

For this service you will need:

- *A wine glass chosen as a gift for the person leaving, filled with good wine or the person's favorite drink*

OPENING SENTENCES

We are here to give thanks for faithfulness,
this faithfulness and all faithfulness:
For God has given us gifts of faithfulness.

We are here to celebrate the gift of ministry,
this ministry and all ministry:
For God has given us gifts for ministry.

We are here to ask a blessing on the future,
this future and for all that lies before us:
For God has given us the gift of hope,
a hope that will carry us into a new day.
Thanks be to God!

DOXOLOGY

CONFESSION

Gracious God,
God who walked our way in Jesus,
we have not always been able to receive
all that was offered in this ministry.

(Person leaving:)

And I have not always been able to give
all that you hoped from me.

(Leader:)

For we are your humble human people,
and we are no longer searching for the Messiah among us.

Even as we toil, the victory has already been won for us
and grace, justice and peace is abroad in all the earth
For Christ has died,
Christ is risen
and Christ will come again!

READING   Isa. 25:1–10

GIVING THANKS

What are the qualities which we value in the life of *(name)*?

(The people offer words which describe these qualities.)

O God, for all these things which we find in *(name)*
our friend and colleague, we give you thanks.
In this service to you and the church
we have experienced your hand upon us,
wiping away the tears of life,
lifting the shroud from the people in love and justice.

We have seen in *(name)* one who gives all that she/he has
in the preparing of your feast for the little and the least.
We are joined today by the unseen presence of those
with whom she/he has stood in many places.
For this we give thanks.
We celebrate his/her life as she/he has followed the Christ.

THE SENDING OUT AND BLESSING

Let us gather around *(name)*
and send him/her forth into God's new day.

(The people gather around the person.)
What are the gifts we ask of God for this new day?

(The people name the gifts.)

(Name), we send you out in the power of the Spirit.
We send you out in love, our love and the love of Christ.
We send you out in faith with a God who is faithful forever.
Go and continue to be part of the transforming of the world.

(A cup of wine is given to the person.)

Carry the wine of life into all the corners of the earth.
But first, stay still for a time our friend, rest in the peace of Christ.
Drink this wine yourself.
This time the wine and the feast are for you.
Amen.

GENERAL BLESSING

Go in peace,
go as though we too are the people for the feast.
And may God's table be spread before us,
Christ Jesus be our host
and the Spirit lead us into the dance of life.
Amen.

(The party follows.)

Tainted Creation

"So God made them all, and was pleased with what he saw." (Gen. 1:25)

CREATOR GOD

*What
makes the
sun to rise?
The power of God.
What makes the seed
to grow? The love of God.
Power of God protect us. Love
of God lead us. Spirit of God strengthen
us. In all
of life
And all creation.*
—David Adam, "Creator God,"
in *Tides and Seasons*[58]

READINGS AND PRAYER FOR THE ENVIRONMENT[59]
(Anglican Church of Canada)

READINGS IN YEAR A

Advent 2: Isa. 11:1–10   (They will not hurt or destroy)
Lent 1: Gen. 2:4b–9, 15–17, 25:3–7   (The Lord God planted a garden in Eden)
Lent 5: Ezek. 37:1–14   (I will place you on your own soil)
Easter Vigil: Gen. 1:1–2   (God saw everything that he had made, and indeed, it was
very good)
Ps. 33   (By the word of the Lord were the heavens made)

Gen. 7:1; 5:11–18; 8:6–18; 9:8–13   (I am establishing my covenant
    with you and your descendants after you, and with every creature)
Ps. 46   (There is a river whose streams make glad the city of God)
Isa. 54:5–14   (In righteousness you shall be established)
Isa. 55:1–11   (. . . everyone who thirsts)
Canticle: Song of Thanksgiving   Isa. 12:2–6
Baruch 3:9–15;32–37, 4:1–4   (The one who prepared the earth for all
    time . . . This is our God)
Ps. 19   (The heavens are telling the glory of God)
Ezek. 36:24–28   (I will sprinkle clean water upon you)
Ps. 42   (As the deer longs for the water-brooks)
Ezek. 37:1–14   (I will place you on your own soil)
Zeph. 3:14–20   (The Lord has taken away the judgments against you)
Ps. 98   (Let the rivers clap their hands and let the hills ring out with joy)
Pentecost: Ps. 104   (O Lord, how manifold are your works)
Proper 1 (Baptism of the Lord): Isa. 42:1–9   (God . . . who created the heavens and
    . . . spread out the earth)
Proper 20: Exod. 16:2–15   (Your fill of bread in the morning)
Proper 30: Ruth 2:1–13   (Let me go to the field and glean among the ears of grain)
Rogation or Harvest: Deut. 8:7–18   (A good land with flowing streams)
        Ps. 65   (You make the dawn and the dusk to sing for joy)
        2 Cor. 9:6–15   (He who supplies seed to the sower and bread
          for food)
        Joel 2:21–27   (Do not fear, O soil; be glad and rejoice)
        Ps. 126   (Restore our fortunes, O God, like the watercourses
          of the Negev)
        Matt. 6:25–33   (Consider the lilies of the field)
        Deut. 26:1–11   (The Lord . . . gave us this land, a land flowing
          with milk and honey)
        Ps. 100   (Be joyful in the Lord, all you lands)

READINGS IN YEAR B

Lent 1: Gen. 9:8–17   (I am establishing my covenant with you and your descendants
    after you, and with every living creature that is with you)
Easter Vigil: (as in Year A)
Pentecost: (as in Year A)
Proper 1 (Baptism of the Lord):   Gen. 1:1–5   (In the beginning when God created
    the heavens and the earth)
Proper 17: 2 Sam. 12:1–14   (The poor man had nothing but one little ewe lamb)
Proper 23: James 1:17–27   (Religion that is pure and undefiled . . . is . . . to care for
    orphans and widows in their distress)
Proper 24: James 2:1–5, 8–10, 14–17   (If a brother or sister is naked . . . and yet you
    do not supply their bodily needs, what is the good of that?)
Proper 31: Deut. 6:1–9   (A land flowing with milk and honey)
Rogation or Harvest: (as in Year A)

PRAYER FOR THE ENVIRONMENT

Creator of the land, the water, and the sky, come and renew the face of the whole earth: **O Lord, hear our prayer.**

Giver of life, we are the sons and daughters of your holy breath; give us new purpose to care in love for the world of your making: **O Lord, hear our prayer.**

Savior of the world, touch our lips in power of your new creation, that we may proclaim your word of life: **O Lord, hear our prayer.**

God of steadfast love, turn our hearts and the hearts of the whole human family to care in thanksgiving and reverence for the world you have given: **O Lord, hear our prayer.**

God of sparrows and wild flowers, teach us to see and preserve the simple beauty of the gifts of your hands: **O Lord, hear our prayer.**

THE JOY OF WATER[60]
(Uniting Church in Australia)

A TRIBUTE TO THE WIDOWS' ASSOCIATION OF HARARE

For this service you will need:

- *Jugs of water*
- *A bowl of salt water*

OPENING SENTENCES

Claim the joy of water for the poor of the earth!
Let it flow and pour and sprinkle for all the people!

Call for the rivers to be shared
And the rain from the heavens

To gather in great ponds of mercy,
That all may know each day the gift of God in water.

(Jugs of water are carried to the table.)

SONG #494 PrH "Out of Deep Unordered Water"

STORY

At the University of Harare for the World Council of Churches Assembly in 1998, the student residence in which some delegates stayed was cleaned by the normally unemployed women of the Widows' Association. Night and day they cleaned the corridors, the rooms and the bathrooms, working long hours for very little pay. They were welcoming women, kindly to the delegates as visitors to their city. Each day the delegates went off to their meals and the WCC meetings and left them to do the cleaning. One morning a delegate returned to get something from her room in the middle of the morning. As she approached the bathroom nearby, she heard unusual noises—ecstatic noises, sounds of happiness, with much laughter and some singing. She looked in the door and there were the cleaning women, clutching tiny fragments of soap, bathing and showering in joy and delight. They were lifting up their arms to feel the water flowing over their bodies, almost dancing under the showers and lying back in the full bath in bliss, encouraging each other in this wondrous moment of access to running water. When they saw her, the sounds suddenly stopped and then they all laughed together, celebrating the moment and her recognition that they had 'seized their day' against the odds.

GRIEVING

We grieve, O God, who gives us water for all life,
that so many of us have only hard-won drops to drink,
while others of us have access to water at every turn
and often waste it with careless abandon.
Forgive us, O God.

We grieve that we rarely even think of this,
that we take the water we have for granted
with little care for others.
Forgive us, O God.

Connect our hearts with those whose tears of grieving
are shed in their need and fear for their thirsty children.
Let us dip a finger in this water and taste the tears of the world,
sharing in its grieving and all its thirsts for justice.

(A bowl of salt water is passed among the people while a silence is kept.)

ASSURANCE

Jesus Christ is our living water,
pouring forth grace towards us who grieve for what we have done.

Open your hearts to receive the life of Christ
and the renewing of grace for this day and the next.
We are forgiven.
Thanks be to God!

READINGS

POEMS ABOUT WATER

SONGS AND PICTURES ABOUT WATER   #18   PrH   "The Desert Shall Rejoice"

DOXOLOGY

COMMITMENT

We will need the living water of God for our task in the world.
O God, we pray for this water, that we may be your faithful servants.

(Silent prayer)

As we are restored by your gifts, these are our hopes for the world:

(The particular hopes relating to work being done by the people are shared.)

We will carry the love of God into the four corners of the earth.
We are the people of God, brought to birth in the rush of water,
washed and sustained day by day in the beauty of water.
We see the wonder of the rivers and streams,
and the endless waves of the mighty seas.
Our faces are lifted up to receive the gentle rain
and the miracle of the greening of the earth as it falls.
In all this, O God, we give thanks for your endless gifts to us
and commit ourselves to move for the just sharing of them with others.

Let us give to each other water for this journey
And commit ourselves to care for each other on the way.

(The people pour water into each other's cupped hands.)

Praise to you, God of all creation!

Praise to you for the gift of water!
Amen.

MUSIC OR SONG   #207   HAM   "Praise to the Lord, the Almighty"

BLESSING

We are blessed forever by the poured out life of Christ.
Let us go and pour this blessing over the heads of all the people.
And may the streams of living water flow beside the road as you go,

the warmth of the love of God move within you
and the Spirit be found in the ripples of grace around you.
Amen.

A HEALTHY WORLD[61]
(Nondenominational)

PRELUDE

HYMN   #431   PsH   "All Creatures of Our God and King"

CALL TO CONFESSION
(on the theme of abuse of the earth)

ASSURANCE OF PARDON

REFLECTION   *"A Healthy World"*[62]

A world in which we know deeply
that we belong to one another:
there is no place of escape from
those who are tiresome,
those from whom we draw back.

> A world in which we pray and work
> for the well-being of business, factory, farm, bank,
> where we search together for meaning and purpose,
> where we repent of what goes wrong between us,
> where we act to put things right,
> where we celebrate what goes well.

A world in which we are alert to signs of God
at work in the way things are being done,
God striving through us to transform
the realms of this world
into the realm of Christ.

> A world in which the contribution
> of those who work in public health,
> in waterworks, sewage farms, civil engineering,
> is valued and held in high esteem.

A world flowing with milk and honey,
with corn and wine and oil,
where salvation is known to be
not less than freedom from deprivation.

A world in which there is sensitivity
towards those who have less than little,
a world in which there is action together
to ensure that all have clean water,
adequate food,
a place to live,
and the opportunity to contribute
to the common good.

A world in which we take corporate action
to challenge and change evil ways
in the policies and practice of corporate bodies
that destroy, deprive, and pollute.

A world in which we care for
the air and water,
the soil and trees,
of the planet we share,
our common earth home.

A world in which nations maturely handle
large-scale changes to eliminate poverty,
changes that are political, economic, military.

A world where we become more healed
by being prepared to bear more
for the sake of those who are less well.

SCRIPTURES   Isa. 58:6–8; Rev. 11:15b

CLOSING HYMN   #197   PsH   "The Trees of the Field"

BENEDICTION

LITANIES FOR ANIMAL PROTECTION[63]
(Anglican)

Despite the theological problems associated with petitionary or intercessory prayer, it remains true that the prayer that Jesus taught is almost entirely petitionary in character. If praying that God's will 'be done on earth as it is in heaven' is preeminently the Christian prayer, then there can be no good reason not to pray that God's will be done in relation to the animal world specifically.

Our prayer, then, should be that God's suffering creatures will be healed, that we will turn away from our wanton exploitation of animals, and that we will repent of our arrogance and spiritual blindness. It will be seen in the following litanies that I think our prayer should equally be for our—as well as the animals'—liberation. I have used elsewhere Jonathan Edwards' image of the Fall as a state of shrunken human sensibilities—a state in which we become less and less sensible to other creatures and more and more obsessed with ourselves. From this perspective, our maltreatment of animals—and our desire to see them and treat them as objects or commodities—stems from a spiritual poverty and hardness of heart. We need, in short, to find a new heart for animals.

We should pray for this new heart: this sensibility, this feeling for animals. For some it comes naturally but for most of us, it does not. In my view, feeling what is now rather pejoratively called 'pity' should be a goal of our spiritual life. Even if we cannot scale the heights of the spiritual sensibility exhibited by the saints, at least we ought to feel a lack of it: a sense of unwholeness, and pray for the grace to feel.

I like the lines from Charles Péguy that we pray to be 'spared from becoming a dead people, a dead nation.' He continues: 'Be spared from mildew. Be spared from going rotten in spiritual death, in the earth, in hell.' Ecclestone, in commentary, suggests that the contrary words—not of death but of life—'are being spoken wherever men and women go that extra mile as "burden-bearers of creation," taking it on themselves to make some acts of reparation and reconciliation or giving themselves generously to patient service of others.' These thoughts have inspired the following three litanies.

—Andrew Linzey

FIRST LITANY

Priest: Our prayer is that the God of the new covenant written into our hearts will enlarge our sense of kinship and fellowship with all living beings.

(One or more of the following may be said:) Ps. 51:10; Ps. 139:23; Jer. 24:7; Ezek. 36:26; Heb. 10:16

Passionate God
we are cold with hearts of stone;
we are deaf to the cries
of your creatures
and blind to their sufferings.

Warm us with your Spirit
so we can feel your passion
raging against injustice
and burning away evil.

Bring us
out of the cold
from our passionless lives
to the heat of your love.

(There follows a pause for reflection.)

(After each line the congregation repeats:)

Give us new hearts, O God.

Priest: For animals neglected and ill-treated

For animals hunted to death

For animals exhibited for entertainment

For animals killed for convenience

For animals in crates and tethers

For animals genetically manipulated

For animals bought and sold in markets

For animals suffering in laboratories

For animals patented as inventions

For animals slaughtered for food

Priest: O God
give us new hearts
that we may feel again
the suffering of our
fellow creatures;

deliver us
from ourselves
and the evil
we inflict
on the animal world.

(There follows a pause for reflection.)

(After each line the congregation repeats:)

Free us, O Lord.

Priest: From our denigration of animals

From thinking of animals as things

From our indifference to cruelty

From our systematic exploitation of animals

From treating animals as machines

From our abdication of responsibility

From our spiritual blindness

From our shrunken sensibilities

From our hardness of heart

Priest: Liberating God
release us from that
spiritual poverty
that sees other creatures
only as commodities for us
and reduces them to things
for our service.

Holy God
you alone
can make all things new;
send your Holy Spirit
upon us;
give us new hearts to feel,
new ears to hear,
new eyes to see
the unity of
all creatures
in Christ;
and to proclaim
all living beings
as fellow creatures
with us in your
wonderful creation.

All: Amen.

SECOND LITANY

Priest: God of flesh and blood
whose Son Jesus Christ
died in agony on the Cross;
help us to hear the cries
of our fellow creatures
who suffer and die
for our sakes.

All: We confess our faith in the true God.

Priest: This is the true God

All: Who comes to us in the flesh.

Priest: This is the true God

  All: **Who suffers in the suffering of the world.**

Priest: This is the true God

  All: **Whose face is seen in the faces of pain in our world.**

Priest: Merciful God
help us to
see that there is
something profoundly
Christ-like about
the innocent
suffering of animals;
give us grace
to feel with you
their pain
and so to share
the burden of suffering
which lies
upon the world.

O God who will free
all creation from evil,
deliver us, we pray,
from our own
spiritual poverty
so that by your grace
we may become
new creatures in Christ
alive with your Spirit.

(There follows a pause for reflection.)

(After each line the congregation repeats:)

Deliver us, O Lord.

Priest: From our hardness of heart

From our littleness of love

From our lack of care

From our greed and cruelty

From our wanton killing

From our desire to dominate and control

From our overwhelming pride

From our contempt for other lives

From our lack of shame

From our inability to repent

From our obsession with ourselves

From our sense of self-satisfaction

From every desire to inflict harm

From every form of violence

Priest: Fill us, O God, with sorrow for the suffering we have inflicted on the animal world; take from us our conceit and pride and give us true humility in our dealings with animals; help us to see through our excuses and rationalizations for our cruelty, and to repent of the evil we have done them. We ask these prayers through your Son, Jesus Christ, who on the Cross identified with all those who suffer and in whose name shall all creation find liberation and fulfillment.

All: Amen.

May the God
who turns
us from evil,
who endures suffering
for our sake,
and who forgives
all who are penitent
grant you lasting
forgiveness that
you may become signs
of light in a
dark world.
Amen.

THIRD LITANY

Priest: We confess our belief in the Triune God, Creator,
Reconciler and Sanctifier who loves each and every creature.

**All: This we believe and know:
animals are our fellow creatures
loved by God the Father
redeemed by God the Son
and enlivened by God the Holy Spirit.**

Priest: Holy Trinity

awaken within us
a sense of feeling
for all the living creatures
you have placed among us;
give us a compassionate heart
for all who suffer
and make us visible signs
of your peaceful kingdom
for which all creation longs.

God of justice and peace
you hear the cries
of all your creatures:

Hear our prayer for
all our fellow creatures that are
imprisoned in zoos

All: and let your mercy be upon them;

(After each line the congregation repeats:)

and let your mercy be upon them.

Priest:: transported overseas

hunted for sport

exploited in circuses

dissected in schools

abused in laboratories

forced into factory farms

butchered in abattoirs

trapped for their fur

Priest: Merciful God
we are made in your image
but we have made gods of ourselves;

we have turned your creatures
into things and machines,
making them objects of our sport
using them for our vanity,
exploiting them for our greed
and stealing their lives;

but you are the Liberating God
who can transform
even ourselves;

> help us to turn from
> our evil
> and embrace
> the vision
> of your peaceable
> kingdom.

READING   Isa. 11:9

(There follows a pause for reflection.)

(After each line the congregation repeats:)

Liberate us, O God.

Priest: From our lack of vision

From our self-centered lives

From our lack of pity and compassion

From our idolatry of ourselves

From our callousness to suffering

From our lack of humility

From our arrogance and pride

From our violent, disordered lives

Priest: Liberate us, O God, from the folly that sees all creatures as simply resources, machines, or commodities here for our sake. Help us to understand that all living creatures are precious in your sight and exist for your glory.

Make us sorry for the continuing crucifixion we inflict on the animal world; of your mercy forgive us, and enable us by your Spirit to lead lives worthy of our repentance: in the name of same God, Creator, Reconciler and Sanctifier who redeems each and every creature and whose kingdom is everlasting peace. **Amen.**

Community Reconciliation

"Esau . . . threw his arms around him." (Gen. 33:4)

MOVEMENT TOWARD RECONCILIATION[64]
(Roman Catholic)

PRELUDE

CALL TO WORSHIP

> **Leader:** What does the Lord ask of you? But to do justice, love mercy and walk humbly with your God.
>
> **People: We worship the God who enables us to walk the way of life.**

HYMN   #398   UMH   "Jesus Calls Us O'er the Tumult"

READING   Matt. 25:31–46

> **Reader:** The Lord says to us: "Blessed are the peacemakers, they shall be called sons and daughters of God."
>
> **Left Side:** Happy are those who build up relationships
> rather than tear them down.
>
> **Right Side:** Happy are those who refuse to ridicule, put down,
> or mock others, especially those different from us.
>
> **Left Side:** Happy are those who see through the shallowness
> of racial prejudice and know we are children of a loving God.
>
> **Right Side:** Happy are those who search out the truth
> and are willing to stand up for justice.

Reader: The Lord says to us: "Blessed are those who hunger and thirst for what is right, for they shall have their fill."

Left Side: Happy are those who stand up for what is right and are not afraid to stand alone in the face of injustice.

Right Side: Happy are those who reach out for fullness of life and work for human collaboration and harmony.

Left Side: Happy are those who help those who are oppressed, who work for human rights, and who defend the helpless.

Right Side: Happy are those who hear the cry of the poor.

Reader: The Lord says to us: "Blessed are they who show mercy, Mercy shall be theirs."

Left Side: Happy are those who are able to forgive themselves as well as others, and who do not hold grudges.

Right Side: Happy are those who love all members of God's family and make friends of their brothers and sisters.

Left Side: Happy are those who accept the limits of those around them— neighbors, friends, parents, and family—and who easily forgive.

Right Side: Happy are those who have the courage to be compassionate.

HOMILY

INTERCESSORY PRAYERS:

Leader: Creator God, you made each of us in love and for love. In baptism we were anointed as prophets and you call us to live holy lives and to participate in the mission of justice.

People: **Grant us the grace, O loving God, to be attentive to your call, to be sensitive to injustice whenever we encounter it, and in all things to act justly, love tenderly and walk humbly with you, our God.**

Leader: We are weak, limited, sinful, O God. We fail to acknowledge the inherent worth of each person as a child of God. We focus on what divides us and makes us different rather than on the great truth that unites us—that we are one body in Christ.

People: **We come before you, O God, parent of us all, asking your grace to appreciate the beauty of our diversity and to celebrate the gift of God incarnate in each one we meet.**

Leader: God of peace, you made us to live in harmony and community, not in chaos and violence. So much of our world is torn by strife, there are so many divisions among us that result in a lack of freedom.

People: **We ask the grace and strength to be instruments of peace in our hearts, our homes, communities, nations and the world.**

Leader: Martin Luther King Jr. wrote: "The cross we bear precedes the crown we wear. To be a Christian we must take up our cross, with all of its difficulties and agonizing and tension-packed content and carry it until that very cross leaves its marks upon us and redeems us to that more excellent way which comes only through suffering."

People: **God of the oppressed and suffering, we pray for all those who suffer in any way. Grant us the strength to bear whatever crosses are in our lives and the grace to know our losses, grief, and pain as part of the mystery of your love for us.**

Leader: The lives of your saints stand as a reminder of what it means to belong to God, to be persecuted for justice's sake, to live and to die for God and for God's people.

People: **We give you thanks, O compassionate God, for the lives of the holy and prophetic leaders of our time and ask you that we can become in our various ministries of serving others the living presence of your son and our brother Jesus. We bring these and all our own needs and the needs of our families and communities to your loving care. Amen.**

THE LORD'S PRAYER

THE CLOSING BLESSING

CLOSING HYMN   #89   UMH   "Joyful, Joyful, We Adore Thee"

REMEMBRANCE, PENITENCE, AND HOPE: MEMORIAL ON 9/11/01[65]
(Interfaith)

This interfaith service may be adapted to include participants from the various faith communities in a particular town/city.

GATHERING PROCESSION

GREETING

Grace and peace to all!

We gather this evening in prayerful remembrance of all that happened one year ago, on September 11, 2001. We come as believers of different faiths, united in prayer for peace, not only for this country, but for all life on this fragile planet. We gather to recall the thousands of men and women who died in the attacks in New York and Washington and in the field of Pennsylvania.

May the prayer of this evening bond us together in our commitment to America as a pluralistic community in the common work of peace making, and in the consolation of those who mourn.

GATHERING SONG   #437   UMH   "This Is My Song"

LIGHTING THE CANDLE OF REMEMBRANCE

We light a candle in remembrance of all those who suffered and died on September 11th in New York, Pennsylvania, and at the Pentagon in Arlington, Virginia. We light a candle to bring to mind those who are still alive and who suffer because of the events of that day.

First Reader,
Baha'i
Community: When we remember the executives, office workers, maintenance workers, restaurant workers, stockbrokers, bystanders, window-washers and all the others who worked together so valiantly to help each other, we can say together:

All: We remember great courage.

Second Reader,
Unitarian
Universalist
Fellowship: When we recall the firefighters who rushed upstairs as most everyone else was racing out, we can say together:

All: We remember selfless service.

Third Reader,
Lutheran
Church: When we recall the police officers who stood to protect and defend the people and performed their duties until the towers came crashing down on top of them, we can say together:

All: We remember selfless sacrifice for the safety of others.

Fourth Reader,
Presbyterian
Church: When we recall the thousands of workers, women and men, old and young, single and married, American-born and those born in countries around the world who did not escape the buildings, we can say together:

All: We remember the loss of human life.

Fifth Reader,
Jewish
Congregation: When we recall those citizens who rushed to help, did all they could to help, we can say together:

All: **We remember and give thanks for dutiful commitment to those in distress.**

Sixth Reader,
    Roman
    Catholic
    Church: When we recall the people who stood in line at the nation's blood banks to make living donations, we can say together:

All: **We give thanks for those who live on to pass on life and love.**

Seventh Reader,
    Episcopal
    Church: When we remember the millions of Americans who gave so generously of their life and labor to endow funds to help the survivors and their families recover from their losses, we can say together:

All: **We are grateful for generosity.**

REFLECTION

Remembrance begins with deep, personal identification. It begins with remembering the affliction of our brothers and sisters, and marking their pain as our own. I invite you to stand at this time and say the name of an individual lost on September 11th whose passing leaves a hole in your life and in the lives of your loved ones.

REMEMBRANCES OF THE PEOPLE
(Concluding remark:)

Remembrance is a sacred moment when we raise up and hold up to the light of the Eternal moment, the good who have passed.

SOLO   "We Remember Them"

In the rising of the sun and in its going down, we remember them.
In the blowing of the wind and in the chill of winter, we remember them.
In the opening of buds and in the rebirth of spring, we remember them.
In the blueness of the sky and in the warmth of summer, we remember them.
In the rustling of leaves and in the beauty of autumn, we remember them,
When we are weary and in need of strength, we remember them.
When we are lost and sick at heart, we remember them.
When we have joys we yearn to share, we remember them.
So long as we live, they too shall live, for they are now a part of us, as we remember them.[66]

LIGHTING THE CANDLE OF PENITENCE

We light a candle, in penitence, recognizing that we have not done enough to address the humanitarian needs of so many who suffer hunger and homelessness, dispossession and despair.

Eighth Reader,
Lutheran
Church: In our sadness, horror and shock we acknowledge that our own fears turned murderous and we have sought revenge, sometimes against even the innocent.

All: **We confess and regret our own anger and recognize its dangers to our spirits, our health, our community, and others.**

Ninth Reader,
Presbyterian
Church: In the midst of the aftermath of the events of September 11, 2001, we have been tempted to seek only our own good, hear only our own truth, acknowledge only our own suffering.

All: **We know that peace will come to us and to our children only when the concerns of justice anywhere become the subject of political and social will everywhere, and that no justice leads to no peace.**

Tenth Reader,
Roman
Catholic
Church: In striving for national security and domestic peace we run the risk of confusing might for right and participating in the very behaviors we condemn.

All: **Guard and guide our country that in our search for security we may not trample the rights of the innocent nor disregard the rule of law. Let us not confuse leadership within the global community as the voice for the whole community.**

ASSEMBLY SONG   "Dona Nobis/Sim Shalom" (Give Us Peace)[67]

Sim shalom tova uv'racha. (2x)
Tova, tova uv'racha, shalom tova, tova uv'racha.
Shalom tova uv'racha, shalom tova, tova uv'racha.

Dona nobis pacem pacem, dona nobis pacem.
Dona nobis pacem, dona nobis pacem.
Dona nobis pacem, dona nobis pacem.

REFLECTION

Repentance means to turn away from wrong deeds. Repentance means choosing instead deeds which require moral restraint, and are more beneficial to all persons who suffer.

LIGHTING THE CANDLE OF HOPE

We light a candle to illumine the way to a better world for our children and our children's children, and all the children of God.

Eleventh Reader,
Jewish
Congregation: We recall with joy the unity we felt in the outpouring of help, kindness, thoughtful words and deeds from at home and around the world.

> **All: We must hold firmly to our unity, borne forward now not of tragedy but of loving-kindness.**

Twelfth Reader,
Unitarian
Universalist
Fellowship: We place fresh confidence in international organizations and conversations that bring the diverse gifts of the world to the problems of poverty, injustice, terror and strife.

> **All: We long for wise policies that forgo short-term gain for long-term stability, justice and peace.**

Thirteenth
Reader, Baha'i
Community: In a year filled with tragedy we dare to hope for an era yet to come in which the slaughter of innocents, greed, the ambitions of power, and cultural, racial and religious bigotries are but memories of a dim and unenlightened past.

UNISON PRAYER

God of the ages, before your eyes all empires rise and fall yet you are changeless. Be near us in this age of terror and in these moments of remembrance. Uphold those who work and watch and wait and weep and love. By your Spirit give rise in us to broad sympathy for all the peoples of your earth. Strengthen us to comfort those who mourn and work in large ways and small for those things that make for peace. Bless the people and leaders of this nation and all nations so that warfare and slavery may become only a historic memory.

REFLECTION

Whatever the motivation, there can be no religious or moral justification for what happened on September 11, 2001. People of all faiths must be united in the conviction that terrorism in the name of religion profanes religion. The most effective counter to terrorist claims of religious justification comes from within the world's rich religious traditions and from the witness of so many people of faith who have been a powerful force for non-violent human liberation around the world.[68] Let us unite in prayer using the Scriptures of the world's great religions read by representatives of these faith traditions from our community:

A BUDDHIST PRAYER
(More than 2,500 years ago, the Buddha taught Metta [loving-kindness] meditation to combat fear and to extend unconditional love to all beings. In light of the recent events, loving-kindness is needed more than ever.)

As a mother would risk her own life
to protect her only child,
even so towards all living beings
one should cultivate a boundless heart.

One should cultivate for all the world
a heart of boundless loving-kindness,
above, below and all around,
unobstructed, without hate or enmity.

May all beings be safe from harm.
May we be happy and peaceful.
May we be strong and healthy.
May we live our lives joyfully.[69]

(Shared, sacred silence follows for 10 seconds.)

(Organ Chime)

A JEWISH PRAYER
(Judaism is the religion of the Jewish people. Judaism created the idea of monotheism, and its greatest gift to the world has been the Hebrew Bible. For three thousand years, the Jews have lived according to the interpretations of the Scriptures—chief among them, the idea that people are created in the Divine image, and that law and ritual make this idea come alive. Judaism is the oldest of the three Western religions, and as such, gave birth to the notions of spirituality, covenant, holiness and ethics.)

Master of the universe,
let there be no good hope that is not a command,
let there be no prayer that does not ask to become a deed,
let there be no promise unless it is kept.

Upon this earth may just and reverent nations arise:
needing no challenge like war,
no more undone by poverty and injustice.
Let them be places where every person matters.
So shall the human community,
rich in beginnings and poor in conclusion,
grow mature in wisdom and ripe in understanding.

Upon this earth may women of spirit arise,
men of integrity and compassion,
creators of God-seeking peoples;
slow to judge others

quick to judge themselves:
so may they be all their days and years.
We ask for messiahs,
a new age of the spirit,
Your kingdom on earth.

Let the Eternal be King of all the earth.[70]

(Shared, sacred silence follows for 10 seconds.)

(Organ Chime)

A BAHÁ'Í PRAYER
(The Bahá'í Faith is the youngest of the world's independent religions. Its founder, Baha'u'llah [1817–1892], is regarded by Bahá'ís as the most recent in the line of Messengers of God that stretches back beyond recorded time. The Bahá'í Faith recognizes the unity of God and of His prophets. It teaches that the fundamental purpose of religion is to promote concord and harmony among the peoples and nations of the world.)

O Thou kind Lord! Thou hast created all humanity from the same stock. Thou hast decreed that all shall belong to the same household. In Thy Holy Presence they are all Thy servants, and all mankind are sheltered beneath Thy Tabernacle; all have gathered together at Thy Table of Bounty; all are illumined through the light of Thy Providence.

O God! Thou art kind to all, Thou has provided for all, dost shelter all, conferrest life upon all. Thou hast endowed each and all with talents and faculties, and all are submerged in the Ocean of Thy Mercy.

O Thou kind Lord! Unite all. Let the religions agree and make the nations one, so that they may see each other as one family and the whole earth as one home. May all live together in perfect harmony.

O God! Raise aloft the banner of the oneness of mankind.

O God Establish the Most Great Peace.

Cement Thou, O God, the hearts together.

O Thou Kind Father, God! Gladden our hearts through the fragrance of Thy love. Brighten our eyes through the Light of Thy Guidance. Delight our ears with the melody of Thy Word, and shelter us all in the Stronghold of thy Providence.

Thou are the Mighty and Powerful, Thou art the Forgiving and Thou art the One Who overlooketh the shortcoming of all mankind.

—Abdu'l-Baha

(Shared, sacred silence follows for 10 seconds.)

(Organ Chime)

A UNITARIAN UNIVERSALIST PRAYER/READING
(Unitarian Universalism is based on a belief in the goodness of all human beings and their universal salvation—that no one is ever removed from the circle of divine grace. Unitarian Universalists also celebrate human interdependence in and with the web of life, as well as the freedom of each person to create his or her spiritual path.)

In the words of Martin Luther King Jr.: We are caught in an inescapable network of mutuality, tied in a single garment of destiny.

Injustice anywhere is a threat to justice everywhere.

There are some things in our social system to which all of us ought to be maladjusted.

Hatred and bitterness can never cure the disease of fear, only love can do that.

We must evolve for all human conflict a method which rejects revenge, aggression, and retaliation.

The foundation of such a method is love.

Before it is too late, we must narrow the gaping chasm between our proclamations of peace and our lowly deeds which precipitate and perpetuate war.

One day we must come to see that peace is not merely a distant goal that we seek but a means by which we arrive at that goal.

We must pursue peaceful ends through peaceful means.

We shall hew out of the mountain of despair, a stone of hope.[71]

Assembly Song   #393   CCH   "Peace Is Flowing Like a River"

A Hindu Prayer

O God, the Giver of Life, Remover of pains and sorrows, bestower of happiness, and creator of the universe, Thou art most luminous, pure and adorable. We meditate on Thee. May thou inspire and guide our intellect in the right direction.

The Gayatri or Guru Mantra

There is peace in the heavenly region; there is peace in the atmosphere; peace reigns on the earth; there is coolness in the water; the medicinal herbs are healing; the plants are peacegiving; there is harmony in the celestial objects and perfection in eternal knowledge; everything in the universe is peaceful; peace pervades everywhere. May that peace come to me!

May there be peace, peace, peace.

Shanti Path—Hymn of Peace
O Supreme Spirit! Lead us from untruth to truth. Lead us from darkness to light. Lead us from death to immortality.

O Lord, in Thee may all be happy. May all be free from misery, may all realize goodness, and may no one suffer pain.[72]

(Shared, sacred silence follows for 10 seconds.)

(Organ Chime)

A Muslim Prayer
(Along with Judaism and Christianity, Islam is one of the three Abrahamic religions. It is founded on the belief in a unique absolutely transcendent God [Allah is the Arabic word for

God] who is Creator and Sustainer of the Universe. God's Word was revealed through his angel Gabriel to the prophet Mohammed, who received the word of God, which he faithfully recorded in the sacred books of the Qur'an [the Koran].)

In the name of God, the Merciful, the Compassionate:
All praise be to God; Lord of all the worlds; Most beneficent, ever merciful; King of the Day of Judgment; You alone we worship, and to you alone we turn for help; Guide us, O Lord, to the path that is straight; The path of those you have blessed; and not the path of those who have gone astray.

I call to witness; the early hours of the morning, and the night when it is dark and still.
The Lord has never left you.
What is to come is better than what has been before.
The Lord will give you, and you will be content.
Did He not find you an orphan and take care of you?
Did He not find you perplexed, and show you the way?
Did He not find you poor and enrich you?
So, do not hinder but help others (orphans, destitute) as the Lord has helped you.

We ordained for the children of Israel (and all the people) that if whosoever slew a human being, unless it is for murder or for spreading corruption in the land, it shall be like killing all humanity; and if anyone saved a life, it would be as if he saved the lives of all the people.

When Mary withdrew from her family to a place Eastward, We sent her our spirit in the form of a man. I seek refuge in the Merciful Lord from you, Mary said. The spirit quietly assured Mary: I am a messenger from the Lord sent to foretell you that you will bear a blessed son. How can I have a son, Mary exclaimed, when no man has touched me, and I am not a sinful woman. Thus will it be, it is the will of the Lord, he intoned; and our Lord will make Jesus a blessed example for all the people.

O mankind, we created you from a male and a female, and made you into nations, that ye may know each other, not that ye may despise each other.

Those who believe in the teachings of the Qur'an, and those who follow the Jewish scriptures, and the Christians, and those who believe in God and work for righteousness, shall have their reward with the Lord. On them shall be no fear, nor shall they grieve.

Let there be no compulsion in religion. Truth stands out clear from error. He who turns away from the forces of evil and believes in God will always find unbreakable strength in his beliefs. God is the friend of those who believe, and He leads them out of darkness and into light. Amen.[73]

(Shared, sacred silence follows for 10 seconds.)

(Organ Chime)

A CHRISTIAN PRAYER/READING
(Christians believe that Jesus Christ, the Son of God, lived, died and rose from the dead to bring salvation to all. Jesus taught that the greatest commandment is to love God with all your heart, with all your soul, and with all your mind. The second is like to the first: to love your neighbor as yourself.)

Matt. 5:1–12

REFLECTION

We have heard Sacred Readings today from members of our local community who represent a number of different faith traditions—among them Buddhist, Jewish, Bahá'í, Unitarian Universalist, Hindu, Muslim, and Christian. If we are to carry one thing away with us tonight, let it be the light of God that is present in each of us no matter what our faith tradition may be.

Let us carry this Light away with us as a memorial of remembrance for those who have died; as a penitence for those who have suffered; and as hope for liberty and justice for all in this world.

CLOSING PRAYER

> **Leader:** Loving God, Protector of the fearful,
> Source of hope,
> Show us the immense power of your goodness and strengthen our faith.
> Comfort the sorrowing.
> Give us courage to carry on,
> To work and pray for a peaceful world, where all are brothers and sisters.
> Give us strength to forgive and hope to see a future
> Where all can live in solidarity together.
> Grant us peace.
>
> **All: Amen.**

CLOSING SONG   #696   UMH   "America, the Beautiful" (Verses 1 & 4)

THE SIGN OF PEACE

Let us begin now, sharing with each other a sign or word of peace by shaking hands and saying, "Peace be with you."

RECEPTION FOLLOWING SERVICE
(You are invited to join us for cookies, juice, and fellowship immediately following the service.)

REPENTANCE AND RECONCILIATION[74]
(Anglican)

THE BURRSWOOD COMMUNITY, TUNBRIDGE WELLS, ENGLAND

An order of worship to encourage the due expression of penitence, and the receiving of forgiveness and reconciliation. Further readings and teaching may be given in the service.

OPENING

We learn in Scripture, in St. Paul's Letter to the Romans, that: "All have sinned, and come short of the glory of God." He adds: "We can have peace with God through our Lord Jesus Christ." St. John, in his First Letter, teaches: "If we say we have no sin we deceive ourselves, and there is no truth in us. But if we confess our sins to God he will keep his promise and do what is right: He will forgive us our sins, and purify us from all wrongdoing."

Through the Book of Nehemiah, we learn: "The Lord our God is a forgiving God, gracious and merciful, slow to anger and full of love; because of his great compassion he will not abandon us. We were disobedient and rebelled against him, yet from Heaven he hears us in our distress, is ready to forgive our sin and deliver us."

We believe God desires we turn to him to be reconciled with him.

SONG   #128   HPW   "Create in Me a Clean Heart O God"

APPROACH

RESPONSORIAL PSALM   From Ps. 139

Verse: Search me O God and know my heart
Response: And lead me in the way everlasting *(repeat after each section)*

O Lord, you have searched us and you know us;
you know when we sit down and when we get up;
you see us at work, you see us at rest,
you know just what we are like. **R.**

Before the word is off our lips,
you know what we are going to say.
Lord, you are all around us
and your hand is upon us. **R.**

Wherever we go, you are there with us—
your hand guiding us, holding us fast.
However dark it gets, it is not dark to you;
your eyes follow us, you can see us. **R.**

For you created us,
formed us before ever we were born—
how wonderfully you made us!

We praise you, Lord:
You know what each day will bring,
and when we wake you are with us. **R.**

O God, you search our hearts,
you lift away our anxieties,
you take away our sin,
you lead us in your eternal way. **R.**

EXAMINATION

Let us be still and reflect upon what the presence of the Lord reveals. Christ the Light of the World has come to dispel the darkness of our hearts. In His light let us examine ourselves: preparing to confess our sins, and to lay before Him our burdens or hurt memories, and offering Him all our sorrows. Together let us pray for the guidance of His Holy Spirit:

Holy Spirit of the everloving God,
trusting in your good counsel,
pray convince us of the truth,
open deaf ears, soften our hearts,
reveal what we do not know,
concentrate our wills,
that lamenting our sins
and those things that burden us,
we may be ready to receive from you,
the God of all mercy,
perfect forgiveness and peace,
through Jesus Christ our Lord. Amen.

(A silence may be kept, and opportunity given to write reflectively and to make symbolic offering of matters to be laid before the Lord.)

(The Kyrie Eleison may be sung.)

Look around you, can you see?
Times are troubled, people grieve.
See the violence, feel the hardness;
All my people, weep with me.
Kyrie eleison, Christe eleison, Kyrie eleison.

Walk among them, I'll go with you.
Reach out to them with my hands.
Suffer with me and together
we will serve them, help them stand.
Kyrie . . .

Forgive us, Father; hear our prayer.
We would walk with you—anywhere,
through your suffering, with forgiveness,
take your life into the world.
Kyrie . . .

CONFESSION AND ABSOLUTION

> **All: Fatherly God, source of all mercy;**
> **We are heavy laden and confess to you now,**
> **dark moments and deep wounds from times past,**

the griefs of today, and fears for the future.
Loose and deliver us, we pray;
setting us free, to serve you gladly,
all the days of our lives, in Jesus' name. Amen.

Leader: Jesus said, "Come to me all who labor
and are heavy laden, and I will give you rest."

All: **Fatherly God, source of all mercy;**
By our many sins we have spurned your love,
and spoiled your image in us.
We admit our own guilt,
and that of our community and society.
We are ashamed and repent in sorrow.
Cleanse us of our sins, we pray;
and in your great mercy forgive us,
restore us and renew us, in Jesus' name. Amen.

Priest: Almighty God, who is loving and merciful,
forgive your sins, and free you from guilt;
deliver you from evil, lifting away your burdens;
to strengthen you in His service,
and keep you in life, abundant and eternal,
through Jesus Christ our Lord. **Amen.**

Receive your forgiveness in the name of our God.
You are loved and accepted by him. As he accepts and forgives you, so may
you forgive yourself, accepting yourself as beloved.
Let the truth sink in: You are God's servant—
He has chosen you and has not rejected you:
Do not fear for he is with you;
Do not be dismayed for he is your God—
He will strengthen you and help you;
He will uphold you with his righteous right hand.
From the past, in the present, into the future,
He is the same, yesterday, today and forever;
We are completely safe in Jesus Christ our Lord.

HYMN   #496   CMP   "O for a Thousand Tongues to Sing"

CONCLUSION

Ever loving God,
grant us grace to desire you with our whole heart;
that so desiring, we may seek and find you;
and so finding, may love you;
and so loving, may put behind us those sins
from which you have delivered us;

and live our days in your peace and joy,
through Jesus Christ our Lord. **Amen.**

THE BLESSING

AN INCURABLE WOUND[75]
(Methodist)

PRAYING FOR THE PAIN OF THE WORLD

(This service by intercession for the world is based upon the experience of Jeremiah and the testimony of John the Baptist, that Jesus is the Lamb of God who takes away the sin of the world. To help in the reflection on the Gospel, you may like to collect a number of photographs from newspapers and magazines of crowd themes or unknown, anonymous figures either from Britain or the U.S. For the prayers of intercession you will need a map of the world, drawing pins, or some other means of marking the map, a supply of candles or nightlights, and matches.)

INVOCATION

O Holy God, sovereign in grace and mercy,
call us to yourself
that we may come in penitence and trust.
Draw us into the circle of blessing,
that we may live in praise.
Remind us in our worship and in our living,
that love and mercy,
love and peace,
love and joy
remain with us
this day and forever. **Amen.**

HYMN   #144   UMH   "This Is My Father's World"

PRAYERS OF ADORATION AND CONFESSION

Loving God, you receive us into your presence,
and we find here a place of welcome.
You bring us into your home,
and we find here a house of hospitality,
where all can come with their need.

(Pause)

O living Creator, O generous Compassion,
you are our place of refuge.
Here we can hide, here we can rest,

here we can learn to face again
our weakness and our frailty.
Here we can be nourished to face again
the fury of the world.

Living God, we seek in you the bread of life.

We do not come for ourselves alone,
but for our community, our nation, our world.
We come in penitence and trust for those around us,
to whom we are bound by ties of faith, knowledge, kinship.

(Pause)

We also come in penitence and trust for those who are not bound to us,
those whom we do not know, and perhaps do not understand;
those who are different, distant, separate, and so many.
We come in penitence because together we have failed in love.
We have failed in mercy. We have failed in justice.
We have not kept your commandments of grace.
We have not carried your cross. We have not fed your lambs.
We have not built up your kingdom.

Living God, we seek in you the mercy of renewal.

Living God, as a community, as a nation, even as your Church
we have turned away from the things which give life,
and have sought the powers of death.
We have lived as people of dust, not as children of heaven.
We recognize our failure.
We confess our wrongdoing.
We acknowledge the evils in our midst.

(Pause)

Yet in Christ, you are calling us again in trust.
Once more, to know ourselves forgiven.
Once more, to turn to our best love, our primary obedience.
Once more, to pledge our allegiance to the One who through
life and death, and life beyond death,
restores what is broken,
binds up what is perilously wounded,
and heals what is desperately diseased.

Living God, we seek in you the grace of healing.

Living God, we come to you bearing the incurable wound of the world,
hearing, all too clearly, the unceasing cry of the world's pain.
We are part of the world, we cannot escape it,
and in our own small way, we have often added to the tale of grief,

but you have received us, forgiven us, and now you seek to
encourage us to be part of the world's healing, agents of the
world's resurrection, seeds of a new beginning.
This task, this transformation
is utterly beyond us, and so in trust and complete dependence
we turn again to you.

Living God, we seek in You the bread of life.
Living God, we seek in You the grace of healing.
Living God, we seek in You the mercy of renewal.

READING   Jer. 8:18; 9:11

PSALM 13

HYMN   #54   LH   "Guide Me O Thou Great Jehovah"

READING   John 1:21–34

REFLECTION ON THE GOSPEL
(Distribute the pictures of crowds and anonymous faces. Invite those present to study their picture during the meditation.)

ONE

You are just one in the crowd,
unnoticed and ignored;
ordinary in expression,
insignificant in dress;
a number, just one in a thousand;
a figure on paper, a name on a form—
signature scrawled unremarkably amongst many—
once seen, forever unremembered.

There is no reason why this one life
should draw attention.
There is no news in faithfulness, poverty, work,
in humor and generosity,
gentleness and grace; all these
are the stuff of anonymity,
a life lived in dull and unrelenting boredom,
unmarked by any spasm of drama,
any spark of heroism,
any demonstration, rise or fall.

You are just one, one in the crowd—
a crowd that has moods, personality, potential
for lynchmobs or carnival—

but you are just one face, one mind, one body,
easily glossed over or wiped out:
>   one more in the queue to the counter,
>   one more in the line along the trench,
>   one more in the train to the gas chambers.
One less Christ in the world.

FOR REFLECTION AND DISCUSSION

1. Do you find it easy or difficult to see the face of Christ in other people?
2. What are the attitudes, beliefs and behavior which make it more difficult to see Christ in another human being?
3. What is it that helps us to see Jesus in others? How do we open our eyes, our minds, our hearts?
4. Should there be limits? What is the cost of such openness?

RESPONSE TO THE GOSPEL

Living God, you have called us to see in each other the face of Christ.
O Lord, open our eyes that we may see.

Living God, you have commanded us to love our neighbors.
O Lord, direct our wills into the way of obedience.

Living God, you require us to love each other as you have loved us.
O Lord, break down our unlawful pride so that we may be one in spirit.

Living God, you draw us to yourself, so that we may find ourselves whole and our communities healed.

O Lord, write your new covenant upon our hearts, so that we may live it out in our everyday.

HYMN #454   UMH   "Open My Eyes, That I May See"

PRAYERS OF INTERCESSION
(As each petition is made, a candle is lit, and a mark made on a map of the world. Alternatively if the service is being held in the round, small nightlights could be used and positioned on a world map laid flat upon a table. Pauses for silence should be allowed, so that unspoken petitions can be offered.)

RESPONSE
(For use after each petition or group of petitions:)

>   **Leader:** Lord, heal us and we shall be healed.

>   **All: Lord, save us and we shall be saved.**

We gather together our prayers in the words that Christ taught us, and which we hold in common. . . . Our Father . . .

OFFERTORY

OFFERTORY PRAYER

Sovereign of all Creation, you who hold all things in your keeping, accept these gifts returned to you with thanksgiving, and grant that we may live our days in trust and hope, as we look for the coming of your glory amongst us. **Amen.**

COMMUNION HYMN *(if appropriate)*

Sovereign God, in the beginning you created us, and despite our unfaithfulness you made covenant with us, a promise which rests upon your own faithfulness and your steadfast love.

Sing praise all you nations: **Shout with joy all the earth.**

Gracious God, in Christ you came to us, showing us by your life the deeds of compassion, and through your death and resurrection the unconquerable possibilities of love.

Sing praise all you nations: **Shout with joy all the earth.**

Holy God, your presence is with us now, calling us to be holy, and to be people of wholeness for the world's healing.

Sing praise all you nations: **Shout with joy all the earth.**

(The words of the Institution of the Lord's Supper may follow here: "We praise you through our Lord Jesus Christ, who on the night in which he was betrayed . . .")

Healing God, you are still bearing the incurable wound of the world.
It is our pain that you have taken upon yourself.
It is our burden that you carry.
It is our cross, on which you died.
It is our failure to love, our sin, our preference for the easy way that you have accepted and embraced.
And in your generosity of heart we are received, reborn, made complete, so that through us the world is made again, recreated as the realm of God, the new country of God's covenant.

Sing praise all you nations: **Shout with joy all the earth.**

(The breaking of the bread and the distribution of the wine may follow here.)

God is in our midst, we praise you as our Maker, Redeemer and Friend. Renew us and enable us to live as your covenant people for the world, this day and forever. **Amen.**

HYMN   #505   PrH   "Be Known to Us in Breaking Bread"

BENEDICTION

May God in majesty look upon you with mercy,
May God in humility walk with you in lowliness,
May God in freedom uplift and encourage you,
from now until the close of the age. Amen.

TO DARE REBIRTH[76]
(United Church of Christ)

PREPARATION
Candles are needed for each person to light at the end of the service. Three candles are needed in the middle of the circle. They are lit at the beginning of the service, are blown out one by one where indicated, and then relit one by one in the Readings section.

GATHERING

One: Invisible manuals of power
Divide us, and call for subtraction.

**All: The angels cry with each new birth,
"May good will reign, may peace prevail."**

One: Relentless vehicles of intolerance
Permeate our patterns of choice.

**All: The angels cry with each new birth,
"May good will reign, may peace prevail."**

One: Distorted windows of economy
Render lives into chaff.

**All: The angels cry with each new birth,
"May good will reign, may peace prevail."**

One: Arrogant storehouses of violence
Poison the web of life.

**All: The angels cry with each new birth,
"May good will reign, may peace prevail."**

SONG   #205   SB   "He Came Singing Love"   Tune: Collin A. Gibson

SCRIPTURE READINGS
  Gen. 4:8–9

(Reader blows out a candle in middle circle.)

  Ezek. 22:25

(Reader blows out a candle in middle circle.)

  Matt. 2:16–18

(Reader blows out a candle in middle circle.)

SONG   "Kindle a Flame to Lighten the Dark" *or* "Shine Jesus Shine"[77]
  Ezek. 11:19

418   Broken World

(Reader lights a candle in middle of circle.)

SONG   "Kindle a Flame to Lighten the Dark"
     Rev. 21:1

(Reader lights a candle in middle of circle.)

SONG   "Kindle a Flame to Lighten the Dark"
     John 3:1–5

(Reader lights a candle in middle of circle.)

SONG   "Kindle a Flame to Lighten the Dark"

RESPONSE

PRAYER FOR REBIRTH

That we might dare rebirth:
Leaving behind
all the ransomed exchanges,
all the narrow corruptions,
all the familiar betrayals.

That we might dare rebirth:
Allowing the breadth of love to give us life,
the depth of justice to rhythm our hearts,
the height of peace to nourish our days.

That we might dare rebirth:
Shaping a world that welcomes gentleness,
a world that dances with joy,
a world where God is at rest;
A world shaped not simply for ourselves,
but for all living yet to come.

(Each person is invited to light a candle and place it in the middle of the circle as a prayer for rebirth in their own lives, and in our world.)

RECOMMITMENT TO COMMON GROUND[78]
(Roman Catholic)

PART I
OPTION A

Option A is used when the commitment to common ground is first made and celebrated.

INTRODUCTORY RITES

GATHERING

Presider: My brothers and sisters in Christ!
We come together to give thanks and rejoice in God's gift to us.
Our time together
has yielded insight and wisdom,
hope and understanding,
and a firm grasp on something which unites us in the face of all that divides.
It is the realization that . . .

(The common ground is briefly named.)

It is a beginning, and in that beginning
we place our hope.
Let us open our prayer together
by giving praise and glory to God.

All: Glory be to the Father . . .

Presider: May the peace and blessing of our God,
who is the source of all reconciliation
be with us.

All: Amen.

OPENING PRAYER

Presider: Let us pray:

Good and merciful God,
source of all wisdom and insight,
gift of forgiveness and promise of peace,
look with kindness upon us
and on the work we have undertaken in your name.
Though the walls that divide us remain strong,
you have given us a glimpse through those walls.
You have given us hope that they can be toppled.
In gratitude and hope

> we ask that you stay with us on our journey,
> till we find, with your help,
> the reconciliation you hold out to us.
> We ask this together
> through Christ, our Lord.

All: Amen.

LITURGY OF THE WORD

(More appropriate readings may arise from the needs and desires of the groups involved. The following are offered by way of suggestion:)

READING   Eph. 4:1–6 *or* 1 Cor. 1:10–25

HYMN   #598   WIII   "Where True Love and Charity Are Found"

HOMILY

RITE OF COMMITMENT TO COMMON GROUND

Presider: You have come together before God
and in the midst of this assembly
to claim and to affirm a common bond
which may lead to reconciliation
beyond all that divides you.
That bond, named among you,
is now yours to claim,
yours to affirm,
yours to follow wherever it may lead.
If you are ready to make this commitment
before God and before us all
please stand,
and let someone from each group
speak the common ground
which both acknowledges and professes.

(The rite continues with the Response *under Option B.)*

OPTION B

Option B is used when the ritual is repeated in the course of the reconciliation process.

INTRODUCTORY RITES

GATHERING

Presider: My brothers and sisters in Christ!
We come together to embrace and rejoice
in God's new gift to us.
Our time together continues to yield
insight and wisdom,
hope and understanding,
and an ever more firm grasp on that which unites us
in the face of all that still divides.
Today we rejoice in a new bond of reconciliation
that has been given to us.

(This new bond may be mentioned here.)

It is once again a time of new beginning,
and in this new sign of God's gracious help among us
we continue to place our hope.
Let us open our new prayer together
by giving praise and glory to God.

All: Glory be to the Father . . .

Presider: And may the peace and blessing of our God,
who is the source of all reconciliation
continue to be with us.

All: Amen.

OPENING PRAYER

Presider: Let us pray:

Good and merciful God,
source of all wisdom and insight,
gift of forgiveness and promise of peace
look with kindness upon us
and on the work we continue in your name.
Though the walls that divide us remain strong,
again you have given us a glimpse through those walls.
Again you have given us hope that they can be toppled.
In gratitude and hope
we ask that you stay with us on our journey
till we find, with your help,
the full reconciliation which you hold out to us.
We ask this together
through Christ, our Lord.

All: Amen.

Liturgy of the Word

(More appropriate readings may arise from the needs and desires of the groups involved. The following are offered by way of suggestion:)

Reading   2 Cor. 5:16–20   *or*   John 17:6–19

Homily

Rite of Recommitment to Common Ground

Invitation

> **Presider:** You have come together before God
> and in the midst of this assembly
> to claim and to affirm once again
> the common bond which you share.
> You come to acknowledge with heartfelt thanks
> that you are closer now to reconciliation
> than when you first began.
> God indeed has been good in your midst,
> and you have been open
> to God's work among you.
> May I invite someone from each group
> to come forward
> and name and claim this new common ground
> that has been given to us to share together.

(The rite continues with the Response *below.)*

Response
(A representative of each group comes forward and speaks in turn, naming the common ground to which each will be committed, or the new level of reconciliation that has been achieved.)

> **Presider:** May God who has begun this good work in our midst
> graciously bring it to completion.

> **All: Amen.**

Instruction
(It would be difficult, if not impossible, to give even a sample instruction at this point, since it needs to be done in light of the specific dispute in question, in light of the common ground that is decided upon and claimed, and in light of the actual level of reconciliation that has been achieved.

The action and commitment of both sides in the dispute should be named here in terms of their significance in God's work of reconciliation. The common ground and the reconciliation achieved should be located squarely in Christ's work of reconciliation, and should affirm or reaffirm the part each group will play in that work.)

PRAYER

Presider: Let us pray now in silence
for the continued blessings of God
upon our common endeavors,
that all divisions may in God's time be healed
and that God may be blessed and praised.

(As the assembly prays silently, representatives from each group come forward and place incense on the burning coals. The incense itself will speak the silent prayer of all. It may be an even more expressive symbol if the representative of each side gives the incense to the representative of the other side before the incense is placed on the coals.)

Presider: *(with hands extended above the representatives)*
Good and gracious God,
we have no power to love or forgive
unless you yourself place that power
within our hearts.
We have no power to understand, to respect,
and to rejoice in the differences
that are ours
unless your Spirit within us calls us
to a deeper and more abiding reconciliation.
Send this Spirit upon us once again
to lead us more firmly to that hope
for which your own Son prayed:
that we be one in you.
We make this prayer through Christ, our Lord.

All: Amen.

CONCLUDING RITE

Presider: And now let us pray
As our Lord Jesus Christ has taught us to pray:

All: (The Lord's Prayer)

Presider: With great hope and confidence
in the Lord's work among us,
let us greet each other in peace.

(Note: As part of the ongoing process toward reconciliation, at the beginning of each deliberation session, some part of the above ritual may be repeated, e.g., the prayer, the instruction, or the passage from Scripture.)

PART II

Part II is intended to ritualize the completion of the reconciliation process. Unlike Part I, in which the tonalities of hope and commitment were stressed, Part II stresses acknowledgement and responsibility and mutual forgiveness. Since the ritual is interpreted as the sacrament of reconciliation in the strict sense, it must also include a prayer and proclamation of God's for-giveness.

INTRODUCTORY RITES

GATHERING

Presider: My brothers and sisters in Christ:
It is indeed a great work of God in our midst
which brings us together to celebrate.
A long journey has come to an end,
and we can taste the victory that is ours.
The walls that have divided you
have been brought to the ground;
the common bond which has been your guide
has shown itself to be strong.
You gather now to give thanks to God,
to ask forgiveness of each other,
and to know that as you forgive each other
so God forgives you all.
May the peace of God,
who is Father, Son, and Spirit,
be with you.

All: And also with you.

OPENING PRAYER

Presider: Let us pray:
Lord, our God,
hear the prayers of those who call on you.
forgive the divisions they have nurtured,
and give them large hearts to forgive each other.
You have led them to this time of reconciliation.
For this we give you praise and thanks.
By the power that is at work within us
you are able to do more than anything
we can ask or imagine.
To you be honor and glory

in the Church and in Christ Jesus,
now and forever.

All: Amen.

LITURGY OF THE WORD

READING   Isa. 55:6–13

RESPONSORIAL PSALM   Ps. 8

> **R. O Lord, our Lord, how glorious is your
> name in all the earth!**

READING   Rom. 6:1–11

GOSPEL ACCLAMATION   John 13:34

**Alleluia . . .
A new commandment I give to you,
that you love one another as I have loved you.
Alleluia . . .**

GOSPEL   John 15:9–17

HOMILY

RITE OF RECONCILIATION

INVITATION

Presider: My brothers and sisters in Christ:
We come to the time of forgiveness and reconciliation,
a time of honesty before God
and before one another.
We are sinners, each and all:
this is our common truth.
And we are forgiven by God, each and all:
this is the revelation of Jesus Christ to us.
On this day of healing grace,
when groups once divided
have found a way to be one,
I would ask
that someone come forward
to speak for each group:

to acknowledge and claim responsibility
for the divisions that have been so costly;
to ask forgiveness of those who have been harmed;
to give forgiveness to those who have harmed.
May God be glorified once again in our midst.

CONFESSION OF RESPONSIBILITY
(Representatives of each group come forward and publicly confess responsibility for their part in the division, apologize even where the division was itself not intended or desired, and express determination never again to contribute to such destructiveness.)

SIGN OF RECONCILIATION

Presider: Before God and before this assembly
you have acknowledged your sin
and have recognized the sinful results
of your own best intentions.
Your thoughts, words, and deeds
have caused division in our world.
From now on you shall bring peace.
I invite you all to turn to those
who were once so distant from you,
and to greet them now in the peace of Christ.

(The greeting of peace is now shared among the members of the groups.)

COMMUNAL ABSOLUTION

Presider: We turn from the Lord, when we turn from each other.
We turn back to the Lord, when we greet each other in peace.
(With hands extended:)
The Lord God has created you
to be brother and sister upon the earth,
to care for one another
and to be agents of peace.
May God continue to create you anew.
May you find God's own loving heart within you.

All: Amen.

Presider: Our Lord Jesus Christ
has called you his friends
and enlisted you in his work
of reconciling all people.
May Christ deepen the reconciliation
that is yours this day
and fill you with his peace.

All: **Amen.**

Presider: The Holy Spirit, Spirit of Love
has softened the hardness of your hearts
and opened your lives
to God's own pardon and peace.
May this same Spirit breathe life into you
and make you true givers of life
to all whom you meet.

All: **Amen.**

Presider: And I absolve you all from your sins
in the name of the Father, and of the Son,
and of the Holy Spirit.

All: **Amen.**

CONCLUDING RITE

Presider: Let us pray together as the Lord Jesus Christ
has taught us to pray:

All: (The Lord's Prayer)

Presider: Let us give thanks and praise to God.

All: **Glory to God in the highest,**
And peace to his people on earth. . . .

(In silence, the representatives of the two groups come forward, each with a lighted candle in hand, and together light the single, larger candle that stands in the midst of the assembly. They then extinguish their own candles and place them aside.)

(The liturgy may conclude with a joyous song.)

HYMN   #726   WIII   "I Come with Joy to Meet My Lord"

HALLELUJAH ANYHOW![79]
(Methodist)

CIRCLE OF HEALING

CALL TO PRAYER

Leader: Peace be to this place, and to all who gather here.

All: **And peace also to you.**

Leader: We come together in the name of Jesus Christ.

All: Yes! We assemble in the power of the whole people of God.

HYMN #512 UMH "Stand by Me"
("Stand by Me" can be done either as a corporate song or as a solo. If no piano is available, the hymn can be read as a prayer response.)

I.

Leader: When the storms of life are raging.

All: Stand by me.

Leader: When the storms of life are raging.

All: Stand by me.

Leader: When the world is tossing me, Like a ship upon the sea; Thou who rulest wind and water,

All: Stand by me.

II.

Leader: In the midst of tribulation,

All: Stand by me.

Leader: In the midst of tribulation,

All: Stand by me.

Leader: When the hosts of hell assail, And my strength begins to fail, Thou who never lost a battle,

All: Stand by me.

III.

Leader: In the midst of faults and failures,

All: Stand by me.

Leader: In the midst of faults and failures,

All: Stand by me.

Leader: When I do the best I can, And my friends misunderstand, Thou who knowest all about me,

All: Stand by me.

IV.

Leader: In the midst of persecution,

All: Stand by me.

Leader: In the midst of persecution,

All: Stand by me.

Leader: When my foes in battle array, Undertake to stop my way, Thou who saved Paul and Silas,

All: Stand by me.

V.

Leader: When I'm growing old and feeble,

All: Stand by me.

Leader: When I'm growing old and feeble,

All: Stand by me.

Leader: When my life becomes a burden, And I'm nearing chilly Jordan, O Thou "Lily of the Valley,"

All: Stand by me.

VI.

Leader: When the storms of life are raging,

All: Stand by me.

Leader: When the storms of life are raging,

All: Stand by me.

Leader: When the world is tossing me, Like a ship upon the sea; Thou who rulest wind and water,

All: Stand by me.

BIBLE READING   Mark 6:7, 12–13; Jas. 5:13–15; 2 Cor. 1:3–5

FREE PRAYERS FOR THOSE WHO ARE SUFFERING

BLESSING THE OIL
(Holding up a bowl of olive or other oil, the leader asks God's blessing with these or similar words:)

> **Leader:** Healing God, giver of life and health: bless this oil, so that, just as your apostles anointed those who suffered, may we who receive this oil gain comfort and peace. Send your Holy Spirit to us here that we may feel your healing power.

> **All: So be it! Amen.**

ANOINTING WITH OIL

(The leader will be seated and start the circle of healing. The leader will put a thumb in the oil and wait for a signal whether to put the oil on the forehead or hand of the person in the next seat.

When the signal is given, the healer will make a sign of the cross on the head or hand while saying words of comfort. The words used by the healer will depend on the circumstances. They may be as simple as, "God bless and heal you," or perhaps, "May God give you the courage to face whatever suffering may come in your life." The person being signed will respond, "Amen," or, "Thanks be to God."

The one who has received the sign will take the bowl of oil and repeat the process until all have received a blessing. The leader who began the anointing will be the last one to be signed and will then replace the bowl on the table.)

PSALM 23

CLOSING PRAYER

> **Leader:** Our study is now over. We pray that the powerful and almighty God, who wraps, clasps and encloses us all around so as to never leave us; will grant us release from suffering, restoration of wholeness, and the gift of inner peace. In the name of Jesus, we pray.

> **All: We say, "Yes to Life!** *Hallelujah Anyhow!* **Amen."**

PRAYING FOR SHALOM[80]
(Reformed Church)

A TIME TO GATHER FOR WORSHIP

PRELUDE   "As the Deer"   arranged by Mark Hayes

MUTUAL CALL TO WORSHIP   #246   MAR!   "As the Deer Pants for the Water"

Greeting from the Lord

Introduction to the Service

A Time to Thank the Lord

Psalm of Thanksgiving   Ps. 121

Hymn   #475   PsH   "Praise, My Soul, the King of Heaven"

A Time to Confess Our Sins

(Although we do not want to convey that specific illness or distress in our families is related to specific sins, we do want to acknowledge that there is a general relationship between sin and the suffering of humankind. We also follow the directive of James 5:15–16.)

Psalm of Confession   Ps. 51:1–12

Hymn   #257   PsH   "O Christ, the Lamb of God"

Affirmation of Our Faith   Rom. 8:38–39

A Time to Listen to God's Word
(The Scripture readings may be read alternately by a woman and a man.)

Scripture   Jer. 17:7, 8, 14; Phil. 4:5–7; James 5:13–16; Mark 10:13–16

Meditation   "Brokenness . . . Prayer . . . Wholeness"
(The Meditation includes the following brief comment on the "laying-on of hands"—not a customary ritual in our congregation:)

In Scripture the placing of hands on someone's head occurs at times of special importance. Jesus and the apostles often place their hands on people as a sign of healing. For example, in Acts 28 Paul heals someone from fever by "praying and putting his hands on the man" (Acts 28:8). At other times the placing of hands suggests a more general giving of God's blessing. You recall in Genesis 48 when Grandpa Jacob blesses his grandsons, he places his hand on their heads and says these wonderful words: "Bless the God who has been my shepherd, bless these boys" (Gen. 48:15–16).

And that reminds us of the Good Shepherd, Jesus himself. We just heard about those busybody disciples who protested that Jesus was too busy with important grown-ups and couldn't be bothered with little kids. Then we hear those grace-filled words of Jesus: "Hey, don't keep the children from coming to me." And then "Jesus took the children in his arms, laid his hands on them, and blessed them."

In our worship, what does it mean when pastors raise their hands over the congregation and say, "The Lord bless you and keep you?" The pastor calls for, assures, declares, proclaims, bestows—no one word quite captures it—the powerful love and the loving power of God on his people.

What does it mean when we put our hands on a person's head during prayer? First, it helps us, as God's people, literally to be in touch with each other. We are, all of us together, called the "body of Christ," and one way to experience that is to be in bodily contact. Second, Peter calls all of us a "royal priesthood" (1 Pet. 1:9). When we pray with and for each other, especially in the context of worship, we also assure each other and proclaim to each other that the Lord will bless us and keep us, make his face to shine on us, and grant us his peace. The laying on of hands symbolizes the healing, restoring power of God in our lives.

HYMN   #450   W&R   "Be Still and Know That I Am God"

A TIME TO PRAY

Jesus says: "Come to me, all who are weary and whose load is heavy, and I will give you rest."

(Prayers for physical healing, emotional and spiritual restoration, and family relations are offered. The worship leader says something like the following: "After a period of communal prayer, we will continue with silent prayer. The silent prayer will begin and conclude with the singing of 'Jesus, Remember Me.' Those who wish to pray with a prayer team are invited to come forward during this time."

   Three prayer teams [a pastor or elder and a deacon; one man and one woman for each team] stand at the front of the sanctuary. Some people come forward individually, some as families. We listen to them, put our hands on their heads or shoulders, and begin the prayer with these [or similar] words:)

We lay our hands on you in the name of our Lord Jesus Christ. May God grant you the healing presence of the Holy Spirit, releasing you from suffering (*or:* granting you his peace) and restoring you to wholeness.

(We then continue with prayer for the particular need in their lives.)

(Some churches sing during the time people come forward, giving the congregation also the role of prayer in a communal way while the groups at the front bring their prayers to the Lord privately. Most hymnals have listings in their topical index under "Healing.")

A TIME TO RESPOND IN GRATITUDE

PSALM OF THANKSGIVING   Ps. 103:1–5

HYMN   #30   PsH   "I Worship You, O Lord"
         stanzas 1, 2, 5: *congregation*
         stanzas 3, 4: *solo*

OFFERING

MUSICAL OFFERING   "O Christ, the Lamb of God"   J. S. Bach

HYMN   #634   PsH   "Father, We Love You"

GOD'S BLESSING

POSTLUDE   "He Is Lord"   Hayes

"Perfect love drives out all fear."
(1 John 4:18)

Chapter 8

Deliverance

INTRODUCTION

For many, deliverance ministries have been greatly misunderstood and too often wrongly used. In my book *The Healing Church*, I discuss the very rare circumstances when they are appropriate, as well as the specific guidelines for the rite of exorcism both of places and people.[1] The most extensive practice and writing on this has been done by Roman Catholics, Episcopalians, Anglicans, and Pentecostal/Charismatic groups. Historically, from New Testament times to the Reformation, exorcisms were regularly practiced, and in the early church they were considered the most important aspect of the healing ministry.

The ministry of deliverance should be seen as an authentic part of the liturgical health ministry. However, it should be limited to very *rare* situations, which are assessed by mature pastors under strict guidelines. The decision to do an exorcism should always be done in consultation with medical professionals and as a treatment of last resort. It should not be used as a substitute for treatment by mental health practitioners. It should never be practiced by solo ministers but with clergy trained in exorcism who are connected with a congregation. An exorcism should not be part of a public healing service.

In the twentieth century, the practice of exorcism has been mainly among Pentecostal and Charismatic groups under the name of the ministry of deliverance. "Their theology is based on being Spirit filled. This can happen only by a total deliverance from spirits that oppress or possess. Although we applaud the centrality of the Holy Spirit in their theology, historical safeguards against the possible abuses of a deliverance ministry may be absent."[2] Some hold a somewhat uncritical view of demon possession. They may not acknowledge the psychological explanations regarding spirits and possession. "If people are possessed, what exactly is possessing them? Are there evil spirit entities from outside that infect people, or are they deep, unhealed areas of the unconscious that manifest in strange ways?"[3]

Obviously, this entire subject is extremely controversial. "In a survey last year by the Mental Health Foundation, entitled 'Spirituality and Mental Health: Voices and Realities,' several respondents said they had been damaged by exorcism."[4] The idea of demonic possession can be extremely damaging when applied to the mentally ill and falsely link evil and ill health. The Rev. Stephen Parsons, author of *Ungodly Fear: Fundamentalist Christianity and the Abuse of Power*, said, "The charismatic movement wants to demonize mental illness so they can deal with it through exorcism."[5] He even asserts this in itself can become a form of abuse.

John Richards, in his helpful book *But Deliver Us from Evil,* observes that in the early and

435

patristic church, the casting out of demons was God's work through the church and a sign of the coming of Christ's kingdom, the doing of Christ's will, and the deliverance from evil for which every faithful person prays; it is God's action, not ours, because the kingdom, the power and the glory belong to God, not to us. The words of exorcism generally include the commands to the demon(s) to harm no one, to come out, and to go somewhere else, Richards adds.[6]

As I discuss in *The Healing Church,* "some practitioners of deliverance describe a three-fold movement of the stages of demonic control: (1) *oppression* occurs in the realm of the mind, where people are influenced to disbelieve God's Word and live worldly lives (Eph. 2:1–3); (2) *obsession* develops when Satan draws a person into deeper subjection—the person no longer desires freedom; and (3) *possession* takes place when Satan has assumed control over one or more areas of a person's body, mind, or spirit. Various orders of demons and personality disturbances and physical illnesses are associated with possession, among them: blindness, deafness, deception, seduction, jealousy, lies, insanity, addictions, and cancers. Indeed the harboring of wrong attitudes—anger, bitterness, hatred, and/or unforgiveness—opens a person to oppression if not possession by a controlling spirit."[7]

CONTEMPORARY VIEWS OF DEMON POSSESSION

Michael Welker, professor of systematic theology at the University of Heidelberg, Germany, argues that demon possession is real, not some antiquated science articulated by writers of the Christian Scriptures. "Are not demons products of unbelief and superstition who in the sober, realistic, enlightened, scientific view of the world disappear like fog in the sunlight?" Welker asks.[8] His response is an emphatic no. Where we find "stabilized and stubbornly defended" suffering in the world today, we find demon possession. Their names might be different from those we encounter in the accounts of Mark 1:26; 9:17–18; and Luke 4:35. In the twentieth century, Welker says, we might recognize demon possession in addiction, greed, ecological ruin, and the debt politics of developing nations. Jesus Christ, bearer of the Holy Spirit, is the liberator from all distress, captivity, and hopelessness and the restorer of coherent and peaceful ways.

Welker's definition of demon possession for some is too broad. He tends to equate corporate sin and demon possession and collapse the various nuances of related phenomena as described in the Church of England Report. Although we cannot explain away all possession in the Christian Scriptures as simply mental illness, neither can we automatically label various manifestations of sin as demon possession.[9] Discernment is essential to determine which cases are demon possession and which are mental illness.[10]

CHURCH OF ENGLAND REPORT

Exorcisms in the Church of England, dating back to 1604, could be performed by priests only with the permission of the diocesan bishop.[11] This type of safeguard and its practice should be adapted to the polity and structure of all denominations. The Church of England has recognized the continued need for exorcisms but mainly has approached previously diagnosed cases in former times as mental illness rather than possession. *A Time to Heal* includes the recent report of the Church of England by a committee on healing ministry chaired by Michael Perry, which contains a discussion of demon possession. Interestingly enough, the *Book of Common Prayer* of the Church of England does not include a rite of exorcism, and the Study Group of the Church of Wales on deliverance ministries did not want their rite reproduced. There is great fear of abuse among most Protestant groups. The rite included here is from the Orthodox Church, which since early Christianity has recognized the place of exorcism as part of the church's healing ministry. One of the best resources on the subject of exorcism was another report prepared by the Church of England's Christian Exorcism Study Group in 1972 (known as the Exeter Report), which can help all churches better understand this phenomenon.

The study group offered guidelines for counselors who are faced with a specific case of suspected possession or satanic involvement. The report highlights various important elements: the interview; diagnosis; preparatory prayer; consultation with the bishop and the medical profession. It states that this ministry must be firmly under the discipline of the church.[12]

The assessment/diagnosis of the particular person's condition may determine that ordinary counseling and psychiatric treatments may suffice without the need for exorcism. Training of specific clergy to discern if possession is present is crucial to avoid the particular dangers of abuse. Clergy working in pairs may be central to assisting in discernment.[13]

The study group also emphasized the importance of understanding phenomena that are related but different from exorcism. "Possession may be a case of psychological projection. It may be the natural defenses of the ego against anxiety, conflict, and guilt. These emotions must be eliminated in the ill person before a pastor attempts to practice an exorcism. There are, of course, a wide range of neurotic and personality disorders, including schizophrenia, which have in the past been confused with demon possession."[14]

As part of the Roman Catholic rubrics on exorcism, it is emphasized that "a priest—one who is expressly and in special wise authorized by the Ordinary—when he intends to perform an exorcism over persons tormented by the devil, must be properly distinguished for his piety, prudence, and integrity of life."[15] In addition, he is required to undergo extensive study and research on these matters so as not to be misled.[16] He needs spiritual wisdom and discernment as to both the person's and the evil spirit's ability to deceive.[17] He must lead the service of exorcism "in a commanding and authoritative voice, and at the same time with great confidence, humility, and fervor."[18]

EXORCISMS OF PLACES AND INSTITUTIONS (SOCIAL EXORCISMS)

"An interesting category of exorcism that recently has been documented in various books on the healing ministry is [an] exorcism performed on social institutions and buildings. There is a deep need for the healing of social institutions, families, congregations, and nations. The word in the Hebrew Scriptures for healing, *shalom*, connotes this social dimension since it defines health and wholeness in communal terms. The Church of England in the previously mentioned study also cites exorcisms of buildings."[19] The reader will note that this chapter includes "Cleansing of a House," which is not strictly an exorcism, as presented here, but acknowledges that a sense of foreboding and evil may pervade a place after wrongdoings have transpired. The report of the bishop of Exeter's commission included the infestation of places as a distinct and serious possibility. Such places include churches, houses, towns, even the countryside, influenced by a variety of causes.

EXORCISM[20]
(Antiochian Orthodox)[21]

(This litany is to be used only with trained clergy. At least three priests should participate if possible.)

Priest: Blessed is our God, always, now and ever and unto ages of ages.

People: **Amen. Glory to You, O Lord. Glory to You.**

Priest: O Heavenly King, O Comforter, the Spirit of truth, Who are in all places and fill all things, the Treasure of good things, and Giver of life, come and abide in us, cleanse us from every stain and save our souls, O Good One.

People: **Holy God, Holy Mighty, Holy Immortal, have mercy on us.**

Priest: Glory to the Father and to the Son and to the Holy Spirit, now and ever and unto ages of ages. **Amen.**

People: **Most Holy Trinity, have mercy on us. O Lord, cleanse us from our sins. O Master, pardon our iniquities. O Holy One, visit and heal our infirmities for Your Name's sake.**

Lord, have mercy, Lord, have mercy. Lord, have mercy.

Glory to the Father and to the Son and to the Holy Spirit, now and ever and unto ages of ages. Amen.

Our Father, Who art in heaven, hallowed be Thy Name. Thy Kingdom come, Thy will be done on earth as it is in heaven. Give us this day our daily bread, and forgive us our trespasses as we forgive those who trespass against us. And lead us not into temptation, but deliver us from evil.

Priest: For Thine is the Kingdom and the power and the glory of the Father and of the Son and of the Holy Spirit, now and ever and unto ages of ages.

People: **Amen.**

Cantor: Lord, have mercy. Glory to the Father and to the Son and to the Holy Spirit, now and ever and unto ages of ages. Amen.

CALL TO WORSHIP

People: **O come, let us worship and bow down to God our King.**
O come, let us worship and bow down to Christ, our King and our God.
O come, let us worship and bow down to Christ Himself, our King and our God.

PSALM 121

Cantor: He Who dwells in the secret place . . . Glory to the Father, and to the Son, and to the Holy Spirit, now and ever and unto ages of ages. Amen.

Alleluia, Alleluia, Alleluia. Glory to You, O Lord.

GREAT LITANY
(After each line the people repeat:)

Lord, have mercy. *Ektenia*[22]

Deacon: In peace, let us pray to the Lord.

For the peace from above and for the salvation of our souls, let us pray to the Lord.

For the peace of the whole world, for the stability of the holy churches of God, and for the union of all, let us pray to the Lord.

For this holy house and for all who enter with faith, reverence and the fear of God, let us pray to the Lord.

For our Metropolitan PHILIP,[23] for the honorable priests and deacons in Christ, and for all the clergy and the people, let us pray to the Lord.

For this country and for every authority and power within it, let us pray to the Lord.

For this city, for every city and country and for those who live in them by faith, let us pray to the Lord.

For seasonable weather, for an abundance of the fruits of the earth, and for peaceful times, let us pray to the Lord.

For those who travel by land, air and sea, the sick and suffering, those under persecution and for their deliverance, let us pray to the Lord.

That He will show mercy to His servant*(s),* and pardon *(him, her, them)* every sin, both voluntary and involuntary, let us pray to the Lord.

That from the goodness of His heart, He will have mercy on His servant*(s),* and will pardon *(his, her, their)* every sin which *(he, she, they have)* has committed from *(his, her, their)* youth to this present hour, and grant peace of heart and soul. Accept *(his, her, their)* sacrifice of praise upon Your heavenly altar; protect *(him, her, them)* from all misery, sickness, and affliction; grant *(him, her, them)* health and length of days, we pray You, O Lord, hear us and have mercy.

O merciful Master and lover of mankind, look down upon Your servant*(s)* _____, and hear our prayers which we offer in faith. You Yourself have said, "Whatever you ask in prayer, believe that you receive it, and you will." Because of this, though we are unworthy, we trust in Your mercy. Grant Your blessings to Your servant*(s)* _____, fulfill *(his, her, their)* good intentions, preserve *(him, her, them)* for the rest of *(his, her, their)* days in peace, health and long life; hasten to hear us and have mercy.

For our deliverance from all affliction, anger, danger and need, let us pray to the Lord.

Help us, save us, have mercy on us, and keep us, O God, by Your grace.

Priest: For you are a merciful God and love mankind, and unto You we ascribe glory: to the Father, and to the Son, and to the Holy Spirit, now and ever, and unto ages of ages.

People: Amen.

GOD IS THE LORD   Ps. 117 (118)

Deacon: *(Refrain)* God is the Lord, Who has shown us light. Blessed is He Who comes in the Name of the Lord. O give thanks to the Lord for He is Good, because His mercy endures forever.

People: God is the Lord, Who has shown us light. Blessed is He Who comes in the Name of the Lord.

Deacon: All nations surrounded me, but in the Name of the Lord I will destroy them.

People: God is the Lord, Who has shown us light. Blessed is He Who comes in the Name of the Lord.

Deacon: I shall not die but live, and declare the works of the Lord.

People: God is the Lord, Who has shown us light. Blessed is He Who comes in the Name of the Lord.

Deacon: The stone which the builders rejected has become the chief cornerstone. This was the Lord's doing; it is marvelous in our eyes.

People: God is the Lord, Who has shown us light. Blessed is He Who comes in the Name of the Lord.

GRADUAL   Prokeimenon[24]

Cantor: Teach me the way I should go, for to You I lift up my soul.

People: Teach me the way I should go, for to You I lift up my soul.

Cantor: Deliver me, O Lord, from my enemies, for I have fled to You for refuge!

People: Teach me the way I should go, for to You I lift up my soul.

Cantor: Teach me the way I should go.

People: For to You I lift up my soul.

Deacon: Wisdom!

Reader: The reading from the Acts of the Holy Apostles.

Deacon: Let us attend!

Reader: (Acts 16:16–34)

Priest: Peace be to you who read.

People: **Alleluia, Alleluia, Alleluia.**

Cantor: The steps of a man are guided by the Lord; and He establishes him in whose way he delights.

People: **Alleluia, Alleluia, Alleluia.**

Cantor: Commit your way to the Lord; trust in Him and He will act.

People: **Alleluia, Alleluia, Alleluia.**

THE GOSPEL READING

Deacon: Wisdom! Let us listen to the Holy Gospel.

Priest: Peace be to all.

People: **And to your Spirit.**

Deacon: The Reading from the Holy Gospel according to St. Luke.

People: **Glory to You, O Lord, Glory to You.**

Deacon: Let us attend!

Deacon: *(Read* Luke 9:37–51)

People: **Glory to You, O Lord, Glory to You.**

Deacon: Wisdom! Let us pray to the Lord.

People: **Lord have mercy.**

THE PRAYERS OF EXORCISM
(Choose those appropriate to the situation.)

PRAYERS BY ST. JOHN CHRYSOSTOM

Priest: O Eternal God, Who has redeemed the human race from the captivity of the Devil, deliver Your servant*(s)* _____ from all the workings of unclean spirits. Command the evil and impure spirits and demons to depart from the soul and body of Your servant*(s)* and not to remain nor hide in *(him, her, them).* Let them be banished from this creation of Your hands in Your own holy Name and that of Your only begotten Son, and Your life-giving Spirit; so that, after being cleansed from all demonic influence, *(he, she, they)* may live godly, justly and righteously and may be counted worthy to receive the Holy Mysteries of Your only begotten Son and our God, with Whom You are blessed and glorified, together with Your all-holy and good and life-giving Spirit, now and ever, and unto ages of ages.

People: **Amen.**

Priest: O You Who have rebuked all unclean spirits and by the power of Your word have banished the legion, come now, through Your only-begotten Son, upon this creature, which You have fashioned in Your own image, and deliver *(him, her, them)* from the adversary that holds *(him, her, them)* in bondage, so that, receiving Your mercy and becoming purified, *(he, she, they)* might join the ranks of Your holy flock and be preserved as a living temple of the Holy Spirit and might receive the Divine and Holy Mysteries, through the grace and compassion and loving kindness of Your only begotten Son, with Whom You are blessed, together with Your all-holy and good and life-giving Spirit, now and ever, and unto ages of ages.

People: **Amen.**

Priest: We beseech You, Lord, Almighty God, Most High, untempted, peaceful King. We beseech You Who have created heaven and earth, for out of You have issued forth the Alpha and the Omega, the beginning and the end; You Who have ordained that the four-footed and irrational beasts be under subjection to humanity, for You have so subjected them. Lord, stretch forth Your mighty hand and Your majestic and holy arm, and in Your watchful care look down upon this Your creature, and send down upon *(him, her, them)* a peaceful angel, a mighty angel, a guardian of soul and body that will rebuke and drive away every evil and unclean demon from *(him, her, them)*; for You alone are Lord Most High, Almighty and Blessed, unto ages of ages.

People: **Amen.**

Priest #1: We make this divine, holy, and awesome invocation and plea, O Devil, for your expulsion, as well as this rebuke for your utter annihilation, O Apostate!

God Who is holy, without beginning, frightful, invisible in essence, infinite in power, and incomprehensible in divinity, the King of Glory and Lord Almighty—He shall rebuke you, Devil! He Who composed all things well by His word from nothingness into being; He Who walks upon the wings of the air.

Priest #2: The Lord rebukes you, Devil!—He Who calls forth the water of the sea and pours it upon the face of all the earth. Lord of Hosts is His Name. O Devil, the Lord rebukes you! He Who is ministered and praised by numberless heavenly orders and adored and glorified in fear by multitudes of angelic and archangelic hosts. O Satan, the Lord rebukes you! He Who is honored by the encircling Powers, the awesome six-winged and many-eyed Cherubim and Seraphim that cover their faces with two wings because of His inscrutable and unseen divinity; and with two wings cover their feet, lest they be seared by His inutterable glory and incomprehensible majesty; and with two wings do fly and fill the heavens with their shouts of "Holy, holy, holy, Lord Sabaoth, heaven and earth are full of Your glory!"

Priest #3: O Devil, the Lord rebukes you! He Who came down from the Father's bosom and through the holy, indescribable, pure, and worthy of all worship,

Incarnation from the Virgin, appeared ineffably in the world to save it and cast you down from heaven in His authoritative power, displaying you as an outcast before all people.

Priest #1: O Satan, the Lord rebukes you! He Who said to the sea, "Be silent, be still!" instantly calming it by His command. O Devil, The Lord rebukes you! He Who made clay with His immaculate spittle and refashioned the deficient member of the man born blind from birth and gave him his sight.

Priest #2: O Devil, the Lord rebukes you! He Who by His works restored to life the daughter of the ruler of the synagogue and snatched the son of the widow out of the mouth of death and gave him whole and sound to his own mother. O Devil, the Lord rebukes you! The Lord Who raised Lazarus from the dead, undecayed, as having not died, and unblemished to the astonishment of many.

Priest #3: O Satan, the Lord rebukes you! He Who destroyed the curse by the blow on the face and by the lance in His immaculate side lifted the flaming sword that guarded Paradise. O Devil, the Lord rebukes you! He Who dried all tears from every face by the spitting upon His precious expressed image. O Devil, the Lord rebukes you! He Who set His Cross as a support, the salvation of the world, to your fall and the fall of all the angels under you.

Priest #1: O Devil, the Lord rebukes you! He Who placed a voice in His Cross and the curtain was torn in two and the rocks were split and the tombs were opened and those who were dead from the ages were raised up. O Devil, the Lord rebukes you! He Who by death put death to death, and by His resurrection granted life to all the human race.

Priest #2: May the Lord rebuke you, O Satan!—that is, He Who descended into hell and cast off its chains and set free those held prisoner in it, calling them to Himself; before Whom the gatekeepers of hell shuddered when they saw Him, and hiding themselves, vanished in the anguish of hell. May the Lord rebuke you, O Devil!—that is, Christ our God Who arose from the dead and granted His Resurrection to all humanity.

Priest #3: May the Lord rebuke you, O Satan!—He Who in glory ascended into heaven to His Father, sitting on the right hand of majesty upon the throne of glory. O Devil, may the Lord rebuke you! He Who shall come again with glory upon the clouds of heaven with His holy angels to judge the living and the dead. O Devil, may the Lord rebuke you! He Who has prepared for you the unquenchable fire, the unsleeping worm and the outer darkness unto eternal punishment.

Priest #1: O Devil, may the Lord rebuke you! For before Him all things shudder and tremble from the face of His power and the wrath of His warning upon you is uncontainable. O Satan, the Lord rebukes you by His frightful Name!

Shudder, tremble, be afraid, depart, be utterly destroyed, be banished! You who fell from heaven and, together with all of you, all evil spirits: every evil spirit of lust, the spirit of evil, a day and nocturnal spirit, a noonday and evening spirit, a midnight spirit, an imaginative spirit, an encountering spirit, either of the dry land or of the water, or one in a forest, or among the reeds, or in trenches, or in a road or a crossroad, in lakes, or streams, in houses, or one sprinkling in the baths and chambers, or one altering the mind of man.

Depart swiftly from this creature of the Creator Christ our God! And be gone from the servant(*s*) of God _____, from *(his, her, their)* mind, from *(his, her, their)* soul, from *(his, her, their)* heart, from *(his, her, their)* reins, from *(his, her, their)* senses, from all *(his, her, their)* members that *(he, she, they)* might become whole and sound and free, knowing God, *(his, her, their)* own Master and Creator of all things, He Who gathers together those who have gone astray and Who gives them the seal of salvation through the rebirth and restoration of divine baptism, so that *(he, she, they)* may be counted worthy of His immaculate, heavenly, and awesome Mysteries, and be united to His true fold, dwelling in a place of pasture and nourished on the waters of repose, guided pastorally and safely by the staff of the Cross, unto the forgiveness of sins and life everlasting.

For unto Him belong all glory, honor, adoration and majesty, together with His beginningless Father, and His all-holy, good and life-giving Spirit, now and ever, and unto ages of ages.

People: Amen.

PRAYERS BY ST. BASIL THE GREAT

Priest #1: O God of gods and Lord of lords, Creator of the flaming ranks and all the bodiless powers, Maker of all things heavenly and earthly, Whom no man has seen nor is able to see, before Whom all creation trembles and fears, Who casts down to earth that archangel who became haughty and because of disobedience forfeited his function, together with all the angels that fell away with him, becoming demons; Who hurled them down into the darkness of the abyss of Tartarus:[25] Grant that this deliverance which is being carried out in Your awesome Name, become efficacious, bringing fear to the leader of evil and all his ranks which have fallen with him from the light-bearing heights; and drive him into banishment and command him and his demons to utterly depart, so that no harm might be worked against Your sealed image. But let those who are sealed receive strength to tread upon serpents and scorpions and upon all the power of the enemy. For Your all-holy Name is praised and magnified and glorified by all breath, the Name of the Father, and of the Son, and of the Holy Spirit, now and ever, and unto ages of ages.

People: Amen.

Priest #2: I command you, the beginner of sin and blasphemy, the leader of rebellion and worker of evil! I command you who were thrown out from the light-bearing heavens and were cast down into the darkness of the abyss because of arrogance. I command you and all the fallen powers that follow your design! I command you, unclean spirit, by God Sabaoth and by all the ranks of the angels of God, Adonai, Elohim, Almighty God! Come out and depart from the servant of God!

Priest #3:   I command you by God! Who created all things through His word and by our Lord Jesus Christ, His only begotten Son, generated before all ages ineffably and dispassionately; Who created the visible and invisible creation and Who fashioned mankind in His own image; Who tutored humanity initially through natural means, and Who protected him by the watchful care of the angels.

Priest #1:   I command you by God! Who from on high flooded sin by water and Who opened the depths of heaven and destroyed the iniquitous giants and shook the tower of the ungodly and reduced the land of Sodom and Gomorrah to ashes by fire and brimstone, where the unending smoke is emitted as perpetual testimony; Who tore the sea asunder with a rod and led the people on dry land and Who destroyed in the waves of the water forever Pharaoh the tyrant and the God-fighting army and enmity of ungodliness; Who in the last days became Incarnate ineffably from the pure Virgin and preserved intact the seal of purity; Who was pleased to wash away in baptism our ancient uncleanness which we had embraced by disobedience.

Priest #2:   I command you by Jesus Christ! Who was baptized in the Jordan and became a type of incorruptibility by grace in water—and before Whom angels and all the powers of heaven stood astonished, beholding incarnate God moderated, for the beginningless Father revealed the beginningless generation of the Son and the descent of the Holy Spirit testified to the unity of the Trinity.

Priest #3:   I command you by Jesus Christ! Who rebuked the wind and calmed the waves of the sea; Who banished the array of demons and ordered the pupils of the eyes, missing from the womb, to be restored to sight by means of clay; Who renewed the ancient creation of our race and restored speech to the dumb and cleansed the sores of leprosy and raised the dead from the graves; Who held converse with humanity to the moment of the grace and Who by His resurrection destroyed hell, and Who made all humanity imperishable by His death.

Priest #1:   I command you by God Pantocreator! Who infused His Spirit into humanity by God-inspired voice, and Who acted with the apostles and filled the world with godliness.

Fear! Flee! Be banished! Depart, unclean and abominable demon! Infernal, abysmal, deceptive, shapeless, visible because of your shamelessness, invisible because of your hypocrisy—wherever you are, to leave or to exit if you are the same Beelzebub, a demon that shakes, or one that is dragon-like, or one with a face of a beast, or one as a vapor or appearing as smoke, or as a male or as a female, or as a creeping thing, or appearing as a fowl, or as one speaking by night, or one that is deaf or dumb, or as one that frightens by invasion or that convulses or attacks or exists in deep slumber or in sickness or in disease or rolling about in laughter, or inciting sensuous tears, or as a lewd spirit or a foul-smelling, or covetous, or lustful, or sorcerous, or erotic, or horoscopic, or dwelling in a house, or one that is shameless, or contentious, or unstable, or changing according to the phases of the moon or one that flees at a certain time, or a morning one, or one of an unseasonable time, or of the dawn or one instantaneously encountered, or if you were sent by someone, or if you approached unawares, or one in the sea or in a stream or out of the earth or out of a well or steep bank or a trench, or a lake or a reed bed or out of matter or an unclean thing, or out of a forest or oak-coppice or a tree or out of a bird or thunder or out of a bath chamber or out of a font of water or from a phantom tomb or from where we know not, either known or unknown, and from an unthought of place.

Priest #2: Be divided and removed! Be repelled by the image created and fashioned by the hand of God! Fear the likeness of the incarnate God and hide not in the servant*(s)* of God _____! For a rod of iron and furnace of fire and Tartarus and the grinding of teeth and the recompense of disobedience await you.

Priest #3: Return not, neither hide with any other evil and unclean spirit! But rather depart to the region which is waterless, desolate, uncultivated, and which no man inhabits, and where God alone watches over and binds all those that perpetrate the spell of the evil eye and assault His image; who with the chains of darkness banished, to Tartarus to a long night and day, you, the Devil, the skillful worker and contriver of all evil! For great is the fear of God and great is the glory of the Father and of the Son and of the Holy Spirit.

People: Amen.

(With the following prayers, the priest should anoint the afflicted person[s] with oil.)

Priest #1: O God of Heaven! God of lights! God of the angels that are under Your dominion, God of archangels that are under Your power, God of the glorious principalities, God of the saints, the Father of our Lord Jesus Christ, You Who loosed the souls that were bound by death; Who by Your only begotten Son illuminated humanity, which was in darkness; You Who set us free from our pains and released us from every burden; Who kept every assault of the enemy away from us.

Priest #2: And You, Son and Logos of God, Who have made us immortal by Your own glory; Who by Your resurrection have granted humanity to advance to God; You Who by Your Cross carried every bond of our sins; Who took on and healed our offense; You Who put us on the way to Heaven, Lord, and changed corruption into incorruptibility:

Hearken to me as I cry out to You in desire and fear, O Lord, before Whom the mountains melt from fright under the heavens and the firmament; before Whom the speechless souls of the elements shudder because of Your power, observing their own bounds; by Whom the fire of revenge does not exceed the bounds ordained for it but rather awaits Your will with groans; for Whom all creation travails, groaning in unutterable sighs and is ordered to await the seasons; from Whom all of nature flees away; and through Whom the army of the enemy has been subdued and the Devil has fallen and the serpent trampled upon and the dragon is destroyed; through Whom the nations which confess You have been illuminated and in You have been made mighty, O Lord; through Whom life has appeared, hope is established, faith is made strong, the Gospel has been preached; through Whom human-ity has been refashioned from the earth, having believed upon You. For Who is there like You, God Almighty?

Priest #3: Therefore we pray to You, God of our fathers and Lord of mercy, eternal and superessential! Receive *(him, her, them)* who has *(have)* come to You in Your holy Name and that of Your beloved child, Jesus Christ, and of Your holy and almighty and life-giving Spirit.

Priest #1: Expel from *(his, her, their)* soul every sickness, every unbelief, every unclean spirit that is convulsive, infernal, flaming, foul-smelling, covetous, greedy, avaricious, fornicating, tempestuous, every unclean demon that is dark, shapeless and shameless! Yes, God, take away from Your servant _____ every working of the Devil, all sorcery, witchcraft, drug-addiction, idolatry, astrology, horoscopy, necromancy, orneoscopy, divination, passion for pleasure, eros, avarice, wrath, contentiousness, instability and every evil fancy.

Priest #2: Yes, Lord our God, breathe into *(him, her, them)* Your peaceful Spirit, so that, being protected by You, *(he, she, they)* might bring forth the fruit of faith, virtue, wisdom, purity, continence, love, kindness, a sound mind, pru-dence, for Your servant*(s)* has *(have)* called upon You in the Name of Jesus Christ, believing in the consubstantial Trinity, with the angels as witnesses, as well as the archangels and the glorious principalities and every heavenly host. Together with *(him, her, them)* protect also our own hearts, for You are mighty, O Lord, and to You we offer glory to the Father, and to the Son, and to the Holy Spirit, now and ever, and unto ages of ages.

People: **Amen.**

Priest: O most pure Mother of God, save us.

People: **Lady worthy of all honor,
More than all the Cherubim,
Glorious beyond all measure,
More than all the Seraphim.
Birth you gave without defilement,**

> **To God's only Son the Word,**
> **Mother of our God most blessed,**
> **May our song to you be heard.**

Priest: Glory to You, O Christ our God and our hope, glory to You!

People: **Glory to the Father, and to the Son, and to the Holy Spirit, now and ever and unto ages of ages. Amen. Lord have mercy, Lord have mercy, Lord have mercy. Father, bless.**

(The priest gives the dismissal of the day, after which he offers the precious cross to the one[s] exorcised to kiss, and sprinkles them with holy water, saying:)

Priest: May the Lord bless you from Zion, granting you freedom from all evil spirits, to the glory of His Holy Name.

People: **Amen.**

CLEANSING OF A HOUSE[26]
(Nondenominational)

Occasion: After an intrusion, robbery, assault or other invasion
Location: The home of the assaulted individual

GATHERING

This ritual we will call a house cleansing. The occasion is the sexual assault and robbery of *(name)* in this the home of *(name)* and *(spouse)*. May God grant them safety and heal them of their wounds.

In this ritual we intend symbolically to strengthen the boundaries of this home, spiritually to cleanse its physical spaces, and to affirm that we are a community that gathers in joy and sorrow.

Let us pray: Spirit of Christ, turn our actions this evening into holy acts of healing and affirmation. Grant to us a sense of strength and connection. We ask for and acknowledge your presence as we face these wounds and fears. **Amen.**

NAMING

Let us begin with a brief time of naming our hopes, fears, strengths and injuries. You may do this silently or audibly.

ANOINTING THE PASSAGES

We now recognize the passageways in this home. I invite the gathered community to smear a small quantity of oil on the lintels, or doorframes, of the passageways in the living room, dining room and kitchen, where the assault took place. The litany for this action will be: "With this oil we pray for safety." I invite *(name)* to lead us.

WATER FOR THE PLACES OF STRUGGLE

We now recognize the places of struggle during the assault on our *(sister) (name)*. I invite the gathered community to sprinkle a small quantity of water on the places of struggle, with this litany: "With this water we pray for cleansing." Again, I invite *(name)* to lead us.

(Following the cleansing:) (name) and *(spouse),* we present you with this vessel as a reminder of this ritual and a sign of this community's continuous presence with you.

PRAYERS

Let us now enter into a time of prayer for *(name), (name),* and all that we are and bring to this moment. You may pray silently or audibly.

HYMN   #630   W&R   "Healer of Our Every Ill"

COMMUNION

As a concluding act of affirmation, let us share together in communion, a sign that what is broken becomes a new creation, a sign that we are not alone but rather live in community, a sign that the Spirit of Christ overflows with love for us. I will set out the juice. You may offer bread to each other as many times as you like, and dip it in the juice as seems appropriate.

LITANY

> **Group 1:** We believe that beyond the violence,
>
> **Group 2:** there can be love;
>
> **Group 1:** That beyond the despair,
>
> **Group 2:** there can be hope;
>
> **Group 1:** That beyond the torment,
>
> **Group 2:** we will find rest;
>
> **Group 1:** That beyond our brokenness,
>
> **Group 2:** there can be healing;
>
> **Group 1:** That beyond our agony,
>
> **Group 2:** we will find joy.
>
> **All: Oh, God, transform our disbelief and gently carry us from darkness to light.**[27]

CLOSING BLESSINGS

"Praise the Lord!"
(Ps. 150:1)

Conclusion

It is my hope that as the reader has studied and used these liturgies, an understanding of the depth and breadth of human need is present, as well as of the ways that pastoral care through worship is possible. I hope too that an appreciation of various Christian traditions may lead to the use of liturgies different from those of one's own denomination. While the language may be strange, it is often in fresh voices that God speaks to us—God's Spirit is never confined to our particular theologies.

May this book raise awareness of our need for God in all seasons of life—as the hymn proclaims, "God of the Changing Years." God is always present with us. However, liturgy, as the word suggests, should be the work of the people. Worship and pastoral care, worship and education, worship and support, advocacy for the weak and marginalized, and worship and concrete acts of mercy must go together. Go forth and claim God's power and healing—*shalom*—in your life and in the lives of others.

Appendixes

Appendix A
Healing Centers

There are a number of healing centers that provide resources for those who want to create their own healing liturgies or participate in healing services. A few of these retreat and spiritual centers, whose creativity and deep Christian faith bring much to the worship experience, are listed below. I have spent time at Burrswood, Taizé, Iona, and the Institute for Christian Renewal and found their ministry a blessing.

BURRSWOOD HEALING CENTER[1]

Burrswood Christian Centre for Healthcare and Ministry
Burrswood
Groombridge
Tunbridge Wells
Kent
TN3 9PY
England
Tel: 01892 863637
www.burrswood.org.uk

Burrswood is a Christian Centre for Health Care and Ministry where people go to find healing through skilled nursing, medical expertise, counseling, and prayer. Set in a beautiful place, it offers a peaceful environment ideal for healing and regeneration. The community of Burrswood, with its individual gifts and abilities, is committed to bringing together mainstream medicine and Christianity. Burrswood seeks to keep the love of Christ at the heart of care and to be a sign of the kingdom of God to a hurting world. It appeals to people of all Christian traditions or none.

Founded by the late Dorothy Kerin in 1948, Burrswood welcomes short-stay patients or guests, visitors to their healing services, and outpatient care. Burrswood gives care, time, love, and respect to every individual in order to discover her or his specific needs and to develop an appropriate path toward healing and peace. Miraculously cured from tubercular meningitis and peritonitis at the age of twenty-two, Dorothy Kerin founded the center in obedience to a vision to "heal the sick, comfort the sorrowing, and give faith to the faithless." Burrswood is intent on interpreting and fulfilling that call in a way that fully respects the integrity of each person. At the same time, it seeks to be dynamic in meeting human suffering with the spiritual resources properly available within the Christian setting.

At the heart of Burrswood's work is the full recognition of the influence of the spiritual upon the well-being of an individual. It combines modern medical facilities with Christian healing ministry to care for the "whole" person—body, mind, and spirit. Burrswood's basic belief is that God works through both medicine and love to achieve God's purposes, so ultimately all true wholeness comes from God, through Jesus Christ.

To treat the fullness of need, Burrswood's hospital team—medical and nursing staff, counselors, chaplains, and therapists—work in close and confidential harmony. Supervised and professional pastoral care and spiritual ministry is available to all who stay in the hospital and guest house. Attentive listening and prayer, often with laying-on of hands, sacramental anointing, Holy Communion, or the ministry of reconciliation, are offered personally. Frequently ministry is shared with the doctor, counselor, or nurse.

In the Church of Christ the Healer, an Italianate building, the reverent public healing services are available to patients, guests, and the working community. A daily Eucharist using Church of England liturgies and varied forms of evening worship complete rich worship possibilities, including the ministry of laying-on hands. Burrswood is in the hands of the Dorothy Kerin Trust, an Anglican foundation, of which the Archbishop of Canterbury is one of the patrons. The bishop of Chelmsford is chairman of the Trust, and the bishop of Rochester is Episcopal visitor.

COMMUNITY OF LIFE[2]

Sisters of Life
198 Hollywood Ave.
Bronx, NY 10465-3350
Tel: 718-863-2264
www.sistersoflife.org

The Sisters of Life is a contemplative/active religious community in the Bronx founded in June 1991 by John Cardinal O'Connor, Archbishop of New York. Prayer for six hours a day is the basis of the Sisters of Life; works and community life flow from "the central act of our faith, the Holy Sacrifice of the Mass." The sisters are dedicated to protecting human life and advancing a sense of the sacredness of all human life beginning with the infant in the womb. Their work includes daylong healing services at the Bronx convent, for both women who have had an abortion, and men who also are wounded by the loss. In addition, the sisters have opened another convent in Manhattan where women who are unexpectedly pregnant can live with the sisters in community in order to gain spiritual guidance and be materially supported while they struggle through their difficulties.

The daylong healing service for abortion begins with silent prayer in the convent chapel. At the morning worship service that follows, a lay leader shares her personal experience with abortion, how it affected her life, and how she was healed. Participants then retire to the comfortable living room of the convent, where they may share their own stories with each other .

A priest is available to hear Confession before the afternoon Mass in the convent chapel.

Women are invited to name their unborn babies and to dedicate their children to the Mass by offering a rose, that is provided, before the altar.

The atmosphere at the convent is relaxed and supportive, with a break for lunch. At any point during the day a woman may leave to talk individually with a sister or be by herself. A booklet of meditations is given to women to read silently when they wish from 1 John 1:5–2:2; Ps. 51:3–4, 5–6, 12–13, 14, 17; Luke 7:36–50; and Luke 15:1–3, 11–32. Included also is Pope John Paul II's pastoral word to women who have had an abortion.

THE INSTITUTE FOR CHRISTIAN RENEWAL (ICR)[3]

148 Plaistow Road
Plaistow, NH 03865
Tel: 603-382-0273
http://netministries.org/churches/ch00682/ICR.htm

In the late 1970s, a number of young clergy, active in charismatic renewal, saw the need for presenting a balanced approach to the integrating of renewal experiences with the liturgical/sacramental, theological and ethical/social aspects of the Christian faith. Teaching and training seminars were initiated in several locations in Massachusetts in 1979, and ICR was incorporated in 1980. The healing ministry became a major focus of ICR in the mid-1980s.

In 1990, Canon Mark Pearson and Dr. Mary Pearson visited the healing homes in England. Their experience reaffirmed an earlier call to establish such a healing center in the United States. Their vision was to combine medicine, pastoral counseling and psychotherapy to treat the whole person: body, soul and spirit. They established the New Healing Creation Center which was incorporated in 1994 which complements the work of ICR. It was dedicated to Christ-centered ministries of Scriptural and theological teaching and spiritual and physical healing. ICR is the primary teaching component, providing programs, conferences and spiritual retreats for individuals and groups. Primary emphasis is placed on the church's healing ministry. It is interdenominational and receives support from churches and individuals throughout the U.S. and Canada. ICR conferences, programs and training events are conducted at the Center in Plaistow, New Hampshire, and other sites throughout the United States, Canada and England. (Additional property is being purchased in 2003 to expand and relocate the ministry.) All events welcome persons seeking wholeness and healing.

THE IONA COMMUNITY[4]

Contact address:
4th Floor, Savoy House
140 Sauchiehall Street
Glasgow G2 3DH
Scotland
Tel: 0141 332 6343
www.iona.org.uk

Iona is a small island off the west coast of Scotland, where in 563 C.E. Columba founded a Celtic monastery that was very influential in its own times. In the Middle Ages it was the site of a Benedictine abbey and over the centuries has attracted many thousands of people on their own pilgrim journeys.

The Iona Community, founded in 1938 by the Rev George MacLeod, then a parish minister in Glasgow, is an ecumenical Christian community that is committed to seeking new ways of living the Gospel in today's world. Initially this purpose was expressed through the rebuilding of the monastic quarters of the medieval abbey on Iona and pursued in mission and ministry throughout Scotland and beyond. The community today remains committed to rebuilding the common life, through working for social and political change, striving for the renewal of the church with an ecumenical emphasis, and exploring new, more inclusive approaches to worship, all based on an integrated understanding of spirituality.

The Iona Community today has almost 250 members, mostly in Britain, over 1,500 associate members and around 1,400 friends worldwide. An ecumenical community of men and women from different walks of life and different traditions in the Christian church, its members share a common rule of: daily prayer and reading the Bible; mutual accountability for their use of time and money; regular meeting together; action and reflection for justice, peace and the integrity of creation.

The Community's mainland home is in Glasgow, the base for: the administration of the Community; its work with young people; its publishing house, Wild Goose Publications, and its magazine, *Coracle*; its association in the revitalizing of worship with the Wild Goose Resource Group. Members meet regularly throughout the year in local groups and in four plenary gatherings, including a week on Iona. As a Community, members corporately and individually pursue some particular areas of concern: justice, peace, and the integrity of creation (opposing nuclear weapons, campaigning against the arms trade, and for ecological justice); political and cultural action to combat racism; action for economic justice, locally, nationally and globally; issues in human sexuality; discovering new and relevant approaches to worship; work with young people; the deepening of ecumenical dialogue and communion; and inter-religious relations.

For further information on the Community and its concerns, please contact the leader of the Community, Rev. Kathy Galloway.

THE TAIZÉ COMMUNITY[5]

71250 Taizé, France
tel: (+33) 3 85 50 30 30
www.taize.fr

Everything began in 1940 when, at the age of twenty-five, Brother Roger left Switzerland, the country where he was born, to go and live in France, his mother's birthplace. For years he had been an invalid, suffering from tuberculosis. During that long illness, the call had taken shape in him to create a community where simplicity and kind-heartedness would be lived out as essential gospel realities.

When the Second World War started, he had the conviction that he should begin at once to offer assistance to people in difficult straits, just as his grandmother had done during the First World War. The small village of Taizé, where he settled, was close to the demarcation line that divided France in half, and so was well situated to be a place of welcome for refugees fleeing the war. Brother Roger was able to buy a house in Taizé that had been uninhabited for years, with the outlying buildings. He asked one of his sisters, Genevieve, to come and help him offer hospitality. Among the refugees they sheltered were Jews.

A "PARABLE OF COMMUNITY"

In 1945, a young man from the region created an association to take charge of young boys orphaned by the war. When he suggested to the brothers that they welcome some of them in Taizé, Brother Roger asked his sister Genevieve to come back and take care of them. She became their mother. On Sundays, the brothers also welcomed German prisoners-of-war interned in a nearby camp. Gradually other young men arrived and joined the original group, and on Easter Day 1949, the first brothers committed themselves for their whole life to celibacy, to material and spiritual sharing and to a great simplicity of life.

Today, the Taizé Community is made up of over a hundred brothers, Catholics and from various Protestant backgrounds, coming from more than twenty-five nations. By its very existence, the community is thus a concrete sign of reconciliation between divided Christians and separated peoples. The brothers live by their own work. They do not accept gifts or donations for themselves, not even their own personal inheritances, which are given by the community to the poor.

Already in the 1950s, brothers went to live in disadvantaged places to be with people who were suffering from poverty or divisions. Today, small groups of brothers are present in Asia, Africa, and South America. As far as possible they share the living conditions of those who surround them, striving to be a presence of love among the very poor, street children, prisoners, the dying, and those who are wounded in their depths by broken relationships, by being abandoned.

Over the years, the number of visitors to Taizé has continued to grow. At the end of the 1950s, young adults between the ages of 17 and 30 began to arrive in ever-greater numbers. In 1966 the Sisters of Saint Andrew, an international Catholic community founded seven centuries ago, came to live in the next village and began to take on some of the tasks involved in welcoming people. Much later, a small group of Polish Ursuline sisters came to help with the welcome of the young.

INTERCONTINENTAL MEETINGS OF YOUNG ADULTS

Every week from early spring to late autumn, young adults from different continents arrive on the hill of Taizé. They are searching for meaning in their lives, in communion with many others. By going to the wellsprings of trust in God, they set out on an inner pilgrimage that encourages them to build relationships of trust among human beings.

Some weeks in the summer months, more than 5,000 young people from 75 different countries thus take part in a common adventure. And this adventure continues when they return home. It is expressed in their concern to deepen an inner life and by their readiness to take on responsibilities in order to make the world a better place to live in.

In Taizé, the visitors are welcomed by a community of brothers who have committed themselves to follow Christ by a "yes" for life. The two communities of sisters present on the hill also take part in the welcome. During the meetings, three times each day all those present gather for prayer, worshiping God together in singing and silence.

Each day, brothers of the community give Bible introductions that are followed by times of reflection and discussion; participants also help with practical tasks. One can also spend the week in silence as a way of letting the gospel illuminate one's life in greater depth.

In the afternoon, groups devoted to specific topics allow people to make the connection between the wellsprings of the faith and the pluralistic reality of contemporary society: "Is forgiveness possible?" "The challenge of globalization," "How can we respond to God's call?" "What kind of Europe do we want?" . . . There are also topics related to art and music.

A week in Taizé is a way of realizing the intimate relationship between an experience of communion with God in prayer and personal reflection on the one hand, and experience of communion and solidarity among people on the other.

By meeting other young people from throughout the world in a climate of openness and listening, participants discover that roads to unity can be opened up amidst the diversity of cultures and Christian traditions. This provides a solid basis to be creators of trust and peace in a world wounded by divisions, violence, and isolation.

In undertaking a "pilgrimage of trust on earth," Taizé does not organize a movement around the community. Each person is invited, after his or her stay, to live out in their own situation what they have understood, with greater awareness of the inner life within them as well as of their bonds with many others who are involved in a similar search for what really matters.

THE UPPER ROOM[6]

1908 Grand Ave.
P.O. Box 340004
Nashville, TN 37203-0004
Tel: 615-340-7200
www.upperroom.org

The Upper Room is a global ministry dedicated to supporting the spiritual formation of Christians seeking to know and experience God more fully. Having started as a daily devotional guide, Upper Room Ministries has grown to include publications, programs, prayer support, and other resources to help believers of all ages and denominations move to a deeper level of faith and service. Upper Room resources are grouped in five different areas:

PERSONAL SPIRITUALITY

The Upper Room believes that the spiritual life is a lifelong process of opening oneself to God. To assist with this process, the Upper Room offers a "Daily Devotional," which has been a spiritual companion used by more than 2.5 million people around the globe. In addition to its daily message on the Web, the daily devotional is available in an e-mail format, regular print, large print, and seventy-two editions and forty-four languages. Upper Room also has a chapel, which was visited by over thirty thousand people last year.

CHILDREN, YOUTH, YOUNG ADULTS, AND FAMILIES

The Upper Room holds that future generations and the family are primary concerns for all Christians. As the family fulfills its calling, its members become empowered to carry out God's ongoing work of love and justice in the world. In order to support the extended family of Christ, the Upper Room offers spiritual resources for believers of all ages, including books and magazines for children and youth and books to help parents help their children to grow spiritually.

SMALL GROUPS

The Upper Room understands small groups to be an integral part of Christian spiritual formation as we watch over each other in love. It offers support for small group ministries in the church so that groups may be more effective arenas for spiritual growth. Recognizing that small groups take many forms and serve many purposes, Upper Room offers different resources for small groups, including accountability groups, study groups, intercessory prayer groups, and devotional materials for small groups.

SPIRITUAL LEADERSHIP

The Upper Room has developed the Pathways Center for the formation and training of spiritual leaders in the ecumenical church. The center, located in Nashville, Tennessee, offers events and retreats in addition to daily morning and evening prayer as a part of the Upper Room's corporate Rule of Life. The Pathways Network links spiritual leaders in a sustained, worldwide ministry of spiritual formation.

CROSS-CULTURAL AND INTERNATIONAL MINISTRIES

The Upper Room *Daily Devotional Guide* is published around the world in seventy-two editions and forty-four languages. The Upper Room also publishes works in Spanish and Korean that both reflect and reach out to diverse Christian traditions.

Appendix B
Worship Resources for Liturgies on Addiction

PRAYERS FOR USE IN RECOVERY[1]

ST. FRANCIS OF ASSISI PRAYER

Lord, make me a channel of thy peace,
that where there is hatred, I may bring love,
that where there is wrong, I may bring the spirit of forgiveness,
that where there is discord, I may bring harmony,
that where there is error, I may bring truth,
that where there is doubt, I may bring faith,
that where there is despair, I may bring hope,
that where there are shadows, I may bring light,
that where there is sadness, I may bring joy.

Lord, grant that I may seek rather to comfort than to be comforted,
to understand, than to be understood,
to love, than to be loved.

For it is by self-forgetting that one finds.
It is by forgiving that one is forgiven.
It is by dying that one awakens to Eternal Life.   Amen.

A PRAYER FROM THOMAS MERTON[2]

My Lord God, I have no idea where I'm going.
I do not see the road ahead of me.
I cannot know for certain where it will end.
Nor do I really know myself, and the fact that I think that I am following your will does
    not mean that I am actually doing so.
But I believe that the desire to please you does in fact please you.
And I hope I have that desire in all that I am doing.
I hope that I will never do anything apart from that desire.
And I know that if I do this you will lead me by the right road though I may know noth-
    ing about it.
Therefore will I trust you always though I may seem to be lost and in the shadow of death.

I will not fear, for you are ever with me, and you will never leave me to face my perils alone. Amen.

A Word about Prayer by Henri Nouwen[3]

In a situation in which the world is threatened
by annihilation, prayer does not mean much
when we undertake it only as an attempt to influence God,
or as an offering of comfort in stress-filled times.
Prayer in the face of nuclear holocaust only makes sense
when it is an act of stripping ourselves of all false
belongings and we become free to belong to God and God alone.
. . . Prayer is not primarily a way to get something done.
. . . Prayer is a real act of death and rebirth.
It leads us right into the midst of the world
where we must take action.
Thus the act of prayer is the basis and source of all action.

Prayers from the Alcoholics Anonymous Text[4]

Third Step Prayer

God, I offer myself to you—to build with me and to do with me as You would. Relieve me of the bondage of self, that I may better do Your will. Take away my difficulties, that victory over them may bear witness to those I would help of Your power, Your love and Your way of life. May I do Your will always. Amen[5]

Seventh Step Prayer

My Creator, I am now willing that you should have all of me, good and bad. I pray that you now remove from me every single defect of character which stands in the way of my usefulness to you and my fellows. Grant me strength, as I go out from here to do your bidding. Amen.[6]

The Serenity Prayer (as used by twelve-step groups)

God, grant me the serenity to accept the things I cannot change, courage to change the things I can, and wisdom to know the difference. Amen

WORSHIP NOTES

I. Scripture and Themes

Ruth 3:1–5; 4:13–17	Loyalty and salvation through courageous action.
Psalm 127	Self-will versus letting go and God's will.
Heb. 9:24–28	Christ as sacrifice and salvation to those who are eagerly waiting and ready.
Mark 12:38–44	Jesus instructs disciples and us to notice and learn from anonymous humble people.
	Personal surrender to God.

II. Background Information about Recovery

A. It begins with admitting there is a problem and getting help. This is called "hitting bottom."

B. Abstinence from and stopping the behavior is necessary. This requires risking new behavior and being in new territory.

C. Help is needed to maintain abstinence on a daily basis. Admitting that one cannot do this on his or her own is part of the process. So the shift is from self-will and isolation to community and depending on God. Healing and wholeness is found in community with others.

D. Twelve-step programs use the simple principles of working with a sponsor to go through the steps. This requires trusting another human being with information and secrets. The risk is telling the truth. The result is self-awareness and forgiveness.

E. Through the step work, one gets honest and takes responsibility for his or her life. The person also stops feeling so alone. Through community with others, one begins to feel God's love. Through feeling loved, one is now more available to love others.

III.

A. Ruth's choice makes no sense, as she relinquishes the familiar for the unknown in a foreign land. Naomi and Ruth represent the bottom of society, yet they follow the love they have for each other and take radical action. Ruth, who would not listen to Naomi's first command, follows the plan for their survival together and a divine blessing through human agents is the result. [7]

B. Psalm 127 speaks to the insanity of anxiety and compulsive activity and recommends trust and confidence in God's power. "Allow God to be your foundation and strength rather than relying on self" is the message of the psalm.

C. In Hebrews 9, Christ is the mediator of a new covenant. His sacrifice puts away sin once and for all so that we can put our sins aside, receive forgiveness, serve the living God, and eagerly await Christ's second coming.

D. The story from Mark of the widow who gives generously out of her poverty is an example of a minor, anonymous character exemplifying the rule of God. Acting with child-like humility, her action expresses her faith. [8]

E. The widow, who gives her coins, like Naomi and Ruth, is of the lowest social status. By surrendering all that they have and trusting God, they lose their lives and, in the process of faithful action, are transformed into God's Word, God's teaching and lesson for us.

IV. Methods of Presenting a Worship Service

A. Take the first five steps (see "Call to Worship)" and apply them to one or all of the Scripture readings.

B. Ask three members of your congregation who are in recovery to share how these Scriptures speak to their experience of recovery.

C. Invite a member of your congregation to share her or his story of recovery: what it was like, what happened, what it is like now.
D. Use the "what it was like, what happened, what it is like now" format to tell the Scripture story as the character of Ruth, Naomi, Boaz, the widow, a scribe, or a disciple.

Notes

PREFACE

1. James F. White, *Introduction to Christian Worship* (Nashville: Abingdon Press, 1990), 254.
2. Ibid., 255.
3. Paul Roberts, "Healing and Reconciliation" in *Liturgy for a New Century,* ed. Michael Perham (London: SPCK, 1991), 63–70.
4. Kathleen Hughes, "Overview of the Constitution on the Sacred Liturgy" in *The Liturgy Documents: A Parish Resource* (Chicago: Liturgy Training Publications, 1991), 3.
5. Ibid.
6. Geoffrey Wainwright, *Doxology: The Praise of God in Doctrine, Worship and Life* (New York: Oxford University Press, 1980).
7. Teresa Berger, ed., *Dissident Daughters* (Louisville, Ky.: Westminster John Knox Press, 2001), 222. For an overview of recent developments, see also Teresa Berger, ed., *Theology in Hymns: A Study of the Relationship of Doxology and Theology according to* A Collection of Hymns for the Use of the People Called Methodist *(1780)* (Nashville: Abingdon Press, 1995), 31–57.
8. Robert Bocock, *Ritual in Industrial Society* (London: Allen & Unwin, 1974), 37, quoted in Chris Harris, *Creating Relevant Rituals: Celebrations for Religious Education* (Harrisburg, Pa.: Morehouse Publishing, 1992), 17.
9. Harris, *Creating Relevant Rituals,* 17.

INTRODUCTION   HEALING LITURGIES: AN ANALYSIS

1. Paul Philibert, "Readiness for Ritual: Psychological Aspects of Maturity in Christian Celebration," in *Alternative Futures for Worship,* vol. 1: *General Introduction,* ed. Regis Duffy (Collegeville, Minn.: Liturgical Press, 1987), 63–122.
2. David Power, "Liturgy and Empowerment," in *Alternative Futures for Worship,* vol. 6: *Leadership Ministry in Community*, ed. Michael Cowan (Collegeville, Minn.: Liturgical Press, 1987), 81–104.
3. Philibert, "Readiness for Ritual," 78.
4. Ibid., 79.
5. Ibid., 77.
6. Ibid., 94.
7. Charles P. Price and Louis Weil, *Liturgy for Living* (New York: Seabury Press, 1979), 34.
8. Ibid., 35.
9. Ibid., 35–36.
10. Chris Harris, *Creating Relevant Rituals: Celebrations for Religious Education* (Harrisburg, Pa.: Morehouse Publishing, 1992), 23.
11. Philibert, "Readiness for Ritual," 81.
12. Ibid., 83.
13. James F. White, *Introduction to Christian Worship* (Nashville: Abingdon Press, 1990), 93.
14. Ibid., 289, 297.

15. Daniel Frankforter, *Stones for Bread: A Critique of Contemporary Worship* (Louisville, Ky.: Westminster John Knox Press, 2001), xii.

16. Robin Green, *Only Connect: Worship and Liturgy from the Perspective of Pastoral Care*, foreword by H. A. Williams (London: Darton, Longman and Todd, 1987), 20–33.

17. William H. Willimon, *Worship as Pastoral Care* (Nashville: Abingdon Press, 1982).

18. Martin Dudley, ed., *A Manual for Ministry to the Sick* (London: SPCK, 1997), 9–13.

19. James F. White, *A Brief History of Christian Worship* (Nashville: Abingdon Press, 1993), 33.

20. John Perry, ed., *A Time to Heal: A Report for the House of Bishops on the Healing Ministry* (London: Church House Publishing, 2000).

21. Power, "Liturgy and Empowerment," 81–104.

22. Robert A. Lambourne, "What Is Healing?" in *Explorations in Health and Salvation: A Selection of Papers by Bob Lambourne*, ed. Michael Wilson (Birmingham: University of Birmingham, 1985), 28.

23. Edward Yarnold, "Media of Spirituality," in *The Study of Spirituality*, ed. Cheslyn Jones, Geoffrey Wainwright, and Edward Yarnold (London: SPCK, 1986), 40.

24. Ibid., 42.

25. Price and Weil, *Liturgy for Living,* 46.

26. Søren Kierkegaard, *Purity of Heart Is to Will One Thing* (New York: HarperCollins, 1986).

27. Mark Santer, "The Praises of God," in *Liturgy for a New Century,* ed. Michael Perham (London: SPCK, 1991), 2.

28. White, *Brief History of Christian Worship*, 37.

29. Philip H. Pfatteicher, *The School of the Church* (Valley Forge, Pa.: Trinity Press International, 1995), 61. Clement begins his *Protrepticus (Protreptikos)*, or *Exhortation,* with a greatly extended metaphor declaring that the musical mythology of ancient Greece has been superseded by the New Song, who is Christ the *Logos*, "the song which is called new, although most ancient."

30. Ibid., 64.

31. Ibid., 65.

32. Ibid., 66.

33. Marva J. Dawn and Martin E. Marty, *Reaching Out without Dumbing Down: A Theology of Worship for the Turn-of-the-Century Culture* (Grand Rapids: Wm. B. Eerdmans Publishing Co., 1995), 87.

34. Ibid., 88.

35. Ibid., 109.

36. White, *Introduction to Christian Worship*, 110.

37. Yarnold, "Media of Spirituality," 41.

38. Michael B. Aune and Valerie DeMarinis, *Religious and Social Ritual: Interdisciplinary Explorations* (New York: State University of New York Press, 1996), 175.

39. Ibid., 177.

40. Ibid., 182.

41. George Steiner, *Real Presences* (Chicago: University of Chicago Press, 1989), 217.

42. Aune and DeMarinis, *Religious and Social Ritual*, 188.

43. A side note to this discussion of music in worship is a growing recognition of the therapeutic nature of music in and of itself. There has been a growing movement in using harp and other music to enhance healing. One such harpist is Jan Faires (folk harpist, http://eiw.com/harplady), who cites research about the diverse effects of music in therapeutic situations. Here are just a few examples:

- At the California State University in Fresno, studies by psychologist Janet Lapp have shown that migraine patients who started and continue to listen regularly to their favorite music have one-sixth as many headaches as before.
- Premature babies at the Medical Center of the University of California in Los Angeles and at Georgia Baptist Medical Center in Atlanta gained weight faster and used oxygen more efficiently, and babies at Tallahassee Memorial Regional Medical Center had shorter stays in the intensive care unit, when music was played for them daily, compared with babies in control groups without music.
- For adult patients, "half an hour of music produces the same effect as ten milligrams of Valium," says Dr. Raymond Bahr, head of the coronary care unit at Baltimore's St. Agnes Hospital.
- When used by surgical patients, music has been shown to reduce the need for anesthesia and pain relievers.

Nurse anesthetist Maureen Reilly of San Antonio, Texas, is involved in research on the subject of music and anesthesia, as is Fred Schwartz, anesthesiologist at Piedmont Hospital in Atlanta, Georgia.

- Dr. Oliver Sacks, the neurologist who has done studies on Parkinson's disease, Tourette's syndrome, and Alzheimer's disease, says, "Whenever I get a book on neurology or psychology, the first thing I look up in the index is music, and if it's not there, I close the book."
- The U.S. Senate Subcommittee on Aging has granted funding for developing the use of music in physical rehabilitation programs.
- The National Institutes of Health has funded research on the use of music in medical settings.

Harpist Faires makes no claims to cure illness with her music. However, studies have shown that people who listen to live music on a regular basis may notice some beneficial results, such as lower blood pressure, slower and deeper respiration, decreased insomnia, greater sense of serenity and personal well-being, reduced heart rate, and increased production of endorphins, which reduce pain. Music is also being used on an experimental basis to aid digestion, as a part of therapy in drug and alcohol detoxification, with Alzheimer's patients, with comatose patients, and as an aid for those with learning disabilities.

44. Yarnold, "Media of Spirituality," 40.
45. White, *Introduction to Christian Worship*, 102.
46. Ibid., 89.
47. Nicholas Constas, "Icons and Imagination," *Logos* 1.1 (1997): 114–27.
48. Pavel Florensky, "Against Linear Perspective," in *Utopias,* ed. Catriona Kelly (London, 1999), 70–75.
49. Yarnold also discusses this subject in his essay "Media of Spirituality," 39–44.
50. White, *Introduction to Christian Worship*, 86.
51. Ibid., 86.

SEASONS OF LIFE

Chapter 1   CHILDHOOD/ADOLESCENCE

1. David Adam, "Consecration," in *Tides and Seasons* (London: Triangle/SPCK, 1989), 6. Used with permission.
2. Erik H. Erikson, *Childhood and Society* (New York: W. W. Norton and Company, 1993).
3. Ibid., 250.
4. Ibid., 251–54.
5. Ibid., 254.
6. Ibid., 255ff.
7. Ibid., 258.
8. Donald Capps, *The Child's Song: The Religious Abuse of Children* (Louisville, Ky.: Westminster John Knox Press, 1995).
9. Ibid., 15.
10. Erikson, *Childhood and Society,* 261.
11. Kenda Creasy Dean, Chap Clark, and David Rahn, *Starting Right: Thinking Theologically about Youth Ministry* (Grand Rapids: Zondervan Publishing House, 2001), 42.
12. Ibid., 43.
13. Dale A. Matthews and David B. Larson, *The Faith Factor: An Annotated Bibliography of Clinical Research on Spiritual Subjects,* vol. 3: *Enhancing Life Satisfaction* (Rockville, Md.: National Institute for Healthcare Research, 1995).
14. American Psychological Association, "Adolescent Behavioral Development," in *Developing Adolescence: A Reference for Professionals*, ed. Jacquelyn Gentry and Mary Campbell, jointly sponsored by Maternal and Child Health Bureau, Health Resources and Services Administration, U.S. Department of Health and Human Services (Washington, D.C.: American Psychological Association, 2002), 33.

FACTORS ASSOCIATED WITH RESILIENCE AND POSITIVE OUTCOMES
Stable, Positive Relationship with at Least One Caring Adult

Numerous studies have found that the presence of an adult—a parent or someone other than a parent—with a strong positive emotional attachment to the child is associated with resilience. This might be a teacher or coach, an extended family member, or a mentor, such as those found in the Big Brothers/Big Sisters Program.

Religious and Spiritual Anchors

A sense of meaning is one of the major pathways through which violent youth find their way to a constructive future, with religious and spiritual institutions and practices being important vehicles for developing a sense of meaning for these youth.

High, Realistic Academic Expectations and Adequate Support

Schools that provide students with a sense of shared cooperative responsibility and belonging, convey high expectations for participation, and provide high levels of individual support for students tend to enhance resilience.

Positive Family Environment

A warm, nurturing parenting style, with both clear limit setting and respect for the growing autonomy of adolescents, appears to be associated with resilience in adolescents. Strong, positive mother-adolescent relations have also been found to be associated with resilience among youth when fathers are absent from the home.

Emotional Intelligence and Ability to Cope with Stress

Although intelligence per se has been reported to be associated with resilience, the factors that may be more important, because they are more amenable to change and are also involved in resilience, are emotional intelligence and the ability to cope with stress.

15. Dean, Clark, and Rahn, *Starting Right,* 49.

16. Paul Philibert, "Readiness for Ritual: Psychological Aspects of Maturity in Christian Celebration," in *Alternative Futures of Worship,* vol. 1: *General Introduction,* ed. Regis Duffy (Collegeville, Minn.: Liturgical Press, 1987), 95.

17. Ibid., 99.

18. Ibid., 98.

19. Ibid., 99.

20. Ibid., 101.

21. Ibid., 102.

22. Ibid., 104.

23. James W. Fowler, Karl Ernst Nipkow, and Friedrich Schweitzer, *Stages of Faith and Religious Development: Implications for Church, Education, and Society* (New York: Crossroad, 1991), 6.

24. Ibid., 20.

25. Ibid., 24.

26. Ibid., 24–25.

27. Dean, Clark, and Rahn, *Starting Right,* 31.

28. Ibid., 30.

29. Ibid.

30. Ibid., 49.

31. American Psychological Association, "Adolescent Behavioral Development," 30.

Weapon Carrying, Fighting, and Sexual Violence

- 17 percent of students have carried a weapon (e.g., a gun, knife, or club) to school on one or more days during the past month, with boys significantly more likely than girls to carry weapons.
- Approximately 36 percent of high school students have been in a physical fight one or more times during the twelve months, with male students (44 percent) more likely than female students (27 percent) to have been in a fight.
- During the past twelve months, approximately 9 percent of students were hit or slapped on purpose by their boyfriend or girlfriend.
- Approximately 9 percent of students have been forced to have sexual intercourse when they did not want to.
- Homicide rates for Black youth ages 10 to 14 are three to four times greater than those for White youth.

32. National Center for Health Statistics, "Teen Birth Rates Decline in All States during the 1990s," 2002 Fact Sheet (http://www.cdc.gov/nchs/releases/02facts/teenbirths.htm, May 30, 2002).

33. Dean, Clark, and Rahn, *Starting Right,* 41.

34. American Psychological Association, "Adolescent Behavioral Development," 29.

35. Ibid., 29–30.

ADOLESCENT RISK-TAKING BEHAVIORS

Cigarette Smoking

- Seventy percent of high school students have tried cigarette smoking, 25 percent before the age of 13.
- About one-quarter of high school students smoke at least one cigarette per day, with male students smoking more than female students.
- Smoking has been on the rise for girls; in 1991, one in eight girls in eighth grade reported smoking (13 percent), but by 1996 more than one in five reported smoking (21 percent).

Alcohol Use

- Eighty-one percent of high school students have tried alcohol; 32 percent had their first drink before the age of 13.
- Half of all high school students report having had more than one alcoholic beverage in the past 30 days, and approximately 30 percent report having had more than five alcoholic beverages at one time during this period. Girls ages 12–18 are now as likely as boys to drink alcohol.
- Male students are more likely than female students to report heavy episodic drinking, as are those in the upper grades (11 and 12) compared to those in the lower grades (9 and 10).
- Thirteen percent of students drove a vehicle more than once after drinking during the past month, with males significantly more likely to do so than females. A third (33 percent) report having ridden more than once during the past month with a driver who had been drinking alcohol.

Other Drug Use

- Forty-seven percent of high school students have tried marijuana, with males more likely than females to report such use; 11 percent tried marijuana before the age of 13.
- Nine percent of high school students have used some form of cocaine, and 4 percent have used cocaine more than one time in the past thirty days.
- Fourteen percent of students have used inhalants to get high; 4 percent more than once in the past thirty days.
- Nine percent of high school students have used methamphetamines, and approximately 4 percent have used steroids.

Sexual Intercourse

- Half of all high school students have had sexual intercourse, with 8 percent having had intercourse before the age of 13, and 36 percent having had sexual intercourse during the past three months.
- Nineteen percent of male high school students report having had more than four sexual partners, as do 13 percent of female students.
- Approximately 25 percent of sexually active students used alcohol or drugs at last sexual intercourse.
- Among currently sexually active high school students, 58 percent used a condom during last sexual intercourse, with males more likely to report using a condom than females. Among sexually active female students, 20 percent report using birth control pills.

Pregnancy

- Approximately 6 percent of students report that they have been pregnant or responsible for getting someone pregnant.
- Between 1991 and 2000, the pregnancy rate for girls ages 15–19 years declined from 56.8 per 1,000 teens to 48.7.

Failure to Use Motorcycle or Bicycle Helmets

- Of the 24 percent of students who report having ridden a motorcycle in the past year, 38 percent rarely or never wore a helmet. Of the 71 percent of students who rode a bicycle in the past year, 85 percent rarely or never wore a helmet.

36. Erin B. Carpenter, "Dating Violence," in *Adolescence: Change and Continuity* (http://www.personal.psu.edu/faculty/n/x/nxd10/adint.htm, January 17, 2003).

37. "Blessing of the Children: Service of Prayer and Healing." Used by permission of the Reverend John Auer, former pastor, First United Methodist Church of San Rafael (California), with some material from the Children's Defense Fund, *National Observance of Children's Sabbaths* (Washington, D.C.: Children's Defense Fund, 2002).

38. "At the Time of Divorce: A Children's Liturgy," in *Human Rites: Worship Resources for an Age of Change*, ed. Hannah Ward and Jennifer Wild (London: Mowbray, 1995), 193. Reprinted by permission of The Continuum International Publishing Group, New York & London, 2002.

39. Charles Parkhurst Baxter, "Evening Hymn," in *The Hospital Service Book* (London: Henry Frowde, Amen Corner, E.C., 1892), 15.

40. "A Service of Darkness and Light," Father Ray Chase, St. Vincent's Center, Timonium, MD, 2002. Used with permission.

41. Baxter, *Hospital Service Book,* 14.

42. "Rainbow Connection," words by Paul Williams and Kenneth Ascher © 1979 Welbeck Music Corp.

43. "Ritual to Affirm the Passage from Girlhood to Young Woman," in Ward and Wild, *Human Rites,* 33. Reprinted by permission of The Continuum International Publishing Group, New York & London, 2002.

44. "For My Daughters: A Liturgy for the Celebration of Your Menarche," in Ward and Wild, *Human Rites,* 63–65. Reprinted by permission of The Continuum International Publishing Group, New York & London, 2002.

45. "Taking Leave," Lana Russell, Princeton Theological Seminary student, Princeton, New Jersey, February 2003. Used with permission.

46. Julie Howard, "Wherever You Go," in Julie Howard, *We Are the Circle: Celebrating the Feminine in Song and Ritual* (Collegeville, Minn.: Liturgical Press, 1993).

47. "Renewal of Baptismal Vows." Reproduced from the *Book of Common Worship.* © 1993 Westminster John Knox Press. Used by permission of Westminster John Knox Press.

48. See "The Woman's Creed," in Rachel Walberg, *Jesus and the Freed Woman* (New York: Paulist Press, 1978), 155–57.

49. Marsie Silvestro, "Blessing Song," in Women's Ordination Conference, *Liberating Liturgies* (Fairfax, Va.: Women's Ordination Conference, 1989).

50. "Sons of Thunder," Rev. Kathleen Smallwood Johnson, Princeton Theological Seminary student, Princeton N.J., February 2003. Used with permission.

51. Cheryl A. Kirk-Duggan, "Graduation and Promotion Days," in *African American Special Days* (Nashville: Abingdon Press, 1996), 26–32. Used by permission of The United Methodist Publishing House.

52. Helen R. Neinast and Thomas C. Ettinger, "Leaving Home: What to Take Along, What to Leave Behind," in *What About God? Now That You're Off to College* (Nashville: Upper Room Books, 1992), 71–75. Used with permission. Adapted by author.

53. Excerpt from *With Head and Heart: The Autobiography of Howard Thurman*, copyright © 1979 by Howard Thurman, reprinted with permission of Harcourt, Inc.

54. Prayers written by author.

CHAPTER 2   EARLY/MIDDLE ADULTHOOD

1. Erik H. Erikson, *Childhood and Society* (New York: W. W. Norton and Company, 1993), 263.

2. Ibid., 267.

3. Ibid., 268.

4. Ibid., 269.

5. Daniel J. Levinson, *Seasons of Man's Life,* ed. Charlotte N. Dorrow, Edward B. Klien, Maria H. Levinson, and Braxton McKee (New York: Alfred A. Knopf, 1978).

6. Gail Sheehy, *New Passages* (New York: Ballantine Books, 1995).

7. Ibid., xii.

8. Hugh Sanborn, *Celebrating Passages in the Church* (St. Louis: Chalice Press, 1999), 117.

9. Carol Gilligan, *In a Different Voice: Psychological Theory and Women's Development* (Cambridge, Mass.: Harvard University Press, 1993).

10. Sheehy, *New Passages,* 201.

11. Ibid., 243.

12. Ibid., 244.

13. Ibid., 254–55.

14. Ibid., 261.

15. Ibid., 273.

16. Frederick Buechner, *Now and Then* (New York: Harper & Row, 1983).

17. Sanborn, *Celebrating Passages in the Church,* 125.

18. Henri J. M. Nouwen, *Reaching Out: The Three Movements of the Spiritual Life* (Garden City, N.Y.: Doubleday, 1975).

19. Ibid.

20. "Blessing of a Pregnant Woman," in *The Book of Occasional Services. Episcopal Church USA* (New York: Church Publishing Incorporated, 1994), 157. Adapted by the author. Used with permission.

21. "The Thanksgiving of Women after Child-Birth," in *The Book of Common Prayer and Administration of the Sacraments and Other Rites and Ceremonies of the Church of England* (Edinburgh: Printed by the Printers to the King's Most Excellent Majestie, 1634).

22. *Dilexi quoniam* is Latin for Psalm 114 (116).

23. *Nisi Dominus* is Latin for Psalm 126 (127).

24. "An Order of Thanksgiving for the Birth or Adoption of a Child" in *The United Methodist Book of Worship* (Nashville: United Methodist Publishing House, 1992), 585–87. © 1992 United Methodist Publishing House. Used with permission. "Prayer of Thanksgiving and Intercession" within liturgy is attributed to Commission on Worship of Consultation on Church Union, which is defunct as of January 2002.

25. "After a Miscarriage or Stillbirth." Excerpted from *Occasional Celebrations* © copyright 1992, 1995, 2001 by the General Synod of the Anglican Church of Canada; published by the Anglican Book Centre, 600 Jarvis Street, Toronto, Ontario, Canada M4Y 2J6; used with permission.

26. "Service of Healing after a Miscarriage" in *Human Rites: Worship Resources for an Age of Change,* ed. Hannah Ward and Jennifer Wild (London: Mowbray, 1995), 221–22. Reprinted by permission of The Continuum International Publishing Group, New York & London, 2002.

27. "A Service of Commemoration and Healing after Abortion," in Ward and Wild, *Human Rites,* 216–19. Reprinted by permission of The Continuum International Publishing Group, New York & London, 2002.

28. David Adam, "For a New Day," in *Tides and Seasons* (London: Triangle/SPCK, 1989), 10. Used with permission.

29. "Renewal of Baptismal Vows." Reproduced from the *Book of Common Worship.* © 1993 Westminster John Knox Press. Used by permission of Westminster John Knox Press.

30. From the *Book of Common Worship.* © 1993 Westminster John Knox Press. Used by permission of Westminster John Knox Press.

31. Ibid.

32. From *Holy Baptism and Services for the Renewal of Baptism,* Supplemental Liturgical Resource 2, copyright © 1985 The Westminster Press. Used by permission of Westminster John Knox Press.

33. Author and publisher unknown.

34. Excerpts from *Autumn Gospel: Women in the Second Half of Life,* by Kathleen Fischer. Robert J. Wicks, ed., *Integration Books: Studies in Pastoral Psychology, Theology, and Spirituality* (New York; Mahwah, N.J.: Paulist Press) © 1995 Paulist Press. www.paulistpress.com.

35. "Blessing for a New Home," adapted by author and Albert Tisdale, from "Celebration for a Home," in *The Book of Occasional Services, 1994* of the Episcopal Church. Permission granted from Sean M. Scheller, Rights and Permissions Director. From the Book of Occasional Services, 1994, © 1995 Church Pension Fund. Service may not be altered without written permission from Church Publishing.

36. "Blessing of Home Animals." Excerpted from *The Book of Alternative Services* © copyright 1985 by the General Synod of the Anglican Church of Canada; published by the Anglican Book Centre, 600 Jarvis Street, Toronto, Ontario, Canada M4Y 2J6; used with permission.

37. "A Turning Season," from *Circles of Grace: Worship and Prayer in the Everyday* by Keri K. Wehlander. The United Church Publishing House, 1998. Pp. 22–25. Used with permission. Adaptation by the author.

38. "Turn! Turn! Turn!" adapted from the book of Ecclesiastes; music copyright Pete Seeger (1954).

39. Mary Frances Duffy, "A Ritual of Healing for Persons in Mid-Life," in *Alternative Futures for Worship*, vol. 7 (Collegeville, Minn.: Liturgical Press), 123–40. Used with permission.

40. Written by the author.

41. Edward Hays, "Psalm for a Woman Who No Longer Bleeds," in *Prayers for a Planetary Pilgrim* (Leavenworth, Kans.: Forest of Peace Publishing, 1989), 154. Used with permission.

42. "Walking the Labyrinth," by the author and Raimundo Barreto, Ph.D. candidate, Princeton Theological Seminary, January 2003. Used with permission.

43. Lauren Artress, *Walking a Sacred Path: Rediscovering the Labyrinth as a Spiritual Tool* (New York: Riverhead Books, 1995), 15.

44. Bruce Morrill, ed., *Bodies of Worship: Explorations in Theory and Practice* (Collegeville, Minn.: Liturgical Press, 1999), 124.

45. Ibid., 125.

46. Ibid., 126.

47. Artress, *Walking a Sacred Path,* 52.

48. Douglas Burton-Christie, "Into the Labyrinth," *Weavings,* 12, 4 (Nashville: Upper Room, July/August 1997), 21.

49. Ibid., 22.

50. Laurie Goodstein, "Reviving Labyrinths, Paths to Inner Peace," *New York Times*, May 10, 1998, 16.

51. Ibid.

52. Melissa G. West, *Exploring the Labyrinth: A Guide for Healing and Spiritual Growth* (New York: Broadway Books, 2000), 23.

53. Ibid., 32.

54. According to West, finger labyrinths are small labyrinths meant to be "walked" with the fingers. For further information on this kind of labyrinth, see West, *Exploring the Labyrinth*, 53ff.

55. Ibid., 66, 67.

56. Ibid., 67.

57. Ibid., 68.

58. Ibid., 76.

59. Jill K. H. Geoffrion, *Praying the Labyrinth: A Journal for Spiritual Exploration* (Cleveland: Pilgrim Press, 1999) and *Living the Labyrinth: 101 Paths to a Deeper Connection with the Sacred* (Cleveland: Pilgrim Press, 2000). The suggestions that follow are an adaptation of the guidelines offered by Rev. Geoffrion in her books.

60. Geoffrion, *Praying the Labyrinth,* 13.

61. Ibid., 33.

62. Ibid., 99.

63. West, *Exploring the Labyrinth*, 156ff.

64. Geoffrion, *Praying the Labyrinth*, 81.

65. Ibid., 77.

66. "The Work of Our Lives," by the Reverend Thomas Evans, Williamsville, New York. Used with permission.

67. "Honouring the Outworkers" in *Prayers for Life's Particular Moments,* by Dorothy McRae-McMahon (London: SPCK, 2001), 108–110. Used with permission.

68. "A Service of Wholeness and Healing for Those Engaged in Ministry," Saturday Morning Worship, in *Welcoming Angels in Our Midst,* 1999 Presbyterian Health, Education and Welfare Association (PHEWA) Biennial National Ministries Division Social Welfare Ministries Conference *Worship Book,* adapted from *Book of Common Worship* prepared by The Theology and Worship Ministry Unit for the Presbyterian Church (U.S.A.) and the Cumberland Presbyterian Church (Louisville, Ky.: Westminster John Knox Press, 1993). Used with permission.

69. "Intergenerational Healing." Excerpts from *Autumn Gospel,* by Kathleen Fischer © 1995. Used with permission of Paulist Press. www.paulistpress.com.

70. "Communal Reconciliation Service." Reprinted with permission from *Prayer Services for the Elderly*, by Sandra DeGidio, O.S.M. Copyright ©1996. Published by Twenty-Third Publications, Mystic, CT 06355.

71. "End of a Close Relationship," in Ward and Wild, *Human Rites*, 170–73. Reprinted by permission of The Continuum International Publishing Group, New York & London, 2002.

72. "At the Ending of a Marriage." Excerpted from *The Book of Alternative Services* © copyright 1985 by the General Synod of the Anglican Church of Canada; published by the Anglican Book Centre, 600 Jarvis Street, Toronto, Ontario, Canada M4Y 2J6. Used with permission.

73. "Liturgy for Divorce," in Ward and Wild, *Human Rites,* 188–92. Reprinted by permission of The Continuum International Publishing Group, New York & London, 2002.

CHAPTER 3   LATE ADULTHOOD/ELDERLY

1. Carl Jung, *The Structure and Dynamics of the Psyche,* 2d ed. (New York: Pantheon Books, 1960), 399.

2. Administration on Aging, "A Profile of Older Americans: 2002—Highlights," http://www.aoa.gov/aoa/stats/profile/highlights.html (accessed February 13, 2003).

3. Jonathan Swift, *Thoughts on Various Subjects.*

4. Fredrica Harris Thompsett, *Courageous Incarnation: In Intimacy, Work, Childhood and Aging* (Cambridge, Mass.: Cowley Publications, 1993), 70.

5. U.S. Census Bureau, *Statistical Abstract of the United States: 1999* (Washington, D.C., 1999), 71.

6. Gail Sheehy, *New Passages* (New York: Ballantine Books, 1995), 419.

7. Ibid.

8. Ibid.

9. Daniel Golden, "Building a Better Brain," *Life,* July 1994, 64, cited in "Healthy Living, Wholly Lives: Achieving Health at Seminary," *Princeton Seminary Bulletin* 21, 3 (2000): 331.

10. Sheehy, *New Passages,* 427.

11. Ibid.

12. Coda Alliance, The Silicon Valley Community Coalition for End-of-Life Care, "Pre-Conference Assessment Tool," in *End-of-Life Care Education for Clergy*, conference proceedings, October 30, 2002, San Jose, California.

13. Thompsett, *Courageous Incarnation,* 72.

14. Coda Alliance, *End-of-Life Care Education for Clergy.*

15. Ibid.

16. Bruce M. Zelkovitz and Karen L. Field, "A Sociology of Aging," *Midwest Medical Ethics* 4, 4 (Fall 1988): 7–10.

17. "The Grace Behind and Before," Rev. Dr. Melinda Contreras-Byrd, New Jersey state-licensed psychologist and ordained elder of the African Methodist Episcopal Church. Used with permission.

18. *This Far by Faith: An African American Resource for Worship* (Minneapolis: Augsburg Fortress Publishers, 1999), 246.

19. *Hymnal for Worship and Celebration* (Waco, Tex.: Word Publishing, 1986), 328.

20. "A Service for the Elderly," in Lawrence Jackson, *Services for Special Occasions* (New York: Continuum Publishing Co., 1982), 119–24. Reprinted by permission of The Continuum International Publishing Group, New York & London, 2002.

21. "A Time to Remember," led by Jean Wright-Elson, parish nurse, and Chaplain Tom Repess, USN Ret., First United Methodist Church of San Diego, Order of Worship, January 16, 1999. Used with permission.

22. "Remembering God: A Liturgy of Naming for Those with Alzheimer's, Their Loved Ones, and Caregivers," by Mary Beth LeCroy, Princeton Theological Seminary student, 2003. Used with permission.

23. See http://www.mercksource.com.

24. Abigail Rian Evans, *The Healing Church* (Cleveland: United Church Press, 1999), 112.

25. Robert Davis, *My Journey into Alzheimer's Disease: A True Story* (Wheaton, Ill.: Tyndale House Publishers, 1989), 18, quoted in *God Never Forgets,* ed. Donald K. McKim (Louisville, Ky.: Westminster John Knox Press, 1998), 87.

26. Written by author.

27. "For the Aged," in *A Manual for Ministry to the Sick,* ed. Martin Dudley (London: SPCK, 1997). Used with permission, including footnotes within the liturgy.

28. *The Book of Common Prayer* (American Episcopal Church, 1979). Extracts from *The Book of Common Prayer for Use in the Church in Wales* © 1984 Church in Wales Publications.

29. *A Prayer Book for Australia* [adapted] © 1995 The Anglican Church of Australia Trust Corporation, published by Broughton Books.

30. *A New Zealand Prayer Book. Prayers from A New Zealand Prayer Book* © 1989 The Church of the Province of New Zealand.

31. "A Retirement Ritual." Excerpts from *Autumn Gospel: Women in the Second Half of Life,* by Kathleen Fischer. © 1995. Used with permission of Paulist Press. www.paulistpress.com.

32. "Ritual for Moving from a Home of Many Years." Excerpts from *Autumn Gospel,* by Kathleen Fischer © 1995 Paulist Press. www.paulistpress.com.

33. "Welcoming a New Resident." Reprinted with permission from *Prayer Services for the Elderly*, by Sandra DeGidio, O.S.M. Copyright © 1996. Published by Twenty-Third Publications, Mystic, CT 06355.

34. "Birthday or Anniversary Ritual." Reprinted with permission from *Prayer Services for the Elderly*, by Sandra DeGidio, O.S.M. Copyright © 1996. Published by Twenty-Third Publications, Mystic, CT 06355.

35. "A Service of Blessing," by the Reverend Terry Thomas Primer, chaplain, Presbyterian Homes and Services of N.J., Inc. Used with permission.

SEASONS OF CRISIS

CHAPTER 4   ILLNESS: AS LIFE-ALTERING

1. David Adam, "Help in Trouble," in *Tides and Seasons* (London: Triangle/SPCK, 1989), 81. Used with permission.

2. Abigail Rian Evans, *Redeeming Marketplace Medicine* (Cleveland: Pilgrim Press, 1999), 74.

3. Thomas Droege, "The Religious Roots of Wholistic Health Care," in *Theological Roots of Wholistic Health Care,* ed. Granger Westberg (Hinsdale, Ill.: Wholistic Health Centers, 1979), 40.

4. Evans, *Redeeming Marketplace Medicine,* 77.

5. Ibid.

6. Ibid., 107.

7. Ibid., 84.

8. William Gaventa, "Pastoral Care with Persons with Disabilities and their Families: An Adaptable Module for Intro Courses," unpublished paper, 2002.

9. Ibid., 2.

10. Stewart D. Govig, *Strong at the Broken Places: Persons with Disabilities and the Church*, Appendix 1 (Louisville, Ky.: Westminster/John Knox Press, 1989), 120–21.

11. Ibid.

12. Ibid.

13. Ibid.

14. Ibid., 120.

15. Ingram C. Parmley and Tresco Shannon, "Ministry and Persons with Developmental Disabilities," *Worship* 66, 1 (January 1992): 10–11.

16. The Commonwealth Fund, "Health Concerns across a Woman's Lifespan: The Commonwealth Fund 1998 Survey of Women's Health, May 1999," in *Domestic Violence Is a Serious, Widespread Social Problem in America: The Facts,* http://endabuse.org/facts/ (accessed February 7, 2003).

17. U.S. Department of Justice, "Violence by Intimates: Analysis of Data on Crimes by Current or Former Spouses, Boyfriends, and Girlfriends, March 1998," in *Domestic Violence,* http://endabuse.org/facts/ (accessed February 7, 2003).

18. National Crime Victimization Survey, 1992–96; Study of Injured Victims of Violence, 1994, in *Domestic Violence,* http://endabuse.org/facts/ (accessed February 7, 2003).

19. Murray A. Straus and Richard J. Gelles, "Physical Violence in American Families" (1990), in *Domestic Violence,* http://endabuse.org/facts/ (accessed February 7, 2003).

20. National Institute of Justice and Centers for Disease Control and Prevention, "Prevalence, Incidence, and Consequences of Violence against Women: Findings from the National Violence against Women Survey, November 1998," in *Domestic Violence,* http://endabuse.org/facts/ (accessed February 7, 2003).

21. See James Newton Poling, *The Abuse of Power: A Theological Problem* (Nashville: Abingdon Press, 1991).

22. Gerald May, *Addiction and Grace* (San Francisco: Harper & Row, 1988), 24.

23. Ibid., 25–26.

24. Anne Wilson Schaef, *When Society Becomes an Addict* (San Francisco: Harper & Row, 1987), 18–19.

25. See Abigail Rian Evans, *The Healing Church* (Cleveland: United Church Press, 1999), 140–52.

26. Supreme Court of the United States, J. Kennedy concurring in judgment, June 22, 1999; http://akmhcweb .org/docs/olmstead/kennedyconcur.pdf (accessed February 12, 2003).

27. Govig, *Strong at the Broken Places,* 9.

28. Fred Cloud, "Pastoral Care of the Mentally Ill and Their Families: Four Perspectives, with Implications for Action" (D.Min. project, Divinity School, Vanderbilt University, 1990).

29. Susan Gregg-Schroeder, *In the Shadow of God's Wings: Grace in the Midst of Depression* (Nashville: Upper Room, 1997), 104.

30. Ibid., 110.

31. Florence L. Kraft, "What Congregations Can Do to Care for Persons with a Mental Illness," *Horizons* (March/April 1996): 16–17.

32. Robert G. Anderson Jr., "The Assessment of Systems in Promoting Collaborative Aftercare: Religious and Mental Health Organizations in Partnership," *Journal of Pastoral Care* 39, 3 (September 1985): 236–48.

33. "A Service for the Handicapped," in Lawrence Jackson, *Services for Special Occasions* (New York: Continuum Publishing Co., 1982), 31–37. Reprinted by permission of The Continuum International Publishing Group, New York & London, 2002.

34. This chorale-improvisation was inspired by the familiar tune for "Now thank we all our God."

35. Bernard De Jonge, "We Are the Church Together," *Reformed Worship* (March 1991): 13. Used with permission.

36. Interfaith Service of Worship at National Alliance of Mental Illness Convention, September 9, 1992, St. Margaret's Episcopal Church, Washington, D.C. Words of hymns written by Margee Iddings. Sponsored by the National Alliance for the Mentally Ill (NAMI) Religious Outreach Network. Nancy Lee Head, coordinator of local arrangements for this service, program coordinator, AMI-DC Threshold; and secretary-treasurer, Presbyterian Serious Mental Illness Network. Used with permission.

37. Author and publisher unknown.

38. "A Service for Wholeness for Use with a Congregation," in *Mental Illness Worship Resource,* ed. Christopher L. Smith (Louisville, Ky.: Office of Health Ministries, Presbyterian Church (U.S.A.), 1999), 28–35. Used with permission.

39. "Alcohol and Drug Awareness Liturgy," in *Substance Abuse Awareness Sunday, Resource for Worship,* General Board of Global Ministries, Cincinnati, Ohio, http://gbgm-umc.org. Used with permission.

40. "Key Statistics: Illicit Drug Production, Trafficking, and Consumption," *Information Sheet No. 2,* United Nations General Assembly, Special Session on the World Drug Problem, New York, June 8–10, 1998, http://www.un.org/ga/20special/presskit/pubinfo/info2.htm (accessed February 26, 2003).

41. "Cocaine Seizures Versus Production," in *Drug Facts and Figures*, U.S. Department of State, International Information Programs, 2000, http://usinfo.state.gov/products/pubs/archive/drugfacts/fig5.htm (accessed February 26, 2003).

42. "Cigarettes and Other Nicotine Products," in *NIDA InfoFacts,* National Institute on Drug Abuse, http://www.nida.nih.gov/Infofax/tobacco.html (accessed February 26, 2003); "Trends in Prescription Drug Abuse," in *NIDA InfoFacts,* National Institute on Drug Abuse, http://www.nida.nih.gov/Infofax/PainMed.html (accessed February 26, 2003); "Substance Dependence, Abuse, and Treatment," in 2001 *National Household Survey on Drug Abuse* (NHSDA), U.S. Department of Health and Human Services, Substance Abuse and Mental Health Services Administration (SAMHSA), Office of Applied Studies; http://www.samhsa.gov/oas/NHSDA/2k1NHSDA/vol1/Chapter7.htm (accessed February 26, 2003).

43. "Substance Dependence, Abuse, and Treatment."

44. Note: Please update these statistics for use in your church, as these figures constantly change.

45. Chuck Risser and Tom Walsh, "Leaving Addiction—One: Admit . . . Get Ready," Office of Health Ministries, U.S.A., Presbyterian Church (U.S.A.), and the Presbyterian Network on Alcohol and Other Drug Abuse, PHEWA. Copyright 1996 by Chuck Risser, Minneapolis, Minnesota. Used with permission. The idea grew largely through the efforts of Elder Tom Walsh, with help from the Presbyterian Committee on Alcohol and Other Drug Concerns and its convener, Chuck Risser.

46. Tamara Hudson, ed., *Celebrating the Miracle: Worship Resources for Addiction Awareness Services,* Office of Health Ministries, Presbyterian Church (U.S.A.), 2–12. Used with permission, including footnotes in the liturgy.

47. *Twelve Steps and Twelve Traditions*, Alcoholics Anonymous World Services, Inc., 1993, 105.

48. Modernized version of "The Third Step Prayer," *Alcoholics Anonymous,* Alcoholics Anonymous World Service, Inc., 1976, 63.

49. Based on the twelve steps, *Alcoholics Anonymous*, 59, and Psalm 46, *Inclusive Language Psalms,* The Pilgrim Press, 1987.

50. Based on the "Third Step Prayer," *Alcoholics Anonymous,* 63.

51. Paraphrased use of paragraph 1, *Alcoholics Anonymous,* Alcoholics Anonymous World Service, Inc., 1976, 164.

52. Paraphrased from "A Vision for You," *Alcoholics Anonymous,* Alcoholics Anonymous World Service, Inc., 1976, 164.

53. Beth Basham and Sara Lisherness, eds., *Striking Terror No More* (Louisville, Ky.: Bridge Resources, 1997), Worship Resources, 88–98. Used with permission.

54. *Lord, Hear Our Prayers: Domestic Violence Worship Resources*, compiled by Kathy Shantz. Published by Mennonite Central Committee Canada, 1994, 3.

55. Ibid.

56. Ruth C. Duck, *Bread for the Journey: Resources for Worship*, Ruth C. Duck ed. (Cleveland: United Church Press, 1981), 35. Copyright © 1981. Reprinted by permission.

57. Ruth C. Duck, *Touch Holiness: Resources for Worship*, Ruth C. Duck and Maren C. Tirabassi, eds. (New York: The Pilgrim Press, 1990), 97. Copyright © 1990. Reprinted by permission.

58. *Leader's Guide: World Community Day for November 1, 1996*. NY: Church Women United, 475 Riverside Drive, Room 812, New York, NY 10115, 4. Used with permission.

59. "Family Ministries and Seniors," Saskatchewan Conference Human Development and Support Committee, volume 8, Spring 1993. Copyright holder unknown.

60. Ibid., 35.

61. *Domestic Violence,* 1, at http://endabuse.org/facts/ (accessed February 7, 2003).

62. Ibid., 2.

63. Note: These statistics need to be constantly updated depending when you use the liturgy.

64. *Leader's Guide: World Community Day*, 6. Used with permission of Mennonite Central Committee Canada.

65. Ibid., 17–18.

66. "Family Ministries and Seniors," 35–36.

67. Excerpted from the 1992 Women's Interchurch Council of Canada *Worship Service* in remembrance of the December 6, 1989, massacre of fourteen women in Montreal. Used with permission of Women's Interchurch Council of Canada.

68. *Lord, Hear Our Prayers,* 21.

69. From Sharon K. Youngs, *Confronting Domestic Violence: Not Just for Adults* (Louisville, Ky.: Curriculum Publishing, 1996), as cited in *Striking Terror No More: The Church Responds to Domestic Violence*, ed. Beth Basham and Sara Lisherness, 94, 95. Bridge Resources, 100 Witherspoon St., Louisville, KY 40202.

70. From *Peacemaking through Worship*, vol. 2, ed. Jane Parker Huber (Louisville, Ky.: Presbyterian Peacemaking Program of the Presbyterian Church (U.S.A.), 1992), as cited in *Striking Terror No More: The Church Responds to Domestic Violence*, ed. Beth Basham and Sara Lisherness, 94. Bridge Resources, 100 Witherspoon St., Louisville, KY 40202.

71. Prayer for "Peace and Family Life," from the book *Flames of the Spirit: Resources for Worship*, ed. Ruth C. Duck (New York: Pilgrim Press, 1985), 45. Copyright © 1985. Used by permission. Worship Resource No. 696, *Hymnal: A Worship Book*, © 1992 The Hymnal Project. Adapted from a prayer by Ruth C. Duck in *Flames of the Spirit* © 1985 Pilgrim Press. Reprinted by permission of Brethren Press, Elgin, Illinois.

72. Youngs, *Confronting Domestic Violence.*

73. Ibid.

74. *Leader's Guide: World Community Day.*

75. Compiled by the author.

76. James Cotter, "More Than Cure," in *Healing—More or Less* (Sheffield: Cairns Publications, 1990), 34–35, 68. Adapted by Abigail Rian Evans. Used with permission.

77. Ibid., 68.

78. "From Victim to Victory." © 1994, CRC Publications, Grand Rapids, MI 49560. www.reformedworship.org. Used by permission.

79. Author and publisher unknown. Adapted by author.

80. James Cotter, "Praying with Those Who Have Been Violently Assaulted or Sexually Abused," in *Healing—More or Less*, 91–95. Used with permission.

81. Elizabeth Goudy, "Hearing the Unheard: Women Walk, Weep and Dance with God," *Criterion*, Bond Chapel worship service led by the Womenspirit group of the University of Chicago Divinity School's Women's Caucus, January 2, 1994. Used with permission, including all footnotes in body of liturgy.

82. "Lot's Wife," from *You Will Hear Thunder,* by Anna Akhmatova.

83. Alice Walker, *The Color Purple* (New York: Harcourt Brace Jovanovich, 1982), 202–4.

84. Ntozake Shange, *For Colored Girls Who Have Considered Suicide When the Rainbow is Enuf: A Choreopoem* (Toronto and New York: Bantam Books, 1981).

85. Prayer inspired by Ntozake Shange's poem "with no immediate cause." Note to reader: Update statistics before using in a service as they may change.

CHAPTER 5   ILLNESS: AS LIFE-THREATENING

1. The author in conversation with Dr. Eric Cassell, clinical professor of Public Health, Cornell University Medical College, in the 1980s; also in Abigail Rian Evans, *Redeeming Marketplace Medicine* (Cleveland: Pilgrim Press, 1999), 121.

2. All statistics were obtained from "HIV/AIDS Statistics," Fact Sheet, National Institutes of Health, December 2002, http://www.niaid.nih.gov/factsheets/aidsstat.htm (accessed February 25, 2003).

3. Abigail Rian Evans, "Bearing One Another's Burden," in "A Response to AIDS: Bearing One Another's Burdens," ed. Jack Spiro, *Journal of Religious Education* (Spring 1988): 179.

4. Robert Lambourne, *Exploration in Health and Salvation: A Selection of Papers by Bob Lambourne* (Birmingham, Eng.: University Press of Birmingham, 1985), 20.

5. "Fast Stats A to Z: Cancer," National Center for Health Statistics, 2000, http://www.cdc.gov/nchs/fastats/cancer.htm (accessed February 25, 2003).

6. "Cancer Facts and Figures 2002," http://www.cancer.org/downloads/STT/CancerFacts&Figures2002TM.pdf (accessed February 11, 2003).

7. Melvyn Thompson, *Cancer and God of Love* (London: SCM Press, 1976), 9.

8. "Stroke Fact Sheet," National Center for Chronic Disease Prevention and Health Promotion, http://www.cdc.gov/cvh/fs-stroke.htm (accessed February 11, 2003). See also http://www.americanheart.org.

9. "Heart Attack and Angina Statistics," American Heart Association, 2000, http://www.americanheart.org/presenter.jhtml?identifier=4591 (accessed February 11, 2003).

10. John Katonah, "Hospitalization: A Rite of Passage," in *Hospital Ministry,* ed. Lawrence Holst (New York: Crossroad, 1985), 56–59.

11. Michael B. Aune and Valerie DeMarinis, *Religious and Social Ritual: Interdisciplinary Explorations* (New York: State University of New York Press, 1996), 297.

12. Ibid., 294.

13. Ibid., 293.

14. Ibid., 294.

15. Ibid.

16. Thomas Talley, *Worship Reforming Tradition* (Washington, D.C.: Pastoral Press, 1990), 52.

17. Abigail Rian Evans, *The Healing Church* (Cleveland: United Church Press, 1999), 10.

18. Charles Gusmer, *The Ministry of Healing in the Church of England as Ecumenical-Liturgical Study*, Alcuin Club Collections, no. 56 (London: Heron and Co., 1974), 32.

19. "Constitution on the Sacred Liturgy," Vatican II, December 4, 1963.

20. Evans, *Healing Church.*

21. Mary Frances Duffy, "A Ritual of Healing for Families of the Terminally Ill," in *Alternative Futures for Worship and Anointing the Sick,* ed., Peter E. Fink (Collegeville, Minn.: Liturgical Press, 1987), 104.

22. Ibid.

23. James Cotter, "More Than Cure," in *Healing—More or Less* (Sheffield: Cairns Publications, 1990), 1–2. Used with permission.

24. "Prayers for the Sick and Anxious," in *A Manual for Ministry to the Sick,* ed. Martin Dudley (London: SPCK, 1997), 22–28. Used with permission, including footnotes in the liturgy.

25. *The Priest's Vade Mecum.* Prayer from *The Priest's Vade Mecum* © 1945 SPCK.

26. Ibid.

27. Ibid.

28. Ibid.

29. "For One Who Is Going Blind," in Barclay, *William Barclay Prayer Book,* ed., Ronnie Barclay (London: Fount Paperbacks, 1994), 274. Used with permission.

30. "For One Who Has Lost the Power to Speak," in Barclay, *William Barclay Prayer Book,* 275. Used with permission.

31. "For One Who Is Going Deaf," in Barclay, *William Barclay Prayer Book,* 276. Used with permission.

32. Charles Parkhurst Baxter, *The Hospital Service Book* (London: Henry Frowde, Amen Corner, E.C., 1892), 11.

33. Ibid., 4–5.

34. Ibid., 14.

35. Ibid., 17.

36. "A Prayer for Restoring Health," The United Methodist Church, General Board of Church and Society. AIDS Interfaith Network defunct.

37. "Prayers for Home and Hospital: For Hospital Staffs," in John Gunstone, *Prayers for Healing* (Godalming, Surrey: Highland Books, 1992), 25. Used with permission.

38. "For Doctors, Nurses and Hospital Staff," in *The William Barclay Prayer Book,* 292. Used with permission.

39. "A Prayer for Operation Day," in Barclay, *William Barclay Prayer Book,* 294. Used with permission.

40. "For One Injured in an Accident," in Barclay, *William Barclay Prayer Book,* 278. Used with permission.

41. "For One Who Knows That He Will Never Be Fully Well Again," in Barclay, *William Barclay Prayer Book*, 284. Used with permission.

42. "Healing Service," created by Rev. Curran Reichert, Rev. Jeffrey Gaines, and Jane Ferguson for the National Health Ministries Association Annual Conference, Asilomar, California, June 23, 2002. Used with permission.

43. "Modern Language Rite," in Dudley, *Manual for Ministry to the Sick,* 67–72. Used with permission, including footnotes in the liturgy.

44. *The Book of Common Prayer* (American Episcopal Church, 1979). Extracts from *The Book of Common Prayer for Use in the Church in Wales* © 1984 Church in Wales Publications.

45. Ibid.

46. Ibid.

47. *A New Zealand Prayer Book* © 1989 The Church of the Province of New Zealand.

48. *Occasional Services: A Companion to Lutheran Book of Worship* © 1982.

49. David Adam, "Three in One," in *Tides and Seasons* (London: Triangle/SPCK, 1989), 29. Used with permission.

50. The Book of Common Prayer (1662) [altered]. Extracts from *The Book of Common Prayer for Use in the Church in Wales* © 1984 Church in Wales Publications.

51. "Worship and Prayer with the Laying on of Hands," The Burrswood Community, Church of Christ the Healer, Ministry and Worship in Development, Tunbridge Wells, England. Used with permission.

52. "Service of Healing," Saint Andrew's Episcopal Church, Saratoga, California, adapted from "A Public Service of Healing." *The Book of Occasional Services*, published by The Church Hymnal Corp., New York, © 1988, Church Pension Fund. Used by permission.

53. "Laying on of Hands and Anointing the Sick," reprinted from *Occasional Services: A Companion to Lutheran Book of Worship*, copyright © 1982. Used by permission of Augsburg Fortress.

54. "Lament for Physical and Mental Loss," excerpts from *Autumn Gospel: Women in the Second Half of Life,* by Kathleen Fischer. © 1995. Used with permission of Paulist Press. www.paulistpress.com.

55. Gerald Calhoun, S.J., and Peter E. Fink, S.J., "Ritual of Anointing for the Long-Term Seriously Ill," in *Alternative Futures for Worship,* vol. 7: *Anointing of the Sick,* ed. Bernard J. Lee, S.M. (Collegeville, Minn.: Liturgical Press, 1987), 95–101. Used with permission.

56. "A Service for Healing and Wholeness," Worship Service, March 25, 1997, National Capital Presbytery, National Presbyterian Church, Washington, D.C. Used with permission.

57. "Service of Healing and Wholeness," Westminster Presbyterian Church, San Diego, California. Used with permission. Additions to service by author.

58. "The Long Way Home," Rev. George R. Pasley, pastor, Garnett Presbyterian Church, Garnett, Kansas. Used with permission.

59. Patricia D. Brown and Adele K. Wilcox, "Healing and Anointing Liturgy," *Worship Resource for HIV and AIDS Ministries* (New York: General Board of Global Ministries), 7–24 (http://gbgm-umc.org). Used with permission.

60. AIDS National Interfaith Network. Adapted from the Interfaith Conference of Metropolitan Washington's *Cry Pain, Cry Hope* service. Responses adapted from Psalm 13, Jerusalem Bible translation. AIDS Interfaith Network defunct.

61. "AIDS: An Interfaith Service of Prayer and Healing," Old Pine Street Presbyterian Church, Philadelphia, Pennsylvania, date unknown.

62. "Blessing Ritual around Therapy for a Disease," in Susan Langhauser, *Blessings and Rituals for the Journey of Life* (Nashville: Abingdon Press, 2000), 112–13. Used with permission.

63. "Blessing of the Gift of Marrow," Rev. Jann Aldredge-Clanton, Ph.D., chaplain, Baylor University Hospital, Dallas, Texas. Used with permission. This service was used for Buck Breland, a senior M.Div. candidate at Princeton Theological Seminary who died from lymphoma while a student in 1999.

64. Leslie Penrose, "Ritual of Healing Touch," in *Shaping Sanctuary: Proclaiming God's Grace in an Inclusive Church,* ed. Kelly Turney (Chicago: Reconciling Congregation Program, 2000), 175. Used with permission.

65. The phrase "fierce tenderness" is from Mary E. Hunt's *Fierce Tenderness: A Feminist Theology of Friendship* (New York: Crossroad, 1991).

66. Carolyn Mackey and Sr. Mary Popoczy, Cancer Prayer Group, St. John Neumann Church, Strongsville, Ohio. Outline of service used with permission.

67. "Daily Novena Prayer to St. Peregrine," Franciscan Mission Associates, Mount Vernon, New York. Used with permission.

68. "Prayer" in *Nine Days of Reflections and Prayers in Honor of St. Peregrine,* National Shrine of St. John Neumann CSsR, Philadelphia, Pennsylvania. Used with permission.

69. "Prayer of the Sick," Missionary Oblates of Mary Immaculate, Belleville, Illinois. Used with permission.

70. "I Have Cancer," in William Rabior, *A Healing Place in a Hurting World: Prayers of Solace and Hope* (Liguori, Mo.: Liguori Publications, 1997), 28. Used with permission.

71. "A Caregiver's Prayer for the Sick," prayer card (Liguori, Mo.: Liguori Publications, 1997). Used with permission.

72. Fr. Larry J. Hess, Our Lady of Good Counsel, 4365 S. 2nd St., Bangor PA 18013 (http://www.OLGC2002 @ptd.net). Contact Fr. Hess for copies of the "Heavenly Father Holy Card" (610-588-5445). Used with permission. All rights reserved.

73. Francisco Maria Aguilera Gonzalez, Auxiliary Bishop of Mexico, "The Miracle Prayer," September 8, 1992, prayer card, © 1993 Servite Fathers, O.S.M. International Compassion Ministry, 20180 Governor's Highway, Olympia Fields, IL 60461, tel. 708–748–6279. Used with permission. The rest of the card reads: "Say this Prayer faithfully, no matter how you feel, when you come to the point where you sincerely mean each word, with all your heart, something good spiritually will happen to you. You will experience Jesus, and HE will change your whole life in a very special way. You will see."

74. William F. Haynes Jr., M.D., F.A.C.C., Princeton, New Jersey (March 2001). Used with permission. See William F. Haynes Jr. and James C. Fenhagen, *A Physician's Witness to the Power of Shared Prayer* (Lincoln, Neb.: www.iuniverse.com, 2000).

75. "Blessing before Surgery," excerpted from *Out of the Ordinary: Prayers, Poems, and Reflections for Every Season,* by Joyce Rupp, O.S.M. Copyright © 2000 by Ave Maria Press, P.O. Box 428, Notre Dame, IN 46556, www.avemariapress.com. Used with permission of the publisher.

CHAPTER 6   DEATH AND DYING

1. David Adam, "Sixfold Kyries," in *Tides and Seasons* (London: Triangle/SPCK, 1989), 71. Used with permission.

2. Thomas Talley, *Worship Reforming Tradition* (Washington, D.C.: Pastoral Press, 1989), 55.

3. William James, philosopher, 1842–1910 C.E.

4. See Robert M. Veatch, *Death, Dying and the Biological Revolution: Our Last Quest for Responsibility* (New Haven, Conn.: Yale University Press, 1976), 235, who disagrees with this view.

5. Lewis Smedes, "Respect for Human Life: 'Thou Shalt Not Kill,'" in *On Moral Medicine: Theological Perspectives in Medical Ethics,* ed. Stephen E. Lammers and Allen Verhey (Grand Rapids: Wm. B. Eerdmans Publishing Co., 1987), 148.

6. Ibid.

7. Elisabeth Kübler-Ross, *On Death and Dying* (New York: Macmillan Publishing Co., 1970).

8. Martin Marty, *A Cry of Absence: Reflections for the Winter of the Heart* (New York: Harper & Row, 1982).

9. From http://www.kolshalom.com/divrei/dvarilana1.html, February 2, 2002 (accessed February 25, 2003). The Amidah is the oldest and considered by many to be the most important prayer in the Jewish liturgy. It has a number of different names, which probably speaks to its importance. It is unclear when Jews started praying it or

why, although Raban Gamliel in the first century C.E. is credited with arranging it. Raban Gamliel was the most influential rabbi in the period following the destruction of the Temple. This was a time when many different rabbis had their own individual domains. He took it as his imperative to standardize rabbinic practice. He was thought to have arranged eighteen benedictions that would be recited daily; hence another name for the prayer, the Shimona Esrey, which is Hebrew for "eighteen."

These benedictions are divided into three categories. The first three are the Benedictions of Praise *(shevach)*. The middle thirteen are Benedictions of Petition *(bakasha),* where we ask God for certain things. And the final three are Benedictions of Thanksgiving *(hodayah).*

10. William H. Willimon, *Worship as Pastoral Care* (Nashville, Abingdon Press, 1982), 102.

11. Mary Frances Duffy, "A Ritual of Healing for Families of the Terminally Ill," in *Alternative Futures for Worship and Anointing the Sick,* ed. Peter E. Fink (Collegeville, Minn.: Liturgical Press, 1987), 109.

12. Foreword to Martin Dudley, ed., *A Manual for Ministry to the Sick* (London: SPCK, 1997), xi.

13. Duffy, "Ritual of Healing," 106.

14. Ibid., 107.

15. Ibid.

16. Ibid.

17. "Rites with the Dying" in Dudley, *Manual for Ministry to the Sick,* 73–81. Used with permission, including all footnotes in body of liturgy.

18. *The Book of Common Prayer* (American Episcopal Church, 1979). Extracts from *The Book of Common Prayer for Use in the Church in Wales* © 1984 Church in Wales Publications.

19. Ibid.

20. Ibid.

21. *A Proposed Prayer Book* (India, 1952) [adapted] © 1952 SPCK and from *The Supplement to the Book of Common Prayer* © 1961 ISPCK.

22. *The Book of Common Prayer* (American Episcopal Church, 1979).

23. *A Proposed Prayer Book* (India, 1952).

24. *The Book of Common Prayer* (American Episcopal Church, 1979).

25. "Rite of Christian Commitment to the Terminally Ill," in Peter A. Clark, "The Transition between Ending Medical Treatment and Beginning Palliative Care: The Reason for a Ritual Response," *Worship,* 72, 4 (July 1998): 350–53. Used with permission, including footnotes in body of liturgy.

26. Margaret Mary Kelleher, "Ritual," in Joseph Komonchak, Mary Collins, and Dermot Lane, eds., *The New Dictionary of Theology* (Collegeville, Minn.: Liturgical Press, 1987), 906–7.

27. "Orders for the Blessing of Adults," *Book of Blessings* (New York: Catholic Publishing Co., 1989) no. 383, 165.

28. "Service for the Withdrawal of Life Support," from Mike Johnston and Vernon K. Rempel, "New Liturgies for Unusual Occasions," *Christian Ministry* 26, 4 (1995): 21–23. Copyright 1995 Christian Century Foundation. Reprinted with permission from the July–August, 1995, issue of the *Christian Ministry.* Used with permission.

29. "Let Them Go Free," in Thomas A. Shannon and Charles N. Faso, O.F.M., *Let Them Go Free* (Franklin, Wis.: Sheed & Ward, 1987), 20–27. Reprinted by permission of Sheed and Ward, an Apostolate of the Priests of the Sacred Heart, 7373 S. Lovers Lane Rd., Franklin, WI 53132.

30. Duffy, "Ritual of Healing," 115–19. Used with permission.

31. "Memory Wreath," by Jean Wright-Elson, parish nurse, First United Methodist Church, San Diego, California. Used with permission.

32. "Christmas Mourning." © 1996, CRC Publications, Grand Rapids, MI 49560. www.reformedworshiporg. Used by permission.

33. The Reverend Christopher J. Heller, adaptation of "Holiday Helps Candle Service," Annual Ministry of Consolation Program, St. Gerard Majella Church, Port Jefferson Station, New York, 1999 and 2000. Used with permission.

34. "Death of an Adult Child," reprinted with permission from *Prayer Services for the Elderly,* by Sandra DeGidio, O.S.M. Copyright © 1996. Published by Twenty-Third Publications, Mystic, CT 06355.

35. Howard Vanderwell and Norma Dewaal Malefyt, "How Long Will You Forget Me, LORD?" *Reformed Worship* 44 (June 1997): 27–28. © 1997, CRC Publications, Grand Rapids, MI 49560. www.reformedworship.org. Used by permission.

36. Written by author, 2002.

37. "After a Suicide," in Dudley, *Manual for Ministry to the Sick,* 84. Used with permission, including all foot-notes in body of liturgy.

38. *A Prayer Book for Australia.* Prayers from *A Prayer Book for Australia* © 1995 The Anglican Church of Australia Trust Corporation, published by Broughton Books.

39. Ibid.

CHAPTER 7   BROKEN WORLD

1. David Adam, "Jesus Lives," in *Tides and Seasons* (London: Triangle/SPCK, 1989), 108. Used with permission.

2. See William F. May, *Beleaguered Rulers: The Public Obligation of the Professional* (Louisville, Ky.: Westminster John Knox Press, 2001).

3. William H. Willimon, *Worship as Pastoral Care* (Nashville, Abingdon Press, 1982), 91, 178ff.

4. James Melvin Washington, ed., *A Testament of Hope: The Essential Writings of Martin Luther King, Jr.* (San Francisco: Harper & Row, 1986).

5. Ibid., 36–37.

6. Ibid., 38.

7. Ibid., 292.

8. Dwight N. Hopkins, *Shoes That Fit Our Feet: Sources for a Constructive Black Theology* (Maryknoll, N.Y.: Orbis Books, 1993), 173.

9. Paulo Freire, *Pedagogy of the Oppressed*, 20th anniversary ed., trans. Myra Bergman Ramos (New York: Continuum, 1993).

10. Gustavo Gutiérrez, *A Theology of Liberation: History, Politics and Salvation* (Maryknoll, N.Y.: Orbis Books, 2001).

11. Howard Thurman, *Jesus and the Disinherited* (Richmond, Ind.: Friends United Press, 1976), 89–109.

12. See Peter J. Paris, "Moral Exemplars in Global Community," in *God and Globalization,* vol. 2: *The Spirit and the Modern Authorities,* ed. Max L. Stackhouse and Don S. Browning (Harrisburg, Pa.: Trinity Press International, 2001), 191–219.

13. Ibid., 207.

14. U.S. Census Bureau news release, September 30, 2002, at http://www.census.gov/Press-Release/www/2002/cb02–127.html (accessed February 24, 2003).

15. Associated Press, "Health Costs Zoom to Decade-high Rates," January 8, 2003, http://www.cnn.com/2003/HEALTH/01/08/healthcare.spending.ap/ (accessed February 24, 2003).

16. Paris, "Moral Exemplars in Global Community," 192.

17. William Barclay, *The Letters to the Corinthians* (Philadelphia: Westminster Press, 1975).

18. "A Service of Healing for a Hurting World," Washington, D.C.: Bread for the World, 5–8. Reprinted with permission from Bread for the World.

19. The Right Reverend William D. Persell, bishop of Chicago, Episcopal Diocese of Chicago, Office of Pastoral Care. Used with permission.

20. "Suggested Prayers of the People," by Rev. Randall R. Warren, D.Min., director, Office of Pastoral Care, Episcopal Diocese of Chicago, adapted from *Gates of Repentance: The New Union Prayerbook for the Days of Awe* (New York: CCAR, 1984) and *The Book of Common Prayer* (New York: Church Hymnal Corporation, 1979). Used with permission.

21. "For the Healing of the Churches," The Burrswood Community, Tunbridge Wells, England. Used with permission.

22. "Apology to My Brothers and Sisters in Developing Countries," excerpted from *Out of the Ordinary: Prayers, Poems, and Reflections for Every Season* by Joyce Rupp, O.S.M. Copyright © 2000 by Ave Maria Press, P.O. Box 428, Notre Dame, IN 46556, www.avemariapress.com. Used with permission of the publisher.

23. "Survival of the Vulnerable Good," in Dorothy McRae-McMahon, *Prayers for Life's Particular Moments* (London: SPCK, 2001), 90–92. Used with permission of SPCK, London.

24. "Blessing of a Victim of Crime or Oppression," *Book of Blessings, The Roman Ritual* © 1988 United States Conference of Catholic Bishops Inc., Washington, D.C. Used with permission. All rights reserved.

25. "Missing Persons," in McRae-McMahon, *Prayers for Life's Particular Moments*, 105–108. Used with permission of SPCK, London.

26. "For the Uprooted Ones," in McRae-McMahon, *Prayers for Life's Particular Moments*, 99–102. Used with permission of SPCK, London.

27. "We Gather to Worship God," First Christian Church (Disciples of Christ), San Jose, California, July 25, 1999. Used with permission.

28. From the United Nations Universal Declaration of Human Rights, 1948.

29. Community Homeless Alliance Ministry (CHAM), Sunday Worship and Healing Service, Rev. Scott Wagers, First Christian Church, San Jose, California. Used with permission. Community Homeless Alliance Ministry is a ministry of the First Christian Church, which has opened its doors to shelter the homeless of San Jose, giving them a place of hope. They hold this informal service that recognizes the dignity and worth of all God's people.

30. "Litany for a Just Health Care System." Author and source unknown. Adapted by author. Note: Figures should be updated to the most recent for use of this litany.

31. Rev. Kathleen Smallwood Johnson, Princeton Theological Seminary, 2002. Used with permission.

32. Linda H. Hollies, "Dr. Martin L. King, Jr. Sunday," from the book *Trumpet in Zion: Black Church Worship Resources, Year A* (Cleveland: Pilgrim Press, 2001), 38–40. Copyright © 1985 Linda H. Hollies. Used by permission, including all footnotes in body of liturgy.

33. Martin Luther King Jr., "I Have a Dream," speech, Washington, D.C., August 29, 1964.

34. "We Shall Overcome," African American spiritual.

35. Linda H. Hollies, "Juneteenth Observance," from the book *Trumpet in Zion*, 134–36. Copyright © 1985 Linda H. Hollies. Used by permission, including all footnotes in body of liturgy.

36. "Come Out De Wilderness," African American spiritual.

37. "Kum Ba Yah," African American spiritual.

38. "God Is a Good God," African American spiritual.

39. "It's Not Easy," in McRae-McMahon, *Prayers for Life's Particular Moments*, 93–95. Used with permission of SPCK, London.

40. "People of Color and the Criminal Justice System," liturgy, from "Justice Jottings" for Race Relations Sunday and Criminal Justice Sunday, February 14, 1993. Rev. Otis Turner and Rev. Kathy Lancaster, Social Justice and Peacemaking Ministry Unit, Presbyterian Church (U.S.A.). "Justice Jottings" was the vehicle for the Program Guide for Race Relations Sunday and Criminal Justice Sunday, which was jointly observed on February 14, 1993, with the theme of "People of Color and the Criminal Justice System." Used with permission, including all footnotes in body of liturgy.

41. Art Solomon, Ojibway Native Canadian prayer, in *Jesus Christ—The Life of the World, A Worshipbook* (Geneva: World Council of Churches, 1983), 71.

42. *In Spirit and in Truth, A Worshipbook* (Geneva: World Council of Churches, 1991), 15–16.

43. James G. Kirk, *When We Gather: A Book of Prayers for Worship, Year C* (Philadelphia: Geneva Press, 1985), 86.

44. Published by the Foundation for Change from essays of Puerto Rican children.

45. Adapted from a "Litany Based on 1 Peter," by Vera P. Swann.

46. Pam McAllister, *Standing in the Need of Prayer: Devotions for Christians in Prison* (Louisville, Ky.: Criminal Justice Program, 1992), Week 31.

47. McAllister, *Standing in the Need of Prayer*, Week 29.

48. Adapted from Task Force on Criminal Justice, Southern California Synodical Association, United Presbyterian Church, 1979.

49. Prayer by Rev. Holly Haile Smith following her sermon, General Assembly, June 5, 1992.

50. "Common Ground: An Act of Witness against Racism," © 1996 Yousouf Gooljary-Wright. From *The Pattern of Our Days: Liturgies and Resources for Worship*, Kathy Galloway (ed.) © 1996, 1997. Wild Goose Publications, Glasgow, Scotland G2 3DH. Used with permission. Excerpts from *The Pattern of Our Days,* ed. Kathy Galloway © 1997. Used with permission of Paulist Press (www.paulistpress.com), including all footnotes within body of liturgy.

51. From a statement made by a Muslim woman in Manchester Cathedral on Human Rights Day 1989, before an audience of Muslims, Sikhs, Hindus, Jews, and Christians.

52. World Council of Churches Statement and Actions on Racism 1948–1979 © 1980 WCC Publications, World Council of Churches, Geneva, Switzerland.

53. "The Road to Damascus," Catholic Institute for International Relations/Christian Aid.

54. "Apostle's Prayer . . . for the Imprisoned and Convicted," Associação de Proteção e Assistência aos Condenados (Association for Protection and Assistance of Prisoners), Brazil. Used with permission of International Centre for Justice and Reconciliation, Prison Fellowship International, Washington, D.C.

55. "Restorees' Prayer," Associação de Proteção e Assistência aos Condenados (Association for Protection and Assistance of Prisoners), Brazil. Used with permission of International Centre for Justice and Reconciliation, Prison Fellowship International, Washington, D.C.

56. Edward DeWeese, *Prayers for Prisoners* (Nashville: Upper Room Books, 1997), 80–81, 118–19.

57. "Celebrating, Sending Out and Blessing," in McRae-McMahon, *Prayers for Life's Particular Moments,* 13. Used with permission from SPCK, London.

58. David Adam, "Creator God," in *Tides and Seasons* (London: Triangle/SPCK, 1989), 54. Used with permission.

59. "Prayer for the Environment." Excerpted from *The Book of Alternative Services* © copyright 1985 by the General Synod of the Anglican Church of Canada; published by the Anglican Book Centre, 600 Jarvis Street, Toronto, Ontario, Canada M4Y 2J6. Used with permission.

60. "The Joy of Water," in McRae-McMahon, *Prayers for Life's Particular Moments,* 3–5. Used with permission of SPCK, London.

61. Written by the author, 2002.

62. James Cotter, "More Than Cure," in *Healing—More or Less* (Sheffield: Cairns Publications, 1990), 3–5. Used with permission.

63. Andrew Linzey, "Litanies for Animal Protection," in *Animal Rites: Liturgies of Animal Care* (London: SCM Press, 1999), 77–90; (Cleveland: Pilgrim Press, 2001). Used with permission.

64. "Service of Reconciliation," author and source unknown.

65. The "September 11 Interfaith Memorial Service: A Litany of Remembrance, Penitence & Hope" is adapted from liturgies by Rev. Eileen W. Lindner and Rev. Marcel A. Welty of the National Council of Churches, with some changes as it was combined with other source material offered by participants in the service. Held September 11, 2002, at St. Mary Church, Los Gatos, California. Used with permission.

66. Rabbi Roland B. Gittelsohn, "Remember Them," in *Gates of Repentance: The New Union Prayer Book for the Days of Awe* (New York: Central Conference of American Rabbis, 1979). Used by permission.

67. Source of this combination of "Dona Nobis" and "Sim Shalom" unknown.

68. Excerpt from "A Pastoral Message: Living with Faith and Hope after September 11," U.S. Conference of Catholic Bishops, November 14, 2001. Used with permission.

69. Verses 7 and 8 from the Metta Sutra (Buddha's words on kindness).

70. "Master of the Universe," in Chaim Stern, *Gates of the House* (New York: Central Conference of American Rabbis, 1984). Used with permission of Rabbi Elliot Stevens, Central Conference of American Rabbis.

71. "A Unitarian Universalist Prayer/Reading," from *Singing the Living Tradition,* Unitarian Universalist Association, 1993.

72. "A Hindu Prayer," in *All in Good Faith: A Resource Book for Multi-faith Prayer,* ed. Jean Potter and Marcus Braybrooke (Oxford: World Congress of Faiths, 1997), 109.

73. Qur'an 1:93; 5:32; 19:16–21; 49:13; 2:62; 2:256.

74. "Repentance and Reconciliation," The Burrswood Community, Tunbridge Wells, England. Used with permission.

75. Howard Booth, "The Incurable Wound," in *Seven Whole Days: A Health and Healing Worship Book* (London: Arthur James Limited, 1992), 47–55. Used with permission.

76. "To Dare Rebirth," in *Circles of Grace: Worship and Prayer in the Everyday,* by Keri K. Wehlander. The United Church Publishing House, 1998, 39–43. Used with permission.

77. Words and music by Graham Kendrick © 1987 by Make Way Music/Integrity's Hosanna! Music.

78. "Rite of Reconciliation," in *Alternative Futures for Worship,* vol. 4, ed. Peter E. Fink, S.J. (Collegeville, Minn.: Liturgical Press), 153–63. Used with permission.

79. "Hallelujah Anyhow!" in Diedra Kriewald, *Hallelujah Anyhow! Suffering and the Christian Community of Faith* (New York: Published by Mission Education and Cultivation Program Dept. for Women's Division, General Board of Global Ministries, United Methodist Church, ©1986), 122–26. Used with permission.

80. "Praying for Shalom," by Harry Boonstra, *Reformed Worship* 46 (Grand Rapids: CRC Publications, December 1997), 16–17 (www.reformedworship.org). Used with permission.

CHAPTER 8   DELIVERANCE

1. See Abigail Rian Evans, *The Healing Church* (Cleveland: United Church Press, 1999), 88–90.

2. Ibid., 86.

3. Ibid.

4. David Batty, "Exorcism: Abuse or Cure," http://society.guardian.co.uk/mentalhealth/story/0,8150,5367 19,00.html (accessed May 2, 2001).

5. Ibid.

6. John Richards, *But Deliver Us from Evil: An Introduction to the Demonic Dimension in Pastoral Care* (New York: Seabury Press, 1974), 165.

7. Evans, *Healing Church*, 86.

8. Michael Welker, *God the Spirit* (Minneapolis: Fortress Press, 1994), 196ff. See especially 195–219 for an insightful passage on demon possession.

9. Evans, *Healing Church*, 86–87.

10. Ibid., 87.

11. Richards, *But Deliver Us from Evil*, 179.

12. Morris Maddocks, *The Christian Healing Ministry* (London: SPCK, 1981), 127.

13. Evans, *Healing Church*, 89.

14. Ibid., 90.

15. Richards, *But Deliver Us from Evil*, 222.

16. Ibid.

17. Ibid., 223.

18. Ibid., 224.

19. Evans, *Healing Church*, 90.

20. "Service of Exorcism," adapted by the Very Reverend Fr. Jack N. Sparks, Ph.D., dean, St. Athanasius Academy of Orthodox Theology, Elk Grove, California, from *Book of Needs*. Used with permission.

21. Antiochian Orthodox refers to a jurisdiction in the Orthodox Church.

22. *Ektenia* is a series of short prayerful requests or pleas, addressed to the Lord, regarding the secular and spiritual needs of the faithful.

23. The hierarchy of the Antiochian Orthodox Christian Church of North America consists of the metropolitan and his four Auxiliary bishops, who oversee the work of the clergy and the welfare of the laity. Since 1975 the metropolitan is Philip Saliba (http://www.antiochian.org).

24. The *Prokeimenon* is a short excerpt from divine Scripture, read together with one or more other verses that supplement the meaning of the *Prokeimenon*.

25. Tartarus is described as a dank, gloomy pit, surrounded by a wall of bronze and, beyond that, a threefold layer of night. Along with chaos, earth, and Eros, it is one of the first entities to exist in the universe. However, in later myths Tartarus becomes a place of punishment for sinners. It resembles hell and is the opposite of Elysium, the afterlife for the blessed.

26. Vernon Keith Rempel, in Mike Johnston and Vernon K. Rempel, "New Liturgies for Unusual Occasions," *Christian Ministry* 26, 4 (July–August 1995): 23. Copyright 1995 Christian Century Foundation. Reprinted with permission from the July–August, 1995, issue of the *Christian Ministry*.

27. "Affirmation of Faith," by Carolyn Holderread Heggen, in *Sexual Abuse in Christian Homes and Churches* (Scottdale, Pa.: Herald Press, 1993). Used with permission. All rights reserved.

APPENDIXES

HEALING CENTERS

1. This information was taken from the Web site: http://www.burrswood.org.uk.

2. Jane Ferguson and author, unpublished paper.

3. Abigail Rian Evans, with Janet Jacewicz, "Church in the Community: Models for Health Ministry," unpublished paper, 2001.

4. Information was taken verbatim from the Web site: http://www.iona.org.uk. Used with permission of Graham Boyle, the Iona Community, 140 Sauchiehall Street, Glasgow G2 3DH, Scotland.

5. Information was taken verbatim from the Web site: www.taize.fr. © Ateliers et Presses Taizé, 71250 Taizé Community, France. Used with permission.

6. Information was taken from the Web site: http://www.upperroom.org. For further information, contact: Office of the World Editor, 1908 Grand Avenue, P.O. Box 340004, Nashville, TN 37212-0004.

WORSHIP RESOURCES FOR LITURGIES ON ADDICTION

1. These resources were originally part of different liturgies.

2. "A Prayer from Thomas Merton," *Thoughts in Solitude,* 3d ed., Alcoholics Anonymous World Service, Inc., 1979. In Tamara Hudson, ed., *Celebrating the Miracle: Worship Resources for Addiction Awareness Services,* Office of Health Ministries, Presbyterian Church (U.S.A.), 8. Used with permission.

3. "A World about Prayer by Henri Nouwen," from "Prayer in Action," *Sojourners,* May 1979. People's Christian Coalition, Washington, D.C. In Hudson, *Celebrating the Miracle,* 9. Used with permission.

4. "Prayers from the Alcoholics Anonymous Text," Alcoholics Anonymous, *Big Book,* 3d ed., Alcoholics Anonymous World Service, Inc., 1979. In Hudson, *Celebrating the Miracle,* 9. Used with permission.

5. Ibid., 63.

6. Ibid., 76.

7. Phyllis Trible, *God and the Rhetoric of Sexuality,* 4th printing (Philadelphia: Fortress Press, 1985), 172.

8. David Rhoads and Donald Michie, *Mark as Story* (Philadelphia: Fortress Press, 1982), 129–33.